READING GENDER IN JUDGES

RESOURCES FOR BIBLICAL STUDY

Editor
Hyun Chul Paul Kim, Hebrew Bible/Old Testament

Number 103

READING GENDER IN JUDGES

An Intertextual Approach

Edited by

Shelley L. Birdsong, J. Cornelis de Vos, and Hyun Chul Paul Kim

SBL PRESS

 **PRESS**

Atlanta

Contents

Abbreviations

AB	Anchor (Yale) Bible
ABD	Freedman, David Noel, ed. *Anchor Bible Dictionary*. 6 vols. New York: Doubleday, 1992.
ABRL	The Anchor (Yale) Bible Reference Library
ACCS	Ancient Christian Commentary on Scripture
ADPV	Abhandlungen des Deutschen Palästina-Vereins
AIL	Ancient Israel and Its Literature
ANET	Pritchard, James B., ed. *Ancient Near Eastern Texts Relating to the Old Testament*. 3rd ed. Princeton: Princeton University Press, 1969.
Ant.	Josephus, *Jewish Antiquities*
ASV	American Standard Version
AT	Annales Theologici
ATSAT	Arbeiten zu Text und Sprache im Alten Testament
AUSS	*Andrews University Seminary Studies*
b.	Babylonian
B. Bat.	Baba Batra
BAR	*Biblical Archaeology Review*
BASOR	*Bulletin of the American Schools of Oriental Research*
BBB	Bonner biblische Beiträge
BDB	Brown, Francis, S. R. Driver, and Charles A. Briggs. *Hebrew and English Lexicon of the Old Testament*. Oxford: Clarendon, 1906.
BHL	*Biblia Hebraica Leningradensia*
BHS	*Biblia Hebraica Stuttgartensia*
Bib	*Biblica*
BibInt	*Biblical Interpretation*
BibInt	Biblical Interpretation Series
BibSem	The Biblical Seminar
BLS	Bible and Literature Series

BN	*Biblische Notizen*
BR	*Biblical Research*
BRev	*Bible Review*
BSac	*Bibliotheca Sacra*
BSNA	Biblical Scholarship in North America
BTB	*Biblical Theology Bulletin*
BWANT	Beiträge zur Wissenschaft vom Alten und Neuen Testament
BZ	*Biblische Zeitschrift*
CANE	Sasson, Jack M., ed. *Civilizations of the Ancient Near East.* 4 vols. New York: Scribner, 1995. Repr. in 2 vols. Peabody, MA: Hendrickson, 1995.
CBET	Contributions to Biblical Exegesis and Theology
CBQ	*Catholic Biblical Quarterly*
CHANE	Culture and History of the Ancient Near East
COS	Hallo, William W., and K. Lawson Younger Jr., eds. *The Context of Scripture.* 4 vols. Leiden: Brill, 1997–2016.
CSHJ	Chicago Studies in the History of Judaism
CurBR	*Currents in Biblical Research*
CV	*Communio Viatorum*
EBR	Klauck, Hans-Josef, et al., eds. *Encyclopedia of the Bible and Its Reception.* Berlin: de Gruyter, 2009–.
ErIsr	*Eretz-Israel*
esp.	especially
ESV	English Standard Version
ET	English Translation
ETS	Erfurter theologische Studien
FAT	Forschungen zum Alten Testament
FCB	Feminist Companion to the Bible
fem.	feminine
FOTL	Forms of the Old Testament Literature
GPBS	Global Perspectives on Biblical Scholarship
HALOT	Koehler, Ludwig, Walter Baumgartner, and Johann J. Stamm. *The Hebrew and Aramaic Lexicon of the Old Testament.* Translated and edited under the supervision of Mervyn E. J. Richardson. 2 vols. Leiden: Brill, 2001.
HAR	*Hebrew Annual Review*
HBM	Hebrew Bible Monographs
HCOT	Historical Commentary on the Old Testament
HSM	Harvard Semitic Monographs

HThKAT	Herders Theologischer Kommentar zum Alten Testament
HUCA	*Hebrew Union College Annual*
IBC	Interpretation: A Bible Commentary for Teaching and Preaching
IBHS	Waltke, Bruce K., and Michael O'Connor. *An Introduction to Biblical Hebrew Syntax*. Winona Lake, IN: Eisenbrauns, 1990.
IEJ	*Israel Exploration Journal*
impv.	imperative
Int	*Interpretation*
ISBL	Indiana Studies in Biblical Literature
IVBS	International Voices in Biblical Studies
JAAR	*Journal of the American Academy of Religion*
JBL	*Journal of Biblical Literature*
JBQ	*Jewish Bible Quarterly*
JETS	*Journal of the Evangelical Theological Society*
JHebs	*Journal of Hebrew Scriptures*
JMJS	*Journal of Modern Jewish Studies*
JPS	*Tanakh: The Holy Scriptures; The JPS Translation according to the Traditional Hebrew Text*
JSJSup	Supplements to the Journal for the Study of Judaism
JSOT	*Journal for the Study of the Old Testament*
JSOTSup	Journal for the Study of the Old Testament Supplement Series
JTS	*Journal of Theological Studies*
KHC	Kurzer Hand-Commentar zum Alten Testament
KJV	King James Version
KRV	Korean Revised Version
LAB	Liber antiquitatum biblicarum
LAI	Library of Ancient Israel
LHBOTS	Library of Hebrew Bible/Old Testament Studies
LUO	Luther Bibel, 1912
LXX	Septuagint
MT	Masoretic Text
NABRE	New American Bible Revised Edition
NAC	New American Commentary
NASB	New American Standard Bible
NCBC	New Cambridge Bible Commentary
NIB	Keck, Leander E., ed. *The New Interpreter's Bible Commentary*. 12 vols. Nashville: Abingdon, 1994–2004.
NICOT	New International Commentary on the Old Testament

NIV	New International Version
NJPS	*Tanakh: The Holy Scriptures; The New JPS Translation according to the Traditional Hebrew Text*
NRSV	New Revised Standard Version
OBT	Overtures to Biblical Theology
OTE	*Old Testament Essays*
OTL	Old Testament Library
OTR	Old Testament Readings
pf.	perfect
RBS	Resources for Biblical Study
REV	Revised English Version
SBS	Suttgarter Bibelstudien
SEÅ	*Svensk exegetisk årsbok*
SemeiaSt	Semeia Studies
SHANE	Studies in the History of the Ancient Near East
SHBC	Smyth & Helwys Bible Commentary
sing.	singular
SJ	Studia Judaica
SJOT	*Scandinavian Journal of the Old Testament*
SP	Samaritan Pentateuch
SSN	Studia Semitica Neerlandica
SR	*Studies in Religion*
StBibLit	Studies in Biblical Literature (Lang)
Syr.	Syriac
TBN	Themes in Biblical Narrative
TDOT	Botterweck, G. Johannes, Helmer Ringgren, and Heinz-Josef Fabry, eds. *Theological Dictionary of the Old Testament.* Translated by John T. Willis et al. 17 vols. Grand Rapids: Eerdmans, 1974–2021.
TOTC	Tyndale Old Testament Commentaries
TynBul	*Tyndale Bulletin*
VL	Vetus Latina (Old Latin)
VT	*Vetus Testamentum*
VTSup	Supplements to Vetus Testamentum
Vulg.	Vulgate
WBC	Word Biblical Commentary
WTJ	*Westminster Theological Journal*
ZAW	*Zeitschrift für die alttestamentliche Wissenschaft*
ZBK	Zürcher Bibel Kommentar

1

Introduction

Shelley L. Birdsong, J. Cornelis de Vos, and Hyun Chul Paul Kim

Judges, Gender, and Intertextuality

The Book of Judges

What is the book of Judges about? It is hard to find thematic coherence, especially when read in isolation. This might be due to its intertextual function. Much of the content of Judges can only be understood when read together with other parts of the Hebrew Bible. Narratives in Judges comment, criticize, and reinterpret other texts from across what became the canon. Oftentimes, these interplays trouble gender, disrupting stereotypical binaries, creating a kind of gender chaos.[1] In particular, the treatment of women mirrors the train of the whole book, which moves in a downward spiral.[2] Judges begins positively with the campaign of the tribe of Judah ordered by YHWH. The first female character in the book, Achsah is a strong and assertive woman and an example for all of Israel, as she secures land as an inheritance for herself.[3] She knows what she wants and gets it. Yet by the time we reach the end of the book, Israel is in pandemonium, and women, presumably without their consent, are taken from their

---

1. For the original discussion on gender trouble, see Judith Butler, *Gender Trouble: Feminism and the Subversion of Identity* (New York: Routledge, 1990).

2. See Gregory T. K. Wong, *Compositional Strategy of the Book of Judges*, VTSup 111 (Leiden: Brill, 2006). Wong argues for an ongoing deterioration in the book of Judges from beginning to end. This is followed by Susanne E. Haddox in ch. 2 in this volume.

3. On the assertiveness of Achsah, see the contributions by J. Cornelis de Vos (ch. 6) and Joy A. Schroeder (ch. 3) in this volume.

homeland. The unnamed *pîlegeš* in Judg 19 is taken from her father's house in Bethlehem, gang raped by Benjaminites in a foreign city, then cut into pieces by her heartless husband, and spread throughout the land. The last women we see, in Judg 21, are abducted from their homelands and forced into marriage with those from the same Benjaminite tribe. Such acts can only forbode bad news for "Lady Israel." Amid, or intertwined with, the gender drama, Judges alludes to previous books and points to subsequent books, thus functioning as an intertextual hinge between them. The death of Joshua, for example, is described both in Josh 24:29–30 and in Judg 2:8–9; the Caleb-Achsah episode of Josh 15:13–19 is partly repeated in Judg 1:10–15. More broadly speaking, the book is often read intertextually with Genesis, since both books include motifs regarding rape (Gen 19; 34; Judg 19–21), child sacrifice (Gen 22; Judg 11), prostitution (Gen 38; Judg 11; 16), and kinship relations.[4] The form of the annunciation scenes also connects Judges to other mothers and children who share the conception and birth process with the divine (Gen 16; 21; 25; 29–30; Judg 13; 1 Sam 1–2).[5] The major themes of leadership and monarchy set up the framework for the rest of the Former Prophets, while the stories of God's salvation allude to Exodus. Judges is also self-referential (intratextual). Male warriors are humiliatingly killed at the hand of a woman (Judg 4–5; 9), fathers fail their daughters (Judg 1; 11; 19), and mothers cannot protect their children (Judg 5; 13–17).[6] Quite quickly, one can see how intertextual and intratextual Judges is, particularly when it comes to the relationships among gendered characters. These connections necessitate more investigation.

Gender

Like intertextuality, gender theory has infiltrated biblical studies, giving us fresh ways to reenvision ancient texts in a postmodern world. While

---

4. See the contribution by Susan E. Haddox (ch. 2) for the connections between Genesis and Judges.

5. See Timothy D. Finlay, *The Birth Report Genre in the Hebrew Bible*, FAT 2/12 (Tübingen: Mohr Siebeck, 2005).

6. For men killed by the hand of women, see the contributions by Zev Farber (ch. 8) and Pamela J. W. Nourse (ch. 4) in this volume. See the contribution by Richard D. Nelson (ch. 9) about father-daughter relationships. See the contribution by Rannfrid I. Lasine Thelle (ch. 7) on motherhood.

feminism, which came before it, did a great service to female characters—liberating them from patriarchal authorship and androcentric interpretation—gender studies goes beyond this to reassess *all* genders, their fluidity, and the complex historical and cultural realities that formed them.[7]

Thus, while this volume spends substantial time on the female characters in Judges, individual essays also question the presentation of male characters, or masculinity, as well as characters who transgress the stereotypical gender binaries within the ancient patriarchal world.[8] As a largely resistant way of reading, gender criticism uncovers oft-ignored power inequalities and deconstructs normative gender roles and stereotypes, such as the assumptions that women should be mothers and wives, who are passive and landless, and that men should be warriors and leaders, who are active and landholders. For example, the stories of Deborah, Barak, Jael, and Sisera in Judg 4–5 have long been known to blur gender lines, since the women perform so-called masculine roles (e.g., judging and killing), and the men perform so-called feminine roles (e.g., being submissive and being afraid). As such, these chapters have been highlighted by gender critics for their gender reversals or genderfucks.[9] So, too, many of the other characters throughout Judges defy gendered prescriptions.

One of the ways that an intertextual approach is useful alongside gender study is that both studies recognize that there are many texts and intertexts at play when ascertaining a character's gender and that character's relationships to their surrounding gendered culture. The author's perspective is simply insufficient. We are called to listen to the characters themselves, the characters around them, the authors and editors, the history of interpreters, and ourselves as readers as we detect the gender

---

7. See, e.g., Butler, *Gender Trouble*, and bell hooks, *Feminist Theory: From Margin to Center*, 3rd ed. (New York: Routledge, 2015).

8. This is one of the unique characteristics of the present work that goes beyond that of Peggy Day, ed., *Gender and Difference in Ancient Israel* (Minneapolis: Fortress, 1989). Day's volume concentrates on feminist readings of female characters, but from throughout the Hebrew Bible. Here, the goal is to broaden the concept of gender while prioritizing intertextuality and the book of Judges in order to create a more focused collection. One should note, however, that *Gender and Difference* includes chapters on Jael (Susan Niditch) and Jephthah's daughter (Day).

9. See Deryn Guest, "From Gender Reversal to Genderfuck: Reading Jael through a Lesbian Lens," in *Bible Trouble: Queer Readings at the Boundaries of Biblical Scholarship*, ed. Teresa J. Hornsby and Ken Stone, SemeiaSt 67 (Atlanta: Society of Biblical Literature, 2011), 9–43.

identity and expressions of a particular character. Depending on our hermeneutical lenses and interpretive ethics, we are free to read with or against these texts. But generally, gender critics utilize a hermeneutic of suspicion, in light of the fact that the Bible was written in an inequitable culture, which continues to affect today's world. Similarly, gender criticism and intertextuality logically align with intersectional lenses, recognizing that the texts of race, ethnicity, class, religion, ability, sex, and sexuality all play a role in how one is gendered.[10] It is no longer enough to look at a character just as a man or a woman. Biblical scholars need to take the intersectional identities of characters and their intertextual environments seriously, and this is what we have begun to do in this volume.

There are many influential scholars who have paved the way for the wide array of contributions in this volume. Regarding gender theory, these include Judith Butler, Michel Foucault, Simone de Beauvoir, Gayle Rubin, Anne Fausto-Sterling, Adrienne Rich, Monique Wittig, Jacob Hale, Cheryl Chase, Kimberlé Crenshaw, Michael Kimmel, and many more. Under the influence of these thinkers, a cadre of biblical scholars has begun to blaze the trail for masculinity studies and a variety of queer readings. Here we will mention a select and instructive few.[11] Peter Ben-Smit has written a short introduction, *Masculinity and the Bible*, for those who want to get the lay of the methodological land, and he has also produced an edited volume with Ovidiu Creangă, *Biblical Masculinities Foregrounded*, which serves as a foundational compendium of essays for the field.[12] The paradigmatic scholars for queer readings are surely Teresa J. Hornsby and Ken Stone, editors of the ground-breaking *Bible Trouble: Queer Reading at the*

10. Hornsby and Stone, *Bible Trouble*, ix, xi. See also Patricia Hill Collins and Valerie Chepp, "Intersectionality," in *The Oxford Handbook of Gender and Politics*, ed. Georgina Waylen et al. (Oxford: Oxford University Press, 2013), 57–87; Gale A. Yee, "Gender, Race, Class, and the Etceteras of Our Discipline," *JBL* 139 (2020): 7–26.

11. The point here is not to give a comprehensive list but simply to demonstrate that there are several scholars bringing creative insight to these burgeoning fields. We use *queer* in this introduction as a capacious umbrella term for persons and perspectives that align with and affirm the LGBTQIA+ community.

12. Ben-Smit, *Masculinity and the Bible: Survey, Models, and Perspectives* (Leiden: Brill, 2017); Creangă and Ben-Smit, eds., *Biblical Masculinities Foregrounded*, HBM 62 (Sheffield: Sheffield Phoenix, 2014). Some other full-length volumes include Stephen Wilson, *Making Men: The Male Coming-of-Age Theme in the Hebrew Bible* (Oxford: Oxford University Press, 2015); Rhiannon Graybill, *Are We Not Men? Unstable Masculinity in the Hebrew Prophets* (New York: Oxford University Press, 2015).

Boundary of Biblical Scholarship.[13] Other volumes of note include those by Guest, Caryn Tamber-Rosenau, and Amy Kalmanofsky.[14]

Without being exhaustive, here we will briefly excerpt some essential remarks by these scholars. In her groundbreaking work, Butler declares that gender defies the rigid binary opposition of male and female but instead is fluidly constituted by way of the "stylized repetition of acts."[15] Gender is neither static nor permanent. It is performed. Picking up Butler's revolutionary concept of gender as performance, Tamber-Rosenau critiques the concept of liminality in relationship to gender, as it assumes that "there is a clear gender boundary or threshold for the characters to straddle."[16] The construction of gender thus goes beyond physicality, as Hornsby and Guest aver: "Though the lived gender may be more or less aligned with one's physicality, the performed masculinity or femininity lives out a subversion that maintains queerness; it is masculinity or femininity with a difference."[17] Here, queerness inherently interrogates, or crashes through, the presumably fixed boundaries that have been socially constructed, and, as Hornsby and Stone claim, the "chaos is indeed a good thing."

Shawna Dolansky and Sarah Shetman similarly develop this fluidity and complexity of gender in that "gender constructs vary with time and social circumstance" as "gender constructions are relational."[18] Likewise, manifold features of intersectionality call for redefinition of "hegemonic masculinity": "As opposed to the strict social hierarchy suggested by the patriarchy paradigm, this results in a heterar-

---

13. See also their influential individual works.

14. Guest, *Beyond Feminist Biblical Studies*, Bible in the Modern World 47 (Sheffield: Sheffield Phoenix, 2012). See also Guest's collaboration with Hornsby in Teresa J. Hornsby and Deryn Guest, *Transgender, Intersex, and Biblical Interpretation*, SemeiaSt 83 (Atlanta: SBL Press, 2016). Guest, like Stone, has contributed extensively to gender scholarship on Judges. See Tamber-Rosenau, *Women in Drag: Gender and Performance in the Hebrew Bible and Early Jewish Literature* (Piscataway, NJ: Gorgias, 2018); Kalmanofsky, *Gender Play in the Hebrew Bible: The Ways the Bible Challenges Its Gender Norms*, Routledge Interdisciplinary Perspectives on Biblical Criticism 2 (New York: Routledge, 2017).

15. Butler, *Gender Trouble*, 174–79.

16. Tamber-Rosenau, *Women in Drag*, 24.

17. Hornsby and Guest, *Transgender, Intersex, and Biblical Interpretation*, 5.

18. Dolansky and Shetman, "Introduction: What Is Gendered Historiography and How Do You Do It?," *JHebS* 19 (2019): 10.

chical organization of society, in which class, age, and gender intersect in various ways to construct complex layers of domination and
subjection."[19] For example, concerning the priestly family rules in Lev
21–22, women can lose or retain their status in relation to priestly
males, while men's status and power too are linked to women. Accordingly, the complex aspects of privilege and power can vary individu-
ally, collectively, and relationally.[20]

Such aspects of relationality and fluidity of gender further extend to
masculinity. Stephen Wilson expounds (biblical) hegemonic masculinity
and contends that masculinity be considered not in contrast to femininity
per se but also to boyhood: "manhood is constructed vis-à-vis *boyhood*
just as much as *womanhood*."[21] Inspired by the study on King David by
David J. A. Clines, Wilson examines the general conglomeration of "culturally exalted" features of hegemonic masculinity. These features consist
of strength (physical military prowess and psychological courage), per-
suasive/intelligent speech, self-control, honor (through competition, hospitality, or grace), kinship solidarity (for family, tribe, and nation), legal
manhood/age, as well as—albeit somewhat dubiously—physical beauty
(youthfulness), womanlessness (real men versus immature/infant), and
virility/marriage (heir/offspring).[22] Wilson opines that "the *failure*-to-
come-of-age theme is used in the book of Judges to indicate symbolically
Israel's national predicament as a fragmented and immature political/reli-
gious entity."[23]

---

19. Dolansky and Shetman, "What Is Gendered Historiography," 10.

20. Dolansky and Shetman, "What Is Gendered Historiography," 11–16. For a
countering epistemological and sociological analysis on gender vis-à-vis historiography, see Susanne Scholz, *The Bible as Political Artifact: On the Feminist Study of the
Hebrew Bible, Dispatches* (Minneapolis: Fortress, 2017).

21. Wilson, *Making Men*, 8, emphasis original. See also Nancy Chodorow,
"Family Structure and Feminine Personality," in *Woman, Culture, and Society*, ed.
Michelle Z. Rosaldo and Louise Lamphere (Stanford: Stanford University Press,
1974), 43–66; Gilbert H. Herdt, *Guardians of the Flutes: Idioms of Masculinity* (New
York: McGraw-Hill, 1981).

22. Wilson, *Making Men*, 29–46. David J. A. Clines, "David the Man: The Construction of Masculinity in the Hebrew Bible," in *Interested Parties: The Ideology of
Writers and Readers of the Hebrew Bible*, ed. David J. A. Clines, JSOTSup 205 (Sheffield: Sheffield Academic, 1995), 212–41.

23. Wilson, *Making Men*, 22, emphasis original.

Therefore, gender constructs comprise multifaceted features. Wilson posits that the story of Jether in Judg 8 and the Samson cycle in Judg 13–16 exhibit cases of "the converse of the coming-of-age theme—that is, they tell the story of youths who fail to transition to adulthood."[24] Interestingly, Samson as a man-child both possesses some of the masculine characteristics ("most notably strength, but also rhetorical skill—a function of wisdom") and lacks others ("self-control, kinship solidarity, marriage, and children").[25] Hence, as Rhiannon Graybill affirms, "masculinity in the Bible, even hegemonic masculinity, is unstable—'shaky indeed.'"[26] The same can apply to femininity, as Tamber-Rosenau argues for the Book of Judith, and (Pseudo-Philo's) LAB 31 claiming that Judg 4–5 is "about women performing femininity, acknowledging the system of sexual exchange of which they are a part, playing with it, and ultimately subverting it, and playing with the signs of maternity while not becoming mothers themselves."[27]

Like these critics, the contributors to this volume are interested in gender issues and their intersections/intertexts, but particularly in the book of Judges. The choice to engage Judges should not be surprising; it is one of the mainstays for gender analysis.[28] The reasons are myriad, but we will highlight three primary ones that are taken up in this volume. First, the intersection of sex, gender, and sexuality litters the book. Second, it is the poster child for gendered violence, including some of the most gratuitous male-on-female brutality in the Bible. Finally, Judges has an array of uniquely gendered characters, with several performing beyond the binary. Many characters play with or transgress the gender norms of the ancient Israelite world, and there seems to be an implicit intertextual invitation to compare and contrast the gender performance of all the characters as a result. These gender-centered questions lead to another host of ques-

---

24. Wilson, *Making Men*, 24.

25. Wilson, *Making Men*, 150. Note also p. 147: "Moreover, both the Jether and Samson stories function as counterpoints to the successful coming of age of David in 1 Sam 17. The relationship between these two tales of failing to come of age and David's successful maturation signifies the transition of Israel from immaturity to nationhood and political power."

26. Graybill, *Are We Not Men?*, 26.

27. Tamber-Rosenau, *Women in Drag*, 21–22.

28. See Kelly J. Murphy, "Judges in Recent Research," *CurBR* 15 (2017): 179–213, esp. 194; Kenneth M. Craig Jr., "Judges in Recent Research," *CurBR* 15 (2003):159–85, esp. 170–71.

tions about rhetorical function. Is gender purposefully being used by the authors to make a point? If so, is it about gender or something else entirely, like the moral depravity of the people of Israel, failed leadership, or heroics of the minoritized? If so, what is the historical context of the book as well as of the editorial layers, and how does that affect its intertextual relationship with other books? The contributors in this volume take up many of these queries in the following pages.

Intertextuality

What exactly is meant by *intertextuality*? The label was coined by Julia Kristeva in 1967, as is well known.[29] By intertextuality she meant that "any text is constructed as a mosaic of quotations; any text is the absorption and transformation of another."[30] Kristeva's intertextuality was influenced by Mikhail Bakhtin's "dialogism" and "polyphony" in that language is both "contextually shaped" and "intentionally relational," amid the plurality of heteroglossia inherent in dissonance and ambivalence.[31] Intertextuality is not about dependence of one, in this case, biblical text from another. It is about a conversation between two or more texts. One text interprets and reinterprets the other and vice versa. Meaning and intention are produced in and by the act of the intertextual conversation. Intertextuality is, thus, reception- and production-oriented at the same time, whereby production does not refer to the origin of either texts but to the reception. Intertextuality might be subdivided into intra-, inter-, and extratextuality.[32] Intratextuality points to intertextuality within the same text or book, for example,

---

29. Kristeva, "Bakhtine, le mot, le dialogue et le roman," *Critique* 23 (1967): 438–65.

30. Julia Kristeva, "Word, Dialogue, and Novel," in *Desire in Language: A Semiotic Approach to Literature and Art*, ed. Leon S. Roudiez, trans. Thomas Gora, Alice Jardine, and Leon S. Roudiez (New York: Columbia University Press, 1980), 66.

31. Patricia K. Tull, "Mikhail M. Bakhtin and Dialogical Approaches to Biblical Interpretation," in *Second Wave Intertextuality and the Hebrew Bible*, ed. Marianne Grohmann and Hyun Chul Paul Kim, RBS 93 (Atlanta: SBL Press, 2019), 180. Mikhail M. Bakhtin, "Discourse in the Novel," in *The Dialogic Imagination: Four Essays by M. M. Bakhtin*, ed. Michael Holquist, trans. Caryl Emerson and Michael Holquist (Austin: University of Texas Press, 1981), 259–422. See also Barbara Green, *Mikhail Bakhtin and Biblical Scholarship: An Introduction*, SemeiaSt 38 (Atlanta: Society of Biblical Literature, 2000).

32. On this division, see Stefan Alkier, "Intertextualität—Annäherung an ein texttheoretisches Paradigma," in *Heiligkeit und Herrschaft: Intertextuelle Studien zu*

within Judges; intertextuality generally refers to intertextual relationships within the same corpus or canon, for example, the Hebrew Bible/Old Testament; and extratextuality can refer to other texts, contexts, or even readers as texts. Although the concept of text is wide in semiotics studies, we adhere to text as written text, as the starting point, in this volume.

Although Kristeva did not adhere to her concept—she adjusted or even revoked it some years later—it was appetizing to biblical scholars. They could "happily continue doing what they have been doing all along, only under a fancier heading."[33] Because Kristeva's intertextuality was welcomed by biblical scholars early on, they have had ample time to refine the methods of intertextual readings of biblical texts. Inasmuch as there have been a plethora of theoretical and philosophical works influenced by Kristeva's intertextuality, biblical scholarship has enjoyed countless monographs and articles on the methodology or praxis of intertextuality in recent decades.

Michael Fishbane's exegetical distinction between "traditum" and "traditio" within the processes of innerbiblical exegesis has been groundbreaking, having reshaped biblical interpretation worldwide ever since its publication.[34] Biblical texts themselves present a mosaic of innumerable yet identifiable intertextual adaptations, be they interactions between the author and the redactor (redaction criticism), comparisons among different manuscripts (text criticism), and the like. Most apparently, among the dual or multiple texts, readers may detect interconnections that comprise a single phrase, a paragraph, or a motif. Cynthia Edenburg differentiates various modes of intertextuality: shared motifs (e.g., "removal of foreign gods," Judg 10:16), formulaic language (e.g., "to look up and see," Judg 19:17), type scenes (e.g., "hostility," Judg 19:3–9, 21–22), genres, parallel accounts, innerbiblical interpretation, allusion, and quotation/citation.[35] Yair Zakovitch essentially sums up with the distinction between "overt" (paraphrase) and "covert" (allusion) innerbiblical interpretation.[36]

Heiligkeitsvorstellungen und zu Psalm 110, ed. Dieter Sänger, Biblisch-theologische Studien 55 (Neukirchen-Vluyn: Neukirchener Verlag, 2003), 1–26.

33. Serge Frolov, "The Poverty of Parallels: Reading Judges 19 with Ezekiel 16 via the Song of Songs," ch. 15 in this volume.

34. Fishbane, *Biblical Interpretation in Ancient Israel* (Oxford: Clarendon, 1985).

35. Edenburg, "Intertextuality, Literary Competence and the Question of Readership: Some Preliminary Observations," *JSOT* 35 (2010): 131–48.

36. Zakovitch, "Inner-Biblical Interpretation," in *Reading Genesis: Ten Methods*, ed. Ronald Hendel (Cambridge: Cambridge University Press, 2010), 92.

Admittedly, biblical scholars have raised numerous probes and debates concerning the aspects of principles, boundaries, or applicability of intertextuality. The most controversial remains the distinction between diachronic and synchronic approaches, or, put slightly differently, between text-centered and reader-centered approaches. On the one hand, "when the reader takes the place of the author the text potentially becomes 'a tale told by an idiot, full of sound and fury, signifying nothing.'"[37] On the other hand, "the conflict of text-centered and reader-centered exegesis proves to be an unnecessary battle lacking reflection on textual theory."[38] Regardless of these contentions, Zakovitch's remark stands legitimate regarding the biblical texts: "No literary unit in the Bible stands alone, isolated and independent, with no other text drawing from its reservoir and casting it in a new light."[39] In fact, amid those interpretive tensions, we acknowledge that "scholars often cross the border between these approaches."[40]

Hence, rather than belaboring the ongoing debates of criteria, our goal primarily remains in what intertextuality can do: Why the authors/redactors did it, how we do it, and even the "so what" of these interpretive approaches. The book of Judges, we believe, can provide a paradigmatic resource for such a goal. The book is itself a conglomeration of many texts. Its hinge status within the Enneateuch (within the transition from the Pentateuch to the Former Prophets) makes it function as a hybrid or interrelated book as well.

Introducing the Essays in This Volume

Gender and intertextuality are the lenses through which the contributors of this volume analyze texts in the book of Judges; some of them more focused on gender, some more on intertextuality, and others on both. Indeed, that might be the value of the volume. Much has already been written about gender in Judges, especially from a feminist perspec-

37. William Irwin, "Against Intertextuality," *Philosophy and Literature* 28 (2004): 236.

38. Stefan Alkier, "Intertextuality and the Semiotics of Biblical Texts," in *Reading the Bible Intertextually*, ed. Richard B. Hays, Stefan Alkier, and Leroy A. Huizenga (Waco, TX: Baylor University Press, 2009), 8.

39. Zakovitch, "Inner-Biblical Interpretation," 95.

40. Karl William Weyde, "Inner-Biblical Interpretation: Methodological Reflections on the Relationship between Texts in the Hebrew Bible," *SEÅ* 70 (2005): 300.

tive.[41] By combining intertextual and gender study, the origin, focus, and meaning of the stories can become sharper than by isolated approaches. The male characters and the many—in comparison to other biblical books—female characters interact with other characters within the book of Judges, without Judges in the Hebrew Bible/Old Testament, and maybe even beyond. Especially the gender aspect might play a decisive role in the intertextual conversation with other texts. Both partners of this conversation gain meaning by and in this process. Judges is popular in biblical research and study, and the last two decades alone have yielded many new commentaries on it.[42]

While numerous feminist, womanist, and minoritized biblical interpretations have been published on the book of Judges, there are few specifically intertextual studies that deal with gender in the book of Judges. The fifteen collected essays in this volume will cover almost all of the key texts, characters, and judges in the book of Judges. This will help readers find examples of how intertextuality together with gender criticism can bring new insight to the book of Judges and, by way of example, to the whole Bible.

Susan E. Haddox identifies the intricate relationship of the triple intertext between Genesis and Judges: Lot and his daughters (Gen 19) with the

41. See, e.g., Athalya Brenner, ed., *A Feminist Companion to Judges*, FCB 4 (Sheffield: JSOT Press, 1993); Brenner, ed., *Judges: Feminist Companion to the Bible*, FCB 2/4 (Sheffield: Sheffield Academic, 1999); Brenner, "Introduction," in Brenner, *Judges*, 13–17; Susan Ackerman, *Warrior, Dancer, Seductress, Queen: Women in Judges and Biblical Israel*, ABRL (New York: Doubleday, 1998).

42. See the research overview by Murphy, "Judges in Recent Research," of which the bibliography spans eighteen out of thirty-five pages! For older research, see Craig, "Judges in Recent Research." See, among others and without commentaries devoted to more than one biblical book, Marc Z. Brettler, *The Book of Judges*, OTR (London: Routledge, 2002); Trent C. Butler, *Judges*, WBC 8 (Nashville: Nelson, 2009); Serge Frolov, *Judges*, FOTL 6B (Grand Rapids: Eerdmans, 2013); Walter Groß, *Richter: Übersetzt und ausgelegt*, HThKAT (Freiburg im Breisgau: Herder, 2009); David M. Gunn, *Judges*, Blackwell Bible Commentaries (Malden, MA: Blackwell, 2004); Ernst A. Knauf, *Richter*, ZBK 7 (Zurich: TVZ, 2016); J. C. McCann, *Judges*, IBC (Louisville: Westminster John Knox, 2011); Susan Niditch, *Judges: A Commentary*, OTL (Louisville: Westminster John Knox, 2008); Roger Ryan, *Judges*, Readings, New Biblical Commentary (Sheffield: Sheffield Phoenix, 2007); Jack M. Sasson, *Judges 1–12: A New Translation with Introduction and Commentary*, AB 6D (New Haven: Yale University Press, 2014); Klaas Spronk, *Judges*, HCOT 7 (Leuven: Peeters, 2019); Barry G. Webb, *The Book of Judges*, NICOT (Grand Rapids: Eerdmans, 2012).

Levite and his wife (Judg 19), Abraham and Isaac (Gen 22) with Jephthah and his daughter (Judg 11), and Judah and Tamar (Gen 28) with Caleb and Achsah (Judg 1). In "Bizarro Genesis: An Intertextual Reading of Gender and Identity in Judges," Haddox points out how Judges reverses Genesis in three main ways, all of which have to do with gender and/or identity. First, Judges lays out the parallel stories in reverse, creating a chiasmus. Second, Judges inverts the gender of the victims, and, finally, it transposes the focus of identity issues, particularly in relationship to the land and God. Genesis moves from extreme violence against out-groups toward a more temperate model of inclusion as the lineage of the promise solidifies, largely via the determination of women. The violence in Judges only accumulates, extinguishing the lives of women and nearly decimating a tribe. Pedigree moves to the background as land rights and the need for political institutions move to the fore. Genesis reinforces kinship ties and God's continual intervention. Judges lacks God's direct involvement and society falls apart. It is almost impossible to read these biblical books and not think of the other. They are both using stories of gender and violence to share community identity, yet in very different ways and with very different points to make.

"The Assertiveness of Achsah: Gender and Intertextuality in the Reception History of Caleb's Daughter" also examines the story of Achsah in Judg 1:11–15 (and Josh 15:13–19). Joy A. Schroeder begins by pointing out the remarkability of Achsah's story because it is only one of two in the Hebrew Bible in which women directly ask for and receive land. Thereafter, she forges through the history of interpretation of this remarkable female character, with emphasis on early modern and nineteenth-century commentators. In general, males of this generation find Achsah a discontented woman and ungrateful daughter. A few praise her, but often in a way that dampens her personality or portrays her requests allegorically rather than literally. Only in the late 1800s, when American and European women began to fight for and gain property rights, did interpreters (mostly women) latch onto Achsah as an exemplar for that aim. Schroeder concludes that Achsah's intertext with nineteenth-century interpreters, and their intertextual readings of her via other biblical passages, ultimately reinforced each interpreter's ideologies of gender.

Unlike most women in the Hebrew Bible, who are usually bound up in their identities as wives, mothers, or daughters, Deborah and Jael are portrayed as leaders and heroes in Judg 4–5. According to Pamela J. W. Nourse, in her essay, "Into the Hand of a Woman: Deborah and Jael in

Judges 4–5," the women are both painted in a positive light, yet their characterizations are distinct when the language used to describe them is scrupulously analyzed. Deborah receives the rare title of "prophetess" and is the sole female depicted as judging Israel. Both descriptions give Deborah a leadership role that comes with communal authority and put her on par with the other prophet-judges, Moses and Samuel. Several of her other actions are rare, and the feminine labels as "wife" and "mother" should not be taken literally, but metaphorical and thus nontraditionally. Deborah is no stereotype. Jael, on the other hand, does seems to fit expected roles. While Deborah is commanding in a military, judicial, and social context, Jael is placed in a domestic setting. While she does not interact with her husband or any children, Jael's actions still evoke stereotypical imagery. She mothers in Judg 4 and is sexualized in Judg 5. Yet Nourse argues that Jael's actions ultimately subvert the assumed connotations. Though motherly, she takes life, and though the presumptive penetrated, she penetrates. Though unique and independent women, together, they conquer an enemy and are praised.

In "Nameless in the Nevi'im: Intertextuality between Female Characters in the Book of Judges," Elizabeth H. P. Backfish examines the rhetorical effect of the named and unnamed female characters who "exert themselves" (following Susan Ackerman) in the story. She argues that when read intertextually, didactic contrasts become apparent; the named figures function as exemplars for Israel's behavior, while the unnamed ones illustrate inappropriate behavior or the consequences thereof. Moreover, there is a structural, chiastic pairing of the women and their male counterparts, which underscores traits that should be deemed commendable (faithfulness) or flawed (unfaithfulness), reflecting the downward spiral of depravity in the book. All this exerts a rhetorical mimetic pressure on the audience to identify with the weaknesses of the anonymous female characters and aspire to be more like the named ones.

J. Cornelis de Vos, in "The Caleb-Achsah Episode: Judges 1:10–15," explores the intertextual relationships between Judg 1:10–15, its parallel in Josh 15:13–19, and the David-Abigail narrative in 1 Sam 25. After demonstrating that the episode in Judg 1 is the latest, de Vos proposes that the authors of Judges adapted the earlier Josh 15 story of Caleb, Achsah, and Othniel and then added it to the beginning of Judges in order to reinforce the Davidic-Judahite predilection of their (likely postexilic) edition. The most obvious edit is the transformation of Caleb's inheritance of Hebron into Judah's conquest of the city instead (Josh 15:13; Judg 1:10). Something more difficult to explain is why they would keep the Caleb-Achsah narrative despite the contradictions that result. Perhaps their overriding purpose was to connect two assertive donkey-riding wives of Calebites, Achsah and Abigail. The intertextual link would draw attention not only to shrewd females (which may or may not have been humorous to a contemporary audience), but also to a shrewd king—David, the Judahite. Ultimately, we cannot know the intentions of the authors, but the intertextual play is undoubtedly entertaining.

In "Motherhood, Violence, and Power in the Book of Judges," Rannfrid I. Lasine Thelle poses the following question: "Does Judges toy with the specter of motherhood as reduced to the mere function of keeping the tribes alive, as breeding machines?" Deborah is referred to as "the mother of the tribes of Israel" and keeps the tribes of Israel alive. However, she is not described as a mother of real children. The other mothers, such as those of Samson and Micah, cannot protect their children—and mothering behavior can even be lethal (for Sisera). At the end of the book of Judges, women become breeding machines in acts of mass rape by the Benjaminites, in order to secure offspring for the tribe of Benjamin. The violence is expressed as taking wombs (רחם), an act Sisera's mother also expects from him. Thus, focusing on the motif of motherhood in Judges elucidates concepts of power and violence.

In "Struck Down by a Woman: Abimelech's Humiliating Intertextual Death," Zev Farber describes how humiliating the death of Abimelech is when read intertextually. In order to do so, he reconstructs several layers of redactional work in the Abimelech account and connects them with compositional phases in related texts, namely the story about Uriah being killed (2 Sam 11) and the story about the death of Saul (1 Sam 31). In the first, as part of the story of the battle in which Uriah was killed, an explicit reference is made to the death of Abimelech by a woman. In the second, Saul asks his armor-bearer to kill him to prevent someone who is uncircumcised from killing him, thereby saving Saul's honor as king of Israel. When these three accounts are read together intertextually, the story of Abimelech becomes even more ignoble. Abimelech is struck down by a woman, whereas Uriah is not. He asks his armor-bearer to kill him so that no one can say that he was killed by a woman and thereby lose his honor. At this request, his servant unhesitatingly kills him. In contrast, the servant of Saul refuses the king's order, and Saul falls on his own sword.

"Fathers, Daughters, and Problematic Verbal Commitments in Judges" are the themes Richard D. Nelson addresses. He analyzes and compares three father(s)-daughter(s) relations in three stories: Caleb and Achsah (Judg 1), Jephthah and his daughter (Judg 10–12), and the fallen fathers and their captured daughters of Jabesh-Gilead and the daughters of Shiloh (Judg 21). Fathers, in a patrimonial society, can give their daughters away as brides. As the Jephthah and Shiloh stories show, the brides should be virgins. Caleb's verbal commitment to give away his daughter as a prize can be considered less problematic than the others. Jephthah's vow leads to the sacrifice of his own daughter and only offspring. The two oaths by the elders of the congregation are clearly problematic because they would lead to the extinction of certain tribes and to the virgin daughters' loss of their potential families. But by the end of Judges, the father-daughter relationship is treated with contempt.

Jennifer J. Williams uses the concept of liminality and the postcolonial notion of unhomeliness to analyze the Judg 13 narrative about the conception of Samson in "A Mother's Womb: The Collision of Politics and the Home in Judges 13." The wife of Manoah is the only one who is informed by the messenger of God about her conception. Even when Manoah wants the messenger to come to both spouses, he reappears only to the wife. Williams scrutinizes the Hebrew wording of the messenger's annunciations and concludes that at the second meeting, the wife *is* pregnant without having had any obvious sexual interaction with her husband. Thus, the pregnancy is initiated by God. This is an invasion of God's politics into the homeliness of the woman who, being pregnant and thus in a liminal state, does not tell her husband that God wants her son to be a military leader. God uses the womb, the homeliest space of a woman, for political aims, whereas the wife wants her son to have a normal life.

Many more males than females cry in the Hebrew Bible, and they cry for more reasons as well, the most common being the loss of someone close. Thus, there is no statistical evidence to suppose that crying is primarily a female act. Nor is there evidence that the Timnite woman used crying as a gendered tool to have Samson tell her the solution of his riddle, argues Shelley L. Birdsong in "Rereading Samson's Weepy Wife in Judges 14: An Intertextual Evaluation of Gender and Weeping." However, this is what exegetes have often stated in the reception history of this tale. Through a close reading of the text and the aid of cultural and psychological studies about crying, Birdsong shows that such a view of the Timnite's crying is a product of cultural gender bias, mainly by males. The Timnite cried to save her family from death; undoubtedly anyone in such a circumstance, regardless of gender, would do the same.

In "One of These Things Is Not Like the Other: Delilah and the Prostitute in Gaza," Tammi J. Schneider expounds the gendered roles Delilah plays
in her intertextual relationships with other characters, such as Samson's
mother, the Timnite bride, the prostitute in Gaza, and especially Samson.
A brief review of the reception history on Delilah vis-à-vis Samson conveys
that over and against Samson the hero, Delilah has assumed the status of
a villainous *femme fatale*. Despite the negative labeling, Delilah stands as
a unique character. As the only named woman in the Samson narrative,
Delilah philologically forms intertextual contrasts with other women whose
depictions as "wife," "whore," or "prostitute" make Delilah stand apart. Without ethnic designation, geographical association, or family ties, Delilah is an
independent character. Eight verbs associated with Delilah as the subject
further underscore her unique role, defying conventional female characterizations. Ten verbs with Delilah as the object also depict her agency and
power, describing events in which she has survived and prevailed in ordeals
against men of immense strength.

Judges 17–18, a seemingly isolated pericope, nonetheless connects the
Danites to Samson the Danite in Judg 13–16 as well as the Levite from
Judah to another Levite of Ephraim in Judg 19–21. In her essay, "'Jonathan's (Great) Grandmother Is a Daughter of a Foreign Priest!': Other
Women, Other Priests, and Other Gods in Judges 17–18," Soo Kim Sweeney expounds the text-critical matters of the hidden, hanging *nun* in the
name of Jonathan's grandfather (Judg 18:30), which can denote either
Moses or Manasseh. Such complexity of the proper names expands to
further interrelated characters pregnant with the issues of intertextuality
and gender. Both Moses, with his son Gershom, and Manasseh, with his
Egyptian mother Asenath, insinuate foreignness and exogamy. Micah too
entails polemic against northern Israel, through the allusions to the Jacob-
Rachel couple and the Ephraimite King Jeroboam. Likewise, these literary
threads portray Luce Irigaray's "womb-earth-factory" metaphor of body
politics, causing Micah's mother, though a leader figure, to disappear into
the private zone and degrading Zipporah the wife of Moses and Asenath
the mother of Manasseh into dangerous foreign/otherness. Nevertheless,
amid the polemics against the Danites and northern tribes, Kim Sweeney
elucidates, these foreign/other characters embraced and looked after their
others for altruistic reasons.

The nameless woman in Judg 19 is described as a "secondary woman,"
"young woman," "slave," and "woman." In "Lost in the Text(s): The פילגש in
Judg 19," Susanne Gillmayr-Bucher intertextually examines various roles

implied by פילגש. Though echoing other occurrences, the term פילגש defies typical portrayals of femininity. This woman is placed on the threshold between inside and outside, between belonging and being the other. She is not merely an allusion to the idolatrous wrongdoings of Israel; rather, this woman displays self-determination, taking initiative and returning to her father's house. Yet, ample intertextual allusions (e.g., Gen 22; Exod 2; Deut 22; 2 Kgs 9; Jer 31; Ezek 16; Hos 2) insinuate comparable expressions and themes of covenant reconciliation. Yet Judg 19 twists any expectation of Israel's virtue or dignity into the depersonalization, devaluation, and dismemberment of the woman, cold-bloodedly executed by male offenders after being led in by her own Levite husband. These images insinuate the fragile and dangerous character of Israel's identity.

Explicating the interpretive tension or mutuality between textual evidences on the one hand and new meanings transposed by readers on the other, Serge Frolov elucidates the gender issues pervading two texts that represent and connect the Enneateuch and the prophets in his essay, "The Poverty of Parallels: Reading Judges 19 with Ezekiel 16 via the Song of Songs." More than the anonymity of Samson's mother and Micah's mother, that even the main characters—the Levite and his spouse—are unnamed is quite unusual. This intertextually parallels the anonymous couple in the Song of Songs, and also the metaphorical couple of male deity (YHWH) and female community (Lady Israel/Zion). Thereafter, Frolov presents and investigates the intertextuality of Judg 19 against Ezek 16. The controversial apostasy or unfaithfulness of the spouse to the husband, leading to the haunting imagery of gang rape, probes issues of theodicy and intervention (or lack thereof) in light of the modern-day Holocaust. Whereas God restores the promiscuous Lady Israel in Ezek 16, the Levite in Judg 19 mutilates the body of his spouse—metaphorically evoking the dismembered body of Israel (both ancient and modern)—even when she returned to him.

Gregory T. K. Wong explores the contact points of the two diametrically opposed approaches of intertextuality, (diachronic) author/reader-centered and (synchronic) reader-centered, in "Synchrony versus Diachrony—Reader- versus Author-Centered: Shall the Twain Ever Meet?" To do so, Wong examines two narratives of pledges where women are victimized—Jephthah's daughter (Judg 11) and the kidnapped daughters who are to be wives for Benjaminites (Judg 21). Both texts contain similar plots and character descriptions, which, Wong opines, adumbrate Judg 11 as the source text (part of the Deuteronomistic core) and Judg 21 as the alluding text (part of a later editorial epilogue in Judg 17–21). Diachronic correlations associated with gender—such as virgins and dances linked to the daughter of Jephthah, virgins of Jabesh-Gilead, and daughters of Shiloh—engender the synchronic dialogues of these two narratives, imbued with meaning through critiques of war, pledge, and (male) leadership.

These essays themselves will thus showcase diverse methodological orientation and hermeneutical outcomes as to how to read the book of Judges with regard to intertextuality (including innerbiblical exegesis and reception history) as well as gender (including feminism, masculinity, and so on). By projecting and presenting multifaceted cases of intertextuality and gender, the essays in this volume can become enlivening dialogue partners toward future directions and developments of gender and intertextual studies.

2

Bizarro Genesis:
An Intertextual Reading of
Gender and Identity in Judges

Susan E. Haddox

The books of Genesis and Judges wrestle with issues of identity and inheritance. Although several stories run in parallel, moving from Genesis to Judges is like walking into bizarro world. The already fraught stories in Genesis are taken to extremes in Judges, where the negative outcomes avoided in Genesis come to grisly fruition. An intertextual reading of three stories in Genesis and their parallels in Judges helps to reveal their respective purposes in the broader contexts of the books. The stories are those of Lot and his daughters in Gen 19, Abraham and Isaac in Gen 22, and Judah and Tamar in Gen 38 in comparison with the Levite and his wife in Judg 19, Jephthah and his daughter in Judg 11, and Achsah and Caleb in Judg 1. In addition to increasing the intensity of the stories, the Judges stories invert three important elements of the stories with respect to their predecessors. The first of these reversals is the order of the stories. The three parallel stories fall roughly at the beginning, middle, and end of the book of Judges, and toward the beginning and end of the family narratives in Genesis, but they appear in reverse order. Second, the stories invert the gender of the victims, with Judges offering female victims. Finally, Judges inverts the focus of identity issues. Genesis works to establish lineage to differentiate a nascent and landless Israel from its neighbors. Judges also wrestles with issues of lineage and identity, but these take place in a landed context and revolve around who has the legitimacy to reside in the land and claim leadership. Notably, God's direct involvement drops off radically from Genesis to Judges.

This analysis will focus on final form readings and will not address issues of dating or authorship, which are murky and only tangential to the argument. Whether the Genesis stories came first and the author(s) of Judges twisted them, or the author(s) of Genesis modified the Judges stories, or both worked from common base stories that they took in different directions, the conclusions are not substantially affected. Instead, I am considering the stories themselves, how they compare and contrast, and how they fit into the larger narratives and purposes of the books of Genesis and Judges, and what a comparative reading highlights.

Lot and His Daughters

The first two stories to be considered in Genesis are part of the Abraham narrative. Genesis 19 describes Lot's fate in Sodom. After God decides to destroy the city because of the outcry against its injustice, Lot is the only one to offer the investigating angels shelter. Lot counters the demand of the men surrounding his house to send out his guests so that they may get to "know" them with an offer of his own virgin daughters, who were betrothed to men of the town. The crowd then turns against Lot as a foreign sojourner who deigns to judge them, but before they can push through Lot's door, the angels blind the men and pull Lot inside to safety. When the angels instruct Lot's family to leave, Lot lingers, the future sons-in-law, who were presumably part of the crowd, refuse to come at all, and Lot's wife famously turns back to her salty regret. When Sodom and Gomorrah are obliterated, Lot's daughters fear that they will never have husbands and the race will die out, so they get their father drunk and sleep with him on two consecutive nights, raping him as he would have let them be raped by the crowd. They bear sons, who grow up to be the eponymous founders of Israel's rival neighbors Ammon and Moab.

This story is complex with many implications, but I will focus on principles related to legitimacy and identity. The first relates to the admonition to stay away from the people of the land. This idea is reinforced throughout Genesis. Lot throws in his lot with the cities of the plain, even planning to marry his daughters to men of Sodom, and that turns out to be a bad idea. The sons-in-law refuse to come with Lot and be saved. Second, the story sets up Israel's neighbors as, to quote Randall Bailey, "nothing but incestuous bastards."[1] Moab and Ammon are tangentially related to

---

1. Randall Bailey, "They're Nothing but Incestuous Bastards: The Polemical Use of Sex and Sexuality in Hebrew Canon Narratives," in *Social Location and Biblical Inter-*

Abraham's lineage, but aspersion is cast on their character. While they are not the product of intermixing with the people of the land, they are suspect as illegitimate and incestuous children.[2] Third, women are used to protect the men and take charge of the lineage. Although the angels do end up preventing any violation of persons in Sodom, Lot was willing to use his daughters to protect the honor of the visitors. The women were set up as sacrifices to protect the bodily integrity of the males who were under threat.[3] In turn, the daughters determine the lineage through raping their father. They bear the sons who start to form the social geography of the region. This female control of the lineage may seem to be the inverse of social norms, but it is a theme throughout Genesis, including Sarah's advocacy of Isaac and the favored status of Rachel's sons, as well as the story in Gen 38, discussed further below.

Abraham and Isaac

The second passage to consider is Gen 22, the binding of Isaac. This story follows immediately upon the conflict over succession between Abraham's son Ishmael from Hagar and his son Isaac from Sarah. Just as Lot's daughters are in charge of the lineage above, Sarah is the one who determines that her son should be the heir, and God supports her position. Once Isaac is left as the sole heir, God asks Abraham to offer him as a whole burnt offering, which he agrees to do. Though Isaac makes a brief inquiry about the absence of the ram to sacrifice, he continues wordlessly with his father through the ordeal. Abraham leaves the servants behind, prepares the altar, binds Isaac, places him on the altar, and raises the knife to slaughter his son when the angel appears and stays his hand. Abraham's willingness to slay his son tells God everything God needs to know, and a ram

---

pretation in the United States, vol. 1 of *Reading from This Place*, ed. Fernando F. Segovia and Mary Ann Tolbert (Minneapolis: Fortress, 1995), 121–38.

2. W. Sibley Towner, *Genesis*, Westminster Bible Companion (Louisville: Westminster John Knox, 2001), 174–75; Kathleen M. O'Connor, *Genesis 1–25A*, SHBC 1A (Macon, GA: Smyth & Helwys, 2018), 281; Susan A. Brayford, *Genesis,* Septuagint Commentary Series (Leiden: Brill, 2007), 322. Mark G. Brett argues that the extreme circumstances of the case, in which the daughters think there is no other man left, mitigates the negative connotation for the lineage (*Genesis: Procreation and the Politics of Identity*, OTR [London: Routledge, 2000], 68–69).

3. Phyllis Trible, *Texts of Terror: A Literary-Feminist Reading of Biblical Narratives*, OBT 13 (Philadelphia: Fortress, 1984), 75.

is provided as an alternative. In the context of Genesis, the story serves to solidify Abraham's intense and zealous faith and to reify Isaac's selection as the bearer of the lineage.[4] Sarah, as Abraham's primary wife, is vindicated, and the secondary status of Hagar as a foreigner and a slave leaves her son Ishmael out in the cold, or at least in the dry desert, though he does get his own legacy of descendants.[5]

Judah and Tamar

The third story for consideration is that of Tamar in Gen 38. In contrast to previous stories, in which marriage to people of the land is expressly condemned, including the marriages of Isaac, Esau, Jacob, and Dinah, Judah marries a Canaanite woman.[6] He has three sons, the first of whom he marries to Tamar. Tamar's identity is uncertain. Although she is sent back to her father's house later in the story, her father's name and ethnicity are not revealed. Considering the extreme concern with intermarriage even

---

4. See Ed Noort, "Genesis 22: Human Sacrifice and Theology in the Hebrew Bible," in *The Sacrifice of Isaac: The Aqedah (Genesis 22) and Its Interpretations*, ed. Ed Noort and Eibert Tigchelaar, TBN 4 (Leiden: Brill, 2002), 4–6, who notes that the linkage of Gen 12, 21, and 22 serve to reveal the "real heir" as Isaac. The Genesis emphasis on lineage is apparent when the story is read in comparison with the version in the Qur'an, as noted by Yvonne Sherwood, "Binding–Unbinding: Divided Responses of Judaism, Christianity, and Islam to the 'Sacrifice' of Abraham's Beloved Son," *JAAR* 72 (2004): 826–27; and John Kaltner, "Abraham's Sons: How the Bible and the Qur'an See the Same Story Differently," *BRev* 18 (2002): 22–23. Contra Brett, *Genesis*, 74–75, who argues that the final editing of the text undermines this exclusivity of lineage by its juxtaposition with Ishmael's story.

5. Hagar is referred to as an אמה in Gen 21:10, which, while not having a definitive meaning, implies a bonded status, perhaps as a concubine. By casting her and her son into the desert, Abraham is also freeing them (Philip Y. Yoo, "Hagar the Egyptian: Wife, Handmaid, and Concubine," *CBQ* 78 [2016]: 226). See also Nahum M. Sarna, *Genesis: The Traditional Hebrew Text with the New JPS Translation*, JPS Torah Commentary (Philadelphia: Jewish Publication Society of America, 1989), 147. For a discussion of the anthropological background for Sarah asserting her status as the primary wife and mother of the primary heir, see Naomi Steinberg, "Kinship and Gender in Genesis," *BR* 39 (1994): 54–55.

6. Abraham's marriage to Keturah in Gen 25:1–6 is not condemned, but the text specifies that the children of that marriage are given gifts but are not included in the primary inheritance or lineage. Towner argues that the lack of condemnation for Judah's intermarriage suggest an early date for the passage (*Genesis*, 250).

up through Dinah's story in Gen 34, this omission is notable. Judah's own choice of wife and Tamar's proximity may indicate that she is Canaanite, which the majority of commentators assume, but she has a Hebrew name.[7] Er is struck down by God, and Tamar is married next to Onan, who is likewise killed after refusing to fulfill his levirate responsibilities. When Tamar later notices that she is still not married to the third son Shelah, she takes matters into her own hands, dressing as a prostitute to seduce Judah when he goes up to sheepshearing. He sleeps with her, leaving his signet ring and staff with her as a pledge. After Judah sentences her to burning for becoming pregnant, she produces the evidence that he is the father, and he relents, calling her more righteous than he. Her twin boys continue Judah's lineage.

This final story before the Joseph novella contributes to our lineage analysis. First, the questions of lineage identity are intriguing. If Tamar is of Abraham's family lineage, then the story bypasses the mixed heritage of Er and Onan and restores the purity of the lineage through Judah. If she is a Canaanite like Shua's daughter, then her actions and acceptance mark a narrative change in what constitutes Israelite identity. Her commitment to the family outweighs genealogy. Second, the woman continues to be the determinant of the lineage. Based on the deaths of his sons, Judah may have feared that she was an unacceptable wife, but her actions proved her loyalty to the lineage.[8] She forced Judah to take responsibility for his actions and to dispense justice, recognizing that he had not fulfilled his duties as a patriarch.[9]

Each of these stories is concerned with lineage. Genesis 19 establishes some lineages as illegitimate, setting up tense relations with neighboring states. Genesis 22 selects a primary lineage from Abraham, which is vulnerable to, but supported by, God's command. Genesis 38 shows that the lineage is also vulnerable to human error and must sometimes be preserved through extraordinary measures. It also shows a slight opening of

---

7. Ephraim A. Speiser, *Genesis: A New Translation with Introduction and Commentary*, AB 1 (Garden City, NY: Doubleday, 1964), 300. Brayford, *Genesis*, 319. Brett also argues for Tamar's foreignness, because of the lack of tribal identification, but notes the ambiguity in the text (*Genesis*, 113).

8. Towner notes that her name is used as a blessing for building up a house of Israel by a foreign woman in Ruth 4:12 (*Genesis*, 253).

9. See also Brett, *Genesis*, 114.

identity, as the lineage becomes settled, to those who pledge loyalty. The Judges stories start from the latter point, before unwinding into chaos.

Achsah and Othniel

Judges marks a new phase in developing identity as landed people. The frame of the book describes an incomplete conquest, with some initial success. Caleb incentivized the capture of Kiriath-sepher by offering his daughter's hand in marriage. Othniel accomplishes the feat and receives his reward. The daughter Achsah is unhappy about her lack of a dowry.[10] First, she urges Othniel to ask for a piece of land, which apparently is given in the desert. This transfer of land is elided in the text, which moves immediately to her second request, when she, as Ken Stone puts it, "gets off her ass" and requests that Caleb also give springs to make the land fertile.[11] He accedes to her request.

This story connects to that of Tamar. In both cases, the father figures have not lived up to their obligations in the marriage of the next generation, risking the lineage. Giving his daughter Achsah away without a good dowry puts the legitimacy of her offspring in jeopardy.[12] She demands her rights, which also ensures the legitimacy and inheritance rights of Caleb's grandchildren. In both her case and Tamar's, the daughter is the one who defies convention and confronts the father to get the necessary resources. In both cases the father acknowledges the righteousness of the daughter's request either through words or deeds.

---

10. Jack M. Sasson (*Judges 1–12: A New Translation with Introduction and Commentary*, AB 6D [New Haven: Yale University Press, 2014], 152) discusses Achsah's dual request for land and water as a suitable dowry in order to assure the stability of her marriage, noting that Caleb had given her away without one. Sasson follows the JPS in translating her complaint that she was given away "as Negeb land," i.e., without a dowry, as does Victor H. Matthews, *Judges and Ruth*, NCBC (Cambridge: Cambridge University Press, 2004), 40; and Richard D. Nelson, *Judges: A Critical and Rhetorical Commentary* (New York: Bloomsbury T&T Clark, 2017), 21.

11. Stone, "What Happens When Achsah Gets Off Her Ass? Queer Reading and Judges 1:11–15," in *Sacred Tropes: Tanakh, New Testament, and Qur'an as Literature and Culture*, ed. Roberta Sterman Sabbath, BibInt 98 (Leiden: Brill, 2009), 409–20. Nelson, *Judges*, 21 also notes this two-part dowry ask.

12. Steinberg, "Kinship and Gender in Genesis," 48–49. Richard D. Nelson, "What Is Achsah Doing in Judges?," in *The Impartial God: Essays in Biblical Studies in Honor of Jouette M. Bassler*, ed. Calvin J. Roetzel and Robert L. Foster, New Testament Monographs 22 (Sheffield: Sheffield Phoenix, 2007), 16.

In addition, both stories wrestle with Israelite identity. Tamar's identity is uncertain, but she is drawn into the tradition by her commitment to the lineage of Judah. Achsah is the daughter of Caleb and the wife of Othniel, whose statuses as Israelites are ambiguous. In Num 13:6 Caleb is identified as a leader of Judah, chosen to reconnoiter the promised land, but in Josh 14:6 Caleb is clearly identified as son of Jephunneh the Kenizzite (כלב בן־יפנה הקנזי), leading up to the doublet of the Judges passage in Josh 15.[13] In Judg 1:13, Othniel is likewise identified as a Kenizzite, but the phrasing is ambiguous: עתניאל בן־קנז אחי כלב הקטן ממנו ("Othniel, son of Kenaz, brother of Caleb, who is younger than him"). Othniel is called the "son of Kenaz," which is sometimes understood as the clan name Kenizzite and sometimes as an individual name.[14] Translations of Kenaz as a proper name obscure the non-Israelite identity of Caleb, Othniel, and Achsah, although the identity of the Kenizzites themselves is uncertain.[15] Significantly, the question of Israelite identity is a dynamic concept in Judges and seems to be influenced by choices and actions, not

---

13. Joshua 14:13–14 has Joshua granting Caleb the territory of Hebron within the territory of Judah, because of his faithfulness, but underscores his Kenizzite identity. The Kenizzites are often associated with Edom, because Kenaz is listed as the grandson of Esau in Gen 36:11, 15 (Carolyn Pressler, *Joshua, Judges, and Ruth*, Westminster Bible Companion [Louisville: Westminster John Knox, 2002], 93).

14. For the former, see JPS. The translation is also complicated by whether to understand Othniel as Caleb's younger brother or nephew. Robert G. Boling understands the term as a military confederate, based on usage at Mari (*Judges: A New Translation with Introduction and Commentary*, AB 6A [Garden City, NY: Doubleday, 1975], 56). Tammi J. Schneider discusses the ambiguity but translates as Othniel being Caleb's younger brother (*Judges: Studies in Hebrew Narrative and Poetry*, Berit Olam [Collegeville, MN: Liturgical Press, 2000], 10–11). Barnabas Lindars suggests the story may demonstrate uncle to nephew inheritance pattern (*Judges 1–5: A New Translation and Commentary* [Edinburgh: T&T Clark, 1995], 22), also seen in Gen 24–28.

15. Ken Stone observes the blurring of the Kenizzite identity in this passage: "Genesis 15.19 goes further, including the Kenizzites among those peoples who already inhabit the land that God will give to Abraham's descendants. Yet here, Caleb and Othniel are involved with the tribe of Judah in bringing about the very Israelite takeover that Genesis 15.19 seems to anticipate" ("What Happens," 418). A. Graeme Auld notes that the Caleb tradition of Josh 15 is subsumed into the lore of Judah in Judges, with Caleb's sole defeat of the sons of Anak at Hebron and assault on Debir (Josh 14:14–15) attributed to Judah (Judges 1:10–11), which reframes the conquest of Debir in a Judahite setting (Auld, *Joshua, Judges, and Ruth*, Daily Study Bible [Philadelphia: Westminster, 1984], 135).

just by lineage.[16] In Num 14:24 Caleb is singled out among the Israelites as the one from that generation who will see and take possession of the promised land, because "he had a different spirit within him and followed me fully." Othniel also possesses this spirit to follow YHWH (Judg 3:10).

Thus, both stories have a role in redefining Israelite status from genetic to spiritual identity. The move is almost overlooked in Genesis, because of Tamar's uncertain identity and because it runs counter to the overwhelming thrust of the family narratives earlier, yet it also opens the door to Joseph's marriage to an Egyptian priest's daughter and the introduction of other foreign women in the lineage.[17] Similarly, Caleb's and Othniel's liminal identity is often overlooked in studies of Judges, where Othniel is lifted up as the ideal Israelite judge from the tribe of Judah.[18] Both stories serve to redefine the lineage. The story of Achsah shows the least inversions of the narrative from that in Genesis, and in fact is the one story in this analysis where the Judges version is tamer than the Genesis version, as the beginning of Judges reflects the most normalcy. While Achsah's actions in confronting her father are unexpected, they certainly have more propriety than dressing as a prostitute and sleeping with one's father-in-law. Yet the result of Achsah's action is less socially typical. Her efforts graft her husband more securely into the Israelite lineage by obtaining land for him in the tribal allotment of Judah, rather than simply preserving that lineage or being grafted in as a wife, as is the case with Tamar.[19] Achsah's role both as a prize for capturing a city and as an advocate for a fertile land dowry also

---

16. J. Clinton McCann, *Judges*, IBC (Louisville: Westminster John Knox, 2011), 32, discusses some of the issues of ambiguous identity, as does Danna Nolan Fewell, "Deconstructive Criticism: Achsah and the (E)razed City of Writing," in *Judges and Method: New Approaches in Biblical Studies*, ed. Gale A. Yee, 2nd ed. (Minneapolis: Fortress, 2007), 131–32.

17. Brayford, *Genesis*, 402, emphasizes the openness to foreign women in the Davidic line.

18. Marc Zvi Brettler, "The Book of Judges: Literature as Politics," *JBL* 108 (1989): 404–5; McCann, *Judges*, 42–43. Barry G. Webb (*The Book of Judges*, NICOT [Grand Rapids: Eerdmans, 2012], 103) also notes the incorporation of Caleb and Othniel into a Judahite identity in Judges.

19. Auld also observes that Othniel is linked to Judah through Caleb (*Joshua, Judges, and Ruth*, 148) though he does not discuss Achsah's role in this. Webb notes the significance of Achsah as an ideal Israelite wife for Othniel in contrast to the intermarriage with people of the land critiques in Judg 3:6 (*Book of Judges*, 161), as does Nelson (*Judges*, 55).

shifts the focus from just the lineage to occupying the land. She ensures that Othniel both holds land within the territory of Judah and acquires Israelite identity, through closer connection with the faithful Caleb.

Jephthah and His Daughter

The question of the legitimacy of identity is again contested through Jephthah and his daughter in Judg 11. Jephthah is named as the son of a זנה. The term has a fairly broad range of meanings related to sexual impropriety, including but not limited to a professional prostitute.[20] Labeling Jephthah's mother as promiscuous leaves his paternity in question. Later in the chapter the other sons call her אשה אחרת ("another woman"), which indicates a nonlegitimate, but not necessarily professional, relationship.[21] The father is named as Gilead, but whether that refers to a specific person or to the region in general is unclear.[22] Thrown out by his kinsmen, Jephthah becomes a mercenary leader, who is later brought back by the leaders of Gilead to fight against the Ammonites. Jephthah engages the Ammonite king in negotiation, arguing for Israel's right to the disputed territory with a thorough knowledge of God's history with the people and the granting of land. The speeches serve to mark Jephthah as a legitimate Israelite through his knowledge and loyalty, despite his own questionable lineage and Gilead's liminal status.[23] Nevertheless, he fails to dissuade the Ammonite king from attacking and goes into battle. Right before engaging, Jephthah vows to sacrifice whatever comes out of his house to greet him if he returns successfully from battle. He is victorious, and his daughter, his only child, runs out to greet him with timbrels and dancing. She encourages him to carry out his vow, only allowing her two months in the mountains to mourn her virginity. After doing the deed, Jephthah engages

---

20. Phyllis A. Bird, "Prostitution in the Social World and Religious Rhetoric of Ancient Israel," in *Prostitutes and Courtesans in the Ancient World*, ed. Christopher A. Faraone and Laura K. McClure, Wisconsin Studies in Classics (Madison: University of Wisconsin Press, 2006), 42.

21. Sasson, *Judges*, 420.

22. Schneider, *Judges*, 162. While the immediate context suggests a person, since the issue of inheritance arises, other elements of the chapter make this identification more ambiguous.

23. Schneider, *Judges*, 173.

in a taunt-off with the Ephraimites, in which the Ephraimites challenge the Gileadites' identity and loyalty. This exchange results in civil war.

The story of Jephthah's daughter reverses the elements of Gen 22 in some important ways. In both stories a father intends to sacrifice as a whole burnt offering a person identified as an only child to fulfill an obligation to God. The Judges version switches the gender of the victim from Genesis. As a male heir, Isaac's death would have greater consequence for Abraham's lineage than the daughter's does for Jephthah.[24] Isaac's offering and salvation highlights the importance of the proper lineage of the promise through his line and not Ishmael's. The death of Jephthah's daughter in a similar sacrifice serves to highlight the lineage problems in Jephthah's story. As a Gileadite, his identity did not fall clearly within the promise to Israel.[25] Jephthah's status within Gilead is even more tenuous. After being disowned, he had come back to the Gileadites when they reinstated him as a battle chief, assuming such an identity with them that he was willing to sacrifice his only child to ensure victory.[26] But his identity is still in flux, and unlike the Abraham narrative, in which the sacrifice scene leads to a restatement of the promise of lineage to Abraham through Isaac and formation of the body of Israel, Jephthah's sacrifice leads to an end of his lineage and dissolution of the body of Israel into civil war. Jephthah himself is never fully integrated into Israel, but instead emerges from and retreats into Gilead, whose identity as part of Israel remains ambiguous in the text. In some ways Jephthah resembles more closely Ishmael, who was

---

24. Deborah W. Rooke, "Sex and Death, or, the Death of Sex: Three Versions of Jephthah's Daughter (Judges 11:29–40)," in *Biblical Traditions in Transmission: Essays in Honour of Michael A. Knibb*, ed. Charlotte Hempel and Judith M. Lieu, JSJSup 111 (Leiden: Brill, 2006), 255. See also Anne Michele Tapp, "An Ideology of Expendability: Virgin Daughter Sacrifice in Genesis 19:1–11, Judges 11:30–39 and 19:22–26," in *Anti-covenant: Counter-reading Women's Lives in the Hebrew Bible*, ed. Mieke Bal, JSOTSup 81, BLS 22 (Sheffield: Almond Press, 1989), 170, 172.

25. Schneider, *Judges*, 185. David Jobling touches on the ambiguity of Gileadite identity with a narratological analysis in "Structuralist Criticism: The Text's World of Meaning," in Yee, *Judges and Method*, 110.

26. Richard E. DeMaris and Carolyn S. Leeb argue that the sacrifice of his child is an expected part of Jephthah's rehabilitation from social death. Ironically, while he is restored to social standing, it does him no good in terms of his lineage ("Judges— (Dis)Honor and Ritual Enactment: The Jephthah Story; Judges 10:16–12:1," in *Ancient Israel: The Old Testament in Its Social Context*, ed. Philip F. Esler [Minneapolis: Fortress, 2006], 184–86).

the son of another woman, disinherited and kicked out of the house, than he does Abraham.[27] Indeed, Jephthah functions as a type of anti-Abraham, because his sacrifice breaks down, rather than solidifying, Israel's future.

A second notable difference from Genesis is that the daughter consented to the sacrifice, whereas Isaac's awareness and participation in his own binding is largely omitted from the narrative account. Jephthah's daughter seems to know about the vow without him explicitly telling her. She does not question the vow or chastise her father for making it, but urges him to fulfill it, while he almost seems to blame her for bringing him low. Through her death she cements Jephthah's place in the Gileadite lineage, but simultaneously ends it, because she was his only child. Her death foreshadows and symbolizes the death of the Israelite social body, as civil war with Ephraim breaks out immediately afterward.

A third difference between the stories is the reversed roles of lineage and land. The war with the Ammonites and the battle with the Ephraimites is over land and who has legitimate claim to it. Lineages and identities are contested, but the major disputes involve which existing group has the right to possess the land. The Genesis story is all about lineage with no land involved. The dispute involves which lineage will bear the promise as it is established.

The Levite and His Wife

The final story of comparison is that of the Levite and his פילגש or secondary wife.[28] Judges 19 is an intensified doublet of Gen 19. A Levite whose wife is either angry with him (LXX) or has fornicated against him (MT) goes to fetch her from her father's house in Bethlehem. Just as Lot had lingered before the destruction of Sodom, the Levite tarries while wined and dined by the father. Finally leaving, he passes up Jebus, then a city of foreigners, and travels on to Gibeah in the territory of Benjamin. The Levite is eventually hosted by an old Ephraimite, who, as Lot had been, is a sojourner in the town, and as in Sodom, the men of the town surround

---

27. Schneider, *Judges*, 178.

28. The exact definition of the term פלגש is widely discussed, but it is generally agreed to mean a concubine or secondary wife. It is usually thought that this secondary status comes because of the lack of a dowry. Sons of a פלגש have some, but not equal, inheritance rights with sons of a primary wife. For a discussion, see Sasson, *Judges*, 376–77; Nelson, *Judges*, 299.

the house and request the Levite be sent out so that they could "know" him. The crowd initially rejects the offer of the host's virgin daughter and Levite's wife, but when someone—it is not clear whether it is the host or the Levite—pushes the wife out to the crowd, they stop bothering the men and gang rape the woman all night. In the morning, the Levite finds her on the threshold, tells her to get up, and when she does not move, puts her on his donkey, takes her home, and cuts her into twelve pieces that he sends throughout Israel, an allusion to Saul's dismemberment of the oxen in 1 Sam 11:7 to call people to battle to rescue Jabesh-gilead. As a result, civil war breaks out against Benjamin.

The Judges version twists the already twisted Genesis version in several notable ways. First, the role of the angels in the Genesis version is played by a Levite in Judges, and it is a poor substitution indeed. He not only does not defuse the threat from the townspeople, but also likely throws out his own wife to be raped and murdered. Second, the Gibeahites are Israelites, not the foreigners of Sodom. Third, the wife is not a virgin and rather than being saved, she is assaulted by the Benjaminites and then hacked into pieces by her own husband. Fourth, in the civil war that breaks out, the city is punished not by God but by fellow Israelites who nearly exterminate the tribe of Benjamin before pulling out at the last minute. They ravage the city of Jabesh-gilead and kidnap virgins from Shiloh in order to save Benjamin by procuring wives for the remnant of four hundred, once again saving men by using women.

These twists reveal several significant themes in each story. In Genesis, the story of Sodom serves as a warning against mixing with the people of the land. Lot chose the seemingly better land for making a living but entangled himself with foreign people who were wicked, cheating the poor and violating the principles of hospitality. The story shows the problem of mixing the good and the bad people. The story in Judges, where the people are mostly settled in the land, problematizes this separation between Israelites and people of the land, mixing up the good and the bad places. The Levite had passed up Jebus, later to be Jerusalem, as the city of foreigners to be avoided. But then the Gibeahites are painted with a Sodomite brush. The safe space became intensely hostile.[29] The Gibeahites were inhospitable, not just to strangers, but to fellow Israelites. They

29. Pressler, *Joshua, Judges, Ruth*, 242–43.

threatened the Levite, the representative of the cult, who should be especially welcomed, and assaulted his wife.[30] In the city of the good people,
there was no salvation for the woman, not from the men of the city, not
from the Ephraimite host, and not from her husband, who further violated her corpse.

These distinctions between people are further revealed in the stories
by the reversal of the gender of the victim, as is the case with Isaac and
Jephthah's daughter, but less obviously so. In the Genesis story, although
he offers his daughters to the crowd, it is Lot himself who is in the most
danger and ultimately the rape victim. The Genesis text is ripe with suggestive words, where the crowd comes near to "break down his door" before
the angels come to the rescue and reinforce his orifices. In the aftermath he
is raped by his daughters, though he is oblivious to the fact. The end result
is the illegitimate births of the neighbors. Thus, Lot's time sojourning with
the bad people leads to future discord with neighboring countries, Moab
and Ammon, who feature heavily in Judges.

In contrast, the Levite in Judges does not seem to be particularly
at risk, despite his claims to the contrary.[31] He never appears outside
when the crowds surround the house, and the concubine is shoved
out the door, rather than pulled behind it. She, not the Levite or the
old man, is raped, but there is no offspring from violence, as she is
dead. Instead, her body is violated and dismembered. Her body is
symbolic of the socio-political structure of Israel, which subsequently
is thrown into dismembering civil war.[32] The story marks discord, not
with neighboring states, but between the tribes of Israel. It serves to
impugn the character of the Benjaminites and, in particular, the city
of Gibeah, Saul's hometown (1 Sam 10:26). It marks the end of the
time of the judges and sets up the country for a monarchy—a Davidic
monarchy. Thus, the focus of identity issues relates to internal gov-
erning power.

---

30. McCann, *Judges*, 129, Dennis T. Olson, "The Book of Judges," *NIB* 2:876, 878–79.

31. Trible, *Texts of Terror*, 73–74.

32. A number of scholars, including Alice Keefe ("Rapes of Women/Wars of Men," *Semeia* 61 [1993]: 85–86) have noted how women's bodies represent the state of the political and social body in Judges. See also Gale A. Yee, "Ideological Criticism: Judges 17–21 and the Dismembered Body," in Yee, *Judges and Method*, 157; Susan Niditch, *Judges*, OTL (Louisville: Westminster John Knox, 2008), 194.

Conclusion

Reading the parallel narratives in Genesis and Judges together helps to reveal the distinctive ways each book uses them to highlight salient issues of identity. The reversal of the story order highlights the roles each book plays in formulation of identity. In Genesis, the stories go from most to least violent. By the end of the book, the crisis of differentiation has passed, and the lineage has coalesced sufficiently to begin to incorporate some of the outside groups that were so violently excluded in the former stories. In Judges, questions of identity are strongly contested throughout, but these issues are linked more closely to possession and governance of the land. Toward the end of the book, the increasing violence and discord serves the polemical purpose of advocating for the institution of monarchy. Loyalty to the values and purpose of the community seem to be more important than genealogy, such that Benjamin was nearly wiped out because of bad behavior.

The changes in gender in the stories are also instructive. In Genesis, women serve mostly as determiners of the lineage. Despite their vulnerability in Gen 19, the daughters take charge in the end and initiate the founding of Moab and Ammon. Although Sarah is absent in Gen 22, it is her son who is the focus of the lineage concerns. Tamar's role in Gen 38 is to ensure continuation of the lineage. In these stories the women control the lineage, but the men are the major victims. As noted above, despite his threat to his daughters, it is Lot himself who is in the most danger from the townspeople and then is manipulated by his daughters. Isaac is the near victim in Gen 22, and Judah's sons are killed off in Gen 38, placing his lineage at risk. Judah himself has to admit that he is less righteous than his daughter-in-law.

In Judges, the victims of the stories are women. As has often been noted, the declining status of women throughout the book is symbolic of the declining state of social affairs.[33] Achsah's story at the beginning represents a relatively healthy society. While initially neglected by her father,

---

33. See, e.g., Tammi J. Schneider, "Achsah, the Raped *Pilegeš* and the Book of Judges," in *Women in the Biblical World: A Survey of Old and New Testament Perspectives*, ed. Elizabeth A. McCabe (Lanham, MD: University Press of America, 2009), 64; Niditch, *Judges*, 191, 194; Olson, "Book of Judges," 872; Danna Nolan Fewell, "Judges," in *The Women's Bible Commentary*, ed. Carol A. Newsom and Sharon H. Ringe (Louisville: Westminster John Knox, 1992), 68.

she earns respect and fertile land by standing up for her rights. Jephthah's daughter has a voice and a will, more so than Isaac, but she subsumes that will to her father's vow, and her death presages civil war. The wife in Judg 19 gets little respect from anyone and suffers grotesque violence at the end of her life and even after. Her death directly leads to civil war and provides justification for a much more centralized and controlling form of government.

These differences all reflect the different focuses on identity. Stories in Genesis use extreme actions and relations that serve to reinforce the ideas of in-group kinship, validation of the lineage, and the establishment of Israelite identity. In the course of these stories, the relations between Israel and its neighbors are set with only minimal attention to possession of the land. Whether this reflects exilic or postexilic concerns with land-less identity is beyond the scope of the paper, but it is notable that explic-itly religious elements, including the direct intervention of God, are more obvious in Genesis, especially in the earlier stories. In Judges, the stories are flipped on their heads and turn the questions about legitimacy inward to a people in the land. Not everyone who lives in the Israelite land is truly Israelite, and conflict over issues of possession of land, and who rules that land, are common. In light of land concerns, the definition of Israelite identity shifts from strict genealogy to include considerations of commit-ment to the community and to God. In Judges, God's direct involvement becomes less obvious as the book progresses. The movement is from the more mundane to the most extreme, as the society falls into chaos and war, lacking legitimate political and religious leadership. This sets the stage for a centralization of power and cult for the Davidic dynasty and the temple.

Reading the stories in Genesis and Judges in tandem helps to high-light the distinctive elements of each, as well as to show how the stories within each book serve a larger purpose in their respective books. In each, gender and violence symbolize the contestation of identity in differ-ent contexts. The element of the land in Judges complicates the question of identity with that of possession and power, reflected in the increasing twistedness of the stories.

3

The Assertiveness of Achsah:
Gender and Intertextuality in the
Reception History of Caleb's Daughter

Joy A. Schroeder

The story of Caleb's daughter Achsah, related in nearly identical accounts in Josh 15:13–19 and Judg 1:11–15, features a newly married woman whose husband Othniel obtained a field from her father as a result of the woman's intervention—either by her prompting Othniel to request it from Caleb or by her requesting it herself at her husband's prompting. After Othniel received the field, Achsah proceeded to request water access—namely, springs or pools of water, presumably to irrigate the dry field. In response, her father granted her "the upper springs and the lower springs" (Judg 1:15). Hebrew scripture relates numerous stories of men acquiring property through inheritance, gifts, grants, requests, purchase, and conquest. Apart from the story of Achsah, only one other text in Hebrew scripture features women who assertively petitioned men in order to receive possession of property: the account of Mahlah, Noa, Hoglah, Milcah, and Tirzah, the daughters of Zelophehad, who—in the absence of brothers—requested to inherit real estate and thus perpetuate their father's name (Num 27:1–11).[1] Both biblical narratives are stories of women who made a request or demand for real estate and, in both cases, they were granted their petition.

Writing in 1898, feminist luminary Elizabeth Cady Stanton (1815–1902) perceived a connection between the story of Achsah and the account of Mahlah, Noa, Hoglah, Milcah, and Tirzah: "In giving Achsah

---

1. Another case of a woman acquiring property occurs in Prov 31:16, which speaks of the hypothetical valiant wife who purchases a field, apparently with her own resources.

her inheritance it is evident that the judges had not forgotten the judgment of the Lord in the case of Zelophehad's daughters."[2] In each case, the
women assertively stated their wishes and were granted their requests on
the grounds of the justice and logic of their claim.

However, until Cady Stanton's time, commentators rarely made the
association between Zelophehad's daughters and Achsah. In fact, whenever they acknowledged that the story was about a woman who requested
literal springs of water, biblical interpreters generally felt conflicted about
the idea of women as active agents initiating a claim on real property. In
this essay, we will see examples of early modern and nineteenth-century
men who criticized Achsah as a spoiled, ungrateful child, unwilling to be
content with the field that her generous father had already granted. She
was like the leech's "daughters" (suckers) in Prov 30:15, perpetually unsat-
isfied. In commentaries, sermons, and homiletical aids, these interpreters
held Achsah up as a negative model, an illustration of behavior that girls
and young women of their own day should avoid at all costs. (In some
cases, it seems that men, who were peeved at women for some reason,
simply used the story of Achsah as an opportunity to vent!) On the other
hand, there were interpreters who emphasized the opposite, praising the
elements of Achsah's humility and obedience that they perceived in the
text. They used these readings of the text to soften the idea of a woman
asking for property.

More often, commentators, including female interpreters, entirely
avoided attention to Achsah's request for *literal* property by reading the
demand for springs as a metaphor or allegory. To accomplish this, they
interpreted Achsah's request in light of scripture passages that could be
used to spiritualize the story. The daughter represented the soul at prayer,
asking for spiritual riches, trusting Jesus's promise that the Heavenly
Father gives good things to those who ask (Matt 7:11). Caleb's granting of
the springs evoked biblical images of wells, springs, and fountains, such
as Isa 12:3, "With joy you will draw from the wells of salvation" (NRSV).

Whether one praised Achsah as submissive, criticized her as outspo-
ken, or spiritualized the text, the underlying gender ideology and rhetorical intent were essentially the same. Either approach to Achsah—blaming
her or taming her—was rooted in the conviction that it was problematic

---

2. Cady Stanton, *The Woman's Bible* (New York: European Publishing Company,
1898), 2:13–14.

for a woman to speak assertively or make requests for property. Reflecting on the literary theories of Michel Foucault, Jay Rothstein and Eric Clayton observed:

> Although every text possesses countless points of intersection with other texts, these connections situate a work within existing networks of power, simultaneously creating and disciplining the text's ability to signify. Foucault insists that we analyze the role of power in the production of textuality and of textuality in the production of power. This entails looking closely at those social and political institutions by which subjects are subjected, enabled and regulated in forming textual meaning.[3]

As we will see below, in the case of Achsah, the text's various meanings were usually shaped by perspectives and ideologies about gender that sought to rein in women's speech, actions, and acquisition of property. Commentators, who themselves were embedded in networks of religious and social power and subjugation, often created textual links or reinforced intertextual associations that perpetuated prevailing ideologies about the need for female passivity and compliance. For several early women's rights advocates, however, this textual netting was too constraining, and so these nineteenth-century interpreters linked Achsah's story to a different biblical text, Num 27, one that they could find more empowering as they worked to reform laws about women's property-holding, inheritance rights, suffrage, and access to power.

A Rash Vow Like Jephthah's?

Before turning to the question of the assertiveness of Achsah and the matter of females negotiating for the ownership of property, a description of the story's opening, with a brief overview of related intertextual associations, is in order. Joshua 15, where the story of Achsah first occurs, and Judg 1, where it is recapitulated, are set within narratives about the Israelites' conquest of the portion of Canaan designated for the tribe of Judah. In the Josh 15 account, Achsah's story comes after a detailed description of Judah's borders (15:1–12) and the report that Joshua granted Caleb a portion of yet unconquered land (15:13). Caleb promised to grant his

---

3. Rothstein and Clayton, *Influence and Intertextuality in Literary History* (Madison: University of Wisconsin Press, 1991), 27.

daughter Achsah as wife to whoever conquered Debir, also called Kiriath-
sepher ("City of Letters"). Othniel, who was either Caleb's brother or his
nephew, seized the city and received Achsah as his prize. In Judg 1, the
same story is set after a report of the death of Joshua (Judg 1:1) and is part
of a sort of prelude to the book of Judges (Judg 1:1–2:5).[4]

A recurring preoccupation of interpreters was the question of Othniel's familial relationship with Caleb: "And Othniel son of Kenaz, Caleb's
younger brother, took [the city], and he gave him his daughter Achsah as
wife" (Judg 1:13). The Hebrew is ambiguous about whether Othniel was
Caleb's brother or nephew. Many ancient Christian and Jewish scholars
believed that Othniel and Caleb were brothers—full brothers or half-
brothers.[5] Textual variants of the LXX offer two options, with Codex Vaticanus reading Othniel as the son of Caleb's brother Kenaz, and Codex
Alexandrinus reading Othniel as Caleb's brother.[6] The Vulgate regards
Caleb and Othniel as brothers: "And when Othniel the son of Kenez, the
younger brother of Caleb, took [the city], he gave him Achsah his daughter
as wife."[7]

In the event that the two men were brothers (making Achsah the niece
of Othniel), Christians ever since the Middle Ages wondered about the
appropriateness of Caleb fulfilling his prebattle vow by giving his daughter
to her uncle, a marriage relationship that Christians understood to be prohibited by Lev 18:14.[8] The scholarly Netherlandish monk Denis the Car-

---

4. Barnabas Lindars, *Judges 1–5: A New Translation and Commentary* (Edinburgh:
T&T Clark, 1995), 3: "It is universally agreed that the original opening of Judges is to
be found in 2.6–10. Thus 1.1–2.5 has been added after the completion of the book in
its original form."

5. Susan Niditch, *Judges: A Commentary*, OTL (Louisville: Westminster John
Knox, 2008), 33. Some rabbinic authors, including Rashi (1040–1105), suggested that
they were half-brothers, in a scenario in which Caleb's mother married Kenaz after the
death of Caleb's father Jephunneh. Others, such as David Kimḥi (1160–1235), believed
that "Kenaz" was a family name designating the Kenizzites, making Othniel and Caleb
full brothers; see Sidney Hoenig and A. J. Rosenberg, eds., *The Book of Joshua: A New
English Translation of the Text and Rashi*, trans. P. Oratz, A. J. Rosenberg, and Sidney
Shulman (New York: Judaica Press, 1969), 106.

6. Codex Vaticanus: "Γοθονιηλ υἱὸς Κενεζ ἀδελφοῦ Χαλεβ ὁ νεώτερος." Codex
Alexandrinus: "Γοθονιηλ υἱὸς Κενεζ ἀδελφὸς Χαλεβ ὁ νεώτερος."

7. Vulgate Judg 1:13: "Cumque cepisset eam Othoniel filius Cenez, frater Caleb
minor, dedit ei Axam filiam suam conjugem."

8. The Hebrew text suggests that a man uncovers the nakedness of his father's
brother by engaging in sexual relations with his paternal uncle's wife. The wording of

thusian (ca. 1402–1471) wondered: "How could Caleb, a righteous man, give his daughter as wife to his brother, his daughter's uncle?"[9]

Medieval Christian scholastic interpreters liked a good puzzle. They occupied themselves with compiling intertextual associations to examine the issue and resolve the contradiction between Caleb's righteousness and his apparent disregard of Moses's laws regarding incest. The Dominican commentator Hugh of St. Cher (ca. 1200–1263), and his consortium of Dominican friars who wrote a massive biblical commentary in thirteenth-century Paris, saw echoes with the story of Jephthah. The warrior Jephthah had solemnly vowed that, in the event of military victory against the Ammonites, he would sacrifice the first being that stepped forth from his house upon his return home. Jephthah fulfilled his vow by sacrificing his unnamed daughter (Judg 11:29–40). In each case, according to the medieval commentators, a well-intentioned but ill-advised prewar promise bound promiser to do something illicit with respect to his daughter, whether sacrificing her upon an altar or offering her up as bride in an incestuous marriage. Caleb should have made a conditional promise, stipulating that the promise of marriage did not apply to a close relative prohibited by the law of Moses. According to Hugh of St. Cher: "It is possible to say that—like Jephthah—he did not make a good vow because he vowed in a rather general way."[10]

Through the centuries, the resolution to which most Christian commentators (including Franciscan exegete Nicholas of Lyra) ultimately resorted was the argument that Caleb was a *good man*. As a righteous man, it was impossible for him to have done something so egregious as to give his daughter to his brother for marriage. Therefore, the comparison with Jephthah was not apt. Franciscan commentator Nicholas of Lyra (ca. 1270–1349), directly rebutting Hugh of St. Cher, wrote: "Some say ... that [Caleb] did not wish to retract his word, just like Jephthah wished to fulfill his vow

---

the Vulgate is a prohibition against sexual relations with one's paternal uncle (*patruus*) as well as the paternal uncle's wife: "You shall not uncover the nakedness of your father's brother, nor [*nec*] shall you approach his wife."

9. Denis the Carthusian, "Enarratio in Librum Josue," in *Doctoris Ecstatici D. Dionysii Cartusiani Opera Omnia* (De Monstreuil: Typis Cartusiae Sanctae Mariae de Pratis, 1897), 3:78: "Quomodo Caleb vir justus, dedit filiam suam uxorem fratri suo, avunculo filiae suae."

10. Hugh of St. Cher, *Postilla super Librum Josue*, vol. 1 of *Opera Omnia in Universum Vetus & Novum Testamentum* (Venice: Pezzana, 1754), 188r: "Vel potest dici, quod sicut Jephte non bene vovit, quia ita generaliter vovit."

regarding the sacrifice of his daughters, as it says in Judges 11. But this is not true, because Caleb was a holy and good man, as it is written in chapter 14 [of Joshua]."[11] This argument continued through the centuries. Paulus Cassel (1821–1892), a nineteenth-century Prussian scholar who had converted from Judaism to Reformed (Protestant) Christianity, went so far as to reject the possibility of incest on aesthetic grounds. According to Cassel, the idea of Caleb and Othniel as brothers "would destroy, not only the historical truth, but also the aesthetic character of the narrative."[12] Nevertheless, many Christians needed additional clarification and biblical justification to argue this point. The puzzle was resolved by referencing Gen 14:14, which referred to Abraham's nephew Lot as his brother. Thus "brother" can mean "kinsman." Nicholas of Lyra wrote: "Where it says here that Othniel is called Caleb's 'brother,' it is in the same manner of speaking that Lot is called Abraham's brother in Gen 14, even though he was his nephew, as is clear there."[13]

A few commentators noted, with approval, the parallels with King Saul offering his daughter Michal in marriage to the victorious warrior David (1 Sam 18:20–27). Like David, Othniel was a manly man, winning the hand of a bride from her father through courage and strength. Cassel wrote: "To obtain the daughter of a house by meritorious actions has in all ages been a worthy subject of ambition set before young and active men. It was only by a warlike exploit that David obtained Michal who loved him."[14] This recalled the romantic days of chivalry, which, in the views of nineteenth-century interpreters, was evidence of women's high status. Peter H. Steenstra, a nineteenth-century American scholar who translated Cassel's Judges commentary for an English-speaking audience in 1872, believed

---

11. Nicholas of Lyra, *Postilla in Librum Iosue*, vol. 2 of *Biblia sacra cum glossa ordinaria … et postilla Nicholai Lyrani* (Venice, 1603), 106: "Dicunt aliqui … noluit retractare dictum suum sicut et Iephthe voluit implore votum suum de immolatione filiae suae sicut habetur Iud. 11. Sed istum non verum tum quia Caleb erat vir sanctus et bonus, ut dictum est c. 14."

12. Paulus Cassel, *The Book of Judges*, trans. P. H. Steenstra, vol. 4 of *A Commentary on the Holy Scriptures: Critical, Doctrinal, and Homiletical*, ed. John Peter Lange (New York: Scribner, 1872), 34.

13. Nicholas of Lyra, *Postilla in Librum Iosue*, 106: "Quod autem Othoniel hic dicitur frater Caleb, hoc est eo modo loquendi quo Lot dicit frater Abraham Genesis 14 qui tamen erat eius nepos, ut patet ibidem.

14. Cassel, *Book of Judges*, 34. Interestingly, though, Cassel cited, as another parallel, the classical Greek story of a Messenian king, Aristomenes, who gave his son in marriage to "a country maiden" who rescued Aristomenes "with heroic daring."

that buying (as in the case of Jacob laboring for Rachel) or winning a wife through armed feats elevated the woman's status:

> It is more honorable to a woman to be "sold" (a term entirely inapplicable, however, to the case in hand), than to have a husband bought for her by her father's gold or lands. When a man stormed the walls of a stronghold, or slew an hundred Philistines by personal prowess, or paid fourteen years of responsible service, for a wife, or when as in the days of chivalry, he ran tilts and courted dangers on her behalf, however grotesque the performance, it indicated not only solidity of character in the wooer, but also a true and manly respect for woman, which is not possessed by all men of modern days.[15]

Grace Aguilar (1816–1847), a British Jewish woman of Sephardic background living in Victorian England, celebrated the supposed chivalry in the text. In her efforts to expand women's rights within Judaism and also to defend Judaism from the ubiquitous slander found in Christian literature of the time, she repeatedly agreed with the popularly held nineteenth-century view that the "age of chivalry is generally supposed to be a powerful proof of the respect and consideration with which women were regarded amongst the Gentile nations during the middle ages." The story of Othniel and Achsah was "the very first instance of chivalry which history records," evidence that Israelites were the forerunners in granting women the status found in chivalric culture that elevated women.[16]

Who Nagged Whom? Othniel and Achsah Acquire a Field

Judges 1:14 contains narrative gaps, ambiguity, and textual variants that open up room for discussing appropriate interactions between husbands and wives.[17] In the Masoretic Text, Achsah urged her husband to ask her father for a field: "When she came [to him], she induced him to ask her

---

15. Cassel, *Book of Judges*, 36. For a scathing critique of this sort of perspective, see Danna Nolan Fewell, "Deconstructive Criticism: Achsah and the (E)razed City of Writing," in *Judges and Method: New Approaches in Biblical Studies*, ed. Gale A. Yee, 2nd ed. (Minneapolis: Fortress, 2007), 127: "Is Achsah another spoil of war? To her father, she is bait. To her future husband, she is his due reward. She is hobbled by her name ["bangle," "trinket," "hobble"] and her ornamental role."

16. Aguilar, *The Women of Israel* (New York: Appleton, 1872), 1:215.

17. In fact, David M. Gunn says of the entire Achsah account: "Told in few words, the narrative demands of its reader mental leaps, while difficulties in the Hebrew

father for some property" (Judg 1:14, JPS). Variant readings allowed for differing ideas of who initiated the request. The Septuagint and Vulgate say her husband prompted *her* to make the request.

In the Septuagint and Vulgate versions, it was Othniel who urged Achsah.

καὶ ἐγένετο ἐν τῇ εἰσόδῳ αὐτῆς καὶ ἐπέσεισεν αὐτὴν Γοθονιηλ τοῦ αἰτῆσαι παρὰ τοῦ πατρὸς αὐτῆς ἀγρόν.
And it came about, when she entered, that Othniel urged her to ask for the field from her father.

Quam pergentem in itinere monuit vir suus ut peteret a patre suo agrum.
And as she was going on her way her husband admonished her to ask her father for a field.

Interpreters who followed the Vulgate and Septuagint reading were generally untroubled by the idea of Othniel asking his new wife to request a field from her father. They interpreted Achsah's subsequent request for springs as obedience to her husband's prompting.

Although Othniel's initiative and desire for property, regarded as natural and logical, usually went unremarked by those who followed the Vulgate and Septuagint, many who followed the Hebrew text and its translations felt the need to deal with Achsah's initiative. Judges 1:14 says that she "induced him" (ותסיתהו) to request the property. Translators have used stronger verbs such as "entice" or gendered words such as "nag."[18] Some commentators rebuked the daughter for her acquisitive and conniving nature, while praising Othniel's "piety and solidity of character," as Cassel termed it, for apparently refusing to ask Caleb for the field.[19]

At this point in the Hebrew text, there is a narrative gap: Judg 1:14a reports that Achsah urged Othniel to ask Caleb for a field; this is followed, in Judg 1:14b, by Achsah's approach to Caleb to request springs. There is

text have also occasioned head-scratching" (*Judges*, Blackwell Bible Commentaries [Malden, MA: Blackwell, 2004], 23).

18. Tammi J. Schneider, *Judges: Studies in Hebrew Narrative and Poetry*, Berit Olam (Collegeville, MN: Liturgical Press, 2000), 13: "The verb *s-w-t* means, 'to allure, incite, instigate.'" Schneider implicitly criticizes "other translators" who "prefer 'nag' for reasons not elaborated," as well as those who add "a more sexual connotation translating, 'seduce, tempt.'" Also see the discussion by Mieke Bal, *Death and Dissymetry: The Politics of Coherence in the Book of Judges*, CSHJ (Chicago: University of Chicago Press, 1988), 149.

19. Cassel, *Book of Judges*, 35.

no intervening statement about Othniel's compliance or resistance to Achsah's urging. Nor is there a specific statement that Caleb had granted the land to Othniel. Thus, in a scenario in which Othniel refused to follow his wife's urging, readers could interpret Achsah's encounter with her father as a demand for the property she had originally wanted Othniel to request. Or, in a situation where Caleb had granted land to Othniel who asked for it at Achsah's prompting, it could be a petition for springs in addition to the dry land (1:15) that her father had granted as a result of the earlier request. Though Othniel speaks no words at all in this account, interpreters through the centuries added imaginative expansions to the conversation between Achsah and Othniel, filled with details that reflected their views of proper or improper marital interactions.

In either scenario, Achsah's desire for land—or for springs as well as the land—was cited as evidence of her acquisitive and conniving nature. Cassel believed that, due to Othniel's "piety and solidity of character," the husband refused to ask Caleb for the property that Achsah desired: "The thing to be especially noted, however, is the firmness of Othniel in resisting his wife's enticements to make requests…. Not many men have so well withstood the ambitious and eagerly craving projects of their wives."[20] Scottish preacher William Mackintosh Mackay (1865–1947), writing in 1912 about *Bible Types of Modern Women,* used Achsah's story to make a comment about discontented women of his own day: "Brides are said to be sometimes difficult to please in the matter of their dowry." Despite the fact that Caleb had "given her a noble dower … she does not seem to have been altogether content with it; for, when she came to her husband, we find her egging him on to make a further request from the old man."[21] Even harsher was Thomas Gaspey (flor. 1840–1860), who authored the devotional *Tallis's Illustrated Scripture History for the Improvement of Youth.* He testily asserted: "The daughter, like some young ladies who have lived since her time, seems to have thought it would be right to get as much as she could from her father for her husband." Even though Achsah was fortunate enough to receive her request, the young readers in his audience should not be too demanding, since "the most selfish are not always allowed to fare the best."[22]

---

20. Cassel, *Book of Judges,* 35.

21. Mackay, *Bible Types of Modern Women* (Garden City, NY: Doubleday, 1929), 1:242.

22. Gaspey, *Tallis's Illustrated Scripture History for the Improvement of Youth* (London: Tallis, 1851), 1:88.

Charles Spurgeon (1834–1892), a Baptist preacher who published popular collections of sermons, praised Othniel's commendable "bashfulness," evident in the rebuff to Achsah imagined by Spurgeon:

> This good woman, before she went to her father with her petition, *asked her husband's help.* When she came to her husband, "she moved him to ask of her father a field." Now, Othniel was a very brave man, and very brave men are generally very bashful men. It is your cowardly man who is often forward and impertinent. But Othniel was so bashful that he did not like asking his uncle Caleb to give him anything more; it looked like grasping. He has received a wife from him, and he had received land from him, and he seemed to say, "No, my good wife, it is all very well for you to put me up to this, but I do not feel like asking for anything more for myself."[23]

As we will see below, Spurgeon regarded Achsah's initiative with her husband to be more praiseworthy when he spiritualized the account as a model of prayer, since it is appropriate for wives to encourage their husbands to ask for blessings from the *heavenly* Father.

In a very different assessment of the interaction between Achsah and Othniel—but one that upheld a similar perspective about the inappropriateness of women assertively giving direction to men—Achsah is transformed into an obedient wife. In his 1702 *Commentary upon the Historical Books of the Old Testament,* Symon Patrick (1626–1707), the Anglican bishop of Ely, conjectured that she asked Othniel for permission to make the request of her father:

> *That she moved him to ask of her Father a Field* [Josh 15:18]. Desired her Husband, unto whom she thought her Father at this time would deny nothing, to bestow a Field upon her. Or, perhaps, she moved him to give her Leave to ask it of her Father; as she did, either by his Permission or by his Desire; who might tell her, it was more proper for her to ask it, than himself.[24]

Puritan minister Matthew Henry (1662–1714), the author of the popular *An Exposition of the Historical Books of the Old Testament,* imagined the conversation between husband and wife. Both agreed that they should

---

23. Spurgeon, *Spurgeon's Sermons on Great Prayers of the Bible* (Grand Rapids: Kregel, 1995), 16 (emphasis added).

24. Patrick, *A Commentary upon the Historical Books of the Old Testament,* 5th ed. (London: Midwinter, 1738), 2:55–56.

request the field. Achsah believed that Othniel was more likely to obtain the land because he was a victorious warrior who enjoyed Caleb's good graces. Othniel disagreed, thinking it was more likely that Caleb, out of fatherly affection, would respond favorably to a request by *her*. Achsah obediently acquiesced to her husband's wishes, and "accordingly she did, submitting to her husband's judgment, though contrary to her own."[25] Achsah is thus the submissive good wife who deferred to her husband. Presumably, devout women who read Henry's commentaries for their own spiritual edification—and female parishioners who listened to sermons delivered by the men who used Henry's *Exposition* in their homiletical preparations—would find Achsah to be a salutary example. Yet, according to Henry, the biblical account also allows for mutuality in marriage, illustrating the fact that "husbands and wives should mutually advise, and jointly agree, about that which is for the common good of their family," though "much more should they concur in asking of their heavenly Father the best blessings, those of the upper springs."[26] More will be said below about these spiritual springs.

Achsah's Encounter with Her Father

As the story continues, Achsah, seated on her donkey, does something to get her father's attention and provoke his response: "She dismounted from her donkey, and Caleb asked her, 'What is the matter?' She replied, 'Give me a present, for you have given me away as Negeb-land; give me springs of water.' And Caleb gave her Upper and Lower Gulloth" (Judg 1:14b–15, JPS). In the NRSV rendering of verse 15a, she says, "since you have set me in the land of the Negeb," referring to a dry desert.

The word translated by JPS as "dismounted," ותצנח, has variously been rendered as "slid down," "sank down," and "cried out" (based on similarity to צוח).[27] The latter option was chosen by the Septuagint, which said, "She grumbled and cried out from her beast of burden," and by the Vulgate, which reads: "And, seated on the donkey, she sighed."[28] Noting that the

---

25. Henry, *An Exposition of the Old and New Testament* (London: Robinson, 1839), 2:82.

26. Henry, *Exposition*, 82.

27. Lindars, *Judges 1–5*, 29–30.

28. LXX (Vaticanus): "καὶ ἐγόγγυζεν καὶ ἔκραξεν ἀπὸ τοῦ ὑποζυγίου." Vulgate: "Quae cum suspirasset sedens in asino."

same root is used in Judg 4:21 to describe Jael's tent peg going through Sisera's head, Mieke Bal comments: "Unfortunately, nobody knows what the verb means exactly, and the coincidence of the occurrences in such different situations is the more disturbing since in both cases there is a woman's insubordination at stake."[29] Since "the problematic word clearly refers to a gesture, a physical action," Bal argued for "clapped her hands" to get Caleb's attention.[30] Cornelis de Vos's suggestion, "spat," is an even stronger speech-act, communicating Achsah's contempt for Caleb's miserly grant of dry, unirrigated land, spitting in her father's presence as she remained seated on her donkey.[31] Medieval commentators following the Latin text, "she sighed" (*suspirasset*), were inclined to spiritualize both Achsah's loud sigh and her donkey. Hugh of St. Cher wrote that "Achsah sighs when the soul desires to be liberated from the prison of the body" (represented by the lowly donkey).[32]

Several twenty-first century female interpreters emphasized Achsah's assertiveness as she got down from the animal. Susan Niditch described Achsah as "leaping from her donkey and offering an angry complaint."[33] Tammi Schneider similarly argued that Achsah's encounter with Caleb was an expression of boldness: "Her descent from the donkey is not as important as her traveling alone and leaving her husband. Her descent in front of her father signifies her arrival at Caleb's place where he was not expecting her."[34] However, in the interpretive tradition, most commentators regarded Achsah's dismounting from her donkey as a sign of humility and respect for her father. Patrick asserted: "And her lighting down, was in Reverence to her Father; unto whom she addressed herself in an humble Posture."[35] Henry, Aguilar, and Spurgeon—who perceived a parallel with Rebekah humbly alighting from her camel when approaching Isaac's tent

---

29. Bal, *Death and Dissymmetry*, 149.

30. Bal, *Death and Dissymmetry*, 150.

31. De Vos, *Das Los Judas: Über Entstehung und Ziele der Landbeschreibung in Josua 15*, VTSup 95 (Leiden: Brill, 2003), 124.

32. Hugh of St. Cher, *Postilla super Librum Josue*, 188v: "Axa suspirat, quando anima a carcere corporis liberari desiderat."

33. Niditch, *Judges*, 41.

34. Schneider, *Judges*, 15. Also see Ken Stone, "What Happens When Achsah Gets Off Her Ass? Queer Reading and Judges 1:11–15," in *Sacred Tropes: Tanakh, New Testament, and Qur'an as Literature and Culture*, ed. Roberta Sterman Sabbath, BibInt 98 (Leiden: Brill, 2009), 409–20.

35. Patrick, *Commentary upon the Historical Books*, 56.

(Gen 24:64)—made similar points.[36] However, Cassel, perpetually suspicious of Achsah's motives, said that, "like a true woman," the daughter staged a scene to get Caleb's attention by *pretending* to fall off her donkey: "She slides from her ass—suddenly as if she fell—so that her father asks, 'What is the matter with thee?'"[37]

Whether Achsah grumbled, sighed, spat, or clapped from atop the donkey (or if, instead, she slid or jumped down from the animal), she made a request of her father, asking for water, in addition to the dry land Caleb had already granted. We will see below that nineteenth-century women commentators highlighted the reasonableness of her request— that agricultural property necessarily requires irrigation in order to be productive. Some of their male counterparts—at least when treating the field and springs as literal property—tended to criticize the request. Achsah should have been contented with what she had already received from her father's generosity.

In the commentary of Rashi (Solomon ben Isaac of Troyes, 1040–1105), which draws on earlier rabbinic tradition, Achsah complains to her father that she was given to an "arid land," namely to a husband poor in material wealth because he spent all his time studying torah. Her father reassured her that she would be all right. The upper springs are Othniel's laudable torah study and the lower springs are material sustenance, which Othniel will also obtain.[38]

Achsah's words, "give me *also* springs of water" (Judg 1:15b, KJV, emphasis added), prompted diatribes against women discontented with what they had. The 1912 "modern woman" illustrated by this story in Mackay's *Bible Types of Modern Women*, is "a girl who, like Achsah, has wedded a very good and worthy man ... a country clergyman." At first, she is happy, "but soon that little word 'also' creeps into her joy." Her idyllic country parsonage in the woods or the hills, far from London, turns out to be "very dull." Longing for fashionable society, "she becomes a discontented bride, and perhaps becomes a hindrance to her husband instead of a help." Mackay concludes this uncharitable tale with a paraphrase of Prov 30:15, about the leech's "daughters," which are the two suckers that attach to the host: "The heart, like the horse-leech, has two daughters which can

36. Henry, *Exposition*, 82; Aguilar, *Women of Israel*, 217; Spurgeon, *Sermons*, 18.
37. Cassel, *Book of Judges*, 35.
38. Hoenig and Rosenberg, *Book of Joshua*, 107.

never have enough, and their names are, 'Give, Give!'"[39] Herbert Lockyer
(1886–1984), bestselling author of *All the Women of the Bible,* subtitled his
entry on Achsah, "The Woman Who Wanted More." Referencing Mackay,
Lockyer repeated the association between Achsah (who had "an element
of covetousness in her disposition"), the proverb about the leech, and the
discontented women of his own day.[40] However, as we see below, when
these same authors applied the story to women's (and men's) prayer lives,
rather than to material possessions, Achsah's request illustrated the pious
soul at prayer.

Spiritualizing the Springs

Up to this point, we have been mostly discussing *literal* land and springs.
Among medieval and early modern Christian interpreters, and well into
the nineteenth century, however, it is typical for arid fields to signify spiritually or morally arid *lives,* lack of faith, and lack of good works. Fruitful, watered fields signify spiritual abundance. Achsah's request for water
symbolizes the Christian's devout prayer. In the writings of the contem-
plative monk Denis the Carthusian, Caleb is God the father, Achsah is
the faithful soul, Othniel is Christ the bridegroom, and the requested real
estate represents celestial fields irrigated with tears. The donkey that she
abandons is carnal desire. Christ exhorts his bride, the faithful soul, to
seek spiritual fertility watered by fountains of tears.[41] Intertextual associations included the Samaritan woman, who asked Jesus, "Sir give me
this water" (John 4:15, KJV); Jesus's promise that "your Father which is
in heaven [shall] give good things to them that ask him (Matt 7:11, KJV);
and the promise that "with joy shall ye draw waters out of the wells of
salvation" (Isa 12:3, KJV).

An anonymous Victorian Englishwoman who published articles
in *The Christian Lady's Magazine* under the pen name of Lydia (flor.

---

39. Mackay, *Bible Types,* 246–47. Also see William W. Hallo, "New Light on the
Story of Achsah," in *Inspired Speech: Prophecy in the Ancient Near East; Essays in Honor
of Herbert B. Huffmon,* ed. John Kaltner and Louis Stulman, JSOTSup 378 (New York:
T&T Clark, 2004), 332. Hallo goes so far as to posit a connection between this proverb
and the name for the basins of water near Debir (*ḥirbet rabūd*) called, in Arabic, the
"upper well of the leech" and the "lower well of the leech."

40. Lockyer, *The Women of the Bible* (Grand Rapids: Zondervan, 1967), 27.

41. Denis the Carthusian, "Enarratio in Librum Josue," 79–80.

1830s–1840s) wove together the story of Achsah and Caleb with the story of Jesus and the Samaritan woman into a devotional pastiche. Achsah speaks, and Christ responds with the words he directed to the woman of Samaria:

> "Give me," said the daughter of Caleb, "a blessing, for thou hast given me a south land; give me also springs of water." "If thou knewest the gift of God, and who it is that saith to thee, Give me to drink, thou wouldest have asked of him, and he would have given thee living water," said Jesus to the Samaritan…. To whom then shall we go to obtain "a blessing"? To him who said "if ye being evil know how to give good gifts unto your children, how much more shall your Father which is in heaven give his Holy Spirit to them that ask him" [Matt 7:11; Luke 11:13]; to him who said, "I will pour water upon him that is thirsty, and floods upon the dry ground" [Isa 44:3]…. And how shall we approach the Father of Spirits [Heb 12:9]? As Achsah approached her earthly parent, with the confidence of a child, but with the low prostration and meek reverence of an inferior, pleading his own rich gift as the ground of a further "blessing."[42]

In a sermon preached in 1889, Spurgeon commended Achsah's actions as a pattern for the Christian at prayer, saying that "the way in which this woman went to her father and the way in which her father treated her may teach us how to go to our Father who is in heaven, and what to expect if we go to Him in that fashion."[43] Furthermore, when the story is applied devotionally, Othniel is not a hen-pecked husband; rather, by urging Othniel to ask for a field, Achsah provides an example for wives to cultivate their husbands' prayer lives: "Still, learn this lesson, good wives, prompt your husbands to pray with you."[44] Spurgeon praises the sweet domesticity of a godly couple's prayer life, initiated by a woman who imitates Achsah *in prayer*:

> So it is a good thing in prayer to imitate this woman Achsah. Know what you want, and then ask others to join with you in prayer. Wife,

---

42. Lydia, "Female Biography of the Scriptures: Achsah," in *The Christian Lady's Magazine* 10 (July–December 1838), 162–63. For a discussion of "Lydia" and an excerpt from this article, see Marion Ann Taylor and Christiana de Groot, *Women of War, Women of Woe: Joshua and Judges through the Eyes of Nineteenth-Century Female Biblical Interpreters* (Grand Rapids: Eerdmans, 2016), 57–62.

43. Spurgeon, *Sermons*, 15.

44. Spurgeon, *Sermons*, 16–17.

especially ask your husband; husband, especially ask your wife. I think
there is no sweeter praying on earth than the praying of a husband and a
wife together when they plead for their children and when they invoke a
blessing upon each other and upon the work of the Lord.[45]

When interpreters associate the Judg 1 text with biblical passages about
prayer and spiritual springs, and when we read these associations back
into the passage, the text and Achsah herself are tamed.

Mackay and Lockyer explicitly made the rhetorical turn from a negative *literal* Achsah, who represents the discontented wife, to a positive *figurative* Achsah who models humble prayer. Lockyer's shift is abrupt:

Solomon reminds us that the human heart is like the horseleech whose
two daughters never have enough, and bear the names of *Give, Give*
(Proverbs 30:15). There is, of course, a divine discontent all of us should
foster. Dissatisfied with our growth in sanctity of life, we should con-
stantly pray, "More holiness give me," and as the bride's father graciously
granted his daughter's request, so our heavenly Father will answer our
yearning for the life more abundant.[46]

Lockyer continues, with an echo of Rashi's explanation about the meaning
of the upper and lower springs:

Caleb gave Achsah the springs of water she desired, and in the upper and
nether springs we have a type of the spiritual and temporal mercies from
our Father above. As heirs of the promise, His children can humbly and
confidently ask and expect great blessings from His generous hand. Both
upper, or heavenly provision, and *nether*, or earthly necessities come
from Him in whom are all our springs (Psalms 81:10; 84:11; Isaiah 33:16;
Luke 11:13; John 4:13, 14; 7:37–39; Ephesians 3:20; 1 John 3:22).[47]

Mackay similarly turned the negative story about Achsah into a positive
message:

---

45. Spurgeon, *Sermons*, 17.
46. Lockyer, *Women of the Bible*, 27.
47. Lockyer, *Women of the Bible*, 27. The explanation of upper and lower springs
as spiritual and material blessings, an echo of the rabbinic tradition, is found in Christian sources such as Matthew Henry, *Exposition*, 82.

> Now the lesson of all this is so obvious that one need hardly drag it home. It is the lesson of prayer. We have a better Father than ever Achsah had, and if at times He seems to lead us into a south land of trial and barrenness, our course is clear. Let us do with our inheritance what she did. Let us "bring it to the Lord in prayer." "If ye, being evil, know how to give good gifts unto your children, how much more shall your Father which is in heaven give good gifts to them that ask Him" [Matt 7:11]. Ask your heavenly Father and he will put it all right for you.[48]

In this way, by spiritualizing the text, Achsah could provide a worthy exemplary model for women to request spiritual riches from a gracious Heavenly Father.

Moving beyond Moses: Expanding Rights for Women

Twenty-first-century people are familiar with early feminist calls for women's suffrage. Less well known are nineteenth-century women's crucial efforts to reform property laws to give women greater economic rights. In England and the United States (where laws varied from state to state), husbands generally acquired control over their wives' property upon marriage. Men could spend the money that their wives inherited or earned. A wife or widow's real estate and other property could be seized by creditors to pay off the husband's debt. A widow also could not necessarily prevent the property that she had brought into the marriage from going to her husband's heirs, who might include the woman's stepsons or her husband's nephews or other relatives. As a *feme covert* (a "protected" or "covered" woman), a wife's legal identity was subsumed into her husband's so that she could not independently enter into certain kinds of legal transactions, such as buying and selling real estate. Beginning in 1839 and continuing through the course of the century, American states began to pass married women's property acts that strengthened the rights of wives and widows. In 1882, the British parliament passed the Married Women's Property Act, granting women the right to own and control their own property. These changes were often supported by fathers who wished their grandsons (their daughters' sons)—rather than their sons-in-law—to inherit the property.[49]

---

48. Mackay, *Bible Types*, 250–51.

49. See Norma Basch, *In the Eyes of the Law: Women, Marriage and Property in Nineteenth-Century New York* (Ithaca, NY: Cornell University Press, 1982); Marilyn

In this context, the story of Achsah, a married woman who acquired property from her father (Judg 1:14) offered a useful biblical precedent.[50]

Aguilar, writing in 1845, found the account to be evidence that Israelite women had the sort of property rights that British women were agitating for: "We learn too from this, that woman must undoubtedly have had the power of possessing landed property in her own right, and in a degree exclusive of her husband; else Caleb would have made over the portion intended for her to Othniel on his marriage, instead of waiting for Achsah to ask, and granting it to her alone."[51] Aguilar recalled Moses's ruling in Num 27, which granted land to Mahlah, Noa, Hoglah, Milcah, and Tirzah in the absence of brothers, but Achsah's story demonstrated that Israelite women's property rights extended even further. Aguilar indicated that her "study of the genealogies in Chronicles" (1 Chr 2:42–50) proved that Achsah was not an only child. Thus, it was significant that she owned property "exclusive also of her brothers; for if landed inheritance were to be man's only she could have had no claim to any portion."[52]

Suffragist Cady Stanton saw in Achsah a powerful example for women wishing to claim their rights. As an activist who had worked to pass the state of New York's Married Women's Property Act (1848), she had delivered several speeches before the New York State Legislature.[53] Nearly five decades later, Cady Stanton edited *The Woman's Bible*, the first feminist bib-

---

Salmon, *Women and the Law of Property in Early America*, Studies in Legal History (Chapel Hill: University of North Carolina Press, 1986); Linda E. Speth, "The Married Women's Property Acts, 1839–1865: Reform, Reaction, or Revolution?," in *Property, Family, and the Legal Profession*, vol. 2 of *Women and the Law: A Social Historical Perspective*, ed. D. Kelly Weisberg (Cambridge, MA: Schenkman, 1982), 69–91.

50. An advocate for women's rights, Elizabeth Wilson (flor. 1849–1850) similarly used the story of Abigail, who offered two hundred loaves, five dressed sheep, and other foodstuffs to appease David (1 Sam 25), to argue for the reform of property laws. Wilson said that Abigail's example demonstrated that married women in biblical times held joint ownership of household property; see Joy A. Schroeder, "Elizabeth Wilson, the Bible, and the Legal Rights of Women in the Nineteenth Century," *Postscripts* 5 (2009): 219–32.

51. Aguilar, *Women of Israel*, 217.

52. Aguilar, *Women of Israel*, 217. Henry (*Exposition*, 82), one of the few male interpreters who connected Achsah with Num 27, had seen Achsah's marriage to her cousin to be an extension of the principle of marrying within the tribe. Reformed commentator Peter Martyr Vermigli (1499–1562) made the same point (*In Librum Iudicum* [Zurich: Froschauer, 1561], 17r).

53. Priscilla Pope-Levison, "Elizabeth Cady Stanton," in *Handbook of Women*

lical commentary, published in two parts in 1895 and 1898. The *Woman's Bible* invokes the story of Achsah as a strong call for justice for women—as well as a critique of the limits of biblical precedent set by Moses in the case of Mahlah, Noa, Hoglah, Milcah, and Tirzah:

> In giving Achsah her inheritance it is evident that the judges had not forgotten the judgment of the Lord in the case of Zelophehad's daughters. He said to Moses, "When a father dies leaving no sons, the inheritance shall go to the daughters. Let this henceforth be an ordinance in Israel." Very good as far as it goes; but in case there were sons, justice demanded that daughters should have an equal share in the inheritance.[54]

Cady Stanton noted the contemporary relevance of the biblical story, which extended even beyond property rights:

> As the Lord has put it into the hearts of the women of this Republic to demand equal rights in everything and everywhere, and as He is said to be immutable and unchangeable, it is fair to infer that Moses did not fully comprehend the message, and in proclaiming it to the great assembly he gave his own interpretation, just as our judges do in this year of the Lord 1898.[55]

Cady Stanton continued:

> Achsah's example is worthy [of] the imitation of the women of this Republic. She did not humbly accept what was given her, but bravely asked for more. We should give to our rulers, our sires and sons no rest until all our rights—social, civil and political—are fully accorded. How are men to know what we want unless we tell them? They have no idea that our wants, material and spiritual, are the same as theirs; that we

---

Biblical Interpreters: A Historical and Biographical Guide, ed. Marion Ann Taylor and Agnes Choi (Grand Rapids: Baker Academic, 2012), 470.

54. Cady Stanton, *Woman's Bible*, 2:13–14. Cady Stanton also attacked the idea that Israelite heiresses should be required to marry their cousins, within the tribe. In *Woman's Bible*, 1:123–24, she conjectured that "crafty old uncles moved in time to get a statute passed," and so, "with their usual masculine arrogance," they limited women's choice in marriage. "If Moses, as the mouthpiece of God, aimed to do exact justice, why did he not pass an ordinance giving property in all cases equally to sons and daughters?"

55. Cady Stanton, *Woman's Bible*, 2:14

love justice, liberty and equality as well as they do; that we believe in the principles of self-government, in individual rights, individual conscience and judgment, the fundamental ideas of the Protestant religion and republican government.[56]

Another contributor to the *Woman's Bible*, a German-American suffragist Clara Neymann, née Loew (b. 1840), argued that women in the Hebrew scripture had more rights than women of New Testament times.[57] She asserted that texts such as 1 Cor 14:34–36, 1 Tim 2:8–15, and Eph 5:22–24 put *new* restrictions on women not found in the Hebrew scriptures or ancient Israelite culture. Neymann looked at the story of Achsah through her feminist perspective, as well as her observations of middle-class German businesswomen who ran family businesses.[58] She conjectured that Othniel, a warrior, did not have Achsah's instinct for business or economic survival. Neymann praised Achsah's initiative as a trait found in sensible women who must provide for their families:

> We begin with Achsah, a woman of good sense. Married to a hero, she must needs look out for material subsistence. Her husband being a warrior, had probably no property of his own, so that upon her devolved the necessity of providing the means of livelihood. Great men, heroic warriors, generally lack the practical virtues, so that it seems befitting in her to ask of her father the blessing of a fruitful piece of land; her husband would have been satisfied with the south land. She knew that she required the upper and the nether springs to fertilize it, so that it might yield a successful harvest.[59]

In families where husbands were impractical or less intellectually gifted, a smart woman needed to be in charge of matters of property and finance. This resonates with Neymann's own assertiveness and financial practicality. As a sought-after speaker on women's rights in Europe and the United States, especially among German-American communities in the Midwest,

---

56. Cady Stanton, *Woman's Bible*, 2:14.

57. For biographical information on Neymann, see Michaela Bank, *Women of Two Countries: German-American Women, Women's Rights, and Nativism, 1848–1890*, Transatlantic Perspectives 2 (New York: Berghahn, 2012), 111–53.

58. On Neymann's admiration for German women who ran family businesses, see Bank, *Women of Two Countries*, 142.

59. Neymann's comments on Judg 1, in Cady Stanton, *Woman's Bible*, 2:217.

she had to contend with the expectation that women would speak for *free*, out of philanthropic motivations. However, Neymann assertively insisted on being paid for her intellectual and oratorical work, writing in a letter: "As I have chosen the occupation, the profession of a lecturer, I will speak only for money."[60]

On the Path with Achsah

This survey of themes and intertextual associations found in reception history has identified three general approaches to dealing with Achsah's assertiveness. We have found forms of taming the daughter and the text, attempts to make Achsah an obedient wife, or a symbol of the soul at prayer. Another approach is to rebuke and blame the daughter for her assertiveness. Finally, some like Aguilar, Stanton, and Neyman claimed her as a positive example needed by women of their own day.

In the introduction to this essay, I suggested that we think of the interpreters' use of biblical intertexts as creating a sort of weaving or netting, which generally served to constrain the meaning of the passage. In his monograph *The Nomadic Text: A Theory of Biblical Reception History*, Brennan Breed uses a different metaphor. He suggests that readers think of the text itself as the protagonist, a sort of nomad: "In order to study the nomad, one must follow the tracks through the steppe and watch for patterns of movement and action that always change over time and space. One must see how the nomad reacts to the ever-changing scenery."[61] According to Breed: "In short, the biblical reception historian asks what a text can do. Here is the mandate: demonstrate the diversity of capacities, organize them according to the immanent potentialities actualized by various individuals and communities over time, and rewrite our understanding of the biblical text."[62] In this essay, we have observed the interpretive contours created by the various "tracks" crisscrossing for centuries between Judg 1 and texts such as those about the Samaritan woman, Jephthah's vow, the leech's greedy daughters, the wells of salvation, and the Heavenly Father who grants the petitions of a faithful child.

---

60. Correspondence dated November 12, 1872, quoted in Bank, *Women of Two Countries*, 114.

61. Breed, *The Nomadic Text: A Theory of Biblical Reception History*, ISBL (Bloomington: Indiana University Press, 2014), 203.

62. Breed, *Nomadic Text*, 141.

Yet if the text is a traveler, it can reveal its disruptive and liberative potential by setting forth in new directions, like Achsah who climbed onto her donkey and journeyed to visit her startled father so that she could claim a new blessing.

4

Into the Hand of a Woman:
Deborah and Jael in Judges 4–5

Pamela J. W. Nourse

Among the themes in the book of Judges are marginalization and anxiety regarding the reliability of Israel's covenantal relationship and the nature of Israel's leadership.[1] These themes are at play in the unexpected gender roles highlighted in Judg 4 and 5. Whereas most women in the Hebrew Bible are defined by their identities as wives, mothers, or daughters, both the prose narrative in chapter 4 and the poetic song in chapter 5 show Deborah and Jael acting as leaders and heroes of the story.[2] Moreover, both narrative and song present the roles of both women as normative, without any expression of disapproval from the narrator.[3] But although the text presents the women in a positive light, it nonetheless presents them quite differently from one another. This essay will analyze the language used in the text to show that, while Deborah is acting in a manner that appears to transcend the gender norm, Jael's actions are expressed in verbs appropri-

---

1. For marginalization, see Michael O'Connor, "The Women in the Book of Judges," *HAR* 10 (1986): 278. For Israel's covenantal relationship, see Eric Christianson, "The Big Sleep: Strategic Ambiguity in Judges 4–5 and in Classic Film Noir," *BibInt* 15 (2007): 524.

2. J. Cheryl Exum, "Feminist Criticism: Whose Interests Are Being Served?," in *Judges and Method: New Approaches in Biblical Studies*, ed. Gale A. Yee, 2nd ed. (Minneapolis: Fortress, 2007), 66.

3. Jo Ann Hackett, "In the Days of Jael: Reclaiming the History of Women in Ancient Israel," in *Immaculate and Powerful: The Female in Sacred Image and Social Reality*, ed. Clarissa W. Atkinson, Constance H. Buchanan, and Margaret R. Miles (Boston: Beacon, 1985), 22.

ate to women's traditional gender identities but are subverted and perverted in a manner that produces the unanticipated narrative result.

Deborah

Given the social structure in premonarchic Israel, it is possible that women
played a more significant role in public life than they would in later times.
There was no centralized government; social structure was based on the
tribes and their component units, the clans. Within such a structural
arrangement, divisions between the domestic/private and public spheres
were much less pronounced than they would become later, in a hierarchical, monarchic setting. In the absence of a centralized standing army, military actions relied on soldiers being provided by the clans when needed;
thus public military functions were inextricably linked to the domestic
kinship groups.[4] Given such an overlap between the public and domestic
domains, it is quite possible that women could indeed have participated,
in some capacity, in military matters.[5] Jo Ann Hackett notes that the status
of women actually tends to improve during "periods of social dysfunc-
tion or social disruption," a phrase that certainly applies to the period
depicted in the book of Judges.[6] The hierarchical breakdown, which tends
to occur during times of war or other crises, can provide the opportunity
"for oppressed groups (particularly women) … to exert more power."[7] It
is not likely that such a role was common in premonarchic Israel, since so
few examples of such women's leadership were recorded. In fact, some of
the terms used to describe Deborah's identity and activity are unusual or
even unique in the biblical text.

Deborah is first introduced in Judg 4:4 as נביאה ("prophetess," or
"female prophet"). The term נביאה is rare, being applied to only five
women in the Hebrew Bible; the Babylonian Talmud, slightly more

---

4. Gale A. Yee, "By the Hand of a Woman: The Metaphor of the Woman Warrior in Judges 4," in *Women, War, and Metaphor: Language and Society in the Study of
the Hebrew Bible*, ed. Claudia V. Camp and Carole R. Fontaine, SemeiaSt 61 (Atlanta:
Scholars Press, 1993), 110–11.

5. Yee, "By the Hand of a Woman," 111; Carol Meyers, *Discovering Eve: Ancient
Israelite Women in Context* (New York: Oxford University Press, 1988), 174.

6. Hackett, "Women's Studies and the Hebrew Bible," in *The Future of Biblical
Studies: The Hebrew Scriptures*, ed. Richard Elliott Friedman and H. G. M. Williamson,
SemeiaSt 16 (Atlanta: Scholars Press, 1987), 149.

7. Hackett, "In the Days of Jael," 19.

generous, lists seven women as "prophetess."[8] She is further identified as שפטה את־ישראל ("one judging Israel") using the feminine singular *qal* participle of the verb root שפט, "to judge." When used in the context of premonarchic Israel (and particularly in the phrase שפטה את־ישראל), the verb evokes a leadership role, and is generally understood to mean "lead" or "rule," although in other contexts the range of meaning also includes judge/decide (in forensic contexts), dispute, or do justice.[9] Wilda Gafney traced the use of the verb from the Torah through the Writings and concluded that "while *shophet* was initially used for dispute resolution, its semantic range includes generic administrative functions as well as governance."[10] The use of the word to denote leadership or authority is supported by other ancient Near Eastern cognates. In the Mari letters, the subject of the verb *špṭ* is always either an official or the king; in Old Babylonian and Assyrian, the verb *šapāṭu* means "determine, decide" and "rule"; in Ugaritic, the meanings of the verb *ṭpṭ* range between "reign" and "judge."[11] All of this suggests that Deborah's role as judge involved acknowledged leadership and significant authority within the community. It appears that Deborah was unique as a woman filling this position; while the verb שפט is fairly common (it occurs 68 times in the participial or "verbal noun" form and over 140 times in other verbal forms), Judg 4:4 represents its only use in a feminine form (although given the inclusive linguistic nature of masculine plural forms, it is possible that other unnamed women did act as judges but were subsumed by collective verb forms).[12] Naming Deborah as both a prophet and a judge further places her in the exclusive

---

8. In addition to Deborah being called a נביאה, there are Miriam (Exod 15:20), Huldah (2 Kgs 22:14; 2 Chr 34:22), the unnamed prophetess (Isa 8:3), and Noadiah (Neh 6:14); although they are not named as "female prophets," prophetic activity (in verbal form) is attributed to "daughters" in Ezek 17:13 and Joel 3:1. For the Babylonian Talmud, see Maurice Simon, trans. "Megillah 14a," in *The Babylonian Talmud: Seder Mo'ed*, ed. Rabbi Dr. I. Epstein (London: Soncino, 1938), 81–83; the prophetesses, in addition to Deborah, are Sarah, Miriam, Hannah, Abigail, Huldah, and Esther.

9. H. Niehr, "שָׁפַט," *TDOT* 15:419–21.

10. Gafney, *Daughters of Miriam: Women Prophets in Ancient Israel* (Minneapolis: Fortress, 2008), 32.

11. Niehr, "שָׁפַט," 415–16.

12. For the verbal noun numbers, see Gafney, *Daughters of Miriam*, 31. For the other verbal forms, see Niehr, "שָׁפַט," 418. For the possibility of other women judges, see Gafney, *Daughters of Miriam*, 32.

company of Moses and Samuel, the only other two judges who were also identified as prophets.[13]

Deborah is further linked to Moses by the unique use of the verb שיר in Judg 5:1. The verb itself is quite common, but it is most often used in the books of Psalms and Ezra/Nehemiah; of the twenty-one uses of the word outside these books, more than half are clustered in three locations: Judg 5 (three uses), Exod 15 (four uses), and Deut 31–32 (six uses).[14] The chapters in Exodus and Deuteronomy both deal with songs of Moses, and the structure of Deborah's song in Judg 5:1 (using a singular verb for a composite subject: ותשר דבורה וברק ["and she sang, Deborah and Barak"]) parallels that of Moses's song in Exod 15:1 (ישיר־משה ובני ישראל ["he sang, Moses and the sons of Israel"]). Again, Deborah's song represents the only use of the verb in the feminine singular form in the Bible.[15]

Another unusual usage, of עור, appears in Judg 5:12. Often translated "awaken," the basic meaning carries a sense of "excite, stir up, become active." When used as an exhortation, it is often addressed to objects that then become active in order to fulfill their functions (e.g., the north wind, spears, stones); in the context of wars, it is applied to nations and peoples setting out for battle.[16] Hackett notes that in the Hebrew Bible, "Awake! Awake!" is a conventional phrase used for a call to arms.[17] The verb is used with a number of feminine nouns, so its appearance in the feminine singular imperative form (as it is used in Judg 5:12) is not unusual; this verse is, however, the only time when the feminine imperative is addressed to a person rather than an object, making Deborah's situation again unique. It is interesting to note as well that the masculine singular imperative form is never addressed to a person; in the verses where the command is not directed toward an inanimate object, the subject addressed is God, and the context is a military one, in which the people are imploring God to awake and do battle with their enemy.[18]

---

13. Gafney, *Daughters of Miriam*, 33.

14. V. Dahmen, "שׁיר," *TDOT* 14:616.

15. A feminine plural participial form is used in 2 Sam 19:36 to refer to a group of female singers. It should be noted that Miriam sings in Exod 15:21 as well, but a different verb (ענה) is used.

16. J. Schreiner, "עור," *TDOT* 10:570–71.

17. Hackett, "Women's Studies and the Hebrew Bible," 156.

18. God is addressed in Pss 7:7; 35:23; 44:24; 59:5; and 80:3. Susan Ackerman, *Warrior, Dancer, Seductress, Queen: Women in Judges and Biblical Israel*, ABRL (New York: Doubleday, 1998), 44.

While a number of unusual and atypical verbs are associated with Deborah in these chapters, she does appear to be described with the more traditional terms of "wife" and "mother" as well, although this appearance may be misleading. In Judg 4:4, in addition to being identified as נביאה and שפטה, Deborah is called אשת לפידות. Most English translations render this "wife of Lappidoth," but that is not necessarily a correct understanding. "Lappidoth" is a *hapax legomenon*. Victor H. Matthews suggests that Lappidoth's subsequent disappearance from the narrative indicates that Deborah "is a postmenopausal female, who, like the 'wise women' of the David narrative, functions as an elder."[19] There are, however, other possible explanations. With a feminine plural ending, "Lappidoth" would be an unusual name for a man, and it is not qualified with a patronymic, as are other male names in Judges.[20] It is possible that the word is not a name at all, but rather represents a feminine plural form of the word לפיד, "torch" (while this is a masculine noun, some Hebrew nouns do occasionally occur in both male and female forms; a feminine plural might have been used to harmonize with the feminine אשה). Such a reading would transform the phrase into "woman of torches" or "fiery woman," and remove any apparent reference to Deborah's (apparently irrelevant) marital status.

Similarly, in Judg 5:7, Deborah self-identifies as אם בישראל, "a mother in Israel." The title is somewhat ambiguous, as we are never told anything about Deborah's children (or whether any even exist); the term may be intended to be understood metaphorically rather than literally. Susan Ackerman notes that Judg 4 makes no mention of Deborah's role as a mother; the fact that the prose version does not, in this instance, provide a literal interpretation of the poem's metaphorical language (as it does throughout the remainder of the text) strongly suggests that "the prose redactor knows of some other, less literalistic definition of 'a mother in Israel' that it is his intention—and also, by implication, the intention of Judges 5—to evoke."[21] Some see the term "mother" as being comparable to the use of the term "father" as a leadership or prophetic title.[22] Ackerman suggests that the

---

19. Matthews, *Judges and Ruth*, NCBC (Cambridge: Cambridge University Press, 2004), 64.

20. Gafney, *Daughters of Miriam*, 90.

21. Ackerman, *Warrior, Dancer, Seductress, Queen*, 38.

22. For leadership, see Hackett, "In the Days of Jael," 28. For prophetic, see Meyers, *Discovering Eve*, 159.

repetition of the word "Israel" in 5:5 (God of Israel) and 5:7 (mother in Israel) is meant to pair the figures of YHWH and Deborah in a cosmic/ earthly, divine/human dichotomy.[23] J. Cheryl Exum analyzed the characteristics of a number of actual mothers in the biblical text, and concluded that "a mother in Israel is one who brings liberation from oppression, provides protection, and ensures the well-being and security of her people."[24] Others have observed that the only other use of the term אם בישראל in the Bible refers not to a woman, but to the city of Abel (2 Sam 20:19). Ackerman, building on the work of Claudia V. Camp, concluded that the term applied not only to the city but to the "wise woman" who mediated the conflict there; the term thus is intended to refer to anyone who embodied the characteristics of the wise woman:[25]

> "A mother in Israel" must be a good and effective counselor and must use her skills in counseling to protect the heritage of Yahweh. Extending such protection on occasion can involve the use of military force, and hence "a mother in Israel" must be willing to step forth as a commander who leads those under her protection in military encounters. Such military endeavors, however, must always be informed by a commitment to Israel's covenantal unity and wholeness (what 2 Samuel 20 describes as peaceableness and faithfulness).[26]

It can therefore be seen that, even when the text appears to assign the traditional female roles of "wife" and "mother" to Deborah, the terms may in fact convey nontraditional meanings that are at odds with their superficial understanding.

Jael

Jael, unlike Deborah, appears to act within the contexts of women's expected roles of "wife" and "mother," although it is not clear that she actually is either one. She is placed in a domestic setting in Judg 5:24, where

---

23. Ackerman, *Warrior, Dancer, Seductress, Queen*, 37–38.

24. J. Cheryl Exum, "'Mother in Israel': A Familiar Figure Reconsidered," in *Feminist Interpretation of the Bible*, ed. Letty M. Russell (Philadelphia: Westminster, 1985), 85.

25. Claudia V. Camp, "The Wise Women of 2 Samuel: A Role Model for Women in Early Israel?," *CBQ* 43 (1981): 14–29.

26. Ackerman, *Warrior, Dancer, Seductress, Queen*, 39–43.

she is identified as one of the "women of the tent," and she is named as אשת חבר הקיני, which could be read as "wife of Heber the Kenite." However, חבר could also be understood as meaning "community, company, or association," in which case Jael would be identified as "a woman of the Kenite community," with no reference whatsoever to her marital status. Nor is there any reference in the text to any children, or the motherhood (whether actual or metaphorical) of Jael. Nonetheless, in both the narrative and the song, we see Jael acting in ways that evoke, if not embody, both of these roles (although to differing degrees).

The expected role of a mother is to nurture and care for her children; the expected role of a wife is to produce those children, which at the most basic level reduces her function to a sexual one. In the narrative of Judg 4, the emphasis seems to be on the mothering aspects (with some sexual overtones); in the song of Judg 5, the emphasis is more sexual (but with a bit of mothering imagery).[27] It is relevant that some scholars (most notably Fokkelien van Dijk-Hemmes) regard chapter 4 as a "male text" (written by, or at least from the perspective of men—the style is that of a "masculine" epic, and Deborah is reduced to an advisory, rather than leading, military role), and chapter 5 as a "female text" (the style is more lyric, based on female tradition, and Deborah's role supersedes that of Barak).[28] The strong sexual overtones to Sisera's assassination in chapter 5 would "strongly [appeal] to the imagination of women, because the violator is in

---

27. There has been much scholarly argument about whether Jael's actions in these texts are maternal *or* sexual, as some scholars appear unwilling to accept the presence of both roles (see, e.g., Mieke Bal, *Death and Dissymmetry: The Politics of Coherence in the Book of Judges*, CSHJ [Chicago: University of Chicago Press, 1988]; and Pamela Tamarkin Reis, "Uncovering Jael and Sisera: A New Reading," *SJOT* 19 [2005]: 24–47). I disagree that one must be selected and the other disregarded. Christianson, using the analogy of film noir, argues that the Jael texts are rife with ambiguity. "To read them closely is to engage with ambiguity borne not of sloppy thinking, but of rigor, tolerance of multivocality and willingness to question conventions and norms. They stand as invitations to deal responsibly with issues of great complexity" ("Big Sleep," 543).

28. Arie van der Kooij, "On Male and Female Views in Judges 4 and 5," in *On Reading Prophetic Texts: Gender-Specific and Related Studies in Memory of Fokkelien van Dijk-Hemmes*, ed. Bob Becking and Meindert Dijkstra, BibInt 18 (Leiden: Brill, 1996), 135–52; Fokkelien van Dijk-Hemmes, "Mothers and a Mediator in the Song of Deborah," in *A Feminist Companion to Judges*, ed. Athalya Brenner, FCB 4 (Sheffield: JSOT Press, 1993), 110–14. Bal, *Death and Dissymmetry*, 211; Ackerman, *Warrior, Dancer, Seductress, Queen*, 31.

turn violated by a woman."[29] Many of the verbs used to depict Jael's actions in both the narrative and the song, however, have nuances or double meanings that serve to subvert her "feminine" actions in unexpected ways.

Jael's first act, in Judg 4:18, is to "go out to meet" (ותצא יעל לקראת) the fleeing Sisera. The combination of the verbs יצא ("go out") and קרא ("meet") can signify a woman's sexual intent, as in Gen 30:16 and Prov 7:15. In both of those instances, however, the sexual intent is explicitly stated (by Leah in Genesis and by the "strange woman" in Proverbs), which is not the case in this passage. The more common—in fact, nearly exclusive—meaning of the construct in its use from Deuteronomy to Judges is a call to war issued by a male speaker.[30] While Pamela Tamarkin Reis notes that even the use of the verb יצא alone, when applied to women, often indicates a sexual outcome (Leah in Gen 30:16; Dinah in Gen 34:1; the daughters of Shiloh in Judg 21:11), in this context such a sexual understanding is subverted by the other appearances of the verb in the text (Judg 4:14 and 5:4), where it is used as a technical military term depicting YHWH "going out" to battle with the enemies of Israel.[31] Just as Deborah was paired with YHWH in 5:5–7, so is Jael paired with YHWH here.

In 4:18, Jael also invites Sisera to "turn aside to me" (סורה אלי), an invitation that could be (and often is) read as sexually suggestive. While she may merely be offering the hospitality of her tent, Reis points out that "whenever a man and a woman, not married to one another, are alone in private there is sex."[32] This phrase also injects a note of ambiguity through its use of foreshadowing: Gen 19:2–3 uses virtually the same phrase ("turn aside to your servant's house ... and they turned aside to him") when Lot offers "an invitation to hospitality ... that leads to disturbing violence."[33]

The next images (4:18–19) appear profoundly maternal. Mieke Bal observes that "what Jael offers [Sisera] are the basic attributes of maternity: protection, rest, and milk."[34] Elsewhere she notes that "the motherly care

---

29. Van der Kooij, "On Male and Female Views in Judges 4 and 5," 148.

30. Christianson, "Big Sleep," 533.

31. Reis, "Uncovering Jael and Sisera," 26. For the military use, see Horst D. Preuss, "יצא," *TDOT* 6:229.

32. Reis, "Uncovering Jael and Sisera," 26–27.

33. Christianson, "Big Sleep," 533.

34. Mieke Bal, *Murder and Difference: Gender, Genre, and Scholarship on Sisera's Death*, trans. Matthew Gumpert, ISBL (Bloomington: Indiana University Press, 1988), 121.

is depicted with insistence."[35] Sisera, upon entering Jael's tent, is covered, given a drink of milk (rather than the water he asked for), and covered again. The pairing of the tucking-in and the offer of milk is seen by Ackerman as "Jael acting here as a mother to Sisera's overwhelmed child … providing him with the only hints of support and compassion that he has seen in his long day of battle."[36] Some midrashim go so far as to suggest that Jael's "mothering" included offering Sisera her own breast milk, despite the fact that the narrative describes her opening a skin of milk in response to his request for water.[37] In fact, the use of the verb פתח adds to the maternal imagery, as it is the term used for "opening" a woman's womb so that she can bear children (Gen 29:31; 30:22).[38]

Despite this emphasis on maternal imagery, some commentators see sexual overtones in these verses as well. Another meaning of פתח is that of a woman "opening" herself to her lover (Song 5:2, 5, 6); it also puns on the verb פתה, which can be translated "entice, seduce, or allure" (this term is in fact used twice in Judg [14:15 and 16:5], in the context of the seductions of Samson).[39] Some scholars argue that the "cover-drink-cover" sequence does not fit the maternal model; Reis notes that "a hot and thirsty runner would be better served by being given a drink *before* he is tucked in," and Lillian R. Klein agrees that "the repetition of 'covering' reinforces the likelihood of intervening sexual activity."[40] Additionally, Reis focuses on the translation of the *hapax* שמיכה, which most scholars translate as "rug," "curtain," or "fly net," instead proposing that the word derives from the verb סמך, meaning "to lean, lay, or rest one's weight on." In other words, "she covered him with laying-on," meaning that she covered him with her body, initiating sex.[41] Robert B. Chisholm disputes this understanding of the word; based on a syntactical analysis: he notes that the *piel* of כסה, "cover," is always followed by a direct object (although this object is implied rather than stated in several cases) and a prepositional phrase

35. Bal, *Death and Dissymmetry*, 213.

36. Ackerman, *Warrior, Dancer, Seductress, Queen*, 90.

37. Leila Leah Bronner, "Valorized or Vilified? The Women of Judges in Midrashic Sources," in Brenner, *Feminist Companion to Judges*, 89.

38. Danna Nolan Fewell and David M. Gunn, "Controlling Perspectives: Women, Men, and the Authority of Violence in Judges 4 and 5," *JAAR* 58 (1990): 393.

39. Fewell and Gunn, "Controlling Perspectives," 393.

40. Reis, "Uncovering Jael and Sisera," 30–31; Lillian R. Klein, *From Deborah to Esther: Sexual Politics in the Hebrew Bible* (Minneapolis: Fortress, 2003), 38.

41. Reis, "Uncovering Jael and Sisera," 28–29.

consisting of ‏בְ‎- and a concrete noun. In no other instance is an abstract verbal noun used in the prepositional phrase, leading him to conclude that, linguistically, ‏שמיכה‎ must refer to some type of material cover rather than an abstract "covering" act.[42] Yet another completely different understanding of the term was proposed in a midrash, presumably by rabbis who also picked up on the sexual overtones of the text and were disturbed by it: "whereas in the more salacious midrashim the act of covering Sisera with a rug might have been seen as part of Jael's seductive lulling of her doomed guest, in this innocent account the word *ś^emîkâ* is interpreted as *ś^emî kōh*, which means 'My Name is here', from which is supposed to follow the implication that God testifies on her behalf that no transgression occurred."[43]

From this primarily maternal interlude, the text returns to sexual imagery in 4:21, with the phrase ‏ותבוא אליו בלאט‎ ("and she came to him in secrecy"). When the genders are reversed, ‏יבוא אליה‎ almost invariably indicates sexual activity (as does the verb alone, without the indirect object ‏אליה‎).[44] ‏לאט‎ "evokes mystery, even romance";[45] the phrase ‏ותבא בלט‎ is used in Ruth 3:7 to describe Ruth's approach to Boaz on the threshing floor, where a sexual context is certainly implied if not explicitly stated.

Numerous scholars have commented on the sexual, "reverse-rape" imagery of the killing of Sisera by means of "an unmistakably phallic tent peg," which follows the description of Jael's "coming in to him" in 4:21.[46] Matthews comments on the narrative's "ironic note since it is the male who is penetrated and it is the female who asserts her power to control the situation."[47] Robert Alter notes, with delightful understatement, that "the driving through of the tent peg into the ground on which the narrator dwells seems to be what our own age would call a phallic aggressive act."[48]

---

42. Robert B. Chisholm Jr., "What Went on in Jael's Tent? The Collocation ‏תכסהו‎ ‏בשמיכהו‎ in Judges 4,18," *SJOT* 24 (2010): 144.

43. Bronner, "Valorized or Vilified?," 91.

44. Fewell and Gunn, "Controlling Perspectives," 393; Klein, *From Deborah to Esther*, 38; Susan Niditch, "Eroticism and Death in the Tale of Jael," in *Women in the Hebrew Bible: A Reader*, ed. Alice Bach (New York: Routledge, 1999), 307; Reis, "Uncovering Jael and Sisera," 34.

45. Niditch, "Eroticism and Death in the Tale of Jael," 307.

46. Fewell and Gunn, "Controlling Perspectives," 394.

47. Matthews, *Judges and Ruth*, 73.

48. Alter, *The Art of Biblical Poetry* (New York: Basic Books, 1985), 49.

Klein bluntly asks, "Can we say that Jael literally 'screwed' [or: 'socially/ sexually abused'] Sisera? That is the implication of the text."[49]

Jael's final interaction in Judg 4 is with Barak. In 4:22, Jael "goes out to meet" him, and he "goes in to her," to find Sisera's dead body. Reis believes this verse depicts an actual sexual encounter between Jael and Barak, arguing that to require *two* exceptions (to the usual understandings of women's "going out" and men's "going in") in a single passage strains credulity.[50] However, the use here of ותצא יעל לקראת parallels that of 4:18, where (as discussed above) it could be understood as an allusion to the phrase's use as a call to arms. Jael's command to Barak (the masculine singular imperative form of הלך) is hardly an invitation to sex, but rather parallels Deborah's report of God's command to Barak in 4:6.[51] Further, the use of יבוא אליה here could be intended ironically rather than literally. Klein suggests that again it is Jael who is "screwing" the men in the narrative: "note the telltale verb choice, here social and ironic rather than sexual.... She has, as Deborah prophesied, conquered the man whom Barak sought, [showing] neither any of the hesitation of Barak nor the feminine constraints of her culture."[52] Furthermore, the pairing of the verbs יצא and בוא is often used in military or cultic terminology, or as antonyms indicating "totality."[53] It is possible that the author intended their adjacent use here (although with a different subject for each) to evoke such alternate and subversive understandings of this pair of sexually suggestive verbs.

In Judg 5, the interaction between Jael and Sisera is cast somewhat differently. There is no approach/"going out" or invitation into Jael's tent, nor is there any "covering" or tucking-in. Alter suggests that "the poetic version avoids direct representation of Jael putting Sisera to bed partly because the poet does not want to mitigate or complicate with maternal associations the image of Jael the triumphant slayer" (he does not, however, address the issue of why the prose author did not seem to feel these qualms).[54] Again, Jael offers Sisera milk, but here it is not paired with the "tucking-in" and is instead presented in a "majestic bowl," making it seem less an act of maternal care and more an extravagant act of epic hospitality that tran-

49. Klein, *From Deborah to Esther*, 39.
50. Reis, "Uncovering Jael and Sisera," 34–35.
51. Ellen van Wolde, "Ya'el in Judges 4," *ZAW* 107 (1995): 243.
52. Klein, *From Deborah to Esther*, 39.
53. Preuss, "יָצָא," 229.
54. Alter, *Art of Biblical Poetry*, 48.

scends ordinary norms.[55] Reis sees the offer of milk and curds/butter here as sexual, rather than maternal, "a salacious bit of biblical bawdry."[56] The only other biblical mention of this specific type of bowl (ספל, in Judg 6:38) suggests that it is a deep, rather than a shallow, bowl, and Reis observes that (deep) churns, butter, and other dairy products all have long histories (ranging from ca. twentieth-century BCE Sumerian hymns to twentieth-century CE American musical theater) as sexual slang.[57]

The depiction of Sisera's death in 5:27 is unambiguously sexual. Susan Niditch notes that "its language is charged with sexuality, sexual submission intertwined, doubling with language of defeat and death, associations found elsewhere in Scripture, but nowhere as exquisitely or compactly."[58] Virtually all of the verbs in the verse carry sexual connotations, and many of them are repeated as an element of the poetic form: "Sisera sinks down (thrice), falls (thrice), and lies (once) between—so the Hebrew—Jael's legs."[59] In the Talmud and several midrashim, the rabbis tally the verbal repetition and determine that the seven verbs in this verse indicate that Jael and Sisera had sex seven times.[60] This total is too extreme even for Reis, who disputes the use of the verb נפל ("fall") as a reference to sexual activity (marking perhaps the *only* time when Reis argues for less, rather than more, sex in the Jael passages!).[61] Yet despite the obviously sexual imagery, some scholars argue for maternal overtones here as well; the verse is "reminiscent of a natural birth scene, when the woman sits on her haunches and the baby has to be caught by somebody, so that it does not fall to the ground (cf. Gen. 30.3)."[62]

The action in 5:27 takes place בין רגליה, "between her feet." Niditch observes that the English translation of the phrase blunts the sexual imagery of the original text.[63] The term "feet" is often used in biblical

55. Alter, *Art of Biblical Poetry*, 48.
56. Reis, "Uncovering Jael and Sisera," 39.
57. Reis, "Uncovering Jael and Sisera," 39–41.
58. Niditch, "Eroticism and Death in the Tale of Jael," 308.
59. Athalya Brenner, "A Triangle and a Rhombus in Narrative Structure: A Proposed Integrative Reading of Judges 4 and 5," in Brenner, *Feminist Companion to Judges*, 103.
60. Bronner, "Valorized or Vilified?," 89.
61. Reis, "Uncovering Jael and Sisera," 41–42.
62. Brenner, "Triangle and a Rhombus in Narrative Structure," 103.
63. Niditch, "Eroticism and Death in the Tale of Jael," 308.

texts as a euphemism for sexual organs or acts.[64] The image of Sisera lying with the phallic tent peg in his head, between Jael's feet, emphasizes the reverse-rape imagery of the scene.[65] (The depiction of reverse-rape in 5:27 is further highlighted by the juxtaposition of this scene with that of Sisera's mother in Judg 5:28–30.) However, it is important to note that feet, and the phrase "between [the] feet," carry a different symbolic meaning as well that also may be at play in this verse, subverting the expected female sexual role. "The symbolism of the foot has to do primarily with sovereignty and subjection. According to Gen 49:10, the ruler's staff (meḥōqēq) shall not depart 'from between' the feet of Judah.... The position of the staff between Judah's feet emphasizes its inherent symbolic power (cf. Jgs. 5:27)."[66]

Although (as discussed above) one of the verbs in the verse (נפל) does not appear to carry any sexual connotations, the remaining three verbs (כרע ["bow down"], שכב ["lie/lie down"], and שדד ["despoil"]) certainly do—but these verbs all carry double meanings of death and destruction as well.[67] While כרע in Job 31:10 is used to refer to a man engaging in intercourse, in Isa 65:12 it refers to those who bow down (כרע) for slaughter.[68] The basic meaning of שכב is "lie down," but in almost one-fourth of its uses (50 occurrences, out of a total of 212 uses in the biblical text) the intended meaning is sexual (and usually illicit sex, at that); its most common understanding, however, is "die" or "be dead" (60 occurrences).[69] The verb שדד, used in this verse as a participle, means "deal violently with, despoil, ruin" and is most commonly applied to the destruction of cities and enemies in war; it is also, however, used as a metaphor in Jer 4:30 for "Israel the loose woman, still beautifying herself with flashy clothes, trinkets, and make-up, [who] is sexually despoiled and ruined."[70] Within this single verse, "double meanings of violent death and sexuality emerge in

---

64. E.g., in Isa 7:20 it is linked to pubic hair; in Judg 3:24 and 1 Sam 24:3 it is linked to urination; in Ruth 3:7, Ruth uncovers Boaz's feet and "lies down"; in Ezek 16:25, unfaithful Israel spreads her feet to the passers-by. In Deut 28:57, where the afterbirth "goes out from between her feet," the imagery might also be linked to maternity, although in a twisted, cannibalistic context.

65. Matthews, *Judges and Ruth*, 73.

66. F. J. Stendebach, "רֶגֶל," *TDOT* 13:319.

67. Niditch, "Eroticism and Death in the Tale of Jael," 309–10.

68. Heinz-Josef Fabry, "כָּרַע," *TDOT* 7:336–39.

69. W. Beuken, "שָׁכַב," *TDOT* 14:660–65.

70. Niditch, "Eroticism and Death in the Tale of Jael," 310.

every line.... The woman Jael becomes not the object of sexual advances ... but herself is the aggressor, the despoiler."[71]

It is perhaps worth noting that a great deal of scholarly discussion has centered on the question of whether Jael and Sisera, whose interactions are depicted in such sexually charged verbs, actually had sex. Reis and the rabbis emphatically state "yes."[72] Others feel that a man running for his life from a defeat on the battlefield would have had neither the inclination nor the energy to engage in intercourse during his escape.[73] I would argue that whether sex occurred or not is irrelevant; it is more important to consider that the use of these sexually loaded words and images in the text established for the reader a certain mindset, an awareness that Jael (in contrast to Deborah) was acting according to the "expected" role of women, which was then completely subverted by her unexpected assassination of the enemy general Sisera.

The actions of Jael decisively challenge the notion that women's identity can be simply reduced to their sexual function or derived exclusively from their mothering role.[74] Deborah and Jael both act in Judg 4 and 5 as leaders and heroes in Israel in ways that transcend women's expected actions, but they do so very differently. The verbs that describe Deborah's actions are rare, and sometimes unique, when applied to women. The verbs that describe Jael's actions are those that are expected of women, yet they produce shockingly unexpected results. While their approaches are very different, they nonetheless remain interconnected: Deborah prophesies that Barak will be deprived of glory because YHWH will sell Sisera into the hand of a woman (4:9); when the deed is done, she sings Jael's praises (5:24–27) as an act of "cooperation and solidarity between women."[75] Together, Deborah's actions, which transcend gender norms, and Jael's, which subvert and pervert them, affirm that even in a society where the perceived value of women is generally defined and constrained by their sexual and maternal roles, the unanticipated narrative result of a text such as Judg 4–5 can still take the patriarchy by surprise.[76]

---

71. Niditch, "Eroticism and Death in the Tale of Jael," 310–11.

72. Reis, "Uncovering Jael and Sisera." Bronner, "Valorized or Vilified?," 88–89.

73. Fewell and Gunn, "Controlling Perspectives," 392, 392 n. 10; Victor H. Matthews, "Hospitality and Hostility in Judges 4," *BTB* 21 (1991): 18.

74. Bal, *Death and Dissymmetry*, 27.

75. Van Dijk-Hemmes, "Mothers and a Mediator in the Song of Deborah," 111.

76. Fewell and Gunn, "Controlling Perspectives," 399.

5

Nameless in the Nevi'im:
Intertextuality between Female
Characters in the Book of Judges

Elizabeth H. P. Backfish

Introduction

I am not the first reader to notice that many characters in the book of Judges, male and female, major and minor, are unnamed. Even some of the characters who occupy center stage in large portions of the narratives remain anonymous. This leads us to wonder why the final editor did not provide these characters' names. Certainly, it would have been clearer and less cumbersome simply to provide at least every major character with a name.

While we cannot psychoanalyze the intentions of the narrators and editors to discern the original reason why some characters are named and some characters are unnamed, we can analyze the rhetorical effect of named and unnamed female characters in the final form of the book of Judges, and that is the aim of this study. Specifically, this essay seeks to show how the four named female characters represent what Israel *should* have been doing and the unnamed characters represent what Israel *should not* have been doing or the *consequences* of doing what should not have been done. The patterned pairing of these characters and the male characters who share their narratives, which is a part of the text's intertextuality, further underscores some of these contrasts, inviting readers to mimetically identify with the exemplary, named characters, who serve as foils for the unnamed characters.

Methodology

There are various layers of intertextuality and rhetorical patterning in the book of Judges, and to make it clear that this study is not an attempt to argue for too much, the patterning observed here is only one of several complementary layers.[1] One potential pitfall in any type of literary criticism is the danger of seeing patterns and features that are not really there. In order to guard against imposing a phantom structure, we must test our findings with collaborative evidence from the text and establish if there are rhetorical reasons for the patterns or correspondences suggested. The overall test question that should guide this inquiry is: How does this pattern or this character fit within and contribute to the theological framework of Judges? In other words, do the relationships that I am arguing for between named and unnamed female characters correspond with consensus views of the overall message and theology of the final form of the book?

So what is the theological message of Judges? Many scholars view the final form of the book of Judges as a cohesive work with a unified message.[2] Alongside Israel's perpetual and increasing unfaithfulness and the ensuing political consequences, the book presents God's persistent and increasing faithfulness in mercifully delivering Israel.[3] According to Lillian Klein,

---

1. E.g., some scholars see a downward spiral (Barry Webb, *The Book of Judges*, NICOT [Grand Rapids: Eerdmans, 2012], 33–34; Daniel I. Block, *Judges, Ruth*, NAC 6 [Nashville: Broadman & Holman, 1999], 145; Tammi J. Schneider, *Judges: Studies in Hebrew Narrative and Poetry*, Berit Olam [Collegeville, MN: Liturgical Press, 2000], xii), or a binary structure (Lillian Klein, *The Triumph of Irony in the Book of Judges*, JSOTSup 68, BLS 14 [Sheffield: Almond, 1989], 15); or a chiasm (D. W. Gooding, "The Composition of the Book of Judges," *ErIsr* 16 [1982]: 70*–79*), or a ring structure (Alexander Globe, "'Enemies Round About': Disintegrative Structure in the Book of Judges," in *Mappings of the Biblical Terrain: The Bible as Text*, ed. Vincent L. Tollers and John Maier, Bucknell Review 33.2. [Lewisburg, PA: Bucknell University Press, 1990], 233–51), or any combination of these. Most scholars note the progressive length of each cycle and the omission of key cycle elements in successive cycles.

2. Gregory T. K. Wong, *Compositional Strategy of the Book of Judges: An Inductive, Rhetorical Study*, VTSup 111 (Leiden: Brill, 2006), 25–26; Trent C. Butler, *Judges*, WBC (Nashville: Nelson, 2009), lviii; Webb, *Book of Judges*, 8–9; Schneider, *Judges*, xiii; Mary Evans describes this unity as an "imposed overall structure"; *Judges and Ruth: An Introduction and Commentary*, TOTC 7 (Downers Grove, IL: InterVarsity Press, 2017), 3.

3. J. Clinton McCann, e.g., describes the theological purpose of Judges as a call for repentance and a warning of the consequences of sin. As such, he (like myself) sees the

these two opposing perspectives that are set up in the introduction of the book play out in the structure and development of the book as a whole, and through irony and other literary techniques "the reader is invited to share Yahweh's judgment of Israel."[4] By the time Israel's unfaithfulness reaches its nadir, it is clear that they are in need of a king, either a faithful human king or acknowledgement of their divine king. By "doing what was right in their own eyes" they set themselves up for self-destruction.

Another final methodological concern is the selection of female characters for analysis. Susan Ackerman, in her important book *Warrior, Dancer, Seductress, Queen*, identifies eleven female characters who "exert themselves in the narratives as actors in their own right."[5] These include Achsah, Deborah, Jael, Sisera's mother, the woman of Thebez, Jephthah's daughter, Samson's mother, the Timnite woman, Delilah, Micah's mother, and the Levite's concubine.[6] Other individual female characters, such as the prostitute in Gaza or Abimelech's mother, do not "exert themselves" in the plot; they neither effect nor reflect turning points in the narrative. This study follows Ackerman's methodology and focuses on these same eleven female characters.

Anonymity and Identity

There appears to be a clear pattern between named and unnamed female characters in the book of Judges, and this pattern reflects the downward spiral of Israel's faithfulness during the settlement period. The table below illustrates three categories of female characters: the first column of char-

---

portrayal of women in the book not as reflection on the narrator or on the patriarchal system in general, but as a means to "highlight the pattern of progressive deterioration" (*Judges*, IBC [Louisville: Westminster John Knox, 2011], 22).

4. Klein, *Triumph of Irony*, 36; quotation from p. 191.

5. Susan Ackerman, *Warrior, Dancer, Seductress, Queen: Women in Judges and Biblical Israel*, ABRL (New York: Doubleday, 1998), 3; see similarly, Yairah Amit, *Reading Biblical Narratives: Literary Criticism and the Hebrew Bible*, trans. Yael Lotan (Minneapolis: Fortress, 2001), 73.

6. In addition to these eleven individuals, Ackerman includes three important groups of women: the wise ladies who counsel Sisera's mother, the companions of Jephthah's daughter, and the dancers at Shiloh (*Warrior, Dancer, Seductress, Queen*, 3–4). While these groups of women are indeed important players in their respective scenes and the overall plot, the current study is limited to individual characters because of the phenomenon of anonymity (which is naturally a feature of groups).

acters includes all of the named characters, who in each case were doing what Israel should have been doing. The middle and right columns identify the characters who were not doing what Israel should have been doing, or were suffering the consequences of others' wrongdoing.

Reference	Exemplary Characters: Doing what Israel *should* have been doing	Nonexemplary Characters: Doing what should *not* be done	Tragic Characters: The consequences of doing what should *not* be done
1:12–15	**Achsah**		
4:1–5:31	**Deborah**		
4:17–22; 5:24–27	**Jael**		
5:28–30		Sisera's mother	
9:53	[Woman of Thebez]		
11:34–40			Jephthah's daughter
13:2–14:4		Samson's mother	
14:1–15:8			Timnite woman
16:4–20	[Delilah]		
17:2–4		Micah's mother	
19:1–30			Levite's concubine
Roles:	mixed roles	all mothers	all daughters

Exemplary Actions

All of the named female characters are doing what the Israelites should have been doing, and they represent all of the major roles within their culture: mothers, wives, daughters, and independent agents. Achsah is the female debut, functioning in a paradigmatic role of a woman who had power to assert herself and receive the respect of men.[7] In this way, she

----

7. Other scholars who consider Achsah's literary role paradigmatic include Schneider (*Judges*, 17); Jo Ann Hackett, "Violence and Women's Lives in the Book of Judges," *Int* 58 (2004): 363–64; and Mieke Bal, *Death and Dissymmetry: The Politics of Coherence in the Book of Judges*, CSHJ (Chicago: University of Chicago Press, 1988), 152–56. However, some scholars consider Achsah's character far from exemplary or

represents not only faithful Israelite women, but also Israel more broadly. She asks for what she needs (springs of water, land), gives intelligent argumentation for her request, and is respected by her father, who gives her more than what she has asked for (two springs of water).[8] Achsah, then, seems to represent what Israel's family relationships should have looked like. By naming Achsah, the narrator gives her not only personal identity and agency in her own right, but also a reference point and foil against which to compare and contrast subsequent characters.[9] If Achsah represents Israel at its best, how then do the other characters measure up?

The second named character, Deborah, is also assertive and respected. As a prophet and a judge, Deborah uses her power to maintain justice among her people and to effect deliverance from foreign enemies, which are two key and exemplary concerns. Deborah is also a wife and a "mother of Israel," two familial roles that are naturally highlighted among the female characters in Judges. However, Deborah is not limited by these roles, and her power is not diminished by these roles or her gender. She asserts power for the good of Israel, and the men in the narrative respect her. In fact, she serves as a foil for the hesitant and insecure Barak. Whereas Achsah represented how Israel was to live within their family relationships, Deborah represents how Israel was to live as tribal chiefdoms: with justice, with faithfulness in YHWH, and with strong military leadership.

The third exemplary female character in the book of Judges is also named. Jael represents what Israel should be doing in their fight against

---

respectable. E.g., Judith McKinlay flatly states, "Achsah is a pawn, three over" ("Meeting Achsah on Achsah's Land," *Bible and Critical Theory* 5 [2009]: 8).

8. Schneider, *Judges*, 15. Caleb's vow to give Achsah away as a prize for military valor strikes our modern sensibilities as strange if not offensive, but the vow needs to be understood in its historical context, wherein Caleb's action is best seen as protective in nature, securing a faithful and courageous husband for his daughter (see Tammi J. Schneider, "Achsah, the Raped *Pileges*, and the Book of Judges," in *Women in the Biblical World: A Survey of Old and New Testament Perspectives*, ed. Elizabeth A. McCabe [Lanham, MD: University Press of America, 2009], 45; Robert B. Chisholm Jr., "The Role of Women in the Rhetorical Strategy in the Book of Judges," in *Integrity of Heart, Skillfulness of Hands: Biblical and Leadership Studies in Honor of Donald K. Campbell*, ed. Charles H. Dyer and Roy B. Zuck [Grand Rapids: Baker, 1994], 37).

9. Klein describes Achsah's character as not only idyllic, but also a symbolic "image of Israel as bride to Yahweh" (*Triumph of Irony*, 34). Just as Achsah and Othniel asked for land and were blessed with it, so also Israel needs to depend on YHWH for its blessings.

their enemies: courageously, even cunningly, defeating their enemies.[10] Jael's named identity highlights her exemplary role as a heroic, honored (and honorary) "Israelite."[11] In the narrative account of 4:17–22, Jael's identity is even emphasized over and against Sisera, who is unnamed from the moment he enters Jael's tent until Barak later enters to find him dead in 4:22. After Jael invites Sisera into her tent, and they are apparently the only people there, the narrator specifies that "Jael, the wife of Hever," killed the enemy (4:21). By naming Jael (and not naming Sisera) in this scene, the narrator highlights Jael's identity as the one exemplifying what Israel was supposed to do: defeat her enemies. If scholarly consensus is correct, that Jael was not an Israelite, but a Kenite, like her husband, then her representative role takes on an added punch: a non-Israelite was faithfully doing what Israel should have been doing.

The fourth and final named female character in the book of Judges is also doing what Israel should have been doing in terms of fighting her enemies and earning the respect of those around her, the Philistines.[12] Delilah is a very powerful character, exerting power over Samson and the Philistines. The lords of the Philistines do not attempt to threaten Delilah (as the Timnite woman was threatened by her fellow Philistines) but they offer her an enormous bribe (over eleven hundred pieces of silver each), acknowledging the unique power that she has over their enemy. They do so at a point in which Israel was so complacent under Philistine oppression that they did not even cry out to God for deliverance (Judg 13:1), and they did not even support God's deliverer, but handed him over to the Philistines so as to maintain the status quo (Judg 15:11–13). Delilah in contrast is a powerful warrior figure who fights for her people, albeit

---

10. Ann W. Engar notes that several women in the Old Testament, even some very exemplary women, use trickery to attain their goals (e.g., Rebekah, Tamar, and Lot's daughters). The frequent use of trickery by exemplary female heroes does not mean that the narrator necessarily condoned the behavior (any more so than he condoned the trickery of Jacob or Ehud) but that the women "more closely at times understand God's purposes than do their male counterparts" ("Old Testament Women as Tricksters," in Tollers and Maier, *Mappings of the Biblical Terrain*, 143).

11. In this way, Jael is much like Rahab, who is also a named, honored, and honorary Israelite (Josh 2:1–21; 6:22–23).

12. The text does not explicitly identify Delilah as a Philistine. Regardless of her precise lineage, Delilah is clearly identified with the Philistines, if not by citizenship or ethnicity, then by loyalty. Susan Ackerman, "What If Judges Had Been Written by a Philistine?," *BibInt* 8 (2000): 37.

against God's people.[13] In my opinion, and from the perspective of the book of Judges, Delilah was a hero on the wrong side of the conflict. Naming Delilah, a representative of Israel's nemesis and the de facto murderer of Israel's chosen deliverer, serves as a sharp critique of Israel's complacency. The suggestion that Israel should have been taking notes from the Philistines was a rhetorical jab that no doubt struck a few Israelite nerves.

All four named characters are exemplifying something that Israel should have been doing: acquiring land for their families, leading their communities, and fighting their enemies. However, one *unnamed* woman also belongs in this group, and her anonymity is an exception to the pattern. "A certain woman," who climbed the tower of Thebez, hurled an upper millstone onto the head of Abimelech, the antijudge and antiking. It has been suggested that the key to her anonymity is a vital part of the literary artistry of the text. Most scholars agree that in Judg 9:53 the numeral in the expression אשה אחת (literally "one woman") should be interpreted as emphatic indefiniteness, so "a certain woman," carries the sense of unimportance, emphasizing that Abimelech was killed by a nobody, a cipher of a character.[14] It is also possible that אחת denotes singularity, which has connections to other scenes in the narrative (e.g., the "one stone" on which Abimelech killed his brothers).[15] Some scholars have pointed out the wordplay between אשה ("woman") and אש ("fire"), which also might account for the anonymity of Abimelech's killer. In the preceding verse,

---

13. Royce Victor even calls Delilah a hero because of her sacrificial efforts to liberate her people from the oppression of Israel; "Delilah—A Forgotten Hero (Judges 16:4–21): A Cross-Cultural Narrative Reading," in *Joshua and Judges*, ed. Athalya Brenner and Gale Yee, Texts and Contexts (Minneapolis: Fortress, 2013), 235–56.

14. Because of Abimelech's misogynistic pride, he asks his armor bearer to kill him so that the woman's deathblow would not be the official cause of death. Of course, his shameful death, along with his misogyny, are now memorialized forever; Robert G. Boling, *Judges: A New Translation with Introduction and Commentary*, AB 6A (Garden City, NY: Doubleday, 1975), 182; Webb, *Book of Judges*, 293. The unnamed woman also functions as an appropriate bookend to Abimelech's unnamed mother, who gave Abimelech life and through whose place in Shechem gave him power. The woman of Thebez brings him down from power by taking his life (Butler, *Judges*, 249). Block states, "The man who had shamelessly played the female card to seize the throne (vv. 1–2) now shamefully falls victim to a representative of this gender" (*Judges*, 333–34).

15. J. Gerald Janzen, "A Certain Woman in the Rhetoric of Judges 9," *JSOT* 12 (1987): 33–37.

indeed two words before the woman is mentioned, the narrator tells us that Abimelech approached the tower in order to burn it with fire, just as he had done to the tower of Shechem. Instead of killing more fellow-Israelites with אש, however, he is killed by an אשה.[16] Any of these levels of rhetoric might be responsible for the deviation from the pattern of named exemplary female characters in the book.

Nonexemplary Characters

The next group of characters represent what Israel should *not* be doing. The exemplary characters included women with various roles and lack of roles, including daughters, wives, mothers, and independent or unspecified agents. Of the nonexemplary characters, however, all three characters share the same primary role (motherhood) and all are unnamed.

The first two nonexemplary characters are mothers of macho, heroic figures, and both suffer from some kind of misunderstanding. The first is Sisera's mother. As an unnamed woman in the Deborah cycle, she stands in stark contrast to the ideal "mother of Israel," Deborah herself, as well as Jael, who cunningly uses her motherly actions to kill Sisera.[17] Sisera's mother is comforted at the thought that her son is late due to the many wombs he is plundering, while he is ironically destroyed by the very sex his culture apparently felt justified in objectifying. This brutal attitude toward women reflects not only what Israel should not have been doing, but even what they were doing, as we see horrifically played out in chapter 21.[18]

Samson's mother, or Manoah's wife, is the most developed anonymous character in the book of Judges.[19] In Judg 13, the author refers to her as "wife" or "woman" (אשה again) no less than fourteen times. She seems to be a relatively devout woman, but she is not depicted as an ideal character because she mirrors Israel in two disastrous ways.[20] First, like Israel, she is

---

16. Robert B. Chisholm Jr., *A Commentary on Judges and Ruth*, Kregel Exegetical Library (Grand Rapids: Kregel Academic, 2013), 323–24.

17. Jael comforts Sisera, covers him with a blanket (4:18), gives him milk/curds (4:19; 5:25), and watches out for him (4:20).

18. Schneider, *Judges*, 96; Chisholm, "Role of Women," 45.

19. While Samson's mother is often referred to as "Manoah's wife," it is her role of impending motherhood that is the central focus of the narrative.

20. James Crenshaw even sees her as an ideal wife, which might be a tempting

disinterested in divine deliverance from Philistine oppression. She accurately relays to her husband everything that the angel tells her, except for the significant detail that the child will deliver Israel. From the perspective of the woman, Israel did not need a deliverer, and neither did she.[21] She needed a child, and that is what consumes her thoughts. Second, she does not accurately understand or communicate to Manoah the angel's charge and prophecy. By adding to the angel's prophetic word that the child would be a Nazarite "to his death" (13:7), she adds what some scholars consider to be Samson's death sentence.[22] Thus in her anonymity she reflects the typical devout Israelite of the day, who was still far from the paradigmatic ideals of Achsah and Deborah.[23] Without a name, she functions as a literary stand-in for any and all Israelites of the time who were devout but misguided.[24]

---

evaluation relative to other characters in the Samson saga and if disconnected from the rest of the book (*Samson: A Secret Betrayed, A Vow Ignored* [Atlanta: John Knox, 1978], 70); Klein also sees Samson's mother positively, primarily because of her connections with Jephthah's daughter; Lillian Klein, "A Spectrum of Female Characters," in *A Feminist Companion to Judges*, ed. Athalya Brenner, FCB 4 (Sheffield: JSOT Press, 1993), 27.

21. In every other judge cycle, the Israelites cry out to God in their oppression, and God in turn raises a deliverer, or judge (3:9, 15; 4:3; 6:6; 10:10). The Samson cycle is the first cycle to completely omit this cyclical element.

22. Adele Reinhartz, *Why Ask My Name? Anonymity and Identity in Biblical Narrative* (New York: Oxford University Press, 1998), 98; and Bal, *Death and Dissymmetry*, 31. The angel had simply stated that the boy would be a Nazarite "from the womb," but he never specified the duration of the appointment. Regardless of whether or not the woman's augmentation had an effect on Samson's fate, it highlights the disjunction between God's message and her reception of it. Far from sharing the angel's prophetic role, her distortion of the prophecy makes her a foil for the angel of the Lord (it also makes her a foil for Deborah, the only character in the book explicitly named as a prophet [Judg 4:4]).

23. Manoah's treatment of his wife likewise reflects Israel's treatment of women, namely the perspective that a woman's testimony could not be trusted (Evans, *Judges and Ruth*, 33). The contrast between their relationship and that of Achsah with the men in her life should not be missed.

24. Reinhartz (*Why Ask My Name?*, 42) explains that anonymous servants can serve as proxies for the named characters they represent (e.g., Abraham's servant serves as his proxy when he goes to Haran to secure a wife for Isaac). The same proxy-function might be at work in the case of Samson's mother, though instead of representing her named husband, she is representing Israel at large. This connection is not a stretch considering that both Israel and Samson's mother are distinguished in this

The third female character who exemplifies what Israel was not supposed to be doing is Micah's mother. A woman of only three verses, she manages to incriminate herself in three ways. First, after her son confesses to having stolen her eleven hundred pieces of silver, she blesses him (17:2), rather than disciplines him (cf. Deut 21:18; Prov 28:24; 29:15). Second, she promises to return the money to her son in the form of a molten image, which is the root cause of the Lord's anger in the book of Judges (2:12). Third, Micah's mother then seems to backtrack on her promise. Instead of using the entire eleven hundred silver pieces for the molten image, she uses only two hundred.[25] In her anonymity, Micah's mother represents Israel's propensity toward idolatry and declining morality.

The Consequences of Israel's Unfaithfulness

In addition to the three characters who do not exemplify what Israel should have been doing, the book of Judges highlights three female characters who fall victim to Israel's nonexemplary behavior, and these two groups are interspersed in an alternating pattern. The three victims are all identified as daughters and fall victim to the men in their lives who should have protected them.

Jephthah's daughter falls under the shadowy identity of her father, who is responsible for her tragic demise. Throughout the cycle, Jephthah's power is seated in his discourse, and when his daughter comes out to meet him, he exerts that power first by blaming her (11:35) and then by appealing to his integrity in keeping his vow (11:35).[26] Both Jephthah and his daughter appear to be unaware of the provisions in the Torah for rescind-

---

cycle by their complacency. Every other action is expected, save for their indifference to be saved from Philistine oppression.

25. This inconsistency between her promise to Micah and its fulfillment foreshadows the Levite's inconsistent (or broken) promise to Micah.

26. For Jephthah's discourse, see, e.g., his negotiations with the elders of Gilead (11:5–11), his lengthy correspondence with the Ammonite king (11:12–27), his foolish vow (11:31), and his altercation with the Ephraimites (12:1–6). The emphatic use of the second-person feminine singular pronoun את along with the second-person feminine singular inflected verb form highlights Jephthah's blame-shifting. In this explanatory clause, Jephthah emphasizes himself as the subject by using a disjunctive *waw* and another redundant pronoun (ואנכי). His pathetic show of self-pity exacerbates his crime and garners no pity from attentive readers.

ing a vow (Lev 27:1–8) and the prohibitions against child sacrifice (Deut 12:31; 18:9–12).[27]

Jephthah's daughter shows a small but significant amount of assertiveness when she shifts the blame squarely back to Jephthah ("My father, *you* have opened your mouth to YHWH. Do to me according to what has gone out of *your* mouth" [Judg 11:36, emphasis added]) and requests that she be permitted to mourn her virginity with her companions for two months (11:37).[28] Her request exhibits a level of assertiveness faintly mirroring that of Achsah, and her father's willingness to meet her request exhibits a level of respect, faintly (very faintly!) mirroring that of Caleb, but these faint parallels probably do more to highlight the contrast between the characters of the two father-daughter scenes—and even these faint glimmers of assertiveness and respect are completely lacking by the time we meet the final anonymous female character.

However, before we meet the tragic concubine, we find the second anonymous victim: the woman of Timnah, Samson's Philistine wife. Her role as a daughter is also highlighted in the narrative, since it is ultimately her father's decision to marry her off to someone else that sends Samson on the rampage that will result in retaliation against the woman and her father. Throughout this narrative, the woman in Timnah is treated like a commodity to be traded and an instrument to be used in men's power games. Just as Samson offered the Philistines an impossible riddle, she is offered impossible options for survival. She is ultimately the victim of per-

---

27. J. Cheryl Exum focuses on the unretractable nature of the vow to support her thesis that Jephthah's daughter was murdered by the narrator as much as by her father; see *Fragmented Women: Feminist (Sub)versions of Biblical Narratives* (Valley Forge, PA: Trinity Press International, 1993), 11. Exum only acknowledges in a brief footnote that the vow was in fact retractable, according to Lev 27. It seems, rather, that this oversight of legal provision is central to the narrator's portrayal of the dire situation: in addition to having a hugely distorted view of what their God required of them (which was certainly not child sacrifice!), Israel had a dearth of torah knowledge. Moreover, in light of the overall structure of the placement of this cycle toward the bottom of the downward spiral gives readers an expectation that things in Israel are far from ideal. Far from committing "literary murder" (Exum, *Fragmented Women*, 23) the narrator (or redactor) is exposing the murderous tenor of Israel at the time of the settlement. In other words, if the narrator has an ax to grind (or a millstone to hurl, or a jawbone to wield) it is against Israel and not against the women trampled under Israel's faithlessness.

28. Exum, *Fragmented Women*, 22.

sonal vengeance and choices beyond her control. Her anonymity highlights her place in the literary pattern of nameless victims and also serves
to generify her so that her identity is absorbed in the people group she
represents, the Philistines.[29]

The final anonymous victim of Israel's unfaithfulness is the Levite's
concubine, arguably the most tragic character in the book. Her father fails
to protect her, and her very own husband is either indirectly or directly
responsible for her violent death.[30] Thus, she is victimized as both daughter and wife. Much like Jephthah's daughter, her death is as unnecessary as
it was preventable, which only adds to the tragedy.

In addition to being nameless, the concubine is also speechless. The
Levite presumably set out to "speak to her heart" but no such conversation
actualized.[31] If each female character is to be read against the gold standard of Achsah, then the concubine represents the farthest deviation from
the ideal. Achsah spoke with confidence and wisdom; the concubine does
not speak at all. Achsah was respected and listened to by the men in her

---

29. As a representative of the Philistines, the woman in Timnah is also a foil for
Delilah. Both women use Samson's apparent lack of love to persuade him to divulge
secret information (14:16; 16:15). However, whereas Samson explicitly loves Delilah
(16:4), his attraction to the woman of Timnah seems to be merely infatuation (14:3),
and whereas Delilah survived and even profited from her work for her Philistine com-
rades, the woman of Timnah neither profits from nor survives their judgment, despite
her efforts.

30. While her husband and the old man who "hosted" them in Gibeah are
obviously to blame for the concubine's fate, her father is likewise culpable. She
is apparently excluded from the multiple day feast and celebration. The singular
imperative verb forms used throughout this scene make it clear that the concubine's father is inviting the Levite in particular to stay longer. Even in English
translation, her exclusion is made clear by such statements as "So the two of them
sat and ate together" (19:6) and "So they ate, both of them" (19:8). Her father's
hospitality is clearly lacking, if not malevolent. By insisting that his son-in-law
remain in Bethlehem until midday, he made it impossible for them to reach the
safety of their home (or at least their tribal region) by nightfall, which otherwise
might have been possible had they left at morning. The distance between Bethlehem and Gibeah is roughly seven to eight miles, while they could have reached
their own tribal land (Ephraim) in less than fifteen miles, a distance that would
require a full day of travel, but would nonetheless be manageable, especially with
a donkey.

31. Schneider, *Judges*, 16–17; see also Schneider, "Achsah, the Raped *Pilegeš*," and
the Book of Judges," 47; Phyllis Trible, *Texts of Terror: A Literary-Feminist Reading of
Biblical Narratives*, OBT (Philadelphia: Fortress, 1984), 68.

life, most explicitly her father; the concubine was disrespected by both her father and her husband. Achsah secured life for her family; the concubine suffered insecurity and death.[32]

The effect of the concubine's anonymity again generifies her. She has no voice, no volitional actions, and no point of view, and as such blends in with her representative people group: women of Israel. The rhetorical effect is that during this time in the settlement period, women were treated horrifically.[33]

Intertextual Pairings of Female Characters

Scholars have pointed out two corresponding pairs of female characters. We have just mentioned the connections between the first pair, who function as an *inclusio* for the book: Achsah and the Levite's concubine. The second noted pair is Jael and Delilah, who both use deception and maternal imagery to bring down their enemies.[34] But is there an overall structure of pairs? I believe that a strong case can be made for the pairs outlined in the table on the following page. Note that the attributes in italics denote commonality, whereas the attributes in bold denote contrasts.

The first pair (A, A'), Achsah and Jephthah's daughter, are both Israelite daughters of powerful fathers and for both women, their marital status is key to the narrative. However, whereas Achsah is honored by her father and given a faithful, valiant husband and life-giving land upon request, Jephthah's daughter is deprived the joys of both husband and life, and she is utterly dishonored. The ideal, honored daughter is contrasted with the tragic, dishonored daughter.

---

32. According to Schneider, these contrasting characterizations are further highlighted by the imagery of riding on a donkey. The book of Judges mentions only these two characters riding on a donkey. Achsah descends her donkey of her own will for her own blessings. The concubine, on the other hand, ascends her donkey as an unconscious or dead victim of a horrendous crime. Schneider notes, too, that both Achsah and the concubine are the only female characters who explicitly live far from their fathers, and both women are from Judah, though their husbands are not; *Judges*, 14–15; Schneider, "Achsah, the Raped *Pileges*, and the Book of Judges," 43–45, 48.

33. The fact that the other tribes were outraged (19:30) does not mean that the woman's fate was the source of the outrage. In fact, given the way that the Levite spun the account to paint himself as the victim (20:5) suggests that his treatment of his concubine could have been normative.

34. Chisholm, "Role of Women," 43.

A Achsah	A' Jephthah's daughter
• *powerful father*	• *powerful father*
• **wife of faithful Israelite**	• **wife of no one**
• **honored** *daughter*	• **dishonored** *daughter*
B Deborah	B' Samson's mother
• *mother* of Israel	• *mother* of Israel's deliverer
• **represents Israel well**	• **represents Israel poorly**
• **assertively fights against enemy oppression**	• **complacently accepts enemy oppression**
• *Barak looks to her for prophetic message and courage,* **and trusts her word**	• *Manoah looks to her for prophetic message and courage,* **but does not trust her word alone**
	[Timnite wife/daughter] The Timnite woman fits the pattern of an unnamed victim, but she does not fit in the intertextual patterning suggested here. She is thus an outlier.
C Jael	C' Delilah
• *deceptive killer of enemies*	• *deceptive killer of enemies*
• **honored in Israel**	• **implicitly dishonored in Israel**
D Sisera's mother	D' Micah's mother
• *wealthy mother of a grown man*	• *wealthy mother of a grown man*
• her worries turn to confidence	• her curse turns to blessing
• *misguidedly blind to her son's sin*	• *misguidedly blind to her son's sin*
• *idolator*	• *idolator*
• *the changed fate of her son* **is unknown by her**	• *the changed fate of her son* **is determined by her**
E Woman of Thebez	E' Concubine
• *no voice*	• *no voice*
• *a nobody*	• *a nobody*
• **active agent**	• **passive agent**
• **female killer of a male victim**	• **female victim of a male killer**

The second pair (B, B′), Deborah and Samson's mother, are both described as mothers who engage with prophecy. Whereas Deborah is a true prophet, Samson's mother hears but does not faithfully relay the angel's prophecy to her husband. Whereas Barak trusts Deborah's words, Manoah distrusts his wife and insists on talking directly with the angel.[35] Whereas Deborah is an active instigator of confronting Israel's oppressors, Samson's mother is passive and complacent under enemy oppression.

The third pair (C, C′), Jael and Delilah, both destroy their victims through deception, using sexual and/or maternal imagery.[36] Both also appear to be outsiders of the people for whom they fight: Jael was a Kenite who fought for Israel, whereas Delilah lived in the Shephelah of Israel (the "Valley of Sorek") and fought for the Philistines. The non-Israelite, Jael, fought on the side of the Israelites in order to take down a foreigner, whereas Delilah fought against Israel in order to take down an Israelite.[37]

The fourth pair (D, D′), Sisera's mother and Micah's mother, are both wealthy mothers who are misguided and blind to the sins of their sons.[38] Sisera's mother is powerless and focused on plunder (wealth). Micah's mother is also focused on her stolen and returned wealth, but she at least considers herself to be powerful in her ability to curse and then bless her son, the thief. Both women are idolatrous, though one is naturally so and the other is unexpectedly so. The idolatrous foreign mother is likened to the idolatrous Israelite mother, and the impotent foolish mother is contrasted with the manipulative foolish mother.

The fifth and final pair (E, E′), the woman of Thebez and the Levite's concubine, are both nondescript, anonymous females without a voice. As for the woman of Thebez, we are told nothing about her father or husband or her role in Israelite society. She is an undeveloped character, but

---

35. Evans, *Judges and Ruth*, 33.

36. Ackerman, "What If Judges," 39–40. The debate over the potential sexual imagery in the Jael narrative was hashed out by several scholars, including the exchange by Pamela Reis ("Uncovering Jael and Sisera: A New Reading," *SJOT* 19 [2005]: 24–47) and Robert B. Chisholm Jr. ("What Went on in Jael's Tent? The Collocation of תכסהו בשמיכהו in Judges 4, 18," *SJOT* 24 [2010]: 143–44; and Chisholm, "What Went on in Jael's Tent? [Part Two]," *SJOT* 27 [2013]: 216–18). See also Serge Frolov, who concludes that most recent attempts at finding sexual imagery in the book of Judges is unfounded; "Sleeping with the Enemy: Recent Scholarship on Sexuality in the Book of Judges," *CBR* 11 (2013): 308–27.

37. Chisholm, "The Role of Women," 42. Ackerman, "What If Judges," 37–38.

38. Reinhartz, *Why Ask My Name?*, 111.

she develops the plot in crucial ways by killing the internal enemy. The concubine has both a father and husband (both unnamed) and she too is an undeveloped character who nonetheless develops the plot through her passive death by an internal enemy. The active, anonymous killer is contrasted with the passive, anonymous killed.

In addition to the intertextuality between female pairs, there are also correspondences between the male characters associated with each female character. These literary connections are shown in the following table:

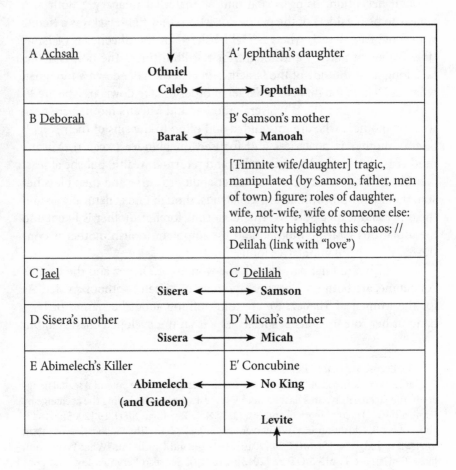

A <u>Achsah</u>
 	
      Othniel
      Caleb ←
	A′ Jephthah's daughter
	
	→ Jephthah

B <u>Deborah</u> **Barak ←**	B′ Samson's mother **→ Manoah**
	[Timnite wife/daughter] tragic, manipulated (by Samson, father, men of town) figure; roles of daughter, wife, not-wife, wife of someone else: anonymity highlights this chaos; // Delilah (link with "love")
C <u>Jael</u> **Sisera ←**	C′ <u>Delilah</u> **→ Samson**
D Sisera's mother **Sisera ←**	D′ Micah's mother **→ Micah**

E Abimelech's Killer
 	
      Abimelech ←
      (and Gideon)
	E′ Concubine
	
	→ No King
	
	Levite

Just as the contrasting images of Achsah and the Levite's concubine formed an *inclusio* around which to interpret the other characters, so also Othniel and the Levite exhibit a strong contrast. Whereas Othniel is a named and heroic husband, the Levite is an unnamed, cowardly, murderous husband. A stronger contrast would be hard to find.

Additionally, just as Achsah and Jephthah's daughter contrasted sharply, so also the fathers of each are radically different. Achsah's father, Caleb, is an exemplary leader in Israel and a devoted father who generously cares for the well-being of his daughter, whereas Jephthah proved to be a horrible leader and an even worse father.

The connections between Barak and Manoah also mirror those between Deborah and Samson's mother. Both men look to the women in their lives for guidance and a prophetic word. Whereas Barak listens to Deborah, however, Manoah is unwilling to trust his wife's rendition of the prophetic message.

The next pair, Sisera and Samson, are both powerful men of war who are deceived by the women in their narratives; their deaths are marked by humiliation and irony. Sisera also corresponds with Micah, both of whom are idolatrous sons of wealthy mothers, and both of whom are deceived.

Finally, Abimelech corresponds with the refrain throughout Judg 17–21 that also introduces the narrative of the Levite and his concubine: "In those days, there was no king in Israel" (19:1). By setting himself up as a king (or an antiking), Abimelech's usurpation of God's throne points to the horrible conditions present when Israel lacked the central leadership decried in the epilogue of the book.

The Overall Rhetorical Effect of Anonymity/Identity and Intertextual Patterning

Thus far we have noted paired relationships between the first five and the final five female characters, as well as their corresponding male characters. These intertextual correspondences emphasize the differences between the paradigmatic features of the exemplary characters and the flaws of the nonexemplary characters. We have also noted a patterning of named and unnamed female characters that appears to correspond with their representation of faithfulness (named characters), unfaithfulness (unnamed characters), or the consequences of that unfaithfulness (unnamed characters). This patterning accords with the downward spiral of faithlessness in the final form of the book.

In addition to reinforcing the theological message of the book, the identity of exemplary characters and anonymity of nonexemplary and tragic characters has an important effect upon the reader. Adele Reinhartz argues that "the absence of a proper name contributes to the effacement, absence, veiling, or suppression of identity," and if Judges is read mimetically, with an effort to imitate that which should be imitated, it is the named characters who should serve as the model reflections of ourselves.[39] Although Israelites during the period of the Judges were more accurately reflected in the unnamed characters, the exilic or postexilic readers of the book in its final form were being exhorted, through a mimetic reading, to associate with the exemplary characters, who stand in sharp contrast with the unnamed characters who represent Israel at its worst.[40]

David Clines, however, argues that mimetic reading is made more fluid through anonymity.[41] The Israelite readers were acting like the anonymous characters, doing what should *not* have been done and experiencing the consequences of those actions. In this way, the ancient readers, as well as modern ones, are drawn into these anonymous female characters who represent us and who cause us to fear and repent.

Perhaps both the identified and the anonymous characters serve mimetic functions in the book of Judges. The identified characters encourage readers to mimic them, whereas the anonymous characters expose to the readers how much they already mimic their sinful ways, and that they must turn and become more like the exemplary characters.

In conclusion, the artistry at the literary and redaction levels of the book of Judges is seen clearly through the female characters of the book. These characters, through their anonymity and identity and through the intertextuality of their patterning, reinforce the theological message of the book, that during this period in Israel's history, God's faithfulness was met with Israel's increasing unfaithfulness.

---

39. Reinhartz, *Why Ask My Name?*, 9.

40. Reinhartz, *Why Ask My Name?*, 10–11. Reinhartz notes the representational quality of other unnamed characters, most notably the first man and woman (before they are named Adam and Eve) who represent all men and women (87).

41. Clines gives as an example the servant songs in Isaiah, wherein the servant's anonymity creates a strong mimetic relationship between the reader and the servant. He argues, "The reader can, in the presence of this, the central persona of the poem, cease to be the active subject interrogating the text, and become the one who is questioned and changed by the text"; *I, He, We, and They: A Literary Approach to Isaiah 53*, JSOTSup 1 (Sheffield: JSOT Press, 1976), 63–64.

6

The Caleb-Achsah Episode: Judges 1:10–15

J. Cornelis de Vos

Introduction

Joshua 15:13–19 and its parallel Judg 1:10–15 are remarkable in at least two ways.[1] First, neither one really fits its context. The story thus must have been regarded as significantly important to be included twice.[2] Second, the narrative course of events is interesting. Achsah is given away to Othniel by her father Caleb as a reward for the latter's capture of Debir.[3] However, Othniel hardly plays any role in the narrative. The interaction is between Caleb and Achsah, and it is Achsah, the former object, who convinces her father to give her a blessing in the form of ponds or a body of water.

In this contribution, I will deal with the background, foreground, and function of the episode, highlighting some intertextual nodes and the narrative roles of Caleb, Othniel, and Achsah.

---

1. The Caleb-Achsah episode of Josh 15:13–19 reoccurs in Judg 1:10–15 with slight differences. In Judg 1, however, Caleb is introduced later, in verse 12, whereas in Josh 15, he enters the stage at the very beginning of the episode. So, the actual Caleb-Achsah episode in Judges is found in 1:12–15 (// Josh 15:16–19). Nevertheless, I adhere to Judg 1:10–15 for this essay. Determining the inner and outer delimitation of Judg 1 is complicated. Is Judg 1:1–36 a unit or Judg 1:1–2:5 or 6? See Susan Niditch, *Judges: A Commentary*, OTL (Louisville: Westminster John Knox, 2008), 36–37. Also, does Judg 1:12–15 belong to 1:10–15 or to 1:8–15? Jack M. Sasson (*Judges 1–12: A New Translation with Introduction and Commentary*, AB 6D [New Haven: Yale University Press, 2014], 139) characterizes 1:8–11 as "to play Janus."

2. See also Sasson, *Judges*, 145.

3. Judith McKinlay ("Meeting Achsah on Achsah's land," *Bible and Critical Theory* 5 [2009]: 1–11) characterizes this as "Achsah, a movable pawn of Israel's myths of empire" (8).

"The authors of Judges 1 write as if Joshua 1–11 had not taken place. At the same time, they know the book of Joshua very well," noted Ernst-Axel Knauf in his commentary on Judges.[4] Not only this, they probably knew the whole book of Joshua as well as the Pentateuch, the books of Samuel and Kings, and the remainder of Judg 2:6–16:31, apart from 2:1–5 (it is commonly accepted that Judg 1:1–2:5 is a later introduction to the book of Judges).[5] Chapter 1, with which I will deal now, is full of allusions to other texts of the Bible. It communicates with them and seeks to set events described elsewhere in a new light. We can only understand what Judg 1 wants to tell us when we read it together with the texts that are alluded to within it. The many allusions, however, make Judg 1 quite complicated. The chapter is already in itself full of tensions and contradictions, though I agree here with Serge Frolov and Knauf, that they are deliberate and part of the alleged "make Judah great again" strategy.[6] It is, for example, no problem for the authors to write that Judah captured Jerusalem (v. 8) but that the Benjaminites were unable to expel the Jebusites from Jerusalem (v. 21).[7] Was not King Saul from the tribe of Benjamin? And was it not David from the tribe of Judah who had captured Jerusalem?

Judges 1 is not only about Judah; it is, again taking from Frolov, about the Judahite David.[8] But its pro-Judahite and pro-David stance is not universally accepted; Gregory T. K. Wong questions whether there is a pro-Judahite slant at all in Judg 1.[9] There is also the matter of the

---

4. Knauf, *Richter*, ZBK (Zurich: TVZ, 2016), 41: "Die Verfasser von Ri 1 schreiben, als hätte Jos 1–11 nicht stattgefunden. Gleichzeitig kennen sie das Josua-Buch sehr gut." Unless otherwise noted, all translations are by the author.

5. Whether or not Judg 17–21 or parts thereof belong to the same stage as Judg 1 is a matter of debate. It is commonly accepted that it is later than the bulk of Judg 2:6–16:31.

6. Frolov, *Judges*, FOTL 6B (Grand Rapids: Eerdmans, 2013), 44–53; Knauf, *Richter*, 41. See also the title of Mareike Rake's third chapter: "'Schreiende Widersprüche' in Ri 1:1–21" in *"Juda wird aufsteigen!" Untersuchungen zum ersten Kapitel des Richterbuches*, BZAW 367 (Berlin: de Gruyter, 2006), 74. Niditch (*Judges*, 37, see also 11–13) evaluates Judg 1 as a compilation of partly old material, in which tensions and contradictions were not erased.

7. Before, they had already brought Adoni-bezek to Jerusalem (v. 7). For a composition-critical analysis, see Rake, "Schreiende Widersprüche," 74–90.

8. Frolov, *Judges*, 50.

9. Wong, "Is There a Direct Pro-Judah Polemic in Judges," *SJOT* 19 (2005): 84–110. Different is the unconvincing article of Philippe Guillaume ("An Anti-Judean Manifesto

Caleb-(Othniel-)Achsah episode in Judg 1:12–15, whereby the parties appear to be connected to Judah, but it is not clear whether they belong to this tribe.[10] If not, this constitutes possibly the only positive representation of non-Judahite persons in Judg 1.[11] Can we, nevertheless, also connect this episode with David?

Judges 1:10–15

As already stated, Judg 1:10–15 has a parallel in Josh 15:13–19, where verses 11–15 in Judg 1 are almost identical to Josh 15:15–19:

Josh 15:13–19[12]

13 According to the command of YHWH to Joshua, he gave [נתן] to Caleb son of Jephunneh a portion among the people of Judah, Kiriath-arba, that is Hebron (Arba was the father of Anak).

14 And Caleb drove out [ויֹרֶש] from there the three sons of Anak:

Sheshai, Ahiman, and Talmai,

the descendants of Anak.

15 From there he went up [ויעל] against the inhabitants of Debir [ישׁבי דבר] (the name of Debir [דבר] was formerly Kiriath-sepher).

16 Caleb said, "Whoever attacks Kiriath-sepher and takes it, I will give him my daughter Achsah as wife."

Judg 1:10–15

10 Judah went [וילך] against the Canaanites who dwelt in Hebron (the name of Hebron was formerly Kiriath-arba);

and they defeated [ויכו]

Sheshai, Ahiman, and Talmai.

11 From there he went [וילך] against the inhabitants of Debir [יושׁבי דביר] (the name of Debir [דביר] was formerly Kiriath-sepher).

12 Caleb said: "Whoever attacks Kiriath-sepher and takes it, I will give him my daughter Achsah as wife."

in Judges 1?," *BN* 95 [1998]: 12–17) who argues that Judg 1:1–18 is anti-Judaean, but not anti-Judah by distinguishing בני יהודה, "Judahites," and יהודה, "Judah."

10. In 1 Chr 2:46–50, the Calebites are even genealogically integrated into the tribe of Judah.

11. The tribe of Simeon is also referred to in a positive light as it fights on the side of the tribe of Judah in battle (Judg 1:3, 17). However, nothing more is said about Simeon.

12. Translations are mostly adapted from NRSV.

17 Othniel, son of Kenaz, the brother of Caleb, took it; and he gave him his daughter Achsah as wife.

13 Othniel, son of Kenaz, Caleb's younger brother, took it; and he gave him his daughter Achsah as wife.

18a When she came to him, she urged him by asking [ותסיתהו לשאול][13] her father for a field [שדה].

14a When she came to him, she urged him by asking [ותסיתהו לשאול] her father for the field [השדה].

18b As she spit [ותצנח][14] from her donkey, Caleb said to her, "What's with you?"[15]

14b As she spit [ותצנח] from her donkey, Caleb said to her, "What's with you?"

19 She said to him, "Give [תנה] me a blessing/pool [ברכה];[16] since you have given me away as Negeb-land [ארץ הנגב],[17] give me ponds of water."

15 She said to him, "Give [הבה] me a blessing/pool [ברכה]; since you have given me away as Negeb-land [ארץ הנגב], give me Gulloth-mayim."

So Caleb gave her the upper ponds [גלת עליות] and the lower ponds [גלת תחתיות].

So Caleb gave her Upper Gulloth [גלת עלית] and Lower Gulloth [גלת תחתית].

It is beyond doubt here that the authors of Judges knew the story in (if not from) Joshua and not vice versa. (1) Kiriath-arba seems to be an older name for the place referred to here as "Hebron" (Josh 15:13); in Judg 1:10 it is the opposite: Hebron is referred to as Kiriath-arba; (2) it is likely that the author of Judg 1 avoided mentioning the mythical Anakites as well as the syntactically awkward "Kiriat-arba … Arba was the father of Anak" (Josh 15:13–14); (3) It is more likely that Judah replaced Caleb in defeating Sheshai, Ahiman, and Talmai than the reverse (Josh 15:14 // Judg 1:10);[18] (4) the author of Judg 1 might not have understood that גלת means "pools" and struck the plural *vav* in the *nomina recta* עליות and תחתיות, thereby making the combinations toponyms. Although it is possible to read them as plurals, it is far more likely that the authors made place names out of

---

13. See below for this translation.

14. See below for this translation.

15. See Sasson, *Judges*, 147–48.

16. ברכה is a word play; vocalized as בְּרָכָה it means "blessing" and as בְּרֵכָה it means "pool."

17. See below for possible translations of כי ארץ הנגב נתתני.

18. The sudden plural as subject of ויכו in 1:10b is awkward whereas יהודה was the subject of 1:10a; maybe this is a way to refer to Caleb as the original victor of the three Anakites (thus in Josh 15:14); see also Rake, "Schreiende Widersprüche," 80.

them because in other cases they inserted *matres lectionis* (1:11);[19] (5) the form השדה (Judg 1:14) instead of שדה (Josh 15:17) could mean that *the* field is now known to author and addressees; (6) Judg 1:11 has three forms in *plene* writing whereas Josh 1:15 has no *plene* there; this, as well as the Aramaic verb יהב in Judg 1:15 (נתן in Josh 15:19) seem to point to a later, probably postexilic stage of Biblical Hebrew.[20]

Adaptations of the Joshua-*Vorlage* are thus very important to understanding the function of the pericope in Judges. Most adaptations occur in Judg 1:10 and 11a. They can easily be explained. In Josh 15:13–14 a portion of the land is *given* to Caleb because it appears within chapters 14–19 in Joshua about the allotment of the land, not about the conquest;[21] the conquest is depicted in the first half of the book of Joshua (chs. 1–12). Only after land has been given to Caleb does he drive the three sons of Anak out of Hebron. In Judg 1:10, it seems to be Judah who goes to Hebron and smites Sheshai, Ahiman, and Talmai, the sons of Anak.[22] Judah does not *receive* Hebron to capture it but *conquers* it on his own initiative. The unimposing verb "to go" (הלך) is important in this context.[23] In verse 2, we can read: "YHWH said: 'Judah shall go up. I hereby give the land into his hand.'" This reminds us of Josh 2:24 where the spies report what Rahab explained to them to Joshua.[24] It reminds us also of Josh 1:3 where YHWH says to Joshua: "Every place that the sole of your feet will tread upon I have given to you." And—now Caleb is on the stage—it reminds us of Josh 14:9 where Caleb tells Joshua,

---

19. Niditch (*Judges*, 30) translates "ponds of water" as well as "the upper and the lower ponds," however, without discussing this.

20. Robert Polzin, *Late Biblical Hebrew: Toward an Historical Typology of Biblical Hebrew Prose*, HSM 12 (Missoula, MT: Scholars Press, 1976), passim; Mark F. Rooker, *Biblical Hebrew in Transition: The Language of the Book of Ezekiel*, JSOTSup 90 (Sheffield: JSOT Press, 1990), passim. For a methodology on using Aramaisms for dating, see Avi Hurvitz, "The Chronological Significance of 'Aramaisms' in Biblical Hebrew," *IEJ* 18 (1968): 234–40.

21. By the way, the verb נתן occurs seven times in Josh 15:13–19 as against five times in Judg 1:10–15.

22. See, however, note 18.

23. Frolov (*Judges*, 34–36) even structures the whole chapter according to movement.

24. See J. Cornelis de Vos, "Violence in the Book of Joshua," in *Violence in the Hebrew Bible: Between Text and Reception*, ed. Jacques van Ruiten, OTS 79 (Brill: Leiden, 2020), 161–76.

Moses swore…, saying [to Caleb], "Surely the land on which your foot
has trodden shall be an inheritance for you and your children forever,
because you have wholeheartedly followed the LORD my God." (NRSV)

In Judg 1, it is Judah who goes and receives the land, and we must understand this as "the whole land." He receives it from YHWH, as Judg 1 begins
by questioning YHWH, who gave the answer just quoted. Reading Judg
1:10 in light of David, on the authority of YHWH it is David himself who
captures Hebron, the city where he was crowned. However, Judg 1:20
is more like Josh 15:13–14a, which sees Caleb as the one who receives
Hebron and drives out the three sons of Anak. This, again, is an obvious
contradiction. It might also be an indication of historical circumstances.

As Caleb is omitted in 1:10–11 compared to Joshua, his appearance
in verse 12 seems somewhat out of the blue. It would have been easy for
the authors of Judg 1 to have replaced Caleb with Judah. However, for
some reason they wanted to retain this part of the Caleb-Achsah episode,
although one can only guess what their motivations were. Maybe there
were, again, historical reasons: Debir is connected to Othniel, the later
judge (3:9–11), or better, to the Othnielites. The Othnielites were originally a non-Israelite, maybe Edomite clan residing in the area of Debir.[25]
Besides, Debir is not the town where David was crowned; this would be
an ideological motive for leaving out this part of the story. Maybe it is an
old folktale that people liked to tell, and the authors wanted to include it.
It could, additionally, be an ironic tale. The context speaks in favor of this
postulate. How large, for example, must the table of King Adoni-bezek
of the little village of Bezek (probably ḥirbet ibzīq) have been that seventy kings could pick up scraps under his table (1:7)?[26] Maybe it was not

---

25. Alexander Sima, "Nochmals zur Deutung des hebräischen Namens ʿOtnīʾēl,"
BN 106 (2001): 47–51: in the southeastern Canaanite dialect to which the Edomite
and Ammonite dialects belong, the name Othniel could mean "God has helped me";
for other translations, see Michael Streck and Stefan Weninger, "Zur Deutung des
hebräischen Namens ʿOtnīʿēl," *BN* 96 (1999): 21–29.

26. For the place name, see Erasmus Gaß, *Die Ortsnamen des Richterbuchs in historischer und redaktioneller Perspektive*, ADPV 35 (Wiesbaden: Harrassowitz, 2005),
9–11. It is highly doubtful that the reference was to the real site of Bezeq. The reference
was on an intertextual level to Saul who gathered Israel in Bezek. So, this might also
be a pun against the Benjaminite Saul. Probably, the reference is also to the king of
Jerusalem as the similarity between the names Adoni-bezek and Adoni-zedek, king of
Jerusalem (Josh 10:1) suggests. Adoni-bezek flees but is caught and brought captive to

only ironical but also full of humor.[27] Unfortunately, it is hard to discover what exactly constituted the humor. Is it the assertive way Achsah acts and can persuade her father Caleb? Was this humorous for males, females, or both?[28]

The answer is complicated by two *cruces interpretationis* in the text. First, who is the subject and who the object of ותסיתהו in verse 14, and what exactly does it mean? Second, what does the verb צנח in verse 14b mean? And back to the initial question: Is there a connection to David in verses 12–15?

Following Paul G. Mosca, I regard Achsah as the subject of סות *hiphil*, rather than Othniel, as some versions do, and Caleb as the object, not Othniel, as many modern translations do.[29] This view is also shaped by how the first verbal construction of Josh 15:18 // Judg 1:12: בבואה is understood. If the suffix ה– is an object, then it could mean "as he came into her" with a clear sexual connotation. Achsah then used the heat of the moment to arouse her spouse Othniel to have him ask for a/the field from her father. However attractive this understanding might be because of its ironical setting, in my mind, it is not the correct view. First, Othniel is not mentioned in verses 15:18 // 1:12. So, the suffix הו– in ותסיתהו is at least ambivalent—besides, the meaning of סות *hiphil*, is not certain at all. Second, in the same verse, it is Caleb who is mentioned explicitly and reacts to something Achsah did. Third, Othniel also does not appear in

---

Jerusalem where he dies (Judg 1:4–7). This could be connected to the inability of the Benjaminites to capture Jerusalem as described in Judg 1:21.

27. Or even satirical; see Adrien J. Bledstein, "Is Judges a Woman's Satire of Men Who Play God?," in *A Feminist Companion to Judges*, ed. Athalya Brenner, FCB 4 (Sheffield: JSOT Press, 1993), 34–54.

28. Bledstein, ("Is Judges a Woman's Satire?") postulates a female author for the whole book of Judges.

29. Mosca, "Who Seduced Whom? A Note on Joshua 15,18 // Judges 1,14," *CBQ* 46 (1984): 18–22. Judg 1:14 LXX (Codices A and B): καὶ ἐγένετο ἐν ᴬτῷ εἰσπορεύεσθαι αὐτήνᴬ / ᴮτῇ εἰσόδῃ αὐτῆςᴮ καὶ ἐπέσεισεν αὐτὴν ᴮΓοθονιηλ τοῦᴮ αἰτῆσαι παρὰ τοῦ πατρὸς αὐτῆς τὸνᴬ ἀγρόν; VL: *et factum est cum ingrederetur ipse, monuit eam Gothoniel ut peteret a patre suo agrum*; Vulg.: *quam pergentem in itinere monuit vir suus ut peteret a patre suo agrum*. Slightly different: Josh 15:18 LXX: καὶ ἐγένετο ἐν τῷ εἰσπορεύεσθαι αὐτὴν καὶ συνεβουλεύσατο αὐτῷ λέγουσα Αἰτήσομαι τὸν πατέρα μου ἀγρόν; Syr.: *wkd hwt lh 'trgrgt dtš'l mn 'bwh yrtwt' dḥql'*; Vulg.: *et factum est, cum ingrederetur ipsa, et consilium habuit cum eo, dicens: Petam patrem meum agrum*; and Judg 1:18 Syr.: *wkd ᶜl 'tgrgrt lmš'l mn 'bwh h ḥql'*.

the verses that follow. Thus, Othniel did *not* ask Achsah's father, Caleb, for a field. Instead, it is Achsah who takes the initiative, and asks for a ברכה, "blessing/pool"; and it is Caleb who reacts to Achsah.

If this is the correct understanding, then, again with Mosca, לשאול cannot mean "to ask" in a final way because then Achsah would instigate her father to ask for a field from her father, but like לאמר, "by saying," as a gerund, "by asking."[30]

The meaning of צנח is not ascertained because it only occurs thrice in the Hebrew Bible, of which two instances are in our parallel verses.[31] Accordingly, there are many translations.[32] The most common is "to dismount," found in most modern translations. I have argued elsewhere that צנח means "to spit."[33] First, the act of spitting can be done from upon the donkey (מעל החמור); second, verses 15:19 // 1:15 play with the scope of opposites: dry–wet. Dry is the ארץ הנגב. But what does it mean within the context? The phrase כי נתתני ארץ הנגב can have various meanings: (1) "You have put me in the land of Negeb"; (2) "You have given me Negeb/arid land"; (3) "You have given me away as Negeb land" (our translation); (4) "You have treated me as Negeb land."[34] In any case, it has to do with something dry. In the third case, it might serve as a pun in relation to verses 12–13. There we read that Caleb gives Achsah away as a wife (ונתתי לו את עכסה בתי לאשה resp. ויתן לו את עכסה לאשה).[35] Did Achsah interpret this as "you gave me away as Negeb land" instead of "as a wife"? This might very well be and makes the tale even more humorous. As yet we have the

---

30. Mosca, "Who Seduced Whom?," 18–22. Cf. the double translation λεγοῦσα Αἰτήσομαι of Josh 15:18 LXX (see note 29).

31. The other occurrence is in Judg 4:21.

32. G. R. Driver, "Problems of Interpretation in the Heptateuch," in *Mélanges bibliques: Rédigés en l'honneur de André Robert*, Travaux de l'Institut Catholique de Paris 4 (Paris: Bloud & Gay, 1957), 66–76; M. H. Gottstein, "A Note on צנח," *VT* 6 (1956): 99–100; Arthur Gibson, "ṣanaḥ in Judges i 14: NEB and AV Translations," *VT* 26 (1976): 275–83; E. W. Nicholson, "The Problem of צנח," *ZAW* 89 (1977): 259–66.

33. J. Cornelis de Vos, *Das Los Judas: Über Entstehung und Ziele der Landbeschreibung in Josua 15*, VTSup 95 (Leiden: Brill, 2003), 122–24.

34. See Richard D. Nelson, "What Is Achsah Doing in Judges?," in *The Impartial God: Essays in Biblical Studies in Honor of Jouette M. Bassler*, ed. C. J. Roetzel, New Testament Monographs 22 (Sheffield: Sheffield Phoenix, 2007), 19–20.

35. On the status of wife for a woman, see Tammi J. Schneider, "Achsah, the Raped Pîlegeš, and the Book of Judges," in *Women in the Biblical World: A Survey of Old and New Testament Perspectives*, ed. Elizabeth A. McCabe (Lanham, MD: University Press of America, 2009), 45–46.

גלת מים, גלת עלי[ו]ת, גלת תחתי[ו]ת, and the blessing, the ברכה, that means "pool" when vocalized as בְּרֵכָה;[36] third, the spitting is a sign of contempt that is a good means to provoke the reaction of Achsah's father: "What is with you?" In contrast, dismounting from a donkey after arriving on one is not quite unexpected and can hardly have been responsible for Caleb's reaction as described in verses 15:18 // 1:14; fourth and finally, the translation also fits the third occasion of צנח in Judg 4:21. After Jael had killed Sisera, she spat on the ground (ותצנח בארץ) as a sign of contempt for Sisera.[37]

Presumably, the authors of Judg 1 used the episode from Josh 15 within the new Judah-David context of Judg 1 so it would, among others, allude to the story of Nabal and Abigail in 1 Sam 25.[38] Although it is a bit hypothetical, and it might only be one way to read this multileveled story, as Danna Nolan Fewell labeled it, I presume that Achsah also functions as a type of Abigail.[39] The connection of Achsah to Abigail in 1 Sam 25 was

---

36. See above note 16.

37. Tsila Ratner ("Playing Fathers' Games: The Story of Achsah, Daughter of Caleb, and the Princess's Blank Sheet," *JMJS* 3 [2004]: 147–61) writes: "By falling off the donkey Achsah expresses both the prostration and respect befitting a 'good daughter' as well as subversive sexual implications. These in turn expand to include 'springs of water,' which is part of the territorial discourse but also alludes to women's fertility/sexuality." This interpretation is allegorizing and far-fetched, and it stands, as argued, on shaky ground. The same applies to the article of Heidi Szpek, "Achsah's Story: A Metaphor for Societal Transition," *AUSS* 40 (2002): 245–56; she maintains that "Achsah's existence is intertwined with Caleb's and then Othniel's. Caleb represents the old ways of society and marriage—the patriarchal dynasty, the time of Wandering and Conquest; Othniel represents Conquest to Settlement—the new ways of society and marriage. Achsah's passage from Caleb's household to Othniel's may metaphorically represent the progression of society from Wandering to Conquest to Settlement" (256). The other extreme is the biblicism of Joseph Fleishman in his "A Daughter's Demand and a Father's Compliance: The Legal Background to Achsah's Claim and Caleb's Agreement (Joshua 15,16–19; Judges 1,12–15)," *ZAW* 118 (2006): 354–73. Fleishman does not critically and diachronically distinguish between 1 Chron and Judg 1. According to 1 Chr 2:42–49 and 4:15, Caleb also has sons. Therefore, for Fleishman, it is an exception that Achsah receives an inheritance. However, there is no mention of sons of Caleb in Judg 1.

38. There is also a clear intertextual nexus to Judg 18–21 and, among others, via the venue of Bezek (Judg 1:4) to 1 Sam 11 (v. 8) as Schneider ("Achsah, the Raped *Pîlegeš*, and the Book of Judges," 43–55) argued convincingly.

39. Fewell, "Deconstructive Criticism: Achsah and the (E)razed City of Writing," in *Judges and Method: New Approaches in Biblical Studies*, ed. Gale A. Yee, 2nd ed. (Minneapolis: Fortress, 2007), 115–37.

already put forward by Richard D. Nelson.[40] I go further in connecting the story in Judg 1 also to David. My arguments are:

1. The Calebite connection: Abigail was married to Nabal, and Nabal was a Calebite (1 Sam 25:3) just like Othniel in Judg 1. This, however, does not mean that Othniel is a type of David. Othniel is, according to Wong, necessary because in the older book of Judges there was no judge from the south at the time, which is why he was inserted as a judge in Judg 3:9–11.[41] The story of Josh 15:13–19 offers a welcome opportunity to introduce him earlier, in Judg 1.

2. The Judahite connection: Whether Caleb, Othniel, and Achsah belong to Judah in Judg 1 is ambivalent, and it would appear, deliberately so. In any case, they are connected to Judah in some way, just like Abigail, probably a Calebite.

3. The personal connection: Abigail is as assertive as Achsah. It is by her actions that David asks her to become his wife. The difference, of course, is that in Judges she receives two villages. According to Frolov, the latter could point to the royal prerogative to offer towns to people of the court.[42] If we translate "the upper" and "lower ponds," or "reservoirs," than there could even be an allusion to the water system in Jerusalem, and the name "Debir" would have, or *also* have the meaning "sanctuary," scilicet in Jerusalem.[43]

4. The donkey connection:[44] Both Abigail and Achsah are riding a donkey, although the action from the donkey is different. In Samuel Abigail dismounts, in Judg 1:14b, in my opinion, Achsah spits (cf. Gen 24). This would have provoked the question of her father Caleb, and it might have been humorous for the contemporary readers.

---

40. Nelson, "What Is Achsah Doing?," 12–22.

41. Wong, "Direct Pro-Judah Polemic?," 105–6.

42. Frolov, *Judges*, 50.

43. For reference to the water system in Jerusalem, see Renate Jost, "Achsas Quellen: Feministisch-sozialgeschichtliche Überlegungen in Jos 15, 15–20/Ri 1, 12–15," in *"Ihr Völker alle, klatscht in die Hände!": Festschrift für Erhard S. Gerstenberger zum 65. Geburtstag*, ed. Rainer Kessler, Exegese in unserer Zeit 3 (Münster: LIT, 1997), 110–25. She refers to Isa 22:9–11 for the lower pool (הברכה התחתונה); and to Isa 7:3 and 36:2 for the upper pool (הברכה העליונה).

44. See also Sasson, *Judges*, 148.

5. The ברכה-connection. Achsah asks for a ברכה from Caleb, Abigail brings a ברכה to David. The verbs used for this sound very similar (הביא/הבה). This could have been deliberate since different verbs are demanded by the different contexts.
6. The geographical connection: The story of 1 Sam 25 is set in the village of Maon and the village and/or field of Karmel. Both Maon (*tell ma'īn*) and Karmel (*ḫirbet el-kirmil*) are not far from Debir, which is probably to be found in *ḫirbet rabūd*.[45] Debir in turn is not far from Hebron. In Judg 1:11, it is still Judah, scilicet David, who goes from Hebron to Debir.[46]

Cumulatively, the arguments present a connection from Achsah to Abigail, through Abigail to David as very likely. As argued above, in Judg 1 there might be puns involved in the relationship between David and Saul. By reading the Achsah story through the lens of this relationship, the story gains depth and is provided intertextual meaning that contemporary addressees might have grasped.

Conclusion

Judges 1 is awkward because it uses material from other biblical texts within new contexts that simultaneously, by allusion, evokes narratives on multiple levels: within Judg 1, within the older parts of Judges, and within a wider context. This makes it full of tensions and contradictions. We do not know what the historical background and the original meaning of the Caleb-Achsah episode might have been, nor do we know how the story's contemporary audience reacted to it. However, in its present state it opens a window to a story about other assertive women, in particular to the story about Abigail (1 Sam 25; see also Gen 24, esp. vv. 64–67). The ancient audience might have thought about the relation of Judah to the Calebites, of David to Saul and the Benjaminites, and of David to women; and about assertive women, either positively or negatively. We also do not know whether Judah and David are alluded to positively in the Caleb-Achsah episode. In any case, it must have been fun for the ancient audience.

---

45. On Maon and Karmel, see de Vos, *Los Judas*, 440–41, 443; on Debir see 427–28, 431; and Gaß, *Die Ortsnamen*, 29–30.

46. A further connection could be that twice "field" is mentioned: "she asked her father for the field" (Judg 1:14); "as we were in the field" (1 Sam 25:15).

7

Motherhood, Violence, and Power in the Book of Judges

Rannfrid I. Lasine Thelle

The book of Judges portrays three mother characters: the mothers of Sisera, Samson, and Micah. In the victory song of Judg 5, Deborah is called a "mother in Israel," and Jael's interaction with Sisera has been described as exhibiting "mothering" behavior. Judges also contains references to motherhood, as well as intriguing instances of absent mothers. In the rich narrative tapestry of Judges, with threads that weave into other biblical books, the mother motif is one such thread to follow in a close engagement with the fabric of the text.[1]

The present essay forms a sequel to my article "Matrices of Motherhood in Judges 5," *JSOT* 43 (2019): 436–52, one form of which I presented at the Society of Biblical Literature Annual Meeting joint session of the "Joshua/Judges" and "Intertextuality and the Hebrew Bible" sections in 2016. I thank the editors for inviting me to include a follow-up in the present volume.

1. With the expression mother-motif, I am not proposing any definition at this point; however, I am naming a motif that I will investigate through the course of the article, which includes figures who are mothers, behavior and roles that may be associated with motherhood, references to matrilineage and parentage through the mother, and poetic formulations such as "mother in Israel." By the end of the article, it is my aspiration that readers will have been able to follow these various threads, and through that experience hopefully gain new insight into the workings and message of the book of Judges. With this contribution, I am joining the ongoing conversation on mothers in the Hebrew Bible. Major past contributions include: Susan Ackerman, *Warrior, Dancer, Seductress, Queen: Women in Judges and Biblical Israel*, ABRL (New York: Doubleday, 1998); Mieke Bal, *Death and Dissymmetry: The Politics of Coherence in the Book of Judges*, CSHJ (Chicago: The University of Chicago Press, 1988); J. Cheryl Exum, "'Mother in Israel': A Familiar Figure Reconsidered?," in *Feminist Interpretation of the Bible*, ed. Letty M. Russell (Philadelphia: Westminster, 1985), 73–85; Esther Fuchs, "The Literary Characterization of Mothers and Sexual Politics in the Hebrew

Violence and Motherhood in Judges 4–5

The three female profiles in the victory poem of Judg 5 each connect to motherhood.[2] Deborah, the protagonist of both the prose account and the poem, and the one who gives voice to the song, rises as "a mother in Israel" (5:7). The mother of Sisera is the enemy leader's mother (5:28–30). Jael, while not a mother, *mothers* Sisera with a lethal outcome (4:17–22; 5:24–27).

Deborah is the figurative mother par excellence. She is the mother of all the mentioned tribes, whom she calls up by name, giving birth to them through song.[3] As a mother in Israel, she may be seen as a counterpart to Jacob, whose sons are the eponymous ancestors of the tribes of Israel.[4] In the poetic account, Deborah is the unifying figure, with Barak at her side. In the military challenge the Israelites face, she musters them to successful battle against the Canaanite coalition in a victory attributed wholly to YHWH. The tribes may not contribute equally, but they have a unified leadership. When Israel has a mother, God is with them, and they succeed. This battle is the final defeat of the Canaanites, completing a narrative arc

---

Bible," in *Feminist Perspectives on Biblical Scholarship*, ed. Adele Yarbro Collins, BSNA 10 (Chico, CA: Scholars Press, 1985), 117–36; Freema Gottlieb, "Three Mothers," *Judaism* 30 (1981): 194–203; Michael O'Connor, "The Women in the Book of Judges," *HAR* 10 (1986): 276–93; Adele Reinhartz, "Samson's Mother: An Unnamed Protagonist," in *A Feminist Companion to Judges*, ed. Athalya Brenner, FCB 4 (Sheffield: JSOT Press, 1993), 157–70. On mothers in fiction, see Brenda O. Daly and Maureen T. Reddy, eds., *Narrating Mothers: Theorizing Maternal Subjectivities* (Knoxville: University of Tennessee Press), 1991.

2. For more detail on motherhood in Judg 4–5, including references to secondary literature, see Thelle, "Matrices," 442–43.

3. Anathea Portier-Young, "I Sing the Body Politic: Stillborn Desire and the Birth of Israel in Judges 5," in *Celebrate Her for the Fruit of Her Hands: Studies in Honor of Carol L. Meyers*, ed. Susan Ackerman, Charles E. Carter, and Beth Alpert Nakhai (Winona Lake, IN: Eisenbrauns, 2015), 376. The word tribe (שבט) does not appear in Judg 5, and the arrangement or order of the tribes does not match any other list, so it is difficult to know what to make of it; for discussion, see Jack M. Sasson, *Judges 1–12: A New Translation with Introduction and Commentary*, AB 6D (New Haven: Yale University Press, 2012), 296–302; D. Charles Smith, *The Role of Mothers in the Geneaological Lists of Jacob's Sons*, CBET 90 (Leuven: Peeters, 2018), 97–100, and the references cited there.

4. Thelle, "Matrices," 442–43.

that began in Josh 6.[5] Read in conjunction with chapter 5, the characterization of Deborah in chapter 4 as one who rose up, as judge, prophet, and
military leader all contribute to informing what it means that she is called
"mother in Israel."[6]

Through the song, Deborah imagines vividly about the thoughts of
the enemy captain's mother (5:28–30). This reflection introduces the dark
side of victory, the inhumanity of the enemy that justifies her own children's acts of war.[7] Deborah, the metaphorical mother, the counterpart
to Jacob, stands successful near the beginning of the book, but the tribes
nearly devour each other by the end. Under the leadership of Deborah,
Israel is successful. Yet, with the figure of Sisera's mother, Judg 5 introduces troubling questions about the rhetorical choices whereby mother
figures spearhead the sanctioning of violence against women. These continue to gnaw at readers and become increasingly difficult to ignore.[8]

Sisera's mother appears as the first actual mother character in Judges.
Readers encounter her through her musings (and those of her "wise
ladies") about why her son is late in returning from battle. The perspective has shifted from the battlefield to the home, where the women wait
for soldiers to return, not knowing what has happened to their sons and
husbands. The striking words describe Sisera as taking women ("wombs,"
רחם) and embroidered garments as booty, as plunder in military victory,
while readers have already seen that the Canaanites took no booty (5:19).
From within the protection of her home, surrounded by her wise ladies,
her fantasy contrasts sharply with the scene of Jael's brutal killing of Sisera,
which the song has just memorialized. Instead of bringing home women
and fine cloth, Sisera lies wrapped in a blanket, his head crushed by a
woman. While the scene of a mother waiting for her son to return safely
from battle offers a way to sympathize with the shared plight of women,
the words of Sisera's mother may have the effect of dehumanizing the
enemy, because they couch the imaginations about victory in terms of the

---

5. Don Seeman, "The Watcher at the Window: Cultural Poetics of a Biblical
Motif," *Prooftexts* 24 (2004): 1–50.

6. Thelle, "Matrices," 438–41.

7. Danna Nolan Fewell and David Gunn, *Gender, Power, and Promise: The
Subject of the Bible's First Story* (Nashville: Abingdon, 1993), 125; Gottlieb, "Three
Mothers," 202.

8. Thelle, "Matrices," 447–48.

suffering of the other.[9] This reflection also reveals the Israelites' justification and normalization of wartime victors' behavior (also codified in Deut 21:11–14). This is what victors do.[10]

The mothering qualities of Jael are clear in Judg 4, where she comforts Sisera with words, gives him refuge, covers him, and offers him milk when he is thirsty. Sisera responds by entering her tent, presumably lying down, asking her to stand guard, taking the milk, and falling asleep. The mother-son image dominates, although many have pointed to sexual undertones.[11] In both Judg 4 and 5, Jael kills Israel's enemy commander by crushing his head with a tent peg, although in Judg 4 Sisera is lying down, whereas in Judg 5 he is standing and falls (5:26–27). Jael is portrayed as hostess gone rogue, in chapter 5 with even stronger sexual allusions and birthing imagery, as Sisera falls between her feet in death.[12]

Together, the two chapters portray Jael as a figure who subverts expected roles, both in her mothering behavior, as hostess, and in her sexually allusive actions and words. She also performs the role of female warrior, for which there is no set expectation in the Hebrew Bible.[13] In fulfillment of Deborah's prophecy (4:9), Jael receives the honor that is denied Barak and is memorialized through the song as one who will be blessed. Both in 4:17–22 and 5:24–27, the accounts of Sisera's death hammer home the striking contrast between the action on the battlefield and the drama within the tent. In the poem, the juxtaposition of Jael's tent with Sisera's

---

9. Daniel I. Block, *Judges, Ruth*, NAC 6 (Nashville: Broadman & Holman, 1999), 242; Barry G. Webb, *The Book of Judges*, NICOT (Grand Rapids: Eerdmans, 2012), 217.

10. Carolyn A. Reeder, "Deuteronomy 21:10–14 and/as Wartime Rape," *JSOT* 41 (2017): 313–36.

11. Nehama Aschkenasy, *Eve's Journey: Feminine Images in Hebraic Literary Tradition* (Philadelphia: University of Pennsylvania Press, 1986), 170; Robert Alter, *The Art of Biblical Poetry* (New York: Basic Books, 1985), 47–49; Danna Nolan Fewell and David M. Gunn, "Controlling Perspectives: Women, Men, and the Authority of Violence in Judges 4 and 5," *JAAR* 58 (1990): 389–411 (392–94); Sasson criticizes this tendency in *Judges*, 275.

12. See the discussion in Thelle, "Matrices," 446.

13. Deborah performs her role as military leader in ways that manipulate the understanding of the relationship between gender and warrior. For the idea that Deborah, Jael, and Abimelech's assassin (9:53) are constructed as metaphors to serve the author's ideological interests, see Gale A. Yee, "By the Hand of a Woman: The Metaphor of the Woman Warrior in Judges 4," in *Women, War, and Metaphor: Language and Society in the Study of the Hebrew Bible*, ed. Claudia V. Camp and Carole R. Fontaine, SemeiaSt 61 (Atlanta: Scholars Press, 1993), 99–132.

mother's chamber behind the lattice heightens both the irony and the absurdity of this defeat of Canaan.

By casting mother figures as affirming violence against women, the poem of Judg 5 actively implicates them in the war enterprise, as carried out by men (normally). Deborah, judge, prophet, military leader, and mother, gives birth to Israel for the children to successfully engage in war, killing the whole enemy army (4:15–16; 5:31).[14] Jael, a woman whose identity is ambiguous, is explicitly given honor and blessing for killing the enemy captain. Although Sisera's mother speaks as enemy other, the fact that Deborah does the singing forth of her thoughts ironically provides further sanction and normalization of the capture of women as a prize for victorious warriors, although with ambivalence.[15] Much as the narrator of 1 Samuel has women praising the exploits of Saul and David as an ideological chorus of sorts (1 Sam 18:7), in Judg 5 the poets appropriate the category of mother in justifying violence against women. The poet incorporates the words of Sisera's mother into the song's underlying ideology.

Sons and Mothers: The Mothers of Samson and Micah

Like Sisera's mother, the mothers of Samson and Micah are also concerned about their sons. The designation "his mother" clusters in the stories of Samson and Micah.[16] Following upon the narratives of the unconventional judge Jephthah with his dodgy parenthood and tragic parenting, the failed ruler Abimelech, who relied on his mother's kin, and the corrupt Gideon, of two minds about his allegiance to YHWH and his role as ruler, readers might now be ready for a true hero's journey.

We meet Samson's nameless mother as the "wife of Manoah," in a version of an annunciation type-story.[17] The introduction of Manoah of the tribe of Dan

---

14. Judges 5:20–21 attributes the victory to forces of nature.

15. Ackerman, *Warrior, Dancer, Seductress, Queen*, 183.

16. Of a total of twenty occurrences in Judges, אמו ("his mother") appears in 14:2, 3, 4, 5, 6, 9, 16; as well as in 16:17; and אביו ("his father") together with אמו in all of the occurrences in chap. 14, plus twice alone in 14:3 and 19. אמו appears twice in each of 17:2, 3, 4, as object and as subject.

17. Or birth-narrative ("barren woman"-scene: Ackerman, *Warrior, Dancer, Seductress, Queen*, 186–93). Boling points out the elements of a "recognition narrative"; Robert G. Boling, *Judges: A New Translation with Introduction and Commentary*, AB 6A (Garden City, NY: Doubleday, 1975), 220; Block calls it "theophany recognition" (*Judges, Ruth*, 397); and Webb, a "call narrative" (*Judges*, 353).

and his wife, who is barren and has had no child, is one that readers recognize from the ancestral narratives of Genesis, and sets expectations accordingly.[18] It also points toward the birth story of Samuel (1 Sam 1), in that both are considered to be Nazirites. Sarah, Rebekah, Rachel, and Hannah are all barren women who, after a message from God, give birth to sons. The Shunammite woman (2 Kgs 4:8–37) is another childless woman who miraculously receives a son. In these stories, the sons either almost die, or they are dedicated as Nazirites.[19] In Judg 13 the angel/messenger of YHWH appears to Manoah's wife (she refers to him as a man of God who looks like an angel of God) and promises her a son, tells her to raise him a Nazirite and that he will begin to save Israel from the Philistines, and gives her instructions about her own lifestyle.

The portrayal of Manoah's wife usually leaves interpreters with a positive assessment of her character.[20] Mary J. Evans sees her as intelligent and Esther Fuchs agrees, adding she is more so than her husband.[21] Daniel I. Block describes her as "calm, collected and knowledgeable" compared to her husband.[22] She is insightful in her immediate recognition of the messenger according to Susan Niditch, while Evans adds that she is independent since the angel speaks to her alone first and she names her child.[23] Evans observes further that she is pious and "spiritually discerning," while Yairah Amit points out that Manoah is "of little faith and lacking the intuitive sense his wife possesses."[24] In contrast, Robert Polzin sees the wife as misunderstanding the message, and Robert G. Boling observes that she "doesn't really know what she is saying, though she is dropping hints all along the way."[25]

---

18. J. Cheryl Exum, "Promise and Fulfillment: Narrative Art in Judges 13," *JBL* 99 (1980): 43–44; Reinhartz, "Samson's Mother," 157.

19. Ackerman, *Warrior, Dancer, Seductress, Queen*, 188–89, 193.

20. J. Cheryl Exum, *Fragmented Women: Feminist (Sub)versions of Biblical Narratives* (Valley Forge, PA: Trinity Press International, 1993), 63–65.

21. Evans, *Judges and Ruth: An Introduction and Commentary*, TOTC (Downers Grove, IL: InterVarsity Press, 2017), 148; Fuchs, "Literary Characterization of Mothers," 124.

22. Block, *Judges, Ruth*, 397.

23. Niditch, *Judges: A Commentary*, OTL (Louisville: Westminster John Knox, 2008), 145.

24. Evans, *Judges and Ruth*, 148; Amit, "'Manoah Promptly Followed His Wife': On the Place of the Woman in Birth Narratives," in Brenner, *Feminist Companion to Judges*, 150.

25. Polzin, *Moses and the Deuteronomist: A Literary Study of the Deuteronomistic History, Part 1; Deuteronomy, Joshua and Judges* (New York: Seabury, 1980), 183; Boling, *Judges*, 221.

A motif that connects Samson's mother to Deborah is the way in which she is given priority and more credibility than her husband, Manoah. In spite of her being unnamed and identified only as the wife of Manoah, she is elevated, while he is portrayed as incredulous and cautious, needing confirmation.[26] Though it is not pronounced, there is an affinity with the Deborah-Barak duo here. In a longer narrative perspective, the mothers of Samson and Micah have been seen as foils for Hannah in 1 Sam 1.[27]

The angel tells the mother-to-be that her son will be a Nazirite to God "from birth" (13:5), while she tells her husband, "from birth to the day of his death" (13:7), and Samson tells Delilah, "from my mother's womb" (16:17). The fact that Manoah is concerned about the instructions for how to raise the child is sometimes bypassed by commentators.[28] Even when he asks specifically, Manoah is not told the rules, only that the wife should not drink wine or eat anything unclean (13:8, 13). Readers know that he is right to be questioning of his wife's version of the encounter with the angel, since she holds back on the instruction about not shaving his hair and the message of Samson's future as one who will begin to save Israel.[29]

Both pieces of information become crucial further on, but the narrator has God keep both parents equally in the dark about his empowering of Samson going forward. The dialogue and interaction between Manoah and his wife set up a potential tension between them that provides a fruitful field for discussion about gender roles in the characterization of the

---

26. Niditch, *Judges*, 145.

27. Robert B. Chisholm Jr., "The Role of Women in the Rhetorical Strategy in the Book of Judges," in *Integrity of Heart, Skillfulness of Hands: Biblical and Leadership Studies in Honor of Donald K. Campbell*, ed. Charles H. Dyer and Roy B. Zuck (Grand Rapids: Baker, 1994), 46–49.

28. See, however, Webb, *Judges*, 353; Chisholm, "Role of Women."

29. David M. Gunn, "Joshua and Judges," in *The Literary Guide to the Bible*, ed. Robert Alter and Frank Kermode (Cambridge: Belknap, 1987), 118; Exum, *Fragmented Women*, 90. In "Literary Characterization of Mothers," 124, Fuchs claims that Manoah's wife reports this to her husband. In her analysis of the annunciation form, Fuchs sees a narrative development of increasing focus on the mother and the gradual decentering of the father, and argues that the annunciation type-scenes thus demonstrate that the power of motherhood lies with God, thereby defining motherhood as a patriarchal institution (119–29). Exum argues that the positive portrayal of Manoah's wife nevertheless serves the patriarchal agenda within the Samson story (*Fragmented Women*, 61–93).

108 Rannfrid I. Lasine Thelle

parents.[30] However, even though this tension is not clearly carried through in the following narrative, the matter of the razor comes back full circle in chapter 16, where his razed head leaves Samson in a state whereby he can be bound and brought into Philistine captivity, the hidden strength just waiting to grow back.

Even though they are not informed of God's plans for Samson in saving Israel, both Samson's mother and father remain heavily involved in his story in Judg 14, mainly with the important parental responsibility of getting a wife. The parents try to dissuade him from marrying a Philistine, but they do not know what we readers do, that this is all a plan from God. The mother stays involved even though Samson asks only his father for the bride (14:3). The repetitive mention of both parents serves to emphasize their relative lack of success in actually influencing their son's future. The parents seem to be keen on keeping up their responsibilities, but Samson himself is out of their control, in some ways preparing readers for Micah's dishonoring of his mother. As they go along with his whims to get him his bride in Timnah, Samson's parents have no idea about his escapades with the lion or where he got the honey. But readers know that something is not right when Samson takes the honey from the carcass, in violation of the Nazirite laws, as well as common purity laws.

The "perfect beginning" of the story of Samson contrasts with the story of the actual hero.[31] The mother character fulfills her role within chapter 13 and is not accorded any independent role in the subsequent narrative. Samson appears to be motivated by impulse and personal grievances. However, this is just the character that YHWH needs to fulfill his plan. Significantly, Samson is powered by the spirit of YHWH from the very beginning (13:25; 14:19; 15:14).

In Judg 14 the narrator portrays a conventional mother and father, who have no clue about their son. In this respect, they are like Sisera's mother. Their portrayal provides a perspective on what is really going on, by contrasting the characters' ignorance and misplaced concerns with

30. Rob Fleenor, "Manoah's Wife: Gender Inversion in a Patriarchal Birth Narrative," in *Women in the Biblical World, 2: A Survey of Old and New Testament Perspectives*, ed. Elizabeth A. McCabe (Lanham, MD: University Press of America, 2011), 24–34.

31. Told with masterful humor and irony, as expounded by Lillian Klein, *The Triumph of Irony in the Book of Judges*, JSOTSup 143, BLS 14 (Sheffield: Almond, 1988), 109–39.

the grave realities that readers have been informed about. This highlights how it is possible for individuals to be appearing to have the right attitude and making the right moves while remaining clueless about the bigger picture. A crucial element in the whole story is the withholding or control of knowledge. With the benefit of the omniscient narrator, readers can put together the elements in chapter 14 from different points of view: a story of Samson following his desires, including not telling his parents about the lion (a point spotlighted later in Samson's dialogue with his wife, 14:16), the parents perhaps attempting to turn the marriage into an advantageous political alliance that is ultimately unsuccessful, while God uses Samson to further his own plans of stirring up trouble that Samson must eventually address.[32]

Delilah, the star female character among Samson's love-interests, is not a mother, nor is she even identified as a daughter or a wife. Yet she is a pivotal character, the narration of whose behavior connects her to Jael. Although Delilah is much more clearly portrayed as a "lover," her behavior also incorporates mothering behavior, such as putting Samson to sleep on her knees (Judg 16:19). Both Delilah and Jael employ methods of trickery, though their motivation is entirely different. There is a common theme of exploiting the protagonist's state of sleep (Judg 4), when he is most vulnerable. How Delilah gets Samson to fall asleep after he has told her the truth and she has taken the money from the Philistines, is hard to imagine, especially since he is aware that the Philistine lords are somehow in cahoots with her, with three ridiculous attempts to capture him already. Presumably, the idea is to foreground the character of Delilah as the active agent here, by contrasting her with Samson and underscoring his weakness, like Sisera in Jael's tent.[33] Both Sisera and Samson trust a woman that they should not have trusted. As J. Cheryl Exum puts it, "The story expresses the male's fear of surrendering to a woman."[34] Both episodes touch on the theme of a woman accorded the honor of a victory, explicitly with Jael, and with Delilah by monetary transaction. Elsewhere in Judges Abimelech does his best to avoid the dishonor of being killed by a woman (Judg 9:54; 2 Sam 11:21), as do Zebah and Zalmunna to avoid being killed by a child (8:21). Delilah does not kill Samson, but completely emasculates him,

---

32. Polzin, *Moses and the Deuteronomist*, 182–87, discusses the role of the "panchronic" narrator in Judg 13–14.

33. Block, *Judges, Ruth*, 461.

34. Exum, "'Mother in Israel,'" 81.

taking away his source of power and exposing his vulnerability, allowing his capture. In one of the attempts to get at his secret, Delilah uses a pin (יתד) to tighten (תקע) his braids, the same word used for Jael's tent peg, with which she strikes (תקע) Sisera, and similar to the word for sinews/cords used to tie Samson up in 16:7.[35]

The third mother character in Judges is the mother of Micah. This story is not about a judge; rather, it introduces the last section of the book, where there is "no king in Israel" (17:6).[36] The Micah text announces itself as odd from the outset. We find ourselves located in Ephraim, but beyond that, no introduction is given of Micah before he launches into his confession of having stolen his mother's savings of eleven hundred pieces of silver, the same amount that each Philistine prince paid Delilah. The mother's first reported speech is a blessing pronounced on her son, a blessing of YHWH. One wonders whether she does so because Micah restores the money, confesses, or because he is the one who stole the money in the first place, so that it stayed in the family.[37] Most likely, her blessing is intended to counteract the curse that Micah says he had heard her speak. Perhaps it is her instinct to protect him from its effects? However, her utterance of the name of YHWH in a curse is a breach of covenant that illustrates instantaneously the fundamental predicament of the era as announced in 17:6, that each man or person (איש), is doing what they consider right in their own eyes (including the piously named man Micah and his unnamed mother). The series of events that follows from the theft illustrates the negative trajectory that self-centered interest takes.

In response to her son's confession Micah's mother is reported to do three things. After blessing her son, she declares that she consecrates the money to YHWH "from her hand to her son" to make a carved image and a molten image. Then, when he returns the money to her, she uses only two hundred pieces of the silver to make the idol. After this, the man

---

35. K. Lawson Younger Jr., *Judges and Ruth*, NIV Application Bible Commentary (Grand Rapids: Zondervan, 2002), 319. A related theme is the use of domestic tools as weapons by women in Judges: a hammer and tent peg for Jael, and a millstone for the unnamed woman who kills Abimelech.

36. On Judg 17–21 and its relation to the rest of the book, see David J. H. Beldman, *The Completion of Judges: Strategies of Ending in Judges 17–21*, Siphrut 21 (Winona Lake, IN: Eisenbrauns, 2017); Gregory T. K. Wong, *Compositional Strategy of the Book of Judges: An Inductive, Rhetorical Study*, VTSup 111 (Leiden: Brill, 2006).

37. Block, *Judges, Ruth*, 477–82.

Micah is on his own and in charge of his shrine; he furnishes it, has his son be a priest, and later hires a real-life Levite.

Here is a different kind of very forward mother. Sisera's mother has what could be seen as reasonable expectations about her son's fate, however optimistic or idealized they may be, or however readers may judge her. Samson's mother appears to act on God's instructions and fulfills her role, however feebly. In contrast, Micah's mother determines on her own accord what the will of YHWH might be without waiting for any instruction about consecrating her son to God's service or anything else. She appears entitled. She utters the blessing on him and decides how to redeem her wayward son (ironically named "who is like [YHWH]"). The fact that the money is tainted is of no hindrance to her. This mother proceeds to control her son's life in ways in which Samson's mother was unable and is confident about what is right for him in spite of there being no cause for optimism. He is a son who steals, confesses only when he likely becomes afraid of the power of a curse, blatantly dishonors his mother, and happily goes along with her idolatrous scheme.

The irony is further compounded because Micah's mother appears to consider it appropriate that her dedication be used to construct an idol. Does she not know the law? Has her son not been educated either? Her behavior contrasts sharply with Samson's mother dedicating her son as a Nazirite in response to a divine communication. Samson's mother was trying to heed God's will, although the eventual outcome of Samson's career was out of her control. Unlike Samson's mother, however, Micah's mother does not even consider wondering what YHWH's plan might be; she has it all worked out. Much as notions of kingship are harassed and ironized over in the Gideon cycle, cultic life is here ridiculed as the story proceeds, with the Danites implementing the settlement of land and cultic practices "as they see fit in their own eyes." Both Micah and his mother disappear from the story, their plans hijacked by the Danites, who transport the shrine and its private contractor Levite priest to their new territory, slaughter the unsuspecting population and set up their own little perverted version of promised land, replete with the grandson of Moses as priest.[38]

What does the mother-figure bring to the Micah-episode? A generous interpretation of this farcical text would be that she wanted the best for

---

38. Gunn, "Joshua and Judges," 118.

her son, but is misguided and poorly educated. She is not malignant, but neither does she seek out divine guidance nor does she raise her son right. However, her wealth somehow speaks against such an approach. A darker interpretation is to see her as someone who knows better, but does not care. Her character would be an example of what happens on the household level when everyone is just looking out for themselves and the law is forgotten or disregarded. You end up with cultic racketeering, which then rises to the tribal level in the subsequent narrative.

In sum, the three actual mothers in Judges are the mother of Israel's enemy (Sisera), the mother of an Israelite leader (Samson), and of a wayward Israelite individual (Micah). Sisera's mother is a fabrication of Israelite imagination, which gives readers insight into Israelite thought about the enemy. Sisera's mother lacks crucial knowledge, the irony of which is accentuated by the presence of the wise ladies. The character of Sisera's mother further serves to articulate a justification for the taking of plunder, including women, as spoils of war. Simultaneously, however, her thoughts raise the issue of taking women as booty up for moral scrutiny. By the end of the book, when the enemy is no longer an outsider and the unified home front is commanding action against its own, echoes from the victory poem will resound clearly in readers' ears and foreground the appalling words of the assembly when it justifies the taking of their own daughters (21:8, 10–11, and 22). The curse of Meroz (5:23) is now upon Jabesh-gilead, and the young women of Shiloh have no one (no man) to protect them.

Samson's mother features in an annunciation story, yet she gives birth to an all but conventional hero. In spite of all her effort to be involved in her son's life, such as acquiring a wife for him and presumably raising him as a Nazirite, she cannot keep up with him. Even though YHWH has divulged to her the knowledge of her son's destiny as a savior of Israel, Samson's mother is ultimately not able to make use of that knowledge, and it functions more for the benefit of readers. In her case, unlike Rebekah, she is impotent in spite of her knowledge. As a character, she is portrayed relatively positively; she has agency, she has been entrusted with a momentous task that she appears to understand. She shows confidence compared to her husband, who appears more apprehensive. She fulfills her role by receiving the instructions from the angel, by encouraging her husband to have confidence in the angel's good will (13:23), and by giving birth to and naming her son. Yet in the subsequent narrative, she fades from view without having significantly impacted the path of her son. YHWH no longer keeps her in the loop (14:4), which causes her and her husband to unknowingly contravene the command to eat anything unclean (the detail about the parents eating the honey is unnecessary to the narrative, and only makes sense in order to underscore the extent to which the parents are kept in the dark, 14:9).

Micah's mother is only known through her one act of assisting her son in doing what she thought was right in her own eyes. In this, she serves as a contrast to Samson's mother, who had instruction from YHWH to follow. Micah's mother controls her son in ways doomed to fail: he steals from her, and when he confesses, she fails to chastise him, but rather rewards him. In the few verses of this short narrative, mother and son succeed in breaking half of the Ten Commandments.

These mothers serve to highlight morally troubling desires, the inadequacy of even the most well-intentioned, dutiful, and divinely guided mothering, and the ludicrous and degenerate outcomes of ignorant and blatantly immoral mothering. With Sisera's mother, it is easy to judge her distantly as the enemy's mother, and recoil from her fantasy of her son degrading women. Upon further review, her figure provides a reflection on how victors' practices in a war situation are justified. As we shall see, this can lead to self-impeachment in contradiction of the text's ideology as articulated in 5:31. The text of Judg 5 contains a loose end, with the potential for unraveling. Samson's mother serves to demonstrate that however enthusiastically a mother acts to fulfill her duty, the son's destiny is not hers to determine. She may follow the rules given her by the angel, but YHWH's spirit slams Samson in his own way. Micah's mother is easily condemned as morally corrupt and doomed to fail. It is a little harder to assess how the fact that she is a mother plays into the narrative, but her story does illustrate the deterioration of Israel at a household level. She appears in the last section of Judges, where the narrative world is coming apart and turning in on itself. She dedicates a portion of her treasure to redeem her son, but all in the wrong ways. It seems that her role in part distributes the blame for Micah's failure and total violation of covenantal concepts of cultic practice.

Motherhood and the (Il)legitimacy of Power

Three references to motherhood in the book of Judges (8:19; 9:1, 3; and 11:1) each connect to issues of power and legitimacy. These are references to mothers who are not characters in the narrative. However, the references play intriguing roles with regard to power relations and figure in the stated rationale for Gideon's assassination of Midianite kings, for Abimelech's bid for power, and play into the narration of Jephthah's troubled origins.

Having captured two Midianite kings (8:11), Gideon questions them about specific men that the two allegedly have killed. They reply that they were like him (Gideon), "they resembled the sons of a king." Gideon then states, "They were my brothers, the sons of my mother" (בני אמי, 8:18–19), and goes on to swear that he would not have had to kill them if they had not killed his alleged brothers. Gideon's reference to his brothers as בני אמי is significant because it is unnecessary for him to refer to them as such, other than to connect the dots to claim that his full brothers were princes, so he is one too.

Only following this do the Israelites ask Gideon to rule (משל) over them, which Gideon declines, although he immediately begins to act like a king.[39] Then, in his death notice, Gideon is described as having seventy sons because "he had many wives" (8:30), another characteristic of royalty. Also provided is the crucial detail that he has one son of a concubine in Shechem (8:31), perhaps indicating a political alliance, and linking the narrative to the episode of this son's kingship, which follows.

"Son of a king" and son of a concubine, Abimelech turns to "his mother's brothers/kin" (אחי־אמו, 9:1, 3) and "the whole clan/all the families of his mother's father's house," (כל־משפחת בית־אבי אמו, 9:1). His mother's brothers, her extended family, are Abimelech's allies in Shechem, who speak on his behalf in support of his proposal that they make him ruler. Unlike his father, Abimelech overtly states his desire and intent to rule. In achieving his goal, he opts for his mother's household of origin from which to develop support and loyalty, seeing only challenge and opposition coming from his father's sons, his brothers, and killing all but the youngest. No good explanation is reported for why his mother's clan would support Abimelech's bid for power, other than the kinship factor. Neither is there any other stated rationale for why the leaders of Shechem would go along with this idea, nor are we told that they needed a ruler or that they had a contender. It may not even have been necessary for Abimelech to kill his brothers in order for him to be made ruler in Shechem.

---

39. Gideon's insincere leadership (saying he does not want to rule but behaving like a king, demolishing his father's altar to Baal, yet instituting a fake cult with an ephod made of the people's jewelry as in Exod 32) anticipates both the failed rule of Abimelech and the illegitimate shrine of Micah.

Abimelech sets up what amounts to a false choice for the Shechemites. He could perhaps simply have claimed rule over Shechem, but his plan involves eliminating the brothers he obviously sees as competition—the "brothers from another mother."

When Abimelech's reliance on his mother's clan and his bid for their support eventually backfires, does the fact that he relied on his mother's kin serve to underscore the wrongfulness of his rule?[40] The contrast with his youngest half-brother Jotham is stark in this respect, a character who does not claim any power for himself, but who takes on the task of condemning poor/evil leadership (9:7–15) as well as seeking fair justice for his brothers in pronouncing the conditional curse on Shechem. Here, Jotham refers to Abimelech as "the son of [Gideon's] slave woman" (אמה, 9:18), using the motherhood of Abimelech to diminish his status. Inevitably, Abimelech and the Shechemites are punished, Abimelech for killing his brothers and the lords of Shechem for supporting his power trip (9:24, 56–57). God's plan works so that Abimelech kills the Shechemites before being killed himself, by a woman (9:53).

Like Gideon's mother, Abimelech's mother has no agency and is not a character in the story. Gideon claims motherhood in order to legitimize vengeance, whereas Abimelech utilizes motherhood to claim a power base. They both might be said to be appealing to a sense of legitimacy and power provided by the idea expressed by that of queen mother, albeit for selfish, though unclear, reasons in Gideon's case, and in a farcical way by Abimelech.[41] For princes and kings, whether they have legitimacy or not, mothers matter, even when they do not appear in the story at all. The Abimelech-episode draws out the consequences of illegitimate rule, leading to inter/innertribal war. Together with 12:1–8 this forms a preamble to Judg 20–21.

The Jephthah cycle opens with the theme of fraternal strife, once again between brothers with different mothers. But while Abimelech eliminated the perceived challenge posed by his father's sons using his mother's clan as a support base, Jephthah does not have that option.

---

40. Athalya Brenner, "Women Frame the Book of Judges–How and Why?," in *Joshua and Judges*, ed. Athalya Brenner and Gale A. Yee, Texts @ Contexts (Minneapolis: Fortress, 2013), 128.

41. O'Connor, "Women in the Book of Judges," 280. On the queen mother motif as it relates to Sisera's mother, see Ackerman, *Warrior, Dancer, Seductress, Queen*, 128–80.

Jephthah is introduced as the son of a prostitute and a warrior, a גבור חיל,
with an even iffier parentage than Abimelech (11:1). Unlike Abimelech,
he is explicitly marred by his mother's status and reputation as a dis-
advantage that he must overcome. Jephthah's father's other, legitimate,
sons drive Jephthah away because he is the son of "another" woman (בן
אשה אחרת). Jephthah, like Abimelech (9:4), gathers worthless men about
him, but returns home when the town needs him to command the war
against the Ammonites, offering to make him their future leader (ראש).
Jephthah agrees, on the condition that YHWH gives them victory in the
battle. This stipulation hints at what might be an added motivating factor
in his ill-fated vow (11:30).

It is only upon Jephthah's return from the successful battle that we
learn that he had a daughter, his only child. We do not hear of any wife or
mother; this child is motherless, as far as the story is concerned, although
it is not easy to assess her absence. It does appear, however, that when
mothers are absent, daughters are in mortal danger, as is also the case with
the Levite's פילגש in Judg 19.

To summarize, references to motherhood play a strategic role in
shaping readers' perceptions. Gideon's brothers are described as looking
like him, like sons of kings. In claiming them as his brothers, Gideon
refers to them as sons of his mother, thereby also accepting the characterization of himself as royal. Abimelech goes to his concubine mother's
family of origin and uses her relatives to support his power base. However, this is perhaps more than he bargained for; as he leans on this connection, he succeeds in eliminating all but one of his brothers, but his
power base turns against him. Jephthah's parentage (son of a prostitute)
shapes the portrayal of his career in significant ways and likely affects
readers' view of him as someone with a bruised ego and eagerness to
prove himself.

Judges 19–21 and the Implication of Mothers in Sanctioning Violence

Mothers are conspicuously absent as actual characters in the final chapters of Judges. This resonates with the crisis that culminates in chapters
20–21, where women must be captured to become mothers and secure the
future. Although her father features prominently in Judg 19, the Levite's
פילגש's mother is never mentioned, and she herself has no mother-role
either. Like Jephthah's daughter, she is sacrificed, here in a warped twist on
rules of hospitality that tells the story of the extent to which the world of

Judges has become an inverted one.[42] Far from being commemorated by a festival (11:39–40), her ravaged body becomes the occasion for all-out civil war. The פילגש's death fulfills no vow, but the events of the aftermath of her brutal mauling lead to the oath that comes to threaten the survival of Benjamin (21:1).[43]

The Israelite tribes decide that they must avenge the abuse of the Levite's פילגש, the account of which he spins into being about an outrage committed against *him* after having callously disposed and dispatched of her body. The Mizpah assembly's decision to punish Gibeah (20:8–11) eventually leads to the חרם against Benjamin (20:37, 48). Thus the Israelites ironically end up perpetrating against their own what they were supposed to do to the indigenous tribes at the beginning of the book. The Israelites regret this self-inflicted predicament (21:3, 6). Compromised as they are after a battle that has killed tens of thousands, they find a loophole in their vow not to give their daughters in marriage to Benjamin (21:1) that, they feel, justifies retribution against those who did not fight against Benjamin (21:5). Is this a twisted form of poetic (in)justice? They annihilate the village of Jabesh-gilead, enacting חרם against it retroactively as punishment, not because it represents a threat. With this, the Mizpah assembly brings back the Benjaminites and offers them peace and four hundred virgins. Since this is not enough, they set up two hundred of their own daughters by abandoning them, thereby washing their hands of their vow and sanctioning the young, dancing women's abduction. This conspiracy to commit mass rape stands in sharp contrast to the proper and successful arranged marriage of Achsah to Othniel by her father Caleb at the beginning of the book (1:12–15). The women of Jabesh-gilead and Shiloh are taken captive and abducted to keep the tribe of Benjamin alive, to redeem the tribe cut off by the others, the "breach" that the tribes blame on YHWH (21:15), all in order to atone for the "original sin" of Gibeah.[44] The upside-down-

---

42. Stuart Lasine, "Guest and Host in Judges 19: Lot's Hospitality in an Inverted World," *JSOT* 9 (1984): 37–59.

43. J. Cheryl Exum, "The Centre Cannot Hold: Thematic and Textual Instabilities in Judges," *CBQ* 52 (1990): 430.

44. Exum, "Centre Cannot Hold," 430. The role of YHWH in the Benjamin vs. the tribes episode is intriguing, but cannot be pursued here. Is YHWH "showing" them, and giving them what they have asked for, by giving the Israelites the final bitter success in battle? Are they getting the answers they deserve, when they inquire of YHWH (20:18, 23, 28)? The contrast with the successful inquiry of 1:1–2 is clear; no fatalities

ness of this world is highlighted once again by the fact that women from Shiloh (in Ephraim) are violated by Benjaminites to atone for Benjaminites' gang rape of the concubine of an Ephraimite.[45] In a collapse of their own making, the Israelites apply the חרם and its consequences equally to Jabesh-gilead and to Benjamin, and violate their own daughters with depraved indifference in Shiloh.

Ironically, once again, this severe narrative of implosion and extermination connects back to the victory poem of Deborah in its evocation of women's roles as wombs (Judg 5:30), the mother role in its most basic, physical form. In the wake of the near extermination of Benjamin, the Israelite tribes act as Sisera's mother imagines that her son does: they take women as wombs, "breeders."[46] Despair leads to desperate solutions. Now, the neat division between enemy and Israelites, that even the song of Deborah cannot completely maintain, completely unravels. Israelites brutalize their own in the manner that Sisera's mother had imagined. Another irony is that Israel commits this crime en masse, so that by the end, as one man (20:1), Israel is "each doing what is right in his own eyes."

With the exception of Deborah as a kind of über-mother, mothers cannot protect their children in the book of Judges. Samson is beyond his mother's control, Micah's mother does not know or do what is good for him, and mothers are absent when daughters are threatened. The portrayal of mothers in Judges demonstrates that while they appear powerless with regard to their sons' destinies, yet the mothers do play a role in shaping the sons' lives and destinies, often in detrimental ways. Mothering behavior proves lethal for Sisera; sons/lovers who trust their women lose their power (Sisera and Samson). Yet, even the protection of Mother Deborah proves to be conditional, as the enemy other and the Israelite other merge in the final chapters of the book. In the breeding process, however, mothers are indispensable (which in 2020 sounds terrifyingly contemporary and *Handmaid's Tale*-ian). Does Judges toy with

---

and collateral annihilation there, versus twenty-five thousand Israelites dead and the tribe of Benjamin nearly wiped out.

45. Ackerman, *Warrior, Dancer, Seductress, Queen*, 255; Beldman, *Completion of Judges*, 103.

46. Sasson, *Judges*, 279. The translations "wenches" (Niditch, *Judges*, 69) and "sluts" (Bal, *Death and Dissymmetry*, 208) emphasize the aspect of soldiers' behavior immediately postvictory more than that of taking women captive as wives. These two aspects are interrelated, see Reeder, "Deuteronomy 21:10–14 and/as Wartime Rape."

the specter of motherhood as reduced to the mere function of keeping the tribes alive, as breeding machines?

A sustained focus on mother figures and the motherhood motif has allowed us to trace and connect a web of threads that contributes to shaping the fabric of the narrative. The mother characters have provided points of contrast and mirroring in fundamentally significant ways throughout the book. Questions of gender in power relations have come into sharper relief with a focus on the motif of motherhood and the concept of matrilineality, serving to justify more or less legitimate claims to power and demonstrating that ideas about motherhood are locked into implicit structures of power. Finally, we observe that with the strategic functions of the mother characters, the book of Judges succeeds in rhetorically appropriating motherhood in the sanctioning of violence against women, and in underscoring YHWH's power over his spirited earthly leadership figures.

8

Struck Down by a Woman:
Abimelech's Humiliating Intertextual Death

Zev Farber

The core of the book of Judges, namely, chapters 3 through 16, is built around a series of stories about שפטים, judges or chieftains, that lead the Israelites during a time of need against foreign enemies.[1] Each שפט comes from a different tribe and is unrelated to the previous שפט.[2] One significant exception to this schema is the story of Abimelech, who is unique for a number of reasons:

1. שפטים are generally heroes, if flawed, whereas Abimelech is a villain.
2. שפטים are never the sons of the previous שפט, whereas Abimelech is the son of Gideon/Jerubbaal, the previous שפט.

---

1. The first chapter is a supplement telling the story of the conquest and settlement in a way that contradicts much of Joshua. Chapter 2 is the Deuteronomistic framing of Judges, which is a pre-Deuteronomistic collection of northern legends at its core. The last five chapters of Judges are a promonarchic appendix, reframing the book (which is antimonarchic at its core).

2. This is an oversimplification. In reality, the שפטים can be subdivided into ones with narratives (Othniel, Ehud, Shamgar, Deborah+Barak, Gideon, Abimelech, Jephthah, Samson) and others simply as part of lists (Tola, Jair, Ibzan, Elon, Abdon). Even this is an oversimplification: Jephthah seems to have been part of both collections; Othniel was added into this corpus by the Deuteronomistic redactor; Shamgar has neither a proper narrative nor a proper listing; Samson's connection to this corpus appears to be artificial. Finally, it seems likely that in a more ancient version of the שפטים corpus, which included only the core stories, Saul was also listed (as per the story in 1 Sam 11); perhaps he was the culmination of it.

3. שפטים take power in response to crisis, whereas Abimelech does so out of personal ambition.
4. שפטים fight Israel's enemies, whereas Abimelech begins a civil war.
5. Abimelech is the only שפט to be given the title "king" (מלך).

In this sense, Abimelech, whose story sits more or less in the center of the book, is really that of an anti-שפט, and his role is to highlight the terrible consequences of abandoning the שפטים system and moving toward monarchy.[3]

The Abimelech Story: An Overview

The overall arc of the Abimelech story is as follows: Abimelech, the son of Gideon and a Shechemite concubine (8:31), wishes to be king of Shechem and convinces the local people to anoint him (9:3–4). He then hires a personal army and kills his seventy brothers in Ophrah (9:5), after which he becomes the king (9:6). Although he and the Shechemites are cursed by his surviving brother Jotham (9:7–21), he rules for three years (9:22).

Later, after the nobility of Shechem turns against Abimelech (9:23–25), and a visiting strongman named Gaal son of Ebed makes a public, drunken promise to take him down (9:26–29), Abimelech removes Gaal (9:30–41) and then attacks the city and destroys it (9:42–45). Then he attacks Migdal Shechem and burns it down (9:46–49). Finally, he lays siege to the city of Thebez and to a large tower there, but before he can burn the tower, a woman drops a millstone upon him and cracks his skull (9:50–53). As he is dying, he asks his armor bearer to end his life (9:54), after which his army disperses and heads home (9:55). With that, this שפט cycle comes to a moralizing close (9:56–57), and the text moves on to the next שפט, Tola ben Puah from the tribe of Issachar (10:1).

---

3. For a discussion of the overall structure of the story and its place in the book of Judges, see Yairah Amit, *The Book of Judges: The Art of Editing* [Hebrew], Biblical Encyclopaedia Library 6 (Jerusalem: Bialik, 1992), 92–104; Gregory T. K. Wong, *Compositional Strategy of the Book of Judges: An Inductive, Rhetorical Study*, VTSup 111 (Leiden: Brill, 2006).

Fissures in the Story Line

The above summary masks a tortuous composition history that is difficult to reconstruct.

Jerubbaal versus Gideon

The first thing to note is that the Abimelech story is grafted onto the Gideon story artificially.[4] Originally, Gideon and Jerubbaal were two separate characters, and Abimelech was the son of the latter. Why the two characters were merged is unclear, but the story about the name change (6:25–32), in which Gideon "fights with Baal," is a classic folk etymology written both to soften the "inappropriate" pro-Baal nature of the name and, more specifically, as a harmonizing supplementation to connect Gideon with Jerubbaal and merge the characters.[5] With this merger of identities, most of the Jerubbaal story appears to have been lost and thus, we do not really have the context for the Abimelech story outside of a handful of hints.[6]

---

4. For a fuller discussion of the secondary nature of the identification between Gideon and Jerubaal, see Herbert Haag, "Gideon—Jerubbaal—Abimelek," *ZAW* 79 (1967): 305–14; Barnabas Lindars, "Gideon and Kingship," *JTS* 16 (1965): 315–26; Reinhard Müller, "Gefahren im Umgang mit Macht: Midraschim und Paradigmata in Jdc 8 und 9," in *Königtum und Gottesherrschaft: Untersuchungen zur alttestamentlichen Monarchiekritik*, FAT 2/3 (Tübingen: Mohr Siebeck, 2004), 96–108; Sara J. Milstein, "Delusions of Grandeur: Revision through Introduction in Judges 6–9," in *Tracking the Master Scribe: Revision through Introduction in Biblical and Mesopotamian Literature* (New York: Oxford University Press, 2016), 147–73. For a critique of this position, see John A. Emerton, "Gideon and Jerubbaal," *JTS* 27 (1976): 289–312. For alternative approaches to the problem, see Baruch Halpern, "The Rise of Abimelek," *HAR* 2 (1978): 79–100; A. Graeme Auld, "Gideon: Hacking at the Heart of the Old Testament," *VT* 39 (1989): 257–67.

5. For an alternative view of why this passage was written, arguing that it is based on an ancient polemic against Baal (though with a layer of Deuteronomistic redaction), see Albert de Pury, "Le raid de Gédéon (Juges 6, 25–32) et l'histoire de l'exclusivisme yahwiste," in *Lectio difficilior probabilior? L'exégèse comme expérience de décloisonnement: Mélanges offerts à Françoise Smyth-Florentin*, ed. Thomas Römer (Heidelberg: Wissenschaftliches theologisches Seminar, 1991), 173–205.

6. Edgar Jans suggests that the story as we have it is missing part of the original introduction to the earlier Abimelech tradition (what he calls the *BAALIM-Erzählung*), which gave Jerubbaal seventy sons, thereby making Abimelech's fratricide an early feature of the account; see Jans, *Abimelech und sein Königtum: Diachrone*

Two Abimelech Strands

The Abimelech story itself is made up of at least two strands.[7] In one strand, the people of Shechem become disillusioned with Abimelech and they begin to set up ambuscades on the hilltops outside Shechem and rob passersby (9:23, 25). This leads Abimelech to attack the city and destroy it (9:42–45). I will call this "the rebellion strand."

In the other strand, which I will call "the Gaal strand," a rival leader named Gaal son of Ebed convinces the Shechemites to abandon their allegiance to Abimelech and follow him. The local governor in charge of the city, Zebul, tells Abimelech about this threat and, as a consequence, Abimelech shows up with an army and forces Gaal out of the city (9:26–41).

The Gaal story is likely more ancient than the rebellion story, as it does not exhibit many of the theological elements found in other Judges accounts.[8] It was not penned by the author of the base text of Judges but was spliced into Judges' own Abimelech story, which was the rebellion account.

The Inexplicable Final Battles and Jotham's Fable

The Abimelech story ends with two battle scenes that lack an obvious connection to either story line. In the first story line, Shechem rebels against Abimelech, and he destroys the city; in the second, Gaal son of Ebed rebels

---

und synchrone Untersuchungen zu Ri 9, ATSAT 66 (St. Ottilien: EOS, 2001), 372. This modifies the similar suggestion of Ernst Sellin, who believed that in the oldest version, Abimelech killed the seventy sons of Hamor, thereby becoming king; see Sellin, *Wie wurde Sichem eine israelitische Stadt?* (Leipzig: Deichert, 1922). In my view, the number seventy was likely added into the Abimelech story, and he simply killed "the sons of Jerubbaal."

7. Although I develop the point further here, I discuss how and why these story lines were combined in Zev I. Farber, "Jerubaal, Jacob, and the Battle for Shechem: A Tradition History," *JHebS* 13 (2013): 5–10. Although the exact division of the strands in these articles is my own, I build upon the work of earlier scholars who also suggest two alternative traditions along these lines. Specifically, see Isabelle de Castelbajac, "Histoire de la rédaction de Juges IX: Une solution," *VT* 51 (2001): 166–85; Walter Groß, *Richter: Übersetzt und Ausgelegt*, HThKAT (Freiburg im Breisgau: Herder, 2009), 485–94.

8. See discussion in Milstein, "Delusions of Grandeur," 153–60. Milstein sees the Gaal account as being expanded by the editor of Judges, and not, as I will argue, as having been spliced into the proto-Judges account at a later point.

against him, and Abimelech banishes him from the city. In both of these cases, the problem appears to have been solved. Why, then, does Abimelech attack Migdal Shechem and then Thebez?[9]

On a simple level, both incidents can be explained against the backdrop of the conclusion of Jotham's fable (9:19–20):

> If, I say, you have acted in good faith and honor with Jerubbaal and with his house this day, then rejoice in Abimelech, and let him also rejoice in you; but if not, let fire come out from Abimelech, and devour the lords of Shechem, and Beth-millo; and let fire come out from the lords of Shechem, and from Beth-millo, and devour Abimelech. (NRSV)

According to this, if the appointment of Abimelech was unjust, then the punishment will be mutual destruction. While the attack on Shechem in 9:42–45 destroys the city, the attack on Migdal Shechem literally burns up Abimelech's enemies in fire, a literal fulfillment of the curse.[10] What is missing from the prophecy fulfillment here, the destruction of Abimelech, takes place in the next story, when during Abimelech's attack on Thebez, he attempts to burn down the tower and is killed himself, thus fulfilling the other half of the Jotham's curse. As such, it is tempting to tie

---

9. Wolfgang Richter sees this disconnect as sufficiently stark so as to lead him to suggest that these stories represent an independent narrative strand; see Richter, *Traditionsgeschichtliche Untersuchungen zum Richterbuch*, BBB 18 (Bonn: Hanstein, 1963), 314–16.

10. Whether the burning of Migdal Shechem fulfills the curse depends on the identity of Migdal Shechem, which is a matter of debate. Some scholars assume that it refers to the name of a tower inside Shechem. If so, then the destruction of this tower is part of the conquest of Shechem. Yairah Amit, e.g., argues that the story was written with a general description (the destruction of Shechem) and then a focus on one part of this action (the destruction of the tower); Amit, *Judges: A Commentary* [Hebrew], Mikra LeYisra'el (Tel Aviv: Am Oved; Jerusalem: Magnes, 1999), 172. Alternatively, Nadav Na'aman has argued that Migdal Shechem is a toponym, and refers to the name of an independent city that Abimelech subdues after he destroys Shechem. Na'aman identifies El-Burnat, a site excavated by Adam Zertal, as Migdal Shechem; see Na'aman, "A Hidden Anti-Samaritan Polemic in the Story of Abimelech and Shechem (Judges 9)," *BZ* 55 (2011): 8–11; Na'aman, "The Tower of Shechem and the House of El-Berith" [Hebrew], *Zion* 51 (1986): 259–80. The appearance of the temple of El/Baal-Berit at the beginning of the story, in association with Shechem's acceptance of Abimelech as their future king (9:4), and then in the Migdal Shechem episode (9:46), as the place where the local leadership is hiding, argues for the first possibility over the second.

the final form of Jotham's fable in with the Migdal Shechem and Thebez stories and suggest that they come from the same hand. And yet, this suggestion is problematic.

First, the stories lack parity as interpretations of the fable. If the Migdal Shechem story was composed to have Abimelech's enemies literally burned in flames to reflect the fable, then why does the Thebez story not end with the inverse, Abimelech burning up in flames? Second, Jotham specifically promises that fire from the Shechemites who appointed Abimelech king will burn him up, and yet the Thebez story is about another city altogether.[11]

If anything, it seems that Jotham's parable has been made to fit the ending of the Abimelech story and not the reverse. More precisely, I suggest that the core parable was indeed added to fit the Abimelech story, but then it was supplemented by an editorial revision that changed its point. This occurred as part of a revision of the whole story.[12]

---

11. The identity of Thebez is debated. The majority of scholars identify it with Ṭubas, as the name is similar to Thebez (though it requires a *tav ṭet* switch, which is uncommon) and it is in the vicinity. Adam Zertal, however, persuasively argues that as Ṭubas does not have remains from this period, while nearby Khirbet Einun in the Tubas valley does, the latter should be identified with Thebez; Zertal, *The Manasseh Hill Country Survey*, vol. 2 of *The Eastern Valleys and the Fringes of the Desert*, CHANE 21.2 (Leiden: Brill, 2001), 59; Zertal, *A Nation Is Born: The Altar on Mount Ebal and the Origins of Israel* [Hebrew] (Tel Aviv: Yedioth Aharonot, 2000), 288–89, 292–93. Finally, Abraham Malamat argues that the word is a scribal error, and that instead of the second letter being a *bet* it should be a *resh*, and that the city was Tirzah; see Malamat, *History of Biblical Israel: Major Problems and Minor Issues*, CHANE 7 (Leiden: Brill, 2001), 127.

12. A number of scholars agree that the Jotham fable has been revised. Richter (*Traditionsgeschichtliche Untersuchungen zum Richterbuch*, 314–16) suggests that the fable was an independent composition and was integrated into the story by the author, and then expanded over time. Ernst Würthwein suggests that the fable was added in at a later stage, along with the curse, but without reference to the killing of Jerubbaal's sons, which was only included once the story was combined with the Gideon account; Würthwein, "Abimelech und der Untergang Sichems: Studien zu Jdc 9," in *Studien zum Deuteronomischen Geschichtswerk*, BZAW 227 (Berlin: de Gruyter, 1994), 12–28. Interestingly, Karin Schöpflin sees a reverse process in which Jotham curses Shechem and Abimelech for their perfidy (9:16–20) and only later was the fable added to enrich Jotham's persona as a wise prophet; see Schöpflin, "Jotham's Speech and Fable as Prophetic Comment on Abimelech's Story: The Genesis of Judges 9," *SJOT* 18 (2004), 12.

The Core of Jotham's Fable

The original parable, which I suggest was part of the rebellion story, describes how the trees (= the Shechemites) could not convince a productive tree (olive, fig, and grapevine) to become their king, so they chose the unproductive bramble (= Abimelech). The bramble accepts but offers a caveat (9:15):[13]

> If in good faith you are anointing me king over you, then come and take refuge in my shade; but if not, let fire come out of the bramble and devour the cedars of Lebanon.

The point of the parable is that the bramble is aware that it is unworthy and thus declares that the trees had better be serious and loyal, for if not, the bramble, which has no productive power, will use its destructive power to destroy them. If we apply this parable to Abimelech's appointment as king, the claim seems to be as follows: Abimelech is a worthless person, and thus of little benefit as king. Once the people realize this, they will tire of him, but then his real power as a destructive force will become apparent, and Shechem will be destroyed.

This is exactly what happens in the rebellion story line. Although it is missing the element of fire, the threat of fire going out from X and consuming Y seems to be a literary trope (see the very similar trope used as a refrain in Amos 1 and Hos 8:14).

Rounding out the Gaal Story Line

In contrast to the rebellion story line, which ends nicely in 9:45, the Gaal story line has a flimsy ending; the entire story feels like an episode in a larger account, of which we have only snippets.[14] Gaal son of Ebed does

---

13. The productive trees refusing to become king may connect to Gideon's refusal of the crown (8:22–23).

14. I am envisioning a lost written account. For more on this, see Farber, "Jerubaal, Jacob, and the Battle for Shechem," 8–10. For the evidence of lost written works in other biblical books (with an emphasis on Joshua), see Farber, "Snippets from a Lost Joshua Cycle: The Prehistory of an Israelite Legendary Hero," in *"Now It Happened in Those Days": Studies in Biblical, Assyrian, and Other Ancient Near Eastern Historiography Presented to Mordechai Cogan on His Seventy-Fifth Birthday*, ed. Amitai Baruchi-Unna et al. (Winona Lake, IN: Eisenbrauns, 2017), 1:43–60. See also the recent and

not seem to be a native of Shechem but from somewhere else (9:36). Moreover, Abimelech appears to be the chieftain of another city, Arumah, which Shechem serves as a vassal. Mark Smith aptly describes this story as "fighting forces led by local leaders pitted against one another."[15]

Gaal's speech, in which he tries to convince the Shechemites to serve him by reminding them how Jerubbaal's son once served the king of Shechem, "so why should we serve him now," hints at pieces of the lost Jerubbaal story. Moreover, we can deduce from this episode that Abimelech is a powerful ruler of a city named Arumah (generally identified as Khirbet el-Urmah), which Shechem and likely other cities now serve, though which once served Shechem.[16] Thus, in the Gaal story, Abimelech should be pictured as the local ruler of Arumah, who dominates his region (including the recently subdued city of Shechem), and who campaigns against other cities as a way to increase his power.

As the Migdal Shechem episode opens with their hearing what happened, I suggest that this was originally connected to the Gaal episode, and what they heard was that their chosen leader was defeated and now Abimelech is coming for them. As for the logic of the Thebez episode, as we are lacking any further context, it is difficult to say if Thebez was connected with Gaal or simply did not pay tribute. Either way, the story fits with the image of a regional chieftain or small-time monarch who goes on campaign with his army to put down any local resistance.

In fact, the reader of the Gaal strand would likely have some grudging respect for the ruthless Abimelech. When Gaal whips up opposition to Abimelech, and publicly declares that if the men follow him, he will tell Abimelech to get lost, Abimelech and his sidekick Zebul respond by

---

persuasive suggestion of Na'aman that Judg 1 contains pieces of a lost northern conquest account; Nadav Na'aman, "Rediscovering a Lost North Israelite Conquest Story," in *Rethinking Israel: Studies in the History and Archaeology of Ancient Israel in Honor of Israel Finkelstein*, ed. Oded Lipschits, Yuval Gadot, and Matthew J. Adams (Winona Lake, IN: Eisenbrauns, 2017), 287–302.

15. See Smith, *Poetic Heroes: Literary Commemorations of Warriors and Warrior Culture in the Early Biblical World* (Grand Rapids: Eerdmans, 2014), 22.

16. See discussion of Khirbet el-Urmah in Robert J. Bull and Edward F. Campbell Jr., "The Sixth Campaign Balaṭah (Shechem)," *BASOR* 190 (1968), 38–41; Erasmus Gaß, *Die Ortsnamen des Richterbuchs in historischer und redaktioneller Perspektive*, ADPV 35 (Wiesbaden: Harrassowitz, 2005), 330–31; Robert D. Miller, *Chieftains of the Highland Clans: A History of Israel in the Twelfth and Eleventh Centuries B.C.* (Grand Rapids: Eerdmans, 2005), 120.

outwitting Gaal, sneaking up on the city and maneuvering him to fight outside the wall, where Abimelech's army has the advantage. Then, when the people of Migdal Shechem hide in their temple, Abimelech exercises charismatic leadership and tactical creativity, having each person follow him in cutting down a branch, bringing it to the temple, and thus burning the inmates alive. It is against this backdrop of a cunning and charismatic military leader successfully putting down Gaal's rebellion, that the third extant incident from this strand has its full, shocking effect.

An Ignoble Death

The manly and wily Abimelech, trying to destroy the tower in Thebez the way he did the temple of Migdal Shechem, faces the unfortunate reality that the escapees are hiding not on the ground floor but on the roof. Thus, by approaching the wall to again set up brambles and burn it down, he exposes himself to death from above.

Even worse, Abimelech is not taken down by an archer or spear-man, but his skull is crushed by a woman dropping a millstone on him. Millstones are not military weapons but objects used for making grain, and can thus be seen as part of the feminine complement of equipment, highlighting the humiliating fact that Abimelech is killed by a woman. As J. Cheryl Exum puts it,

> A millstone is a domestic tool, associated with women's work, not a weapon of war. If a man had killed Abimelech from the wall, it would not have been with a millstone but with a man's weapon, perhaps with arrows (as in 2 Sam 11:20).... In that case, Abimelech would not have needed to ask his armor bearer to kill him, but his death would still be shameful, for he was foolish in coming so close to the tower in the first place (cf. 2 Sam 11:20–21). It appears that the narrator of the Judges story wants not only to punish Abimelech for his wickedness but also to shame him as much as possible.[17]

The image of a woman killing a warrior appears elsewhere in Judges, in the story of Deborah, in which Yael kills Sisera by feeding him milk and then

---

17. Exum, "Encoded Messages to Women," in *Feminist Biblical Interpretation: A Compendium of Critical Commentary on the Books of the Bible and Related Literature*, ed. Luise Schottroff, Marie-Theres Wacker, and Martin Rumscheidt (Grand Rapids: Eerdmans, 2012), 118.

crushing his skull with a tent peg (Judg 4:19–21; 5:25–26). In both cases the woman uses a nonconventional weapon, and in both cases the man is killed by having his skull crushed. In the case of Abimelech, the woman is unnamed, one of the faceless hundreds that Abimelech was about to have burned alive. This is a fitting end to the antihero Abimelech, who, unlike the שפטים, rules as king and uses his military skill to subdue fellow Israelites, and not in defense of his people from outside threats.[18]

When Jotham's Fable Met the Gaal Story

The author of the rebellion strand uses Jotham's fable to foreshadow the inevitable turning of the Shechemites against Abimelech and their mutual destruction. Nevertheless, the rebellion story is not really about Abimelech, but about monarchy. The fact that Abimelech is a bramble is just par for the course, since anyone who understood the will of YHWH would never have been interested in kingship in the first place. The core of the book of Judges is about a succession of leaders who take power in times of necessity; kingship is not an ideal other than in the promonarchic appendix (chs. 17–21).

After the stories were spliced together, the entire account was recast as being about the betrayal of Gideon and not the very fact of monarchy. To do this, the redactor added verses 16b–19a, as Reinhard Müller persuasively argues, which reinterpret the point of the parable entirely.[19] It is no longer about the foolishness of appointing a bramble—useless when embraced and dangerous when angered—but about the inappropriateness of supporting the man who murdered Jerubbaal's (other) sons. This makes nonsense of the parable, since the parable itself says "be loyal or else" while the explanation says "if appointing Abimelech was wrong, you will be destroyed," that is, even if you are loyal.

----

18. Although it is very possible that Shechem in the period in which the story is set was Canaanite, and the Gaal strand may not have been thinking in terms of Israelite versus non-Israelite identity, the biblical authors who included the story in Judges seem to be thinking of them as Israelites.

19. Müller suggests that this passage is a supplement or expansion (*Erweiterung*) added to shift focus from the poor choice of Abimelech to the failure of the Shechemites to properly respect Gideon's legacy. The addition is clear not only from the shift in content, which is at odds with the simple meaning of the parable, but from the resumptive repetition (*Wiederaufnahme*) of אם באמת ובתמים, "if in good faith and honor," in 9:16a and 19a, as well as the אם טובה, "if [you have dealt] well," picking up on the "if" language, in 9:16b. Müller, "Gefahren im Umgang mit Macht," 108–9.

This expanded version of the parable solves another problem. As already noted, the parable connects well with the destruction of Migdal Shechem by fire, even if this connection is secondary. In contrast, the original fable connects poorly to the Thebez story, as the people of Thebez have no part in having appointed Abimelech king.

The parable's new layer, however, recasts it to be not about loyalty but about the wicked getting their just deserts. The Thebez story fits with this framing, since Abimelech's death is part of this divine punishment; he is, after all, the wicked person who murdered his own. This edit changes the act of the woman from a humiliating accident to an expression of the hand of God working behind the scenes.

The compiler of Judg 9 is not the only editor who made use of the story to make a point. The redactor of an entirely different story in Samuel reflects on the Abimelech story in such a way as to make Abimelech's ending even more ignoble.

Abimelech's Ignoble Death in Samuel

The Bible is filled with intertextual allusions. Nevertheless, as Hava Shalom-Guy points out,

> Whereas, for the most part, analogies in biblical literature are hidden, allusive, or deductive, the reference to Abimelech's death at Thebez (Judg. 9.52–53) in the David and Bathsheba narrative (2 Sam. 11) constitutes a rare example of an explicit analogy between characters, circumstances, and events.[20]

Much has been written on the connection between the two from a literary level.[21] Here, I would like to narrow the focus to composition history and see what we can learn about the driving force behind the redaction of both passages.

---

20. See Shalom-Guy, "Three-Way Intertextuality: Some Reflections of Abimelech's Death at Thebez in Biblical Narrative," *JSOT* 34 (2010): 420, adapted from the Hebrew version of this paper, Shalom-Guy, "Why Recall Abimelech's Death in the David and Bathsheba Narrative?" *Beit Mikra* 54 (2009): 5–13. For the ease of the English reader, I will refer to page numbers in the English version in the following notes.

21. See, e.g., Yair Zakovitch, *Through the Looking Glass: Reflection Stories in the Bible* [Hebrew] (Tel Aviv: Hakibbutz Hameuchad, 1995), 28; Zipporah Talshir, "Narrative Ties in Early Biblical Historiography" [Hebrew], *Shnaton* 5–6 (1982): 69–74.

In the book of Samuel, David asks his general, Joab, to make sure that
Uriah the Hittite, the loyal soldier whose wife David impregnated while
her husband was out fighting on the frontlines, does not survive the siege
of Rabbah, the Ammonite capital. David suggests this be accomplished
through simple treachery, namely, that the army abandon him during a
battle and let him be struck down (2 Sam 11:15). Joab, however, accomplishes this task by putting Uriah at the head of a group who runs at the city
wall, baiting an elite force to come out and strike them down (11:16–17):

> As Joab was besieging the city, he assigned Uriah to the place where
> he knew there were valiant warriors. *The men of the city came out and
> fought with Joab*; and some of the servants of David among the people
> fell. Uriah the Hittite was killed as well. (NRSV, emphasis added)

According to this, Uriah was killed in hand-to-hand combat by valiant warriors that ran out of the city into the field to attack Joab's front lines. The
story continues when Joab sends David a message that the request has been
fulfilled. His instruction to the messenger about what to say is multipronged:

> When you have finished telling the king all the news about the fight-
> ing, then, if the king's anger rises, and if he says to you, "Why did
> you go so near the city to fight? *Did you not know that they would
> shoot from the wall?* Who killed Abimelech son of Jerubbeshet [LXX:
> Jerubbaal]? Did not a woman throw an upper millstone on him
> from the wall, so that he died at Thebez? Why did you go so near the
> wall?" then you shall say, "Your servant Uriah the Hittite is dead too."
> (emphasis added)

Joab is worried that David will be angry about the rookie mistake of
coming too close to the wall, as that exposes soldiers needlessly to arrows
shot or stones dropped from the roof. He even assumes that David will
pull out the famously humiliating story of Abimelech being killed by a
woman. Yet, why would David jump to this conclusion if Uriah was killed
by a soldier's fighting him in hand-to-hand combat?

This same ambiguity appears in the messenger's actual message
(11:23–24) which, in the MT, avoids David's reaction (and in LXX is in
response to the very reaction Joab predicted):[22]

---

22. The MT of Samuel is well known as an inferior text to other witnesses in many
cases. Nevertheless, in this case, the LXX is so repetitive that one is tempted to suggest

The men gained an advantage over us, and *came out against us in the field*; but we drove them back to the entrance of the gate. *Then the archers shot at your servants from the wall*; some of the king's servants are dead; and your servant Uriah the Hittite is dead also. (emphasis added)

Here we have hand-to-hand combat that leads to an approach to the wall, and then the archers shooting and the death of Uriah. Shalom-Guy notes the inconsistency between the messenger's claim that Uriah was killed by arrow fire from atop the wall and the narrator's description of his being killed in battle on the field, and argues that this is part of a larger pattern of how the author of the passage in Samuel reworked the Thebez account in Judges.[23]

For example, in Judges, the woman is standing on the roof of a tower, but when the story is retold in Samuel, she is standing above a wall. This difference stems from the desire of the Samuel passage to tie the Abimelech story in with the Uriah story more closely. Adding the motif of Uriah's death by arrow fire from the wall of Rabbah is a similar editorial adjustment.

This may be the case, but it points to the likelihood that the entire quotation of the Abimelech story is a later addition, since if the narrator's depiction of the death of Uriah and reference to Abimelech's death were penned by the same hand, why not make them cohere better?

Thus, I suggest the following: In the earlier layer of the story, Joab's purposeful tactical mistake was positioning his army in such a way as to give enemy ground troops an advantage in the counterattack. Nevertheless, the proximity of the battle to the wall suggested to a later editor the story of Abimelech.

This editor made use of the anecdote as the quintessential mistake in siege warfare. "Everybody knows" David is to say, "how the powerful warrior Abimelech was felled by a woman due to a foolish mistake." Abimelech is thus not merely an example of *a* warrior killed by a woman, but his place in Israel's history is to be remembered by military men as *the* warrior who was killed by a woman; he is paradigmatic.

This explains the otherwise cumbersome formulation of being attacked then beating the enemy back. If the point was just to get Uriah

---

that it represents an "expansive style" addition familiar from the SP; see discussion in Shalom-Guy, "Three-Way Intertextuality," 428 n. 37, and literature cited therein.

23. Shalom-Guy, "Three-Way Intertextuality," 423–24.

killed by arrow fire, it would have been simpler just to have Joab rush the walls. Again, I suggest that we are seeing the result of a redaction. To further integrate this supplement, the editor added the death of Uriah the Hittite by arrows into the mouth of the messenger.

Originally, the message was simply that the army was attacked and although they beat the enemy back to the gates, soldiers were lost, including Uriah the Hittite. This is also why David simply responds with this message to Joab (1 Sam 11:25), "Do not be distressed about the matter. The sword always takes its toll. Press your attack on the city and destroy it!" Although it is not impossible that this could be a response to his learning about a poorly thought-out siege and arrow fire, it fits better as a response to a surprise attack from enemy ground troops, leading to casualties from the sword.

Poking Fun at Abimelech: The Final Redaction

One final manipulation of the Abimelech and Thebez story appears again in the Judges version. According to the story, the woman on the tower drops a millstone onto Abimelech's skull and crushes it. Like what happened with Sisera, I suggest that in the older layer of the story, this simply killed him. In the current text, however, Abimelech survives the blow and asks his armor bearer to euthanize him (9:54):

> Immediately he called to the young man who carried his armor and said to him, "Draw your sword and kill me, so people will not say about me, 'A woman killed him.'" So the young man thrust him through, and he died.

As has been noted by others, the story has a textual resonance with the death of Saul (1 Sam 31:4–5),

> Then Saul said to his armor bearer, "Draw your sword and thrust me through with it, so that these uncircumcised may not come and thrust me through, and make sport of me." But his armor-bearer was unwilling; for he was terrified. So Saul took his own sword and fell upon it. When his armor bearer saw that Saul was dead, he also fell upon his sword and died with him.[24]

---

24. Shalom-Guy ("Three-Way Intertextuality," 424) describes this as a motif, common to stories like this, as opposed to an intertextual reference.

Abimelech suffers in the comparison here, since Saul wants to protect his honor as king of Israel, by not allowing the uncircumcised Philistines to mock him. He also is greatly respected by his armor bearer, who will not do it, and he ends up killing himself by falling on his own sword.

Abimelech, in contrast, wants to protect not Israel's national honor but his personal honor—as it was an Israelite (woman) who killed him, no one was going to use Abimelech's death to mock Israel. Abimelech is also laying the groundwork for a lie since a woman did, in fact, kill him; he was already dying from the wound on his skull. Finally, unlike Saul's armor bearer, Abimelech's does not shy away from doing the job. In fact, the contrast is even starker when we note that Saul's armor bearer kills himself as well in solidarity; something that does not happen with Abimelech's.

Yet another connection appears with the follow up to the story of Saul's death, when an Amalekite man tells David that it was he who dealt Saul the final blow (2 Sam 1:9–10):

> He said to me, "Come, stand over me and kill me; for convulsions have seized me, and yet my life still lingers." So I stood over him, and killed him, for I knew that he could not live after he had fallen.

Here, too, we have a dying man asking to be killed, but Saul just wants to end his pain whereas Abimelech wants to create the false impression that he was killed by a man.

I suggest that an editor familiar with at least the first story of Saul's death, and perhaps both, added 9:54. On one hand, by adding this anecdote, Abimelech is saved from dying at the hands of a woman. On the other hand, the story serves to make Abimelech seem even more pathetic, as the final stroke is a farce and highlights the reality of who really killed him.[25]

An Intertextual Irony

One support for this redaction critical suggestion is the fact that the passage in Samuel does not seem to know anything about the armor bearer's

---

25. Jacob Wright has argued that the theme of female power, obvious in this story and that of Yael but implicit in a number of others, are all examples of "an overall conception by the post-exilic editor of the book of Judges who uses the subversion of male power as a theme to highlight the ultimate power of YHWH over Israel"; see Wright, "Yael and the Subversion of Male Leaders in Judges," *TheTorah.com* (2017); https://tinyurl.com/SBL03109a.

final stroke.[26] Instead, it is just taken for granted that Abimelech was killed by the woman. If this is correct, then a final form reading of the text yields a great irony.

The original meaning of the gloss in Samuel was meant to invoke Abimelech as the ultimate example of someone who made a classic military blunder during a siege and as a consequence died a humiliating death. Once, however, the canonical form of Samuel is read together with that of Judges, Abimelech's final act in life is entirely futile. He says that his armor bearer should kill him so people do not say that Abimelech was killed by a woman, and yet the only other time he is mentioned in the Bible is when the great general Joab, channeling King David himself, says, "because of this very mistake, Abimelech was struck down by a woman."

---

26. Talshir ("Narrative Ties in Early Biblical Historiography," 72) notes this as well but she does not see it as sufficient reason to call this a redaction, and instead argues that the detail was unnecessary in Samuel. Shalom-Guy ("Three-Way Intertextuality," 425–26) argues that Abimelech's desire to conceal his death at the hands of a woman lies behind elements of the David and Bathsheba story, namely, David's wish to conceal that Uriah's death is really at the hands of a woman (Bathsheba), as is David's own shameful sin.

9
Fathers, Daughters, and
Problematic Verbal Commitments in Judges

Richard D. Nelson

Judges incorporates three narratives relating how a questionable pledge activates an episode involving the relationship between fathers and daughters. Assertive Achsah gets what she wants in the first chapter, Jephthah's acquiescent yet self-assertive daughter leaves her mark in the middle of Judges, and the abducted daughters of Shiloh supply the book's conclusion. These three accounts touch on issues such as the inviolability of spoken obligations, the bond between fathers and daughters, wise and persuasive speech, and the fundamental importance of inheritance and progeny. When analyzed for their narrative shape and rhetorical strategy and read in narrative sequence, these stories influence how readers are prompted to create meaning out of the book as a whole.

Historical critics cogently argue that these three stories appear in three different redactional levels of Judges originating in different historical periods. The story of father Jephthah and his daughter is an element of the cyclically structured Deuteronomistic core of the book, 2:6–16:31. The story of Caleb and Achsah is part of the book's introduction, 1:1–2:5. This block of text was assembled out of material mostly from Joshua to create an overture for Judges when it was no longer part of a continuous Joshua-Judges-Samuel sequence. The third section, Judg 17–21, is generally recognized as a conclusion secondarily added in the last stage of the book's development. A recurring formula observes that reported outrages happened when there was no king in Israel (17:6; 18:1; 19:1; 21:25).

Plot and Narrative Structure

Achsah

The story of Caleb and Achsah exhibits a telegraphic style with narrative gaps and ambiguities of vocabulary and syntax. Following Caleb's promise, Othniel's victory, and her marriage, Achsah takes center stage:

> When she came, she urged him to ask her father for a field. She dismounted from her donkey, and Caleb said to her, "What can I do for you?" She said to him, "Give me a blessing because you have treated me like the land of Negev. So give me a bowl of water."[1]

Judges 1:14aα establishes Achsah's desire for territory, but the expected follow-up by Othniel is abruptly broken off. Instead, the narrative action is carried forward by a direct encounter between Achsah and Caleb, precipitated by the conclusion of what the reader must assume is a donkey journey on her part (1:14aβ–b). She makes a request and supports it with argumentation (1:15a). So, Caleb grants her two water sources (1:15b).

Caleb gives Achsah away as a reward for services rendered. The situation of a father promising a daughter as a motivational gift in a military situation is also described in 1 Sam 17:25; 18:17–27. Othniel's capture of Debir may be seen as a sort of bride price (מהר) like the Philistine foreskins handed over by David (1 Sam 18:27). The field and water sources that Achsah seeks fall under the category of dowry, property brought into a marriage by the bride (1 Kgs 9:16), over which the wife retained certain potential rights.

Joshua 15:15–19 is the source of the Achsah story. The Jephthah incident shares with it a context of war and victory, and, like Achsah, Jephthah's daughter makes a request that her father choses to grant. Achsah's story involves a pledge to give in marriage and the concept of blessing (1:15). The forced marriages of chapter 21 have a similar but skewed setting: an oath swearing *not* to give in marriage (21:1, 7) and the concept of curse (21:18).

Jephthah and His Daughter

Judges 10:6–12:7 holds together as a single narrative constructed of several interconnected episodes. The initial narrative problem is Israel's

---

1. Unless specified otherwise, all translations are mine.

abandonment of YHWH and YHWH's resulting anger. Divine anger leads to oppression and invasion by the Ammonites, the overarching narrative crisis about which the reader is repeatedly reminded (10:7, 9, 17; 11:4). YHWH shockingly announces that deliverance of Israel will no longer take place (10:13). Even after Israel repents, YHWH's willingness to deliver them remains uncertain. Judges 10:16 describes only YHWH's internal state of mind (and does so in ambiguous language), so that at the level of the story characters, the problem of divine anger remains unresolved.[2]

The first attempt to undo the invasion crisis leads to a subplot involving the search for a leader (10:18). This is blocked by various difficulties in installing Jephthah until resolution is reached with 11:11. The next subplot has to do with Jephthah's failed attempt to use diplomacy to resolve the invasion crisis, bracketed by the resumptive repetition of 11:12 and 28 (וישלח, "and [Jephthah] sent"; and אשר שלח, "that he sent").

Finally, the main plot resumes as YHWH's spirit comes on Jephthah (in reaction to the failure of diplomacy), and he moves against the enemy (11:29, continued by vv. 32–33). But this main plotline is briefly sidetracked when yet another narrative problem is introduced in the shape of his vow in 11:30–31. This detour raises reader tension to a high pitch. How will this vow, which is so obviously fraught with danger, work out? The main plot action then resumes, and Jephthah's victory sorts out the main crisis (11:32–33). The vow subplot reaches a climax in the revelation scene of 11:34–35, followed by the denouement of 11:36–38. The vow subplot is resolved when 11:39a describes the daughter's fate in as euphemistic a way as possible, but by referring directly back to the vow, communicates that she was indeed sacrificed. The tragedy is underscored in 11:39b, which reemphasizes that she never had intercourse with a man. Judges 11:40 moderates matters somewhat by describing a ceremony performed annually by the daughters of Israel.

The Daughters of Shiloh

Judges 21 recounts how an oath sworn by the men of Israel concerning their daughters resulted in a brutal misuse of the practice of חרם,

---

2. Is YHWH no longer able to bear to see Israel suffer (NRSV), or is YHWH impatient with the trouble Israel was causing?

ḥērem, followed by a scheme to undermine the authority of the fathers (and brothers) of the daughters of Shiloh. Judges 21:1–5 serves as exposition, introducing location, the active characters, and the narrative problem of how to provide wives for the surviving warriors of Benjamin. This problem has stemmed from disproportionate violence directed against the civilian population of Benjamin (20:48), compounded by a foolish oath only revealed to the reader by 21:1 and later referred to in 21:7 and 18.

> Now the men of Israel had taken an oath at Mizpah, saying, "None of us will give his daughter as wife to Benjamin." (21:1)

This is a classic example of delayed exposition in that a prohibition of marriage had not been mentioned before. The characters in the story consider their oath to be unbreakable (as do Jephthah and his daughter with respect to his vow).

The narrative problem comes to the fore when the rest of Israel realizes that Benjamin is doomed to extinction (21:2–3), and repetition emphasizes this concern (21:6–7, 15–17). Israel's belated, tearful realization is not unlike Jephthah's anguished discovery of the consequences of his vow. However, a *second* oath revealed only in 21:5 (again through delayed exposition) provides a twisted sort of way to solve the problem the first oath has created. A warped application of חרם-slaughter against Jabesh-gilead provides virgin brides for Benjamin.

This first-stage solution proves to be insufficient (21:14b). The narrative problem persists, and further resolution must be sought. The narrator's observation in 21:15 that YHWH(!) had made a gap in the tribes of Israel moves the story on to the next phase. The second plan is devised by the *elders of the congregation* rather than by the entire assembly, perhaps because success requires secrecy. This plan of ambush (21:20–21) directs the Benjaminites to hide in the vineyards, suggesting that the dancing is part of a vintage celebration, a time when social constraints are relaxed (cf. Ruth 3). The kidnappers are to head directly back to Benjaminite territory, avoiding predictable paternal outrage.

Judges 21:22 describes a subordinate scheme intended to deal with the male protectors of the captured women. Outraged fathers and brothers are to be told that it will be best if they do not insist on normal marriage processes, but rather passively accept these marriages by capture and subordinate themselves to larger community interests.

> When their fathers or brothers come out to complain to us, we shall say
> to them, "Be generous to them for our sake, because we could not take
> a wife for any of them in battle and because you for your part could not
> give wives to them at this time without incurring guilt."

To avoid the peril of a broken oath and a lethal curse, the plot resolution
must avoid any action on the part of fathers to *give daughters as wives*
(21:1, 7, 18). The situation for the fathers and brothers of the daughters
of Shiloh is perilous. By not taking action to protect the young women,
are they in effect giving those daughters to Benjamin? Judges 21:22 provides a legalistic way out. The curse does not apply. We Israelites for our
part did not *take* enough wives in military action, and *you* (emphatic
pronoun) fathers and brothers did not actually *give* your daughters. You
did not do anything of your own accord, so you are innocent of the curse.
Equal to their own number in 21:23 signals a complete resolution of the
narrative problem.

Pledges, Vows, and Oaths

Problematic Commitments

All three of these verbal commitments to act or avoid acting have an open-
ended character. Reflecting this, translations sometimes express indeterminacy by using "whoever" (e.g., 1:12; 11:31 NRSV). Caleb's open-ended
announcement is problematic. What if someone from a non-Israelite
group or a clan not in harmony with Caleb's family were to conquer Debir?
Jephthah's vow is notoriously reckless and dangerously open-ended,
pledging the sacrifice of "the coming out one that comes out of the doors
of my house" (11:31). Many interpreters believe that Jephthah's wording
allows for him to mean either a person or an animal kept in the house.
Some translators acknowledge this possibility by using "whatever" rather
than "whoever" (ESV, NIV). But what would Jephthah do if this turned
out to be an animal unclean for sacrifice like a dog or a donkey? The reader
may hope that a domestic animal may come out, but cannot overlook the
much greater likelihood that this would be a human being, and most likely
a woman greeting the returned hero (Exod 15:20–21; Jer 31:4; 1 Sam 18:6–
7; Ps 68:26).
The open-ended nature of the first oath taken at Mizpah (21:1, 7,
18) led to unforeseen consequences when the victory reported in 20:48

resulted in a complete massacre of Benjaminite wives and other women available for marriage. Now no father could voluntarily *give* a daughter to one of the warriors left to Benjamin. Moreover, the second oath taken at Mizpah (21:5) also turned out to have an unforeseen outcome. Clearly intended to maximize the response rate for the muster against Benjamin, in the end it unexpectedly provided a partial solution to the problem created by the first oath.

Caleb's Promise

Caleb's pledge or offer is less formal than either a vow or an oath, but is a specific promise that he could hardly fail to honor. An anticipatory clause or protasis (אשר and imperfect followed by *waw*-consecutive perfect) is followed by a main clause (apodosis) using a first-person *waw*-consecutive perfect. The protasis functions as a condition (e.g., Exod 21:13), and the apodosis describes what will happen for the person who fulfills that condition. Similar positive pledges are Judg 14:12 (Samson's riddle) and 1 Chr 11:6 (David and Joab). Saul in 1 Sam 11:7 incorporates a negative promise, that is to say a threat. Caleb's promise is an obligation he lays on himself, but it is not a vow or oath. A *vow* is offered to God to motivate the deity's behavior; Caleb's pledge operates entirely on the human level. An *oath* involves a potential self-imprecation if the promised behavior is not fulfilled. In contrast, it is the public character of Caleb's pledge that requires it to be kept, in order to avoid shame and community censure. Such a promise must be a somewhat public statement so that it can advertise for candidates to fulfill the protasis.

Jephthah's Vow

Jephthah instead vows a formal vow to YHWH. A vow may be understood as an emphatic prayer for a specified divine response involving a particular form of self-obligation. The one who vows voluntarily commits to give something to God or do something for God if the deity fulfills a set condition. The verb נתן ("give") is commonly used, implying a sort of mutual transaction. This verb may appear either in the condition (as in the Jephthah example; Gen 28:20; Num 21:2; 1 Sam 1:11) or in the pledge (Gen 28:22; 1 Sam 1:11). What the one vowing promises to do or deliver varies widely: to consider YHWH as one's personal God and pay a tithe (Gen 28:21–22), to devote cities to destruction (Num 21:2), to give over a person to temple service (1 Sam 1:11), or to worship YHWH (2 Sam 15:8). The content of the vow may be a sacrifice, including a burnt offering (Ps 66:13). In a vow, the protasis is addressed to YHWH, stating a condition expressed by אם, "if," (Gen 28:20; Num 21:1; 1 Sam 1:11; 2 Sam 15:8). The promised behavior is signaled by a *waw*-consecutive perfect (והיה, "and it will be"; Gen 28:21–22; Num 21:2; 1 Sam 1:11; 2 Sam 15:8).[3]

Jephthah's vow is rhetorically complex. Some suggest that this complexity is a representation of Jephthah's uncertainty or emotional stress.

> If you really will give the Ammonites into my hand, then no matter what comes out of the doors of my house to meet me when I return safe and sound from the Ammonites, shall belong to YHWH and I will offer that one as a burnt offering. (Judg 11:30–31)

The condition to be fulfilled in the protasis is two-fold: victory and safe return. What Jephthah vows requires not just victory, but that he return safely. This is logical in that the identity of the one coming out of the door can only be known if Jephthah comes back home. Similarly, the apodosis consists of a double promise. Someone (or something) will both belong to YHWH and also be offered as a whole burnt offering. The emerging greeter will not merely be YHWH's possession, as a sanctuary slave or dedicated person might be. This apodosis begins with the standard *waw*-consecutive perfect והיה ("shall [belong to YHWH]") and then a second *waw*-consecutive perfect ("I will offer"). Perhaps the second outcome is intended to be seen as a result of the first (cf. NRSV, "shall be the LORD's, to be offered up").

The Oath at Mizpah

The assembled Israelites swore an *oath* at Mizpah of Benjamin. Oaths and vows are different categories of self-obligation.[4] A vow is addressed to God, both as the one who may fulfill the stated condition and the potential recipient of what is vowed. In contrast, in an oath, a person or persons put themselves under a potential threat if the oath is breached. God may serve as a witness or guarantor of an oath, but is not a beneficiary of anything to

---

3. Otto Kaiser, "נָדַר," *TDOT* 9:242–55; Micha Roi, "Conditional Vows—Where They Are Made and Paid," *BN* 167 (2015): 3–24.

4. Ingo Kottsieper, "שָׁבַע," *TDOT* 14:311–36.

be received. Oaths contain an element of self-imprecation, but the dangerous specifics of this element are commonly suppressed. Judges 21 contains
the standard vocabulary of oath taking. The *niphal* verb שבע appears in
21:1, 7, 18, and the noun שבועה in 21:5. The content of the oath about
marriage is described in 21:1 and 7, and in 21:18 the imprecatory formula
of cursing (with ארור) is cited in direct discourse. Saul's oath in 1 Sam
14 provides a close narrative parallel. It also utilizes the category of curse
(14:24, 28) to proscribe an action. In Judges the people evidently consider
their oath to be irrevocable, but in 1 Samuel the community manages to
ransom Jonathan (14:44–45). The second oath, cited in Judg 21:5, is said
to be a *great oath* and involves laying the apodictic death formula (מות
יומת) on violators. This language implicitly justified the חרם slaughter of
the inhabitants of Jabesh-gilead (cf. Lev 27:28–29).

Rhetoric

Achsah

The relationship between fathers and daughters in these three narratives revolves around the verb נתן ("give"). In Judg 21, נתן appears for the
act of providing in marriage in 21:1, 7, and 18 (twice) with reference to
"daughter" and in 21:14 and 22 with "women" or an equivalent pronoun
as direct object. The condition of Jephthah's vow and YHWH's fulfillment
of it is based on God's act of giving (נתן) the enemy into Jephthah's hand
(11:30,32). Achsah's subservient social position is signaled by the notion of
giving (1:12, 13, and 15), but through skillful speech she is able to flip this
around to her benefit. The narrative exhibits a balanced structure based
on Caleb's acts of giving, using the verb נתן except in the first part of 1:15a:

> I will give him Achsah my daughter as wife (1:12b)
> He gave him Achsah his daughter as wife (1:13b)
> "Give [impv. of יהב] me a blessing (1:15aα)
> Because as Negev land you gave me (1:15aα)
> So give me a bowl of water" (1:15aβ)
> Caleb gave her the upper pool and the lower pool (1:15b)

The transition from 1:14a to 1:14b–15 is shockingly abrupt, perhaps communicating Achsah's strength of purpose and role as true protagonist. This
awkward text most likely conveys the idea that Achsah first urged her new

husband Othniel to ask Caleb for a field but then in a subsequent action requested a water source from her father in 1:15. It is possible, however, to construe Achsah as the subject of the infinite construct לשאול ("to ask") and translate 1:14a as "she persuaded him [referring to Caleb] by asking from her father." This would indicate that Achsah came to her father at the beginning of 1:14aα, not to her new husband.

Achsah's unexpected donkey is a rhetorical signal of assertiveness. The key is 1 Sam 25:18–35. In a moment of crisis, Abigail rides a donkey to make her case to David and deliver a request (25:20, 23). She hurries to dismount to make her appeal, and David grants her petition. Later, Abigail again hurries to ride off again on her donkey to become David's bride (25:42). Early readers would understand that Achsah's dismount from her donkey points to the end of a determined, resolute, goal-directed journey. She does not engage in negotiations from the back of her animal, but dismounts to show appropriate respect for Caleb as her father and social superior.

Achsah moves from a passive to an active role. In 1:12–13 she is the object of actions proposed and carried out by her father. She is an object of her father's patriarchal privilege and male patterns of land ownership. Her first action in 1:14a (apparently) reveals deference to her new husband. However, after that she becomes strikingly assertive and speaks with rhetorical skill. She now becomes the grammatical subject: she *urged* … she *dismounted* … she *said*, pushing the envelope of the father-daughter relationship to get what she wants.

Jephthah and His Daughter

Context

The rhetoric of the Jephthah narrative guides readers to consider his vow in light of his situation as Israel's leader and the military situation. The vow comes near the end of a long discourse that begins with Israel's apostasy with alien gods (10:6) and uncertainty concerning YHWH's willingness to deliver Israel (10:11–13, 16). The reader is likely to find the motivation for Jephthah's vow in the ambiguity about whether he can actually expect victory. He never receives the usual promise from YHWH that the enemy will be given into his hand (contrast 3:28; 4:7, 14; 7:7, 9, 15) and therefore must include exactly this language in his vow ("if you really will give the Ammonites into my hand"). In contrast to the other military judges, YHWH does not send or raise up Jephthah. Moreover, the larger context of Israel's acceptance of foreign religious behavior is evoked by the willingness of both Jephthah and his daughter to engage in or consent to human sacrifice.[5]

Jephthah speaks his vow soon after the notice that YHWH's spirit has come upon him (11:29a; cf. Othniel, Gideon, and Samson). Is this a rhetorical indication that he is being obtuse or inexplicably faithless or even that YHWH is inspiring the vow? Actually, the syntactical structure of 11:29–31 links the arrival of the spirit, not to the vow, but to the negative response of the king of the Ammonites in 11:28 and to Jephthah's military maneuvers. The *waw*-consecutive imperfect beginning at 11:29 points back to the previous failed negotiations. The king does not listen; then the spirit comes. The spirit's advent comes as YHWH's response to the declaration "let YHWH the Judge decide" in 11:27. The vow is separated from the spirit by Jephthah's multistage journey in 11:29aβ–b: ויעבר ... ויעבר ... עבר, "and he passed through … and he passed through … he passed through." This campaign itinerary is continued directly by 11:32–33, so that the vow incident of 11:30–31 is bracketed off and distanced from the arrival of YHWH's spirit by a resumptive repetition between 11:29b and 11:32a: עבר בני עמון [pf.], "he passed on to the Ammonites," ויעבר אל בני עמון [*waw*-consecutive imperfect], "he passed on to the Ammonites." This *Wiederaufnahme* highlights the act of vowing and the content of the vow, but also sets it firmly into and subordinates it to Jephthah's movement toward the enemy.

It is possible to understand Jephthah's vow as a sort of cunning ruse motivated by a crisis of military danger, failed negotiations, and lack of confidence about YHWH's willingness to save. Readers might see the open-ended vow as a sort of negotiating technique in that it actually leaves the choice of victim up to YHWH. YHWH can choose what sacrifice YHWH thinks is fitting: animal, human, or even daughter! Jephthah's fate (and that of his daughter) is in YHWH's hands.[6] If nothing else, Jephthah's vow shows that he believes that sacral war victory is the sole provenance of YHWH.[7]

---

5. Robin Baker, "Double Trouble: Counting the Cost of Jephthah," *JBL* 137 (2018): 41–43.

6. Hans-Dieter Neef, "Jephta und seine Töchter (Jdc. xi 29–40)," *VT* 49 (1999): 216.

7. Jephthah might have been seen as a positive figure by traditionalist readers accepting of human sacrifice; Alice Logan, "Rehabilitating Jephthah," *JBL* 128 (2009): 665–85.

Syntactical Analysis

Several features strengthen the internal unity of the vow episode. For example, יצא ("go out") is used in 11:31 (twice), 34, and 36; and שוב ("return") is used in 11:31, 35, and 39. A *Wiederaufnahme* bracket is created by 11:30 ("he vowed a vow") and 11:39a ("the vow he had vowed"), exhibiting a characteristic verb and subject reversal (וידר ... נדר and את נדרו אשר נדר). This makes the vow story stand out from its larger narrative context, thereby stressing its importance. It also sets off 11:39b–40 from the core of the vow story as a persuasive appendix, underscoring the tragedy by repeating the fact of virginity with language stronger than that of 11:37–38 (cf. 21:12) and supporting the veracity of the story by means of an etiology.

The point of view of the Jephthah story is that of an omniscient narrator until the הנה ("behold") of 11:34 briefly shifts the narrative to depict matters though Jephthah's eyes and highlights the description of his emotional reaction in 11:35. The narrative is marked throughout by Jephthah's repeated speech acts designated by ויאמר ("and he said": 11:7, 9, 30, 35, 38). After his vow, Jephthah continues to be main character as 11:32–33 carry on the actions of 11:29b. However, his daughter is then introduced as a new character by the piled up circumstantial clauses of 11:34: "his daughter coming out, she his only child" and "there was no other son or daughter." Jephthah's domination as speaker (ויאמר) is interrupted by two speech acts by the daughter (ותאמר) in 11:36 and 37. When he then speaks for the last time, he responds to her request with only a single word: "Go." The center of gravity has shifted from father to daughter.

Syntactical analysis indicates that, when interrupted, the foregrounded main narrative line is repeatedly resumed by *waw*-consecutive imperfects of "to be." This main line consists of the *waw*-consecutives of 11:29 (introduced by ותהי), 30, 32–33, the first four words of 11:34, 35 (introduced by ויהי), and 39a (introduced by ויהי) where daughter and Jephthah share the role of grammatical subject. This main line is interrupted at three points by "off line" material in the remaining words of 11:34, 36–38, and 39b, in which the daughter is the dominant topic. This analysis shows that the narrative's emphasis shifts from Jephthah to his daughter.[8]

---

8. Klaas Spronk, "Judging Jephthah: The Contribution of Syntactic Analysis to the Interpretation of Judges 11:29–40," in *Tradition and Innovation in Biblical Interpretation:*

Surprise

The text inculcates reader tension about the identity of the victim of Jephthah's vow so that the appearance of his daughter is a surprise. The reader is likely to presume that a human is meant, but the advent of an animal would probably remain as a background possibility. The expression "go out to meet" (יצא plus לקראת, 11:31, 34) can be used for both humans and animals (Job 39:21). The vow uses the default masculine gender to avoid prematurely signaling the outcome. "Will belong to YHWH" is an unusual way of referring to a burnt offering, and could suggest to the reader that there might be some doubt about what will happen to the one who will come out. Yet this phrase also seems to signal that a human being is meant (Num 3:12; Jer 24:7; Mal 3:17). Tension is created in that the culturally competent reader is likely to expect a woman, but would also know that giving up one's child as a gift of the utmost value is the proper form for human sacrifice. But until 11:34, the reader does not even know that Jephthah has a daughter or only one child, something emphasized by repetitive grammar ("only child, neither son nor daughter").

Distancing

Efforts are made to insulate the reader from the horror of human sacrifice. The nonspecific language of "do to me" and "he did to her" in 11:36 and 39 avoids brutal details. Similarly, any mention of a reaction on the part of YHWH (indignation? acceptance?) is suppressed. Nevertheless, although the Iron Age reader might be outraged that the young woman was slaughtered and her whole body incinerated, this would not have been something completely outside the realm of expectation (2 Kgs 16:3; 21:6; Mic 6:7). Second Kings 3:27 has exactly the same syntax as Judg 11:31bβ. Giving Jephthah a chance to grant his daughter's wish and citing the ceremony through which her story is commemorated somewhat ameliorate readers' horror. By describing the annual festival that emerges, the text provides communal meaning for the sacrifice and a sense of orderliness or closure.

Studies Presented to Professor Eep Talstra on the Occasion of His Sixty-Fifth Birthday, ed. Wido Th. van Peursen and Janet Dyk, SSN 57 (Leiden: Brill, 2011), 299–315.

Emotions and Responsibility

The emotional load of the encounter scene is intense. Happiness and honor ("come out to meet" and "tambourines and dances") collide directly with anguish ("tore his clothes" and "alas, my daughter"). Jephthah's two "you" statements in 11:35 sound like accusations in our ears, sensitive to the penchant for blaming the victim. Certainly, the dreadfulness of his position is emphasized, and the verbal root כרא ("driven to one's knees") is bought into coordination with עכר ("to trouble, thwart achievement of a goal") by means of alliterative wordplay (בראותו ... ויקרע ... הכרע הבראעתני ... בעכרי ...).

Then again, Jephthah recognizes that his behavior is the ultimate causative factor in this tragedy. In 11:35aβ–bα, the subject pronouns are emphatic and make a balanced contrastive statement: "you [for your part] have driven me to my knees and you have become ... I [for my part] have opened my mouth." In other words, he acknowledges his fault with his emphatic first-person pronouns, and declares what his vow has caused her to become. Verse 35aβ ought to be translated "you have become one of my troublers." This expression focuses on her status as troubler, not on her troubling actions.[9] Nevertheless, his statement mentions her involvement first in the sentence and in so doing seems to deemphasize his own fault.

By using the intense verb פצה rather than the more neutral and usual פתח for the act of opening his mouth, Jephthah seems to point to the thoughtlessness or folly of his vow and implies self-criticism. Psalms 22:14; 66:14; Job 35:16; and Lam 2:16 suggest connotations for פצה corresponding to "open wide" or "tear open." His words were too quick, too unrestrained. Perhaps a good contemporary translation would be "I shot off my mouth." In her reply in 11:36, his daughter passes over his comments emphasizing his heart-rending predicament and her role in causing it, and repeats only his rash act of shooting off his mouth. In doing this, she shows that she is no mere pushover or passive victim, but already is seizing some independent agency in the situation.

---

9. NABRE "brought calamity upon me" and NIV "made me miserable and wretched" are overly negative. NJB is more accurate, "You have joined those who bring misery into my life!"

The Daughters of Shiloh

The narratives about obtaining wives for the remnant of Benjamin form
two balanced paragraphs (21:1–14 and 15–24) recounting two successive
solutions to the narrative problem. Judges 21:1 and 15 serve as paragraph
markers, each beginning with a disjunctive *waw* plus grammatical subject
followed by a perfect verb. The chapter is held together by a repetition of
themes, among which are oath (21:1, 5, 7, 18), wives and virgins (21:1, 7,
12, 14, 16, 18, 21–23), Benjamin's plight (21:3, 6, 15, 16), and inheritance
(21:17, 23, 24). The two incidents are told entirely from the perspective of
the warriors and elders of Israel, the deprived Benjaminites, and the male
relatives of the young women, but never from that of the women themselves. Even though the earliest readers of Judges were used to marriages
that did not involve the bride's completely voluntary participation, the
rhetoric of the narrative instills a sense of outrage in harmony with the
overall context of the last chapters of Judges. The surviving young women
of Jabesh-gilead suffer the loss of their entire family structure. The verb חטף
("abduct") has violent connotations (21:21; Ps 10:9; *HALOT*, 307), and this
is also true of גזל ("seize") in 21:23 ("snatch away by force, rob," Gen 31:31;
HALOT, 186). The two atrocities are rationalized by means of transparently
casuistic interpretations of, first, the custom of חרם (21:10–11) and then
the precise wording of the Mizpah oath. The language used by Israel and
its elders obscures their moral responsibility. They speak of the slaughter
of Benjamin in the distancing passive voice (21:6, 16, 17), and the narrator
even fixes responsibility for it on YHWH (21:15). The directions to Shiloh,
perplexingly given to Benjamin in 21:19, have a similar distancing effect.
Although Benjamin has just received its first installment of wives there
(21:12, 14), Shiloh is treated as though it were "offstage," as a little-known
place where the atrocity of kidnapping could be acceptable. The repetition
of נחלה ("inheritance") in 21:23 and 24, first for Benjamin and then for
Israel, signals that the narrative problem has been solved and indicates that
the contending parties have returned to unity and integration.

Themes and Topics

Fathers and Daughters

That the women involved in these stories are daughters is specified in 1:12,
13; 11:34 (twice), 35, 40; and 21:1, 7, 18. Young women gathered for a

communal action are designated "daughters" in the sense of young women belonging to a group or locality in 11:40 (of Israel) and 21:21 (of Shiloh). The one who determines their fate is explicitly designated as "father" in each narrative as well (1:14; 11:36, 37, 39; 21:22). In the Achsah and wives for Benjamin narratives the father arranges for or accedes to marriage. Jephthah's role as father is defined by his relationship to his daughter and her actions with respect to him (11:36, 37, 39). She addresses him as "my father," speaks to him to make a request, and returns to him of her own accord. "My father" is an address of respect, if not affection (11:36; Gen 48:18; 1 Sam 24:11; 2 Kgs 13:14), and the same is true of "my daughter" (11:35; Ruth 3:1, 10). Achsah signals her respect for her father by descending from her donkey. Both Caleb and Jephthah respond positively to an assertive entreaty by their daughter.

Nathan's parable in 2 Sam 12 reflects what ancient readers would recognize as a father's affection and attachment to a beloved daughter. But it is telling that the parable equates daughters and pet lambs (12:3). Like a domestic animal, the daughter falls under the patriarchal authority of the father's house. This cultural reality is reflected in Jephthah's vow of a domestic entity, daughter or animal, from "my house" over which he has life and death control.

The most basic relationship between fathers and daughters in Judg 1 and 21 centers on giving in marriage (1:12–13, 15; 21:1, 7, 18, 22). This is the heart of the problem facing the fathers and brothers of the Shiloh women. The fathers would be dishonored and suffer financially because these marriages are bypassing the usual negotiations over bride price. Brothers are protectors of their unmarried sisters (Song 8:8–9).

Much of the narrative interest in the Jephthah and Shiloh stories derive from conflicting responsibilities. Jephthah faces a conflict of duties between his role as leader and his role as father. The fathers and brothers of Shiloh's marriageable young women are urged to subordinate their responsibilities and desires to larger community interests.

Achsah and Jephthah's daughter exercise what today we call agency. Achsah uses her verbal skills to get what she deserves, namely, not to be treated as dry Negev land. Jephthah's daughter may seem to be merely a passive victim as she speaks in Judg 11:36, but the reality is that she chooses to support her father in what she thinks he has to do as Israel's leader. She is not forced to return, but comes back willingly. The seemingly extraneous notice in 11:39b that she had never had sexual intercourse with a man may communicate that during her time without paternal supervision she had not done anything to undermine her virgin status. The triumphal context of Judg 5:11 indicates that the verb תנה in 11:40aβ does not really imply "lament" (as NRSV) but "recount in an antiphonal performance" (*HALOT*, 1759–60). The ritual to honor her did not grieve over her victimhood, but celebrated her boldness.

Wise and Persuasive Speech

Wisdom was concerned with the danger of thoughtless vows (Qoh 5:3–5; Prov 20:25). Both Judg 11 and 21 can be read as example stories that warn against foolish vows and oaths.

Achsah engages in the verbal skill that the wisdom movement promoted (e.g., Prov 16:23; 22:11). Her request for a blessing involves indirect wordplay in that "blessing" (בְּרָכָה) sounds much like "pool" (בְּרֵכָה), though the latter word is not actually used in the story itself. She asks ambiguously for "a bowl of water" (as though to drink?), contrasting with the arid implications of *Negev*. She contends that she has been treated poorly by her father, and her strategy works. She asks for one bowl of water but ends up with two pools. Her rhetoric is richly effective.

Jephthah's daughter also exhibits verbal wisdom. In 11:36 she picks up and reflects his own words about his *mouth* ("you have opened your mouth … what has gone out of your mouth") in her insistence that he cannot go back on his vow. Her father's original purpose or intention does not matter, only the raw fact of what came out of his wide-open mouth. She accepts her fate with a balanced statement. "Do to me" (עשה לי) is the appropriate correlative to what YHWH has done for her father (עשה לך). This is the wise person's recognition of the balance between act and consequence.

The argument that the elders of Israel plan to use in 21:22 to persuade the fathers of Shiloh to abandon their rights uses the strategies of wise speech to convince them. There is an appeal to group solidarity (NJPS, "be generous to them for our sake"; NIV, "do us a kindness by helping them"). A careful parsing of the words of the oath and the realities of the situation is set forth in a balanced equation ("we could not take … you could not give").

Descendants and Inheritance

The issue of patrimony and progeny materializes in the Jephthah and Benjamin narratives. Concern for the heritage of Benjamin permeates the latter: weeping (21:2), "one tribe" missing or cut off (21:3, 6), and compassion (21:15). The narrative problem, "What shall we do for wives for the ones left?," is repeated word-for-word in 21:7 and 16. Resolution of the problem means restoration of Benjamin's possession (ירשה, 21:17) and inheritance (נחלה, 21:23).

Rhetoric surrounding the sacrifice of Jephthah's daughter communicates the fall of his house and termination of his line of descent. There is most likely an intentional intertextual allusion in 11:34–36 to Abraham's aborted sacrifice of his beloved heir (יחידה to יחיד, Gen 22:2, 12, 16; "my daughter" to "my son," 22:7, 8; "my father," 22:7). Israel's classical story of duty to God and paternal sacrifice is inverted. Abraham chose the path of faithful obedience to God and Isaac was rescued. Jephthah chose to obey his vow, but his daughter was not saved. Unlike Abraham, Jephthah's future life through her potential children was extinguished and his family line became extinct. That she was his only daughter and never had the chance to conceive is emphasized by overfull, repeated language (11:34, 39b) and by weeping (11:37, 38). The narrative also plays out under the shadow of Jephthah's problematic parentage and loss of inheritance (11:1–2, 7). The fulfillment of his vow is staged at his "house," perhaps a subtle allusion to the theme of progeny and inheritance (11:31, 34; cf. "father's house" in 11:2, 7). The term "the Gileadite" brackets his biography (11:1, 40; 12:7), surrounding the whole textual unit with the topic of family and lineage and calling attention to his irregular status as Gilead's unvalued son.

A comparison of 12:7 with five similar formulas in 10:1–5 and 12:8–15 shows that Jephthah was part of an earlier source list that catalogued the tenure, achievements, and burial location for six clan worthies, the so-called minor judges. Jephthah's lack of future offspring is highlighted by contrast with the fruitfulness and family prosperity of those figures who bracket his story. Jair, Ibzan, and Abdon have numerous offspring. The enumeration of their descendants increases from thirty (Jair) to sixty (Ibzan) to seventy (Abdon). In contrast Jephthah has but one daughter and she dies childless. Of the six, his tenure of six years is the shortest.

Overall Rhetorical Impact

The evaluative arc of Judges traces a downward track. The leadership qualities and personal characters of the judges deteriorate from successful Othniel through hesitant and vengeful Gideon to inept Samson. The three narratives discussed here trace this downhill path, although the

assertive agency claimed by Achsah and Jephthah's daughter moderate
the downward spiral to a degree. Caleb may give Achsah away carelessly
and without sufficient dowry, but she assertively gets the water sources she
wants, negotiating by means of effective rhetoric. Jephthah's ambiguous
leadership qualities continue Gideon's insecurity (6:17, 36–40), and his
rash vow prepares for Samson's impetuous words and actions. Nevertheless, his daughter stands up for the religious and social principles of Israel,
addresses her father with proper respect, and secures a delay in order to
observe the tragedy of her fate in a socially constructive way.

Israel's fidelity to YHWH reaches its nadir in Judg 17–21. The fathers
of Israel swear a communal oath about their daughters that would lead to
the extinction of a brother tribe and the alienation of their heritage. By
perverting the custom of sacral warfare, women who seem to be valued
primarily for being virgins are deprived of their families and taken as
wives, without the consent of their slaughtered fathers. Then a kidnapping
scheme tramples on the rights of fathers to give daughters in marriage and
of brothers to protect their sisters.

Achsah was able to leverage the father-daughter relationship into
a blessing for herself. Faced with the consequences of her father's vow,
Jephthah's daughter was able to preserve some positive elements of the
father-daughter relationship and wrest from it something at least for herself. But as the book of Judges finishes in chaos, the father-daughter relationship is treated with contempt. Prospects for a marriage close to home
and family for hundreds of young women are sacrificed to achieve the
reintegration of Benjamin.

10

A Mother's Womb:
The Collision of Politics and the Home in Judges 13

Jennifer J. Williams

Motherhood in the biblical text is typically understood as a joyous event, and the frequent theme of women's barrenness heightens the sense of celebration when a child is conceived. Once-barren mothers are read as elated to conceive and bear children, especially as many of these women bear sons who shape Israel's future. However, a closer reading of Judg 13 and Manoah's wife's response to the envoy's message suggest alternatives to this maternal enthusiasm. Why is there this ambivalence to an otherwise joyous occasion? Answering this question will help us understand broader themes involving women's roles, liminality, and unhomeliness throughout the book of Judges. Specifically, the ambivalence in Manoah's wife's response to her conception of Samson reflects larger narratival ambivalence about the Lord's role in the book of Judges, namely, through the invasion of politics into domestic spaces.

In this essay, I will first examine the discrepancies between the messenger's announcement and the woman's reiteration of the message and how the digressions serve as a vehicle for highlighting the ambivalence in the narrative. I will then consider fertility and liminality and how Manoah's wife is the perfect person to experience and reflect such ambivalence; her liminality marks her with ambiguity and makes her more receptive to a divine encounter. Finally, I will explain the concept of unhomeliness and the discomfort of blurred boundaries when the woman's womb bears Samson, a public and political Israelite leader.

The Testimony of the Woman and the Envoy's Message

Manoah's wife's story accords with the narratives of many other barren (עקרה) women who receive an announcement that they will miraculously bear a son. Her tale resonates specifically with that of Rebekah in Gen 25 and Hannah in 1 Sam 1 and the divine involvement in conception.[1] As in the story of Samson and his mother, Hannah's son will be dedicated to the Lord and forbidden the use of a razor (1 Sam 1:11). This mother fits nicely within the other type scenes of special birth narratives.[2] Judges 13:5 contains the birth announcement formula (כי הנך הרה וילדה) that indicates divine intervention and remains almost constant throughout the Hebrew text.[3] In all cases, this announcement concerns the birth of a boy with special quali-fications.[4] Dennis Olson remarks that the "opening episode is saturated with allusions to the wider biblical tradition ... barren mothers, Nazirite vow, angels visiting, wrestling with Jacob, seeing God face to face ... all point to the birth of this son as an extraordinarily momentous event."[5]

There are two announcements of Samson's birth in Judg 13: one from the divine messenger and one from Manoah's wife. The messenger announces the new child and gives the woman instructions in 13:3–5. The divine envoy says,

> Even though you are barren and you have not given birth, you will con-ceive, and you will bear a son. Now, be careful, do not drink wine or strong drink. And do not eat anything unclean. Indeed, you are now pregnant and you are going to bear a son. A razor shall not go upon his head, for the lad will be a Nazirite of God from the womb. He will be the deliverer of Israel from the hand of the Philistines.[6]

After the woman describes the divine messenger and her encounter with him, she repeats the messenger's instructions in 11:6–7, yet she digresses

---

1. Also Sarai in Gen 11:30 and Rachel in Gen 29:31.

2. However, in contrast to these other biblical women, we get surprisingly little background information on Manoah's wife (including the fact that she lacks a name); see J. Cheryl Exum, *Was sagt das Richterbuch den Frauen?*, SBS 169 (Stuttgart: Katholisches Bibelwerk, 1997), 47.

3. Magnus Y. Ottosson, "הָרָה," *TDOT* 3:458–61; see also Gen 16:11; Isa 7:14.

4. Ottosson, "הָרָה," 461.

5. Olson, "The Book of Judges," *NIB* 2:846.

6. All translations are mine, unless otherwise noted.

in important ways. She reports to Manoah, "And he said to me, 'Indeed you are pregnant, and you are going to bear a son. Now do not drink wine or strong drink. And do not eat anything unclean, for a Nazirite of God will be the lad from the womb until the day of his death.'"

The inaccurate report of the divine messenger's missive suggests her ambivalent response to the situation and her son's future. The woman omits and adds certain elements to the divine envoy's pronouncement. Her testimony is accurate, and in the ways that it differs from the messenger's dispatch, it is judicious and even more precise than the messenger's original message. Thus, the woman's digressions from the messenger's announcement are not insignificant.

The woman adds words to the message. While the messenger reports that the lad will be a Nazirite of God "from the womb" (13:5), the woman's account of the message to her husband mentions that the lad will be a Nazirite of God from the womb "until the day of his death" (13:7). The messenger's lack of mention of the child's death does not necessarily mean that this child will be superhuman and immortal. However, the mother's addition of "until the moment of his death" is noteworthy. Her mention of a life from womb to death arguably indicates her understanding, maybe wishful thinking, that the child will be normal and will have a typical life pattern. He will die.[7]

The mother's words simultaneously acknowledge that her son will have an *uncommon* form of Nazirite status. Vows need to have a term of operation, and the mother's words emphasize not only that her son will die, but that this Nazirite vow that binds her son will be in effect throughout his entire life. It is atypical to have a lifetime of Nazirite status. Her words, "until the moment of his death," also note an important juxtaposition concerning the character of Samson. On the one hand, she highlights the way in which his life will be normal (i.e., he will die), but on the other hand, he will be uniquely Nazirite.

The woman also digresses from the messenger's dispatch by omitting key elements. The envoy explains that refraining from using a razor is directly linked to the child being a Nazirite of God from the womb. Manoah's wife makes no mention of a razor to her husband. It is hard to know why the pregnant woman's testimony leaves out this piece of

---

7. She also provides an end time to the Nazirite vow. Nazirite vows are typically taken for a duration of time, not forever, so perhaps the woman can only conceptualize a Nazirite vow if it has an end date; see Num 6.

information in her report. Perhaps the information seems superfluous
because a Nazirite is often known by his long locks. Notably, the woman
links the Nazirite status (not to the razor) but to her addition of the
moment of Samson's death. Thus, by eliminating the important element
of the razor, the woman's words (or lack thereof) provide a noticeable
lacuna to an attentive reader and the addition of something ominous:
death. The absence of mention of the razor becomes the narrative foreshadowing of her son's demise: death because of the razor.[8] It is true, as
Barry Webb suggests, that "certainly she speaks better than she knows."[9]
Her message is prophetic. The mention of a razor does not occur again
until the end of Samson's narrative and life in 16:17. At the end of Samson's story, it becomes apparent that the razor bears much more significance to Samson than simply being part of his Nazirite status; the razor
removes the source of his superhuman strength.

The woman also omits a key element in the envoy's announcement
when she leaves out Samson's public role. The messenger tells her, "He
will be the deliverer of Israel from the hand of the Philistines" (13:5), but
the woman makes no mention of her deliverer son when she speaks to
Manoah. She never addresses the political impact her son will have on
their people. In this way, both the woman's words and narrative repetition
of her restrictions (in 13:4, 7, and 14) divert attention away from the political ramifications of the son and focus instead on personal and domestic concerns. It seems she would *rather* highlight his normal life, even his
death, than his special role as deliverer.

It is striking that when the messenger appears again, and Manoah asks
for instructions, the messenger does not repeat his original announcement
to Manoah's wife, but instead changes the dispatch and in important ways,
more closely follows the woman's version of the announcement. The envoy
instructs in 13:14, "Of all that I said to the woman, let her be careful. Of
all that comes from the grapevine, she may not eat. Wine and strong drink
she may not drink. And all that is unclean she may not eat. All that I commanded let her be careful." So, the messenger's report to Manoah becomes
incomplete, like the wife's message. The messenger leaves out mention of

---

8. Benjamin Johnson, "What Type of Son Is Samson? Reading Judges 13 as a
Biblical Type-Scene," *JETS* 53 (2019): 269–86; and Daniel I. Block, "Echo Narrative
Technique in Hebrew Literature: A Study in Judges 19," *WTJ* 52 (1990): 325–41.

9. Webb, *The Book of Judges: An Integrated Reading*, JSOTSup 46 (Sheffield: JSOT
Press, 1987), 166.

a razor and that the boy will be God's deliverer for Israel. The messenger neither gives her away, nor corrects her, nor indicates that her announcement was incomplete.

In terms of the announcements about and instructions for the coming son, Manoah is predominantly left out. He is not given the message directly while the messenger gives the woman specific instructions that impact what *she* must do to prepare for the son's birth (e.g., refrain from eating and drinking certain things). The man of God repeatedly repositions his message toward the wife, even though the husband insists on knowing about "the regulations of the lad and his work" (משפט הנער ומעשה, 13:12). The messenger evades Manoah's questions and requests and does not give him any new details. Instead, the messenger redirects the conversation to focus solely on the woman and what she must do. This response to Manoah includes an *inclusio*, with the introductory line in 13:13 "Of all that I said to the woman, let her be careful," and the reiteration in 13:14 "All that I commanded her she must keep."

J. Cheryl Exum and Yairah Amit argue that she has a central role and is more favorably pictured than her husband.[10] Following biblical conventions, the narrator has the messenger initially appear to only her (13:3). Then, after Manoah requests that the messenger come to both Manoah and his wife (13:8), the narrator makes a point to indicate that the messenger again only appears to the woman (13:9). This is emphasized in two phrases in 13:9. Although "God heard the appeal of Manoah" (וישמע האלהים בקול

---

10. Exum, "Promise and Fulfillment: Narrative Art in Judges 13," *JBL* 99 (1980): 43–59; and Amit, "Manoah Promptly Followed His Wife" (Judges 13:11): On the Place of the Woman in Birth Narratives," in *A Feminist Companion to Judges*, ed. Athalya Brenner and Lillian R. Klein, FCB 4 (Sheffield: JSOT Press, 1993), 146–56. See also Adele Reinhartz regarding Manoah's wife's centrality and anonymity: "Though defined throughout the passage as Manoah's wife, her words, actions, and interactions both amplify and challenge this mode of identification … her centrality to the passage belies the insignificance implied by her anonymity … by forcing the reader to use 'the wife of Manoah' … anonymity draws attention to the interplay between the wifely role and her narrative portrayal and thereby the uniqueness and individuality which personal identity expresses" (Reinhartz, *Why Ask My Name? Anonymity and Identity in Biblical Narrative* [New York: Oxford University Press, 1998], 12). Esther Fuchs notes that Manoah is the fourth character described and that the wife is the clear protagonist (Fuchs, "The Literary Characterization of Mothers and Sexual Politics in the HB," *Semeia* 46 [1989]: 151–66); see also Michael J. Smith, "The Failure of the Family in Judges, Part 2: Samson," *BSac* 162 (2005): 424–36.

מנוח), the narrator provides that the messenger "came again to the woman" (ויבא מלאך האלהים עוד אל האשה) when she was in the field and then further supplies "but Manoah her husband was not with her" (ומנוח אישה אין עמה). In regard to the birth of the son, the narrative concentration settles chiefly on the anonymous woman.

The Liminality of the Woman

Liminality and Pregnancy

Manoah's wife, who begins the scene barren and ends the narrative pregnant with Samson, is a liminal figure and the perfect candidate for a divine encounter. By liminality, I refer to a transitional period, like pregnancy, that is characterized by ambiguity, openness, and indeterminacy. According to Victor Turner, this is a time removed, even liberated, from "normative constraints" wherein usual self-understanding and behavior are relaxed or shifted.[11] A new way of being becomes possible. Frequently such transitional periods are marked as a rite of passage and indicate social instability from one social or religious state to another. Turner describes the characteristics of liminality as "necessarily ambiguous, since this condition and these people elude or slip through the network of classifications that normally locate states and positions in cultural space. Liminal entities are neither here nor there."[12]

Arnold van Gennep argues that in many cultures pregnancy is recognized as a transitional period. Sometimes there are rites of separation at pregnancy and states of isolation for the woman, either because she is considered dangerous or impure or because her pregnancy puts her in a physiologically and socially abnormal condition. Van Gennep describes the rites associated with pregnancy and childbirth as "actual bridges, chains, or links ... to facilitate the changing condition."[13] Susan Hogan's study on maternity rituals in Britain and Ireland similarly highlights the evaluation of the liminal state of mothers. Mothers giving birth "may be viewed as 'liminal' entities because they straddle the line between purity and pollution; self and other; and

---

11. Turner, *The Ritual Process: Structure and Anti-Structure* (Chicago: Aldine, 1969), 6.

12. Turner, *Ritual Process*, 16.

13. Van Gennep, *The Rites of Passage* (Chicago: University of Chicago Press, 1960), 16, 41, and 47. Not only is pregnancy treated as a liminal period, but there also often exists a transitional period after childbirth (46–47).

indeed life and death."[14] Because of these unclear boundaries, Mary Douglas goes so far as to say that such liminal events and persons can be disturbing or polluting.[15] They create anxiety and might be considered dangerous or ambiguous because they are threatening to established structures.

The woman, whose pregnancy is announced in Judg 13, becomes betwixt and between. This facilitates a sense of ambiguity and discomfort for Manoah and for the reader. Her transitional state specifically threatens male/female power relations.[16] This is clear when Manoah's very first response is to entreat God (13:8) and request that the messenger come again to "us." This potential threat to gendered power relations similarly occurs when the unnamed woman continues to be the recipient of the message. The woman is also the sole human participant in the conception of the child. Further, the special power she carries is also highlighted when she calms her fearful husband in 13:23. Thus, it is in this pregnant and liminal, albeit ambiguous and potentially threatening, state that the woman's true social power is realized; "die Frau ist machtvoll als Mutter des Retters."[17] Finally, the woman's power in her liminality is realized when she takes the liberty to change the divine message. This is perhaps a more precise moment when the woman speaks "better than she knows." The woman's ambivalent response to her pregnancy highlights the narratival ambivalence to the Lord's machinations.

Liminality and Fertility for Divine Purposes

The moment and details of the beginning of the woman's liminal state require scrutiny, as it becomes clear that conception is a divine initiative and not necessarily motivated by human interest.

---

14. Hogan, "Breasts and the Beestings: Rethinking Breast-Feeding Practices, Maternity Rituals, and Maternal Attachment in Britain and Ireland," *Journal of International Women's Studies* 10 (2008): 141–60.

15. Douglas, *Purity and Danger: An Analysis of Concepts of Pollution and Taboo* (New York: Praeger, 1966).

16. Hogan, "Breasts and the Beestings," 141. Hogan writes, "Or if I may put this more crudely, childbirth was, and remains, (perhaps because of its very liminality), a political, and ideological 'hotspot' and a contested site with regards to male/female power relations, and the application of rituals; consequently, every aspect of the management of the event was potentially highly inflammatory, and subject to rival proscriptions."

17. Renate Jost, *Gender, Sexualität, und Macht in der Anthropologie des Richterbuches*, BWANT 9.4 (Stuttgart: Kohlhammer, 2006), 295–303.

Scholars debate the envoy's message to Manoah's wife and if she *is* pregnant or if *she will conceive* at a future point. Scott Ashmon says that she is not pregnant; we need to use the future tense "you will be pregnant" throughout the narrative. This conflicts with Robert Boling and Lillian Klein's translation "you are pregnant" for 13:5.[18] The first announcement by the divine messenger in 13:3 should be read, "Even though you are barren and have not given birth, *you will conceive* and bear a son." However, the envoy announces the woman's state in 13:5 with a different phrase: "Indeed! You are *now* pregnant and are going to bear a son," using the adjective "pregnant" (הרה) and the *qal* perfect consecutive "you will bear." This statement in the present tense "you are now pregnant" might be considered problematic for multiple reasons, resulting in the misuse or misinterpretation of certain words and phrases to avoid discomfort or something seemingly fantastic. But this discomfort and fantasy is precisely the point as it marks the woman's liminal and ambiguous state. In the messenger's announcement, she is not pregnant and then she is!

The phrase "you are pregnant and you are going to bear a son" (כי הנך הרה וילדת בן) is used in Gen 16:11 and in Isa 7:14. In both cases, the phrase reflects a present state. Both narratives require that the women *already* be pregnant. Isaiah 7 is a helpful example as it uses Ahaz's pregnant wife to predict the near future, a future wherein the king of Assyria squelches the Syro-Ephraimite resistance. Isaiah says,

> Look here, see: this young woman is pregnant and will bear a son … and when this child is of the age that he can refuse the evil and chooses the good, the lands of Syria and Ephraim will be forsaken. (Isa 7:14, 16)

Judges 13:5 follows a similar pattern and should reflect a present rather than future state.

---

18. See Ashmon's argument, "Birth Annunciations in the Hebrew Bible and Ancient Near East: A Synchronic and Diachronic Comparison of Their Forms and Functions" (PhD. diss., Hebrew Union College-Jewish Institute of Religion, 2010), 169–70 with n. 196. See Boling, *Judges*, AB 6A (Garden City, NY: Doubleday, 1975), 220; and Klein, *The Triumph of Irony in the Book of Judges*, JSOTSup 68, BLS 14 (Sheffield: Almond Press, 1988), 112–15. As will be discussed, I do not think that Ashmon's argument takes into account the various ways of reading הנה and the particles in 13:3–5 and the fact that there is no indication that "she conceived" later in the narrative. Thus, I support Boling and Klein's translation of the הרה in 13:5, but for slightly different reasons.

The question of Manoah's wife's current or future pregnancy relates to the preceding phrase in 13:5, כי הנך. Translations usually link 13:4 (the prohibitions of drink and food) to 13:5 by translating כי as "for." Bruce Waltke and Michael Patrick O'Connor claim that too often כי gets translated in this logical sense "because of the fact" or the "Biblical English" "for." Waltke and O'Connor state, "This translation is often used where it, and the understanding behind it, are simply wrong, that is, where there is no evident logical link of the clause to what precedes."[19] In the case of Judg 13:5, כי could be used in the emphatic sense "indeed" and thus render the phrase, "Indeed, you are pregnant!" Similarly, adding הנך, an exclamation of immediacy that emphasizes the "here-and-now-ness" of the situation, further supports the emphatic sense of כי over the logical sense.[20] The phrase כי הנך heightens the presentative exclamation, and the phrase is best translated, "Indeed, you are *now* pregnant."

In fact, a case can be made for either the emphatic or the logical use of כי only if the phrase uses the adjective in the present, "you are pregnant." If the logical sense of כי is used, the proscriptions to consume wine and strong drink and unclean food relates specifically to the woman. Do not drink or eat these things "*because* you are pregnant." More than simply relating to her unborn son's Nazirite status, refraining from wine could indicate concern with the woman's liminal state and her physiological health. Regarding the woman's health, ancient Southwest Asian and Egyptian documents inform us about various restrictions on and rituals surrounding diet before giving birth.[21] Refraining from wine could also reflect the special status, specifically through separation and isolation from normal practices, that liminal pregnant women experience. Wine was commonly consumed since water was often contaminated, and wine was also an integral part of social gatherings.[22] The woman's liminal state might make her incapable of participating in certain parts of social life.

The logical sense of כי does not make sense with the future "you will be pregnant" because there are not typically prohibitions to refrain from

---

19. *IBHS*, 665.

20. *IBHS*, 675; and Thomas O. Lambdin, *Introduction to Biblical Hebrew* (New York: Scribner, 1971), 168.

21. See Geraldine Pinch, "Private Life in Ancient Egypt," *CANE* 1:363–81; and Fiorella Imparati, "Private Life among the Hittites," *CANE* 1:571–86.

22. Philip J. King and Lawrence E. Stager, *Life in Biblical Israel*, LAI (Louisville: Westminster John Knox, 2001), 101.

drink when trying to get pregnant. In fact, there is not necessarily a logical link between refraining from drinking wine and strong drink or eating
unclean things and the ability to conceive.

The emphatic and immediate nature of כי הנך is bolstered by the
other particles and phrases used in 13:3–4. הנה נא in 13:3 refers to and
reiterates 13:2 and the statement about the woman's barrenness. This
may fit Thomas O. Lambdin's position that this is a "logical consequence,
either of an immediately preceding statement or the general situation in
which it is uttered."[23] The phrase is also stated in a nonvolitional context.
There is no command that proceeds; the woman is not commanded to
be barren, conceive, or bear. Rather, 13:3 is a statement of fact and what
is about to happen. Thus, "even though" best fits the situation and the
translation for הנה נא, affording the phrase in 13:3, "Even though you
are barren and you have not given birth, you will conceive and bear a
son."[24] The phrase ועתה השמרי נא in 13:4 is a volitional form, telling
the woman what she must do. However, there is a possible temporal
and emphatic use, emphasizing that the woman must do these things
now because of the extraordinary circumstances.[25] "Now be careful" and
avoid certain substances.

The rule of three applies to these particle-filled phrases. כי הנך becomes
the surprising culmination. "Indeed, you are now pregnant!" Reading all
three of these phrases in terms of temporal immediacy (here and now)
and in the emphatic sense heightens the miraculous moment. The perfect
tense of הרה and the emphatic immediacy of כי הנך also makes sense with
the omission of key terms like "he knew" and "she conceived" and the
shock that is conjured in the narrative.

Related to this, there are a few last pieces of evidence that Manoah's
wife is announced as pregnant in 13:5. The announcement that the woman
is pregnant evokes even more fear and discomfort about her liminality
and pregnancy. Manoah's wife's experience does not follow typical biblical birth procedures. When most biblical narratives describe some degree
of the husband's involvement in the process of conception, Manoah has
nothing to do with this pregnancy. Manoah is shocked, and he entreats
God *after* the announcement of her pregnancy and not as a plea to have

---

23. *IBHS*, 578 and 684; Lambdin, *Biblical Hebrew*, 170.

24. See *IBHS*, 579.

25. See *IBHS*, 578–79, 667.

the woman conceive.[26] Importantly, neither Manoah's wife nor Manoah entreat or pray to the Lord for a child. Manoah entreats God to know what to do with the child that has already been announced. There is also no customary announcement *after* the encounter with the angel that Manoah "knew his wife." After Manoah's wife pacifies her husband and convinces him that the Lord will not kill them, the text simply supplies, "And the woman bore a son, and called his name Samson."

The tale also lacks the typical phrase "she conceived," because conception has already happened according to 13:5. Thus, the narrative contains no remembering by or entreating the Lord to become pregnant, no knowing by the husband, and no conceiving. The reader observes no human attempt to acquire a son.[27] This makes the Lord the sole initiator in Samson's conception. God seems to be acting on God's own.[28]

In the Hebrew understanding of conception, God oversees fertility.[29] God is able to close and open wombs. The Hebrew Bible does contain some evidence that the human father contributes, but the texts tend to emphasize above all (or only) God and the mother as vital parts of the life-creating process.[30] The woman's ability to procreate puts her in the "quasi-divine nature of the female," as wombs allude to the chaos waters within, and the waters and children that can overflow from wombs. Such references become like a reenactment of God's creation.[31]

If fertility is a divine enterprise, then it is likely that a divine reason for the fertility precedes. Further, it is clear that in a number of barren women and birth annunciation narratives, the Lord utilizes fertility for the Lord's purposes. Many commentators emphasize God's faithfulness in granting fertility and opening wombs.[32] But fertility, while a blessing, is also a mixed bag. The child is no longer the woman's, perhaps never was and is

---

26. As is typical, Isaac entreats the Lord for his wife because she was barren (Gen 25:21).

27. Johnson, "What Type of Son," 274.

28. Johnson, "What Type of Son," 274.

29. Johanna Steibart, "Human Conception in Antiquity: The Hebrew Bible in Context," *Theology and Sexuality* 16 (2010): 209–27.

30. Steibart, "Human Conception," 220 and 225.

31. Steibart, "Human Conception," 222.

32. Ashmon comments on the wider impetus of conception in Gen 25 and that God answering Isaac's prayer "shows that God faithfully remembers and graciously fulfills God's promise/covenant of many offspring and nations to Abraham, Sarah and Isaac" (*Birth Annunciations*, 167).

subject to God's direction. The biblical writers were primarily interested in how the fruit of the woman's womb contributes to group identity and a larger theological agenda, not the course of a woman's life. Wombs opened by God do not mean autonomous lives for these women and their families. This realization of divine intervention into private lives becomes terrifying at both the levels of character and reader responses.

Unhomeliness: The Perfect Candidate for the Unhomely Invasion

The Public versus Private Dichotomy

In Judges, a flat reading might note that many of the women in Judges occupy and act in domestic and private spaces. However, all of the women's private and domestic maneuvers in the Judges tales have important political and public ramifications. Women in Judges have public influence, yet this is ambiguously presented.

The blurring of the lines between public and private and the response the blurring creates requires analysis.[33] Private, family affairs in Judges are also public; and the private sphere is never safe from invasion by that which is public. It becomes abundantly clear for the reader of Judges that what happens between individual characters and in families reverberates in Israelite communal life and social structures—and this can be a disturbing realization.

---

33. The public/male and private/female spheres is a western construct that needs to be reexamined and problematized; see esp. Karla G. Bohmbach, "Conventions/Contraventions: The Meanings of Public and Private for the Judges 19 Concubine," *JSOT* 24 (1999): 83; and Subha Mukherji, "Introduction," in *Thinking on Thresholds: The Poetics of Transitive Spaces*, ed. Subha Mukherji (London: Anthem, 2013), xvii–xxviii. Consider the discussions in L. J. Nicholson, "Feminist Theory: The Private and the Public," in *Beyond Domination: New Perspectives on Women and Philosophy*, ed. Carol C. Gould (Totowa, NJ: Rowman & Allanheld, 1984), 221–30; A. Yeatman, "Gender and the Differentiation of Social Life into Public and Domestic Domains," *Social Analysis* 15 (1984): 32–49; Janet Sharistanian, "Introduction: Women's Lives in the Public and Domestic Spheres," in *Beyond the Public/Domestic Dichotomy: Contemporary Perspectives on Women's Public Lives*, ed. Janet Sharistanian, Contributions in Women's Studies 78 (Westport, CT: Greenwood, 1987), 1–10; and Sharistanian, "Conclusion: The Public/Domestic Model and the Study of Contemporary Women's Lives," in Sharistanian, *Beyond the Public/Domestic Dichotomy*, 179–84.

A Terrifying Condition

The blending of the public and private spheres, included in the stories of liminal, odd, and subjugated characters, illustrates a strange and disturbing reality within the Judges stories. Homi Bhabha's postcolonial concept of "unhomeliness" provides helpful language and a useful theoretical framework for articulating what the narrator has the characters experience and what brings about a disconcerting sense of the state of things for the intended reader of the book of Judges.

If liminality denotes a temporarily blurred line, a transitional threshold, and a moving to something or becoming something new, then Bhabha's concept of unhomeliness signifies the realization that presupposed domestic and public lines *have* blurred. Liminality references a rite of passage or movement between two spaces or statuses within one culture, and unhomeliness represents the doubling of cultures at once such that the subject is not fully at home in either. Where liminal figures and spaces imply potential threats or danger to the greater community because of the character of their in-betweenness, unhomeliness is a condition experienced by the individual of being caught between two worlds. Bhabha identifies the condition of unhomeliness as an invasion and a blurring of distinctions:

> The recesses of the domestic space become sites for history's most intricate invasions. In that displacement, the borders between home and world become confused; and uncannily, the private and public become part of each other, forcing upon us a vision that is as divided as it is disorienting.[34]

Bhabha focuses primarily on female literary characters in his description of the expression of unhomeliness in literature. This expression is often heard distinctly "in fictions that negotiate the powers of cultural difference in a range of transhistorical sites."[35] For example, unhomeliness is experienced, when Henry James's Isabel Archer, in the *Portrait of a Lady*, takes the measure of her dwelling in a state of "incredulous terror." This is a moment of realization and articulation of everything that should have been secret suddenly coming to light. A boundary has been broken.

---

34. Homi K. Bhabha, *The Location of Culture* (New York: Routledge, 1994), 9.
35. Bhabha, *Location*, 9.

When she brings the public into the private, namely when she makes her domestic space the "perfect cover for gun-running," Aila's reality in *My Son's Story* also displays the condition of unhomeliness.[36] These literary examples illuminate the conflation of a variety of related dichotomous pairs including public versus private spaces, men's work versus women's work, men's spaces versus women's spaces.

The convergence and overlapping of the concepts of liminality and unhomeliness can be observed in Bhabha's work and Supriya Chaudhuri's chapter in *Thinking on Thresholds*, two unrelated pieces that analyze the character of Bimala in *The Home and the World*.[37] According to Bhabha, the experience of unhomeliness is present in Bimala's voice through the transgressing of boundaries. She is "drawn forever from ... the secluded women's quarters ... (and) crosses that fated verandah into the world of public affairs."[38] Chaudhuri reflects on the context of colonial India wherein traditionally the architecture of homes reflects the inner quarters designated for women and outer precincts reserved for men. In a westernizing bourgeois house that suggests the movement toward modern socialization, women move out into public apartments. According to Chaudhuri, the main character, Bimala, displays a liminal emotional state of "not only private desire but public hope" and also through "the nostalgia she expresses at the start of the novel for a lost way of life (and) the urgency with which she embraces a future that is always out of reach." She dwells in a liminal physical state as she inhabits "the boundary between inside and outside." While he does not use Bhabha's language (i.e., experiencing the condition of unhomeliness), Chaudhuri does present Bimala's liminal state as a "transition attended by extreme risk and difficulty" and "marks her with the signs of radical discontent."[39] Also, much like the idea of unhomeliness, the liminal state experienced by characters like Bimala represents the failure of "the opposition of inner and outer, home and world."[40]

---

36. Bhabha, *Location*, 13–15.

37. See Bhabha, *Location*, 14; and Chaudhuri, "Dangerous Liaisons: Desire and Limit in the Home and the World," in Mukherji, *Thinking on Thresholds*, 87–95.

38. See Bhabha, *Location*, 14.

39. Chaudhuri, "Dangerous Liaisons," 88–89, 92.

40. Chaudhuri, "Dangerous Liaisons," 95. Chaudhuri repeatedly posits that the process of social modernization creates the possibility for the liminal state Bimala experiences, which could pose a problem in reading this particular kind of liminality (i.e., the threshold between public and private spaces) into an ancient text like the Hebrew Bible. However, the Judges narratives include enough instances of the

Unhomeliness in Judges 13

The condition of unhomeliness often becomes realized at the location of a threshold or liminal space. This episode in Samson's tale is no exception. The pregnant woman, in her liminal state, is not only the perfect candidate for a divine encounter, but also the perfect candidate for experiencing the condition of unhomeliness.

A deeper reading through Bhabha's postcolonial lens enables a new perspective and way to articulate what is so troubling about the Judges narratives. Specifically, Manoah's wife's particular speech, or more accurately, the omissions in her speech, demonstrate a realization and a *resistance* to the invasion of the public into the private. In fact, Manoah's pregnant wife's particular speech demonstrates a resistance to the invasion of the *Lord's* political and public initiatives into the private experience of a family and a woman's womb.

It is notable that the instructions to the woman, while they might pertain to the lad's Nazirite status, also concern the domestic realm: food, drink, and personal hygiene. There are no instructions about how to train this deliverer in military tactics, and there is no mention of specific religious or social responsibilities for this Nazirite. In fact, the request that Manoah makes to know about the regulations and work for the boy is completely ignored (13:12). Thus, the announcement about the son, the instructions for preparing for his arrival, and the instructions for his care are directed chiefly to the woman and address domestic matters.[41]

The narrator places the birth of this son not only in the domestic but specifically in the maternal realm by making the woman the recipient of the divine message, giving her the only significant role in preparing for the birth of the son, and permitting her to edit the divine message.[42] Following Exum's argument about how this character might serve the interests of

---

ambiguous treatment of both men and women occupying public and private spaces such that the breakdown of clearly defined gendered spaces seems to be apparent, even if it is not the result of a modern or westernizing process.

41. See Tammi J. Schneider, *Judges: Studies in Hebrew Narrative and Poetry*, Berit Olam (Collegeville, MN: Liturgical Press, 2000), 20.

42. Exum similarly argues that the narrative stresses the importance of the woman: "The narrative arrangement in Judges 13 teaches us, as well as Manoah, a lesson: in the events surrounding the birth of this wonderchild, the father is not more important than the mother" ("Promise and Fulfillment," 58).

the implicit patriarchy within the narrative, the emphasis on the woman as a mother and on her domestic and maternal activity is an indication of how this character cooperates with the text's patriarchy and poses no threat.[43] It is true that she works for the messenger of the Lord, relays his message, and serves the interests of her husband and son. However, her significant omission of her son as a deliverer is one element in the narrative that pushes beyond dichotomous strategies that separate domestic/maternal/feminine spheres from public/political/masculine spheres. She edits the message in such a way that highlights her resistance to the convergence of the public and private.

The woman's exclusion of crucial components of the messenger's announcement is intentional and enables what Bhabha calls an "unhomely moment."[44] While it might be speculative to rehearse the character's unspoken thoughts, it is still a potential unhomely moment for both her as a character and the reader who is paying close attention to the narrative.

The woman becomes faced with a complicated and terrifying reality: Her child will bear not only the honor and fame of being a hero for her people but also the potential personal risk that comes with being a military leader. It is one thing to learn that her son is predetermined to be a set apart and dedicated Nazirite to God for life, but it is another thing entirely to have a son who will be the leader and deliverer for a whole people. So, she omits this detail.

The reader grasps the stark reality that the things that are political sometimes invade family life. In the moment of the realization of her pregnancy, the woman's "world shrinks then expands," moving from the inward womb to the Israelite war with the Philistines, and becoming a narrative articulation in which the "recesses of the domestic space become sites for history's most intricate invasions."[45] What could be more domestic than a womb, and what could be more invasive than the declaration of war coming from your own doorstep? Powerful in narrative subtlety but still accessible for an observant reader, the additions and omissions by the

---

43. See J. Cheryl Exum, "Feminist Criticism: Whose Interests Are Being Served?," in *Judges and Method: New Approaches in Biblical Studies*, ed. Gale A. Yee, 2nd ed. (Minneapolis: Fortress, 2007), 78; and Exum, "Was sagt," 47. See also Corinne Lanoir, *Femmes fatales, filles rebelles: Figures féminines dans le livre des Juges*, Actes et recherches (Geneva: Labor et Fides, 2005), 115–16.

44. Bhabha *Location*, 13.

45. Bhabha *Location*, 13.

woman highlight a reality in which the borders between the home and the world are (terrifyingly) confused.

This condition of unhomeliness resounds in many narratives involving pregnant women. Rebekah laments in Gen 25.[46] Manoah's wife omits, remaining silent on critical political repercussions.[47] Importantly, both women fail to acknowledge political implications of the divine message. Rebekah does not respond to the oracle, and she does not share it with her husband. The wife of Manoah emphasizes the son's mortality, and she does not share his political destiny. In their own ways, each mother responds with ambivalence to their children's futures. These are responses that avoid the inevitable, that avoid speaking something painful into being. Each woman refuses to fully acknowledge the political implications of their pregnancies. Barren women soon find out that not only do politics enter the home and family, but also that which is political invades a woman's actual womb.

The news from the messenger means that the woman realizes that she is also an essential but compelled participant of public life and politics. The woman becomes an accomplice in military efforts as she bears, raises, and educates this deliverer of her people. In this way, the narrator reemphasizes a theme that runs throughout the Judges narratives: the complicated portrayal of women and the way in which women participate in political endeavors. Women both reap the rewards of success and bear the consequences of defeat alongside the military men they promote. As a mother, she wields a degree of power because of her reproductive abilities, but she is also subject to a patriarchal and political power that is out of her control.[48]

---

46. This moment in Judg 13 is treated in a similar way to Gen 25. Rebekah knows something is amiss when she feels the twins struggling in her womb. She laments this. And the Lord responds to her with an ominous oracle, as it describes the political discord that will ensue between the twins in her womb; see Roger Syrén, *The Forsaken First-Born: A Study of a Recurrent Motif in the Patriarchal Narratives*, JSOTSup 133 (Sheffield: JSOT Press, 1993), 81–82.

47. Similarly, Hannah delays giving her son to the Lord (1 Sam 1:22–24).

48. Adrienne Rich provides a helpful distinction between two connotations of motherhood, "I try to distinguish between two meanings of motherhood, one superimposed on the other: the *potential relationship* of any woman to her powers of reproduction and to children and the *institution* which aims at ensuring that that potential—and all women—shall remain under male control" (Rich, *Of Woman Born: Motherhood as Experience and Institution* [New York: Norton, 1976)], xv, emphasis original).

Conclusion

While her liminal state makes her ambiguous, potentially threatening to established structures, Manoah's wife is the one who responds ambivalently to the announcement of her pregnancy. She is not entirely on board. This redirects the subject of ambivalence away from her and toward something else. In fact, it is really the Lord who creates the ambiguity, not the woman, because the Lord is responsible for the woman's fertility. Ultimately, what the woman says and what she leaves out highlight the troubling aspects of fertility by God, when the public and the private collide.

Characters, especially liminal characters, throughout the book of Judges experience similar transgressions by public and political affairs into the private and familial situations, such that a sense of blurring of public and domestic spaces regularly occurs. Bhabha's idea of unhomeliness helps articulate why the Judges narratives have a constant interplay between family narratives and stories that involve political conflict or battles. Private family life and public political conflict become part of each other. The disorienting sensation of the conflation of all things private and public is made all the more troubling in Judg 13 when it is clear that the Lord is responsible for these events and that the human characters are not entirely on board with God's plan. Ambivalence exists in the blurring of public and private; ambivalence to God's actions similarly exists in the narrative.

11

Rereading Samson's Weepy Wife in Judges 14:
An Intertextual Evaluation of Gender and Weeping

Shelley L. Birdsong

Introduction

Throughout the Bible, women are often proprietary pawns in the tales of men. The woman from Timnah in the book of Judges is no exception. Her story begins under the male gaze; then men exchange and threaten her. Unless she can extract a riddle's answer from her bridegroom, Samson, a male mob will kill her and her family by fire. So, she cries upon Samson, pressing him for the solution. After days of weeping, Samson relents, and she successfully saves her family from peril. Tragically, though, Western male interpreters have disparaged her heroic tears as predictably feminine and thus sexualized and deceitful.[1] However, by putting the Timnite into intertextual dialogue with other criers—both ancient and modern—such gendered stereotypes become untenable. Instead, Samson's "weepy wife" rises from the ashes of misogynistic scholarship and reveals herself as essentially *human*. She is not an emotional seductress or a nefarious traitor. She is a strategist and savior of her people, even if only for a moment.

---

1. See J. Cheryl Exum, "Feminist Criticism: Whose Interests Are Being Served?," in *Judges and Method: New Approaches in Biblical Studies*, ed. Gale A. Yee, 2nd ed. (Minneapolis: Fortress, 2007), esp. 77.

Refuting the False Stereotypes via Intertextuality

Weepy Woman? Reading the Timnite in Dialogue with Biblical Criers

Male scholars have demeaned the Timnite's weeping in Judg 14:16 and 17 as "womanly wiles" for millennia.[2] The Christian bishop Ambrose (fourth century CE) accused the Timnite of weakening Samson with her "womanly charms," claiming that her emotions were a treacherous charade.[3] In the seventeenth century, Anglican John Trapp puts her on par with the devil and declares, "tears are women's weapons."[4] For the eighteenth-century pastor Jonathan Edwards, the Timnite represents "those lusts which infatuate men" and then "do us [men] a great deal of damage."[5] Two centuries later, Arthur Cundall and Leon Morris proclaim, "the woman ... used the last resort of her sex, a flood of tears."[6] For these men, female tears are synonymous with seduction and treachery.

Despite such unanimity regarding the Timnite woman (and apparently all women), a meta-analysis of crying in the Hebrew Bible exposes such conclusions as overtly gender-biased.[7] The root *bet, kaph, he*, which conveys "weeping" or "crying," occurs 175 times in the Hebrew Bible.[8] Of these, there are only eleven separate instances of individual female criers and four of groups of female criers, making up just under 9 percent of all

---

2. Exum, "Feminist Criticism," 79.

3. John R. Franke, ed. *Joshua, Judges, Ruth, 1–2 Samuel*, ACCS 4 (Downers Grove, IL: InterVarsity Press, 2005), 150.

4. John Trapp, *Genesis to Second Chronicles,* ed. W. Webster and Hugh Martin (Edinburgh: Dickinson, 1867), 383.

5. Jonathan Edwards, quoted in David M. Gunn, *Judges*, Blackwell Bible Commentaries (Malden, MA: Blackwell, 2005), 198.

6. Arthur E. Cundall and Leon Morris, *Judges and Ruth: An Introduction and Commentary*, TOTC 7 (Downers Grove, IL: InterVarsity Press, 1968), 160.

7. I am focusing exclusively on crying (בכה) rather than including mourning (אבל) and lamenting (ספד) because these actions include a larger array of ritualistic behaviors that may not include the shedding of tears. For a comprehensive account of mourning in the Hebrew Bible, see Saul M. Olyan, *Biblical Mourning: Ritual and Social Dimensions* (Oxford: Oxford University Press, 2004). His study correlates with the conclusions drawn here about crying as a social behavior managed by cultural norms.

8. There are 142 verbal forms and 33 noun forms. Due to space constraints, I was unable to include my complete data analysis. I have tried to provide comprehensive statistics and instances of import throughout this essay.

occurrences.[9] In contrast, there are forty-three instances of individual male criers and nine of male-exclusive groups of criers, comprising roughly 30 percent of all occurrences. That means men cry more than three times more often than women in the Hebrew Bible! The large category not yet accounted for is what I am calling a "mixed group." These are mainly masculine plural instances of בכה, which do not necessarily exclude women. Unfortunately, the gender bias of the Hebrew language disallows us from accurately calculating how many of these instances should fall under the category of a male-exclusive group. Nonetheless, the data still reveal two important facts: (1) most of the weeping in the Hebrew Bible is communal, and (2) the crying community most often consists of male and female actors. The data clearly show that both men and women cry; it should not be understood as a primarily female act. Consequently, to suggest that the Timnite's crying is somehow innately feminine is contextually indefensible.

It is also a false presumption to claim that biblical women cry for sexually devious purposes. Of the nine individual females who cry in the Hebrew Bible, almost all of them are responding to a lack of or threat to family, particularly children.[10] The data for groups of women follow the same trend. Thus, in almost every instance, women cry due to death, separation, or tragedy in relationship to their family or tribe.[11] No occurrence is sexual, manipulative, or deceitful. Thus, it is erroneous to assume that women in the Hebrew Bible, including the Timnite, cry in order to sexually manipulate.

---

9. Individual female criers: Hagar cries over the near death of Ishmael (Gen 21:16); female prisoner of war laments death/separation from family (Deut 21:13); Jephthah's daughter bewails nonmarriage status (Judg 11:37, 38); Timnite woman cries to save family (Judg 14:16, 17), Hannah laments lack of a child (1 Sam 1:7–8, 10 [2x]); *nefeš* of YHWH cries over people's pride and captivity (Jer 13:17); Rachel weeps for loss of children and is commanded to stop weeping (Jer 31:15 [2x], 16); (Daughter) Zion has no comforters and her children are destitute (Lam 1:2 [2x], 16); and Esther weeps over threat to Jews (Esth 8:3). Groups of female criers: Daughters of Israel (2 Sam 1:24), women (Ezek 8:14), widows of priests of Israel (Ps 78:64, made no lamentation), widows of the wicked (Job 27:15, make no lamentation), Orpah, Ruth (and Naomi?) (Ruth 1:9, 14).

10. See previous note.

11. The one exception might be the weeping for Tammuz, who was a god. However, if the women are adherents of Tammuz, then they are part of a religious tribe that would mourn the loss of this central figure.

To put the false gendered assumptions to rest, we should also note why *men* cry in the Hebrew Bible. They cry for almost all the same reasons and more. They weep over death within their tribe, the destruction of their land or defeat in battle, and other extenuating circumstances.[12] There are a few instances where male tears are part of a supplication to God or expressions of joy when reunited with family.[13] Some of the most exalted men in biblical tradition are criers: Abraham, Jacob, Joseph, David, Hezekiah, Josiah, Elisha, and Isaiah. Their tears are never deemed suspicious, and their crying has yet to be described as treacherous "masculine wiles." Instead, their tears are interpreted as symbols of sincerity.[14] The discrepancy between how male and female tears have been interpreted becomes lucidly clear when put into such intertextual relief.

Weepy Woman? Reading the Timnite in Dialogue with Modern Psychological Research

Putting the Timnite's story into dialogue with psychological research on gender and crying also substantiates her crying as unfairly gendered. First, studies show that if there are gender differences in crying, they are more influenced by culture and other societal factors rather than biological sex.[15] According to researchers, male and female infants show

---

12. Death within their tribe, e.g., Abraham for Sarah (Gen 23:2), Joseph for Jacob (Gen 50:1), David for Abner (2 Sam 3:32) and Absalom (2 Sam 19:1–2). Destruction or defeat, e.g., Israelites defeated by Benjaminites (Gen 33:4; Judg 20:23), Nehemiah's loss of Jerusalem (Neh 1:4), and Moab's destruction (Isa 15:2–12). Extenuating circumstances, e.g., all of Israel for broken covenant (Judg 2:4), psalmist in despair and fear (Pss 6:9; 69:11; 102:10), Hezekiah's illness (2 Kgs 20:3), Paltiel's separation from Michal (2 Sam 3:16).

13. E.g., Joseph and Benjamin reunited (Gen 45:14). Only men cry for positive reasons or happy occasions in the Hebrew Bible.

14. There is not space here to review the literature on the interpretation of these men's tears. However, after much searching, I have not uncovered any instance where these men have been belittled for their tearful episodes.

15. The distinction between "sex" and "gender" has helped draw a line between biological difference (e.g., variants in genitalia or chromosomes) and social roles (e.g., behaviors and expressions of identity) shaped by society and culture. The latter is a pattern of meaning-making that, historically speaking, has often been used to subordinate the female sex by claiming that certain culturally determined gender roles are actually the result of biological difference (see Ken Stone, "Gender Criticism: The Un-Manning of Abimelech," in Yee, *Judges and Method*, 184–85). However, there is a hot

no sign of sexual difference in crying for the first two years of their life. Only later, in adolescent development, do they begin to show traces of difference, suggesting that those variances are informed by cultural and societal context rather than pure biology.[16] Such societal contexts include relationship dynamics, power structures, and socialized expectations regarding gender roles.[17] For example, cross-cultural studies on emotion show that gender difference is higher in individualistic societies rather than collective ones. In other words, the more collective the society, the less gender difference there is when it comes to displays of emotion.[18] Moreover, crying occurs more often in affluent, democratic, and extroverted countries regardless of gender.[19] Such studies have led most researchers to move away from hypotheses focused on how sex impacts crying; instead, they are investigating how cultural and societal assumptions about gender shape when and how men and women are allowed to cry in their particular contexts.

---

debate in the field of gender and sexuality studies regarding the constructed binary of biology versus culture or sex versus gender. Some argue that sex is also a culturally situated concept and should be deconstructed.

16. Marrie H. J. Bekker and Ad J. J. M. Vingerhoets, "Adam's Tears: The Relationships between Crying, Biological Sex and Gender from Various Perspectives," *Psychology, Evolution and Gender* 1 (1999): 11–31. Bekker and Vingerhoets define crying as "a typically human complex secretomotor response to an emotional situation." The main characteristics include "shedding of tears" often "accompanied by alterations in the muscles of facial expression, vocalizations and, in some cases, sobbing" (12). While most studies on adult crying find that women do cry more often than men in contemporary society, the causes are largely societal and cultural; see Ad Vingerhoets and Jan Scheirs, "Sex Differences in Crying: Empirical Findings and Possible Explanations," in *Gender and Emotion: Social Psychological Perspectives*, ed. Agneta H. Fischer, Studies in Emotion and Social Interaction (Cambridge: Cambridge University Press, 2000), 143–65, esp. 145–49.

17. Bekker and Vingerhoets, "Adam's Tears"; Mathell Peter, Ad J. J. M. Vingerhoets, and Guus L. Van Heck, "Personality, Gender, and Crying," *European Journal of Personality* 15 (2001): 19–28; D. G. Williams, "Weeping by Adults: Personality Correlates and Sex Differences," *Journal of Psychology* 110 (1982): 217–26.

18. Agneta H. Fischer and Antony S. R. Manstead, "The Relation between Gender and Emotion in Different Cultures," in Fischer, *Gender and Emotion*, 72–89.

19. Dianne A. van Hermert, Fons J. R. van de Vijver, and Ad J. J. M. Vingerhoets, "Culture and Crying: Prevalences and Gender Differences," *Cross-Cultural Research* 45 (2011): 399.

The analysis of gender and crying in the Hebrew Bible appears to parallel these contemporary conclusions.[20] The results show that men and women both cry, and they cry for similar reasons. This lack of significant gender difference in crying articulated in the Hebrew Bible is likely the result of their collective, nondemocratic, tribal society. Consequently, it would be unfounded to claim that the Timnite cries because she is a woman expressing her innate feminine qualities. One would be more justified in arguing that she is crying due to the relationship dynamics, power structures, and personalities at play in the story.[21]

Second, psychological studies show that when Westerners interpret the emotions of others, including crying, they tend to use their own gender biases as an interpretive lens. For example, one study revealed that the farther away an interpreter is from an event involving an emotional experience, the more that interpreter uses gendered stereotypes to interpret the other person's emotions.[22] This finding sheds light on the history of interpretation. Western male interpreters were quite a distance from the events portrayed in Judg 14. Thus, it is reasonable to suspect that they fell into the same trap of using gendered stereotypes when interpreting the Timnite's emotions. Moreover, these Western men were in an environment prone to view crying through a lens of gender difference, since they were writing in more affluent, democratic, extroverted, and individualistic societies. Thus, even though they were analyzing a very different time and culture, where gender difference in crying was not as substantial, they read the emotions of the Timnite through a Western lens, forcing their own cultural and biased views of crying onto her.[23]

---

20. As Stephanie A. Shields notes, "we must be very cautious before generalizing across cultures or historical times" when drawing conclusions about gender and emotion ("Thinking about Gender, Thinking about Theory: Gender and Emotional Experience," in Fischer, *Gender and Emotion*, 5). Nonetheless, the themes across studies can be instructive or at least used in a supplementary fashion as I am doing here.

21. These factors will be taken up shortly.

22. Shields, "Thinking about Gender," 9.

23. The major researchers on crying regularly comment on Western assumptions. Fischer and Manstead lament, "Western cultures share the stereotypical belief that women are more emotional than men. This stereotype has long featured in Western philosophy, where a binary between emotion and reason has been closely associated with the opposition between masculinity and femininity" ("Relation," 71). As a result, "One of the most pervasive stereotypes of sex differences in our [Western] culture is that of the emotional, labile woman versus the rational, strong man" (Bekker and

Seductive Woman? Reading the Timnite in Dialogue with Delilah and Samson

The Timnite's tears have also been interpreted by Western males as a tactic to sexually conquer Samson. Again, there is little to support such a claim. The Timnite engages in four primary actions: she cries (ותבך, 14:16), speaks (ותאמר, 14:16), cries again (ותבך, 14:17), and presses (הצקתהו, 14:17). None of these actions are explicitly or implicitly sexual. As we have seen thus far, people cry for a variety of reasons, but none of them is to seduce someone sexually. The Timnite does accuse Samson of not loving her, even hating her, but such comments are not inherently sexual; instead, they are about love and trust. Samson confirms this with his retort. He does not charge her with being flirtatious or treacherously feminine. He just says that he will not even tell his parents the riddle, so he is not going to tell her. His reply comparing her to his parents points to the fact that the issue at hand is familial not sexual.[24] She is pressuring him to confide in her like family, but, for Samson, she is not yet family and not yet deserving. Ironically, he does not trust his own family either. Samson's comment exposes his lack of filial duty. He goes against his parents' will when choosing to marry a Philistine, and he regularly withholds information from them that could indict him as a Nazirite.[25]

All of this suggests that Samson is being put into dramatic contrast with the Timnite regarding familial loyalty. Samson disrespects his parents while the Timnite demonstrates filial righteousness.[26] In the discourse between Samson and the Timnite, Samson states his disrespect for his father and mother when he implies he cannot trust them with the

---

Vingerhoets, "Adam's Tears," 12). See also Vanda L. Zammuner on Western gender bias in lay theories of emotion ("Men's and Women's Lay Theories of Emotion," in Fischer, *Gender and Emotion*, 48–57).

24. James L. Crenshaw has previously remarked that much of the Samson saga is about competing loyalties, esp. between parents and a spouse (*Samson: A Secret Betrayed, a Vow Ignored* [Atlanta: John Knox, 1978], 65–66).

25. E.g., he touched a carcass and ate honey.

26. Judges 14:4 claims that the Timnite is "from YHWH," and she is called "right" in 14:3 and 7. Most scholars have ignored the fact that Judg 14:4 can be read as the woman being "from YHWH" rather than "this" or "it," i.e., the situation. The only two commentators that I have found who note this ambiguity or freeness in the text are J. Cheryl Exum (*Fragmented Women: Feminist (Sub)versions of Biblical Narratives* [Valley Forge, PA: Trinity Press International, 1993], 61) and Crenshaw (*Samson*, 9).

riddle. In contrast, the Timnite is going to the greatest lengths to show
her allegiance to her paternal household by saving them from the threat
of death by fire. The disparity shows that the true test is one of devotion
not sexual strength.[27]

But what of Judg 14:15, when the Philistine men command the Timnite to "force open your man" (פַּתִּי אֶת־אִישֵׁךְ)? The root פתה connotes
opening, and in Judg 14:15 it is in the *piel* form. According to BDB, the
causative form of פתה can be translated as "persuade," "seduce," "entice,"
or "deceive."[28] Many of the causative instances of פתה in the Hebrew Bible
have to do with using speech (or one's lips) to make another weak or vulnerable. The action is primarily a power shift that allows the speaker to
gain access to or influence over the other. While context in several cases
makes the translation of "seduce," "entice," or "deceive" reasonable, the
heart of the verb is about power versus weakness, predator versus prey.
Of the twenty-six occurrences of the verb, only two are explicitly aligned
with sexual encounters.[29] Therefore, the instance in Judg 14:15 need not
be sexual in nature, especially since it follows the pattern of using one's
speech to weaken the listener into a malleable role. The Timnite takes control of her situation by wearying her opponent with her words not her
sexual prowess.

The last counterclaim to be addressed also revolves around the verb
פתה. It occurs in Judg 16:5 as well. There, Delilah is asked by Philistine
men, who want to "overpower" and "subdue" Samson, to פַּתִּי אוֹתוֹ, "force
him [Samson] open!" Like the Timnite, Delilah is asked to acquire information from Samson by the power of persuasion. Also, like the Timnite,
Delilah uses "her words" to press Samson "day after day," questioning his
love (Judg 16:16).[30] Because of their similarities, these two women are

---

27. Questions abound concerning whether or not Samson and the Timnite ever
consummated their marriage; see, e.g., Mieke Bal, *Death and Dissymmetry: The Politics of Coherence in the Book of Judges*, CSHJ (Chicago: University of Chicago Press,
1988), 78; Tammi J. Schneider, *Judges: Studies in Hebrew Narrative and Poetry*, Berit
Olam (Collegeville: MN: Liturgical Press, 2000), 138–39.

28. BDB, s.v. "פָּתָה."

29. Exod 22:15; Job 31:9; and perhaps Hos 2:16. The other occurrences are Gen
9:27; Deut 11:16; Judg 16:5; 2 Sam 3:25; 1 Kgs 22:20, 21, 22; 2 Chr 18:19, 20, 21; Job
5:2; 31:9, 27; Ps 78:36; Prov 20:19; 24:28; 25:15; Jer 20:7 (twice), 10; Ezek 14:9 (twice);
Hos 7:11.

30. Here is an example of where Exum believes the "text encourages us to confuse
and to conflate" the women in Samson's story and Bal "warns against" the "tendency to

often conflated and so suffer the same fate of sexist interpretation. Unfortunately, since Delilah is one of the most infamous *femmes fatales* in the West, the Timnite has been found guilty by association.[31] But, as J. Cheryl Exum has astutely pointed out, "the text does not say that the women used sexual favors to get the answers out of Samson. In both cases 'he told her' (14.17; 16.17) 'because she harassed him' (14.17; 16.16). The Timnite uses tears; Delilah presses Samson 'with her words' (16.16)."[32] Their acts are not explicitly sexual, and the commentators who suggest such are doing so based on their own bias.[33]

---

superimpose the pictures of the women" (*Fragmented Women*, 70). Cf. Susan Ackerman (*Warrior, Dancer, Seductress, Queen: Women in Judges and Biblical Israel*, ABRL [New York: Doubleday, 1998], 233), who suggests that the intertextual connections between the Timnite and Delilah highlight their differences and essentially belittle the Timnite.

31. Both women are read as such because interpreters continue to put their own gender bias into the story. When they translate פתה, and when they see a woman overcome a man, they presume the woman is in the wrong. Shields explains why we see this adverse reaction to a woman overcoming a man. Researchers have discovered that people with lower statuses (e.g., women who are viewed as subordinate because of their sex or gender) who violate biased social expectations (e.g., excel in the workplace or overcome a man in a battle of wits) are viewed as more appropriate targets for anger and attack. Because they are seen as less deserving, when they do succeed, others react with offense. As Shields rightly points out, this is primarily about power and status rather than gender/sex ("Thinking about Gender," 17). So, when male interpreters see that the women in Judges (whom they view as lower in status) prevail over Samson, the response is to attack them. The fault here is with the interpreters not the women.

32. Exum, *Fragmented Women*, 86.

33. Despite this, some of the most prominent feminist scholars who write on Judges read פתה this way. Both Schneider and Exum comment on the fact that the verb פתה refers to seducing virgins in Exod 22:16 and conclude that the Philistines are commanding a similar attack (Schneider, *Judges*, 210; Exum, *Fragmented Women*, 79). Susan Niditch translates the verb as "seduce" and remarks that the command is for the Timnite to "pry open her man psychologically and sexually" (*Judges*, OTL [Louisville: Westminster John Knox, 2008], 148, 152). Niditch apparently buys into the gendered assumptions that the Timnite and Delilah (along with Jael) do, in fact, "employ feminine wiles to subdue, defeat, and betray the enemy" (157). In contrast, Schneider rejects the "depiction of her as a foreign temptress luring Samson" and calls it "completely unfounded" (*Judges*, 210). Similarly, Exum points out that, despite what the men may have intended, the text does not say the Timnite followed their directions (*Fragmented Women*, 86).

Malevolent Deceiver? Reading the Timnite in Dialogue with Ishmael, Shiphrah, and Puah

As previously mentioned, in Judg 14:15, the Philistines ask the Timnite to פתי את־אישך, which can be translated as "Deceive your man!"[34] It is possible that the Philistines had deception in mind when they gave the command to the Timnite. But the narrator does not say that she follows their instructions exactly. She cries, she speaks, and she presses; she does not פתה. So even if a reader demands that פתה be understood as deception, the Timnite is not guilty of it.

The only thing the Timnite says to Samson is "You hate me; you do not really love me. You have asked a riddle of my people, but you have not explained it to me" (14:16). She also cries repeatedly (14:16–17). At face value, neither the statements nor the actions are dishonest. Why *should* she believe that Samson loves her? She barely knows him, and his response belittles her as less valuable than his parents, whom he clearly does not value much at all. In addition, he *has* asked a riddle of her people and not explained it to her. Finally, we have no reason to believe her tears are not earnest. She is in a highly stressful situation, her family has been threatened, and she still needs the information that can save her life. Context warrants tears. This cause for tears is supported by the data on crying in the Hebrew Bible. Individuals cry when their family is endangered. What the evidence does not support is the idea that people cry to deceive.

There is one exception—a single male character who feigns tears to treacherously deceive. He is Ishmael ben Nethaniah, murderer of Gedaliah ben Shaphan, governor of Judah. After his assassination of the governor (Jer 41:2), Ishmael lures men into Mizpah by taking on the actions of a mourner, misleading the Jerusalem pilgrims. Once in the city, he slaughters them (Jer 41:1–8). In this singular incident, Ishmael cries for a reason unlike any other in the Hebrew Bible. His purposes are explicitly to deceive and kill, and he does so.

Ishmael could be the doppelgänger our biased interpreters are looking for to condemn the Timnite. However, the Timnite is nothing like Ishmael. She is not a rogue character nor a murderer. Moreover, her aim

---

34. The Greek translators understood it this way. The LXX provides a form of the verb ἀπατάω, generally meaning "to deceive" or "mislead."

in crying is not to kill but to save. To put Ishmael and the Timnite into the same category would be a mistake. Even if we grant that she uses a similar tactic in forcing tears to influence the situation, the intent behind those tears is drastically different. The Timnite is unwillingly put in a situation where she must get information she needs in order to save her family. Ishmael willfully wreaks havoc in Judah and kills anyone he has to in order to do it.

If the Timnite was to be paired with others who expediently omit information, she should be paired with the midwives, Shiphrah and Puah, in Exod 1, who also choose their words wisely to save lives. They do not cry, but power is at play just as it is in Judg 14. All three women use their intellect, not their sexuality, to navigate a high-stakes situation. They successfully take advantage of their opponent's ego and use it against them. In Exodus, the actions of the midwives are portrayed as heroic; God even rewards them. Similarly, in Judges, the Timnite is deemed by the narrator as "from YHWH" (Judg 14:4). Such a statement cannot go unaddressed. When we see the Timnite in light of her similarities with Shiphrah and Puah, it becomes apparent that past interpreters have misjudged her. The Timnite woman should not be understood as a sexual predator who manipulates to betray Samson. She is a savior figure, who puts her own life on the line to protect her loved ones.

Effective Strategist:
Reading the Timnite in Dialogue with
Modern Psychological Research

So, what is the reason the Timnite cries? As already suggested by the data on those who cry in the Hebrew Bible, it is possible, perhaps even likely, that the Timnite is crying because she and her family are in a near-death situation. However, that need not be the only or primary reason for her weeping. In light of the intertextual connections between the Timnite and Ishmael in Jeremiah and Shiphrah and Puah in Exodus, it is imperative that we question her motives for crying. When read intertextually with psychological research, the Timnite can be interpreted as using her tears as a behavioral strategy. She weeps to communicate her needs and get them met, to increase the probability of getting what she wants, and to assuage Samson's belligerence.

First and foremost, the Timnite becomes a proactive problem-solver. Before she cries in Judg 14:16, she was a passive woman. She was merely seen and spoken to by men (Judg 14:1, 7, 15).[35] But in 14:16, she becomes the subject and not the object. *She* initiates the dialogue with Samson, and she acts upon and against him when she cries. Thereafter, she continues to act—weeping, pressing, and explaining (14:17). Such an active context reduces the supposition that she is crying for cathartic purposes, which is one of the two main reasons humans cry. Instead, she is crying to communicate that she is in need of comfort or support—the second main reason people cry.[36] The Timnite is not just emoting; she is in a life-or-death crisis. Psychologists identify this type of crying as a coping mechanism for stress-induced situations. It is called a "problem-focused" coping mechanism, which is proactive in nature.[37] It does not just communicate a need; it incites action to get that need met. Both men and women use this "problem-focused strategy," and the Timnite is clearly one of them.[38] She cries to get what she needs—the information to save herself and her family.[39]

By crying, the Timnite is also improving her odds for getting what she wants. Research shows that tears give criers a better chance of receiving support than a noncrying person.[40] So the Timnite's tears are not arbitrary or excessive nor do they signify the helplessness of a female. On the contrary, they are witness to her discriminating calculations and concerted effort to ensure that she will outwit Samson.

Finally, the Timnite uses tears in her attempt to avert an impending conflict for all involved. She is aware of the sizable wager between Samson

---

35. In both Judg 14:7 and 15, the woman is spoken *to*, not *with*. She is only a passive listener not an active interlocutor. Ackerman has commented on the Timnite as primarily object versus subject; however, she dismisses the Timnite's moments of action as largely irrelevant (*Warrior, Dancer, Seductress, Queen*, 233).

36. Vingerhoets and Scheirs, "Sex Differences," 143.

37. Vingerhoets and Scheirs, "Sex Differences," 143–44.

38. Vingerhoets and Scheirs, "Sex Differences," 144.

39. One could argue that the Timnite's choice to press Samson for the answer to the riddle rather than just tell him that she has been threatened highlights that she is not just a "helpless woman." Instead, she takes it upon herself to get what she needs through her own powers of persuasion rather than hoping Samson is going to rise to the occasion of helping a "damsel in distress."

40. Michelle C. P. Henriks, Marcel A. Croon, and Ad J. J. M. Vingerhoets, "Social Reactions to Adult Crying: The Help-Soliciting Function of Tears," *Journal of Social Psychology* 148 (2008): 35. They note that some persons may exploit their own weakness in order to solicit help; however, the supplicant can run the risk of being perceived negatively by others thereafter (36). Whether or not the Timnite is actually playing off her own weakness is unclear.

and the thirty Philistines; she knows lives are in the balance; and she has likely deduced Samson's conniving and violent disposition.[41] It may be she cried in order to reduce Samson's aggression and stimulate social bonding, which have been linked in psychological research.[42] In other words, her tears disarmed Samson and disoriented his singular focus on the Philistines while refocusing his energy toward her, his betrothed. She may have believed that if she could shake him out of his hypervigilant desire to win and bring him to a place of compassion, then maybe he would not only show her trust but perhaps he would also be gracious with the Philistines.

Of course, Samson is not gracious to the Philistines, but he is gracious to the Timnite, demonstrating that she was clearly an effective strategist. She assessed her situation and then used the appropriate tactics to get what she needed. She cried, not because she was a woman or a seductress or a deceptive traitor but as part of her efforts to save herself and her family.

Will She Have Cried and Died in Vain?

Rereading Samson's so-called weepy wife reveals her as a representative of everywoman, at least in the history of Western civilization. She is quite complex, yet so many have devalued her as a mere extra in the saga of men. She is a calculated and successful strategist, yet her emotions and actions are dismissed as feminine and therefore untrustworthy. Such unjust interpretations of the Timnite woman are emblematic of the incessant sexism in the history of biblical interpretation and in modern women's lives. We cannot allow this to continue, and we cannot allow the Timnite to have died in vain, twice. Her story demands that we vigilantly examine our interpretive biases, particularly when it comes to gender and emotion. In this endeavor, intertextuality can serve as a powerful heuristic tool. By juxtaposing our own interpretations of the actions and emotions of those with different genders, we can potentially expose our biases, which may have previously gone unnoticed. In doing so, we can potentially become better scholars and more just human beings.

---

41. She certainly knows about the wager, but she may also know about the lion he tore to pieces.

42. Van Hermert, van de Vijver, and Vingerhoets, "Culture and Crying," 401. See also Henriks, Croon, and Vingerhoets, "Social Reactions."

12

One of These Things Is Not Like the Other: Delilah and the Prostitute in Gaza

Tammi J. Schneider

The story of Delilah is unusual in that she is not depicted like most women in the book of Judges, or any book of the Hebrew Bible. Many have argued that the figure of Delilah is in conversation with other characters in the Samson narrative, and most scholars agree that Samson is the last judge of the core of the book of Judges.[1] This is noteworthy since the book of Judges contains more stories than many other biblical books about women carrying out actions beyond the traditional sphere of marrying, birthing, and raising children, such as Jael and Deborah (Judg 4–5).

Regardless of her conversation partners, the way Delilah is treated by the text is unique. On some levels, were she not grouped with other key women in Samson's life (mother, Timnite bride, prostitute in Gaza), one might argue that she is actually not engaged intertextually. The fact that she is grouped with these other women and yet stands so far outside of them suggests something different about her and, as will become apparent, might suggest more about Samson, which is indicative of where the Israelites are within the narrative time of the book of Judges in general.[2]

---

1. For Delilah in conversation with other characters, see Susan Ackerman, *Warrior, Dancer, Seductress, Queen: Women in Judges and Biblical Israel*, ABRL (New York: Doubleday, 1998), 232–35; James L. Crenshaw, *Samson: A Secret Betrayed, a Vow Ignored* (Atlanta: John Knox, 1978), 70; Susan Niditch, *Judges*, OTL (Louisville: Westminster John Knox, 2008), 168–71. For Samson as the last judge, see Victor H. Matthews, *Judges and Ruth*, NCBC (Cambridge: Cambridge University Press, 2004), 6.

2. There are two main camps of scholarship on Judges: those who take a diachronic versus synchronic approach. Since the point of this volume is to treat the text intertextually, the focus here will be purely synchronic. Thus, while some scholars may

This essay will first provide a brief overview of how Delilah has been treated in the history of scholarship in general, which will suggest where and how she has been situated as a character. After that, Delilah will be considered by verbing her, meaning she will be evaluated based on how she is described, where she appears as a subject and object of verbs, and her relationships.[3] This will show how the text actually presents her. Through this process she will be compared to some of the other women in the Samson story and Judges in general to reveal what a unique character she is and what that might suggest about the role her character plays within the narrative.

Past Views of Samson and Delilah

The character of Samson is one of the few figures from Judges who appears in the New Testament. Samson manages to find his way onto the list of Heb 11:32. While modern Christians may struggle with Samson and his appearance on a list of faithful, ancient scholars were less bothered. Ambrose praises Samson.[4] Caesarious of Arles interprets Samson's death as prefiguring the crucifixion of Jesus.[5] Samson and Christ are further linked because both of their births are foretold by angels (Judg 13:3; Luke 1:26–38).

With Samson as a clear hero, Delilah, who turns him over to the Philistines who then blind him (Judg 16:18–21), cannot fare well. According to Josephus, Delilah is a prostitute (*Ant.* 5.306). In Pseudo-Philo she is both a prostitute and Samson's wife.[6] Ambrose claims, "Did not the woman Delilah's love of money deceive Samson, the bravest man of all?… Love of money, then, is deadly."[7] Jodi Magness has recently discovered mosaics from early synagogues depicting Samson at the excavation of Huqoq.[8] The

---

want to focus on when that period of Judges occurred, it is not relevant for topics in this essay.

3. Tammi J. Schneider, *Mother of Promise: Women in the Book of Genesis* (Grand Rapids: Baker Academic, 2008), 11–12.

4. John R. Franke, ed., *Joshua, Judges, Ruth, 1–2 Samuel*, ACCS 4 (Downers Grove, IL: InterVarsity Press, 2005), 141–75.

5. Franke, *Joshua, Judges, Ruth, 1–2 Samuel*, 166–67.

6. Frederick J. Murphy, *Pseudo-Philo: Rewriting the Bible* (Oxford: Oxford University Press, 1993), 172.

7. Franke, *Joshua, Judges, Ruth, 1–2 Samuel*, 160.

8. Magness, "New Mosaics from the Huqoq Synagogue," *BAR* 39.5 (2013): 66–68.

mosaics and their interpretation are in the first stages of scholarly discussion. Such exciting new finds of visual data mean that the earliest interpretations of Samson will be under serious review. While the debate rages as to whether Samson is disreputable or messianic, the opinion on Delilah is clear: she is bad.

Delilah's role does not improve over time. For example, in the nineteenth century, "this racy narrative drew little comment from nineteenth century women interpreters, who typically avoided interpreting texts involving sexuality."[9] Certainly in the twentieth century she is treated as the *"femme fatale par excellence."*[10]

Many scholars have noted a few key aspects about Delilah. Despite claims that she is a prostitute, or even prostitute-like in her behavior, the text does not state that she is.[11] No ethnic affiliation is attributed to her; in other words, the text does not label her as a Philistine, Israelite, or any other "ite." The text is explicit that Samson loves Delilah; her feelings are not included (Judg 16:4). Finally, most argue that, unlike Samson's bride, Delilah is not threatened and so her only reason for turning in Samson must be the money and/or that she is a Philistine.[12] Terms such as *betrayal* are frequently used to describe her actions.[13] The above references suggest attributions to Delilah from the text where they do not exist. What is slightly more obscured is what the text does state about Delilah. What will be highlighted here is also how unique many of those attributes are.

Delilah's Description

Delilah has a name. This may not appear too shocking, but she is the only woman in any kind of a relationship with Samson who is named. Even his mother is not named. Precisely what her name means, and if it connects to the story, is a debated point. Hebrew דלל means either "loose, long hair"

---

9. Marion Ann Taylor and Christiana de Groot, eds., *Women of War, Women of Woe: Joshua and Judges through the Eyes of Nineteenth-Century Female Biblical Interpreters* (Grand Rapids: Eerdmans, 2016), 231.

10. Danna Nolan Fewell, "Judges," in *The Women's Bible Commentary*, ed. Carol A. Newsom and Sharon H. Ringe (Louisville: Westminster John Knox, 1992), 73.

11. Ackerman, *Warrior, Dancer, Seductress, Queen*, 231.

12. Mark E. Biddle, *Reading Judges: A Literary and Theological Commentary*, Reading the Old Testament (Macon, GA: Smyth & Helwys, 2012), 163.

13. See the title of Crenshaw's book (*Samson: A Secret Betrayed, a Vow Ignored*); Niditch, *Judges*, 168.

or "small" while the root means "flirtatious" in Arabic.[14] While it does not appear to be etymologically connected to the Hebrew word לילה for night, it sounds like it and has led scholars to note how it appears to be a play on words with Samson's name, connected to שמש, "sun."[15] Delilah's introduction with this name already suggests a series of contrasts: night and day, light and dark (where Delilah will cause Samson to dwell after he is blinded). If Samson is considered a hero (a debated point but one made by Heb 11), is she by definition the antihero?

Delilah is described with only one term: woman. The term used is אשה (Judg 16:4). The term means both woman and wife in Hebrew.[16] This same term is included as the introductory reference to all of the women in Samson's life. His mother, when first introduced, is described as a "barren woman" (Judg 13:2). The use of the term for many readers is obscured because most English texts here translate "wife." In this case, since Manoah is the main focus of the text, "wife" seemingly works better than "woman" (English texts considered include: Wycliffe, Geneva, KJV, NRSV, and the NJPS).[17] So too is Samson's future bride initially introduced when he "saw in Timnah a woman," and then she is described as from the daughters of the Philistines (Judg 14:1).[18] Most translations retain some version of this where "woman" is included. Not so with the third female in Samson's life, the prostitute in Gaza (Judg 16:1). While the Hebrew text refers to her as a "woman prostitute," few translations include the reference to her being a woman. Of the five considered here, only Wycliffe translates the role of this woman as a "whore woman." The rest of the translations simply use some variation of whore, harlot, or prostitute.

The woman in Gaza is particularly relevant for understanding Delilah, as some suggest that Delilah is more than just a prostitute who catches Samson's eye, or that because he was recently visiting a prostitute, Delilah is somehow more likely to have that profession.[19] Some interesting issues flow from their

---

14. Biddle, *Reading Judges*, 162.

15. Biddle, *Reading Judges*, 162.

16. BDB, s.v. "אשה."

17. This list is used as it includes three of the earliest English translations, possibly a source for some of the later translations, as well as two more modern translations including both Christian and Jewish traditions.

18. Unless otherwise stated, all translations are mine.

19. Matthews, *Judges and Ruth*, 159; Ackerman, *Warrior, Dancer, Seductress, Queen*, 231.

connection. By deleting the reference to her being a "woman" prostitute, the actual philological (intertextual) connection between the three women is diluted. Deleting "woman" limits the ability to link the woman in Gaza to Jephthah's mother, also identified as a "woman prostitute" (Judg 11:1). In the earlier case, there is a fair amount of variation in the English translations about Jephthah's mother's occupation. Again, only Wycliffe translates in both cases "whore woman." Both the NRSV and KJV translate the same term for both women, though each uses a different term (NRSV labels them both "prostitute" whereas in the KJV they are both "harlot"). NJPS and the Geneva Bible treat them differently: with Jephthah's mother being a prostitute and the woman in Gaza a harlot for the Geneva, and NJPS features the woman in Gaza as a whore while Jephthah's mother is a prostitute.

The wide array of translation techniques suggests a few issues. Despite the woman in Gaza carrying the identical label as Jephthah's mother, some translators are uncomfortable with that association. What makes all translators uncomfortable, either philologically or theologically, is that every one of Samson's female associates are first introduced as some kind of a woman. Furthermore, for purposes here, Delilah is the only character from the entire array who is not otherwise described.

One might argue that Delilah is described by her location: Wadi Sorek. Robert G. Boling identified the Valley of Sorek with the modern Wadi es-Surar, about 13 miles southwest of Jerusalem.[20] It also places her directly at the border between the Philistines and Israelite settlement, according to the narrative time of Judges, obfuscating her ethnic identity. The text and her location cannot categorically identify her as a Philistine, Israelite, or any other "ite" roaming around the area. One possibility is to connect שרק (Sorek) with "red grapes," suggesting it is likely the chief agriculture product of the region at the time.[21] It could also come from the verb "to comb," hinting at the hair that will soon be cut.[22] Regardless of the specifics, the suggestion, if either of these translations or roots is correct, is that Samson, as a *nazir*, definitely should not be there.[23]

---

20. Boling, *Judges: A New Translation with Introduction and Commentary*, AB 6A (Garden City, NY: Doubleday, 1975), 248.

21. Biddle, *Reading Judges*, 162.

22. Biddle, *Reading Judges*, 162.

23. Samson is told he will be a Nazir from his birth. For more about the role of Nazirites see Tammi J. Schneider, *Judges: Studies in Hebrew Narrative and Poetry*, Berit Olam (Collegeville, MN: Liturgical Press, 2000), 197–98.

In the final analysis, Delilah's only description ties her to the other women in Samson's orbit. Despite that, the fact that she has a name, has no ethnic designation, and no other defining characteristics suggest she is unique. Unlike other women, she does not have a father, husband, or son. She has no family and is completely independent.

Delilah's Actions

Delilah is the subject of eight different verbs, though most of them she only carries out one time. The nature of those verbs is fairly unique, again highlighting how Delilah is not like the average woman, even in Judges.

The first verb, where she is the subject, she carries out seven different times and is the most common verb in her repertoire. In Judg 16:6 she first speaks, and thus is the subject of the verb אמר "to say."[24] The first time she is the subject of this verb is when she initially asks Samson what makes him so strong. This verb makes obvious what Danna Nolan Fewell has observed previously regarding Delilah, "she does not, however, as many commentators are eager to assert, deceive him. She asks him directly what she wants to know. Samson is the one who deceives her."[25] Since Samson does not answer her truthfully, she is the subject of this verb a number of times, such as in Judg 16:10 and 16:13 where in both cases she suggests that Samson deceives her. Finally, in Judg 16:15 she says to him that he cannot say he loves her when he will not confide in her, noting that he has deceived her three times.

Delilah's situation is similar to that of the Philistine woman Samson tries to marry during their wedding week but uses very different terminology. In that case too, the Philistine bride suggests that Samson hates her and does not love her because he has not told her the riddle (Judg 14:16). With the exception of the word "say" being used in both and "love," though conjugated and used differently, the terminology is different. As a result, while commentators suggest they are both doing the same thing, that is, using their feminine ways to learn a secret from him, the reality is that the Hebrew terminology does not demand the verses be read together. Furthermore, in terms of creating a character profile, the bride cries, Delilah appears almost angry.

---

24. BDB, s.v. "אמר."
25. Fewell, "Judges," 73.

Delilah's situation differs also because of two other occurrences of the word. Delilah is trying to learn the secret to his strength and carries out what he says will weaken him. So, in Judg 16:9 and 16:12, after carrying out precisely what Samson says would weaken him, she says to him that the Philistines are upon him. Of course, unbeknown to Samson, a Philistine ambush awaits him in the next room. Samson finally tells her the truth and so it should be no surprise to him or the reader that she carries out the action (Judg 16:20). In this final use of the term "say," when Delilah says to Samson that the Philistines are there, they are. Following this verse, Delilah disappears from the text.

The only other verb where Delilah is the subject more than once is to bind (אסר). In both cases she acts because Samson suggests that if he is bound by various materials he will lose his strength (Judg 16:7, 11). As noted previously, it is hard to suggest that she is deceiving Samson when she asks overtly for the source of his strength, and immediately after he tells her she carries out the action. So the only reason she carries out this action twice is because he uses this ruse twice.

The rest of the verbs occur only once with Delilah as the subject. In Judg 16:12 she "takes" (לקח), in this case new ropes. This is a verb that means a task as simple as taking but can have sexual connotations, though that appears unlikely here. In this context, it is in direct response to Samson's second explanation of the source of his strength.

Delilah finally resorts to nagging and pressing (צוק) him (Judg 16:16). Apparently nagging works with Samson because his bride did the same to get the answer to the riddle from him (Judg 14:17). In her case, the nagging was accompanied with tears, but with Delilah it is accompanied by more forceful action. In this case, the two are connected by a term not regularly employed. The reference to nagging connects them while the associated actions serve to differentiate them.

Delilah's last actions are all associated with Samson finally telling her the source of his strength. In Judg 16:18, Delilah realizes that Samson has told her the truth and so she sends (שלח) for the Philistines. In fact, she is so confident that she includes a message for them. In the first two attempts, the Philistines are waiting for Samson (Judg 16:9, 12). In the third attempt they are not there (Judg 16:14). It might be that they are no longer trusting Delilah, hence the need for the message. Once Samson is asleep, she also calls (קרא) a man who will shave him (Judg 16:19). The suggestion is that Samson is sleeping so soundly that he does not notice another person in the room. Note that in the first two attempts at weakening Samson, a

Philistine ambush is awaiting Samson and he does not hear or notice them either. It is either a commentary on how Delilah is binding Samson or how deeply he sleeps that he does not notice either an ambush awaiting him or a man entering his room.

In this last case, Delilah intentionally causes Samson to sleep on her knees (Judg 16:19).[26] In the first two cases, Delilah manages to carry out the actions without Samson noticing, suggesting he is asleep while she is doing it (Judg 16:8, 12). Since both of those cases suggest he is bound, it is possible he allowed her to bind him while awake, though the text includes no data as to whether or not he is awake. In the third case, pegging his hair, the text includes that he has to wake up when she says the Philistines are on him (Judg 16:14). This final case is the only one where Delilah specifically carries out some action that leads him to fall asleep.

Since this text follows immediately upon Samson's nocturnal visit to the prostitute in Gaza, something sexual in her actions leading to his exhaustion is certainly a possible reading. It also leads some to associate this intertextually with Jael's tent and the death of Sisera in Judg 4:17–21; 5:25–27. In both cases it is possible Jael has some sort of sexual encounter with Sisera leading to his exhaustion and slumber, allowing her to put a mallet through his temple.[27] Note that in Judg 4 Sisera is apparently sleeping prior to Jael's efforts with the mallet (Judg 4:21), whereas in Judg 5 he falls at her feet (Judg 5:27). Again, as is the case with the finding out the source of Samson's strength, while the scenario between Delilah and Jael is similar, the Hebrew terminology used in both is not the same. For example, Samson is on Delilah's knees, whereas Sisera falls between Jael's legs. They are similar but, had the text wanted us to read them tightly together, the same terminology could have been employed with the same impact for the internal story. Instead, the text uses different language.

Once Samson is asleep, Delilah calls a man into the room but the subject of the verb "to shave" (גלח) is feminine. So why Delilah needs a man in the room to shave Samson's locks is not clear. What is fitting is that this is yet another unique verb used by Delilah. In this case, there are no parallels in the biblical text of a woman shaving a man's head, especially while he sleeps.[28]

---

26. In this case, it is the third-person feminine singular *piel* form of ישן.

27. Colleen M. Conway, *Sex and Slaughter in the Tent of Jael: A Cultural History of a Biblical Story* (Oxford: Oxford University Press, 2017).

28. The only reference to this verb associated with a woman is Deut 21:12 concerning what to do with a beautiful captive woman. She must shave her head.

This final act weakens Samson. While technically she begins to humble him (עִנָּה), the term is used in cases of abuse (Sarah of Hagar, Gen 16:6) and in scenes with sexual connotations, such as what Hamor does to Dinah (Gen 34:2). The notion of beginning to do something to Samson aligns neatly with Samson's role from his birth: to begin to save the Israelites from the Philistines (Judg 13:5). Delilah does precisely what Samson himself claims would happen if various things were done to him. Because of Delilah Samson loses his strength as the Israelite deity leaves him.

In summary, Delilah's actions are represented by normal verbs, even for women, like speaking, and unique like shaving and binding. There are places in the narrative where she easily could be linked, through verbs suggesting actions she is already carrying out in the present text, to other women in the Samson cycle and the book of Judges in general, and yet those terms are not used. Since she is connected to Samson's other women, the implication has to be that the use of different terminology for similar situations is intentional. The text does not want the reader to link Delilah too closely with either Samson's bride or Jael.

Delilah as the Object of a Sentence

Delilah is the object of ten verbs but many of the cases are direct speech where she is speaking to Samson and she refers to herself as the object. There are a number of different verbs used for speech where she is the object. Thus, even when she is the object of a verb she appears to be in a position of power. This is true for most of the places where Delilah is the object with one big exception.

The first verb with Delilah as the object is in her introduction, when the text informs the reader that Samson loves a woman named Delilah (Judg 16:4). Love is a complicated notion in the Hebrew Bible with only one woman recorded as loving a man (Michal loves David [1 Sam 18:20] and this does not turn out well for her). Samson's love of Delilah is later used by her when she suggests that it is not the case; she argues, after he does not tell her the source of his strength three times, that he says he loves her but his heart is not with her (Judg 16:15). In this case, she is the object even though it is in the midst of her direct speech. Note Samson's Timnite bride uses a similar tactic by telling him, "You really hate me; you do not love me" (Judg 14:16) when she seeks the answer to his riddle. As is the case with how they attempt to elicit answers from Samson, the terminology is similar but not identical.

Delilah is next an object when the lords of the Philistines went up to her (Judg 16:5). This is also the first time that someone speaks to her using the term אמר. Delilah is the object of speech acts more often than anything else. This first speech act is notable for its content and the way it is delivered. While the Philistines say something to her, the first two items are direct imperatives to her. An imperative is an order to someone, "do x," without including the second person pronoun "you." Technically that means that the person being ordered "you" is the subject of the verb. Here they are imperatives, they are in second person delivered to Delilah so technically she is the subject of those verbs (you). Since the Philistines' direct speech is directed to her and they are imperatives, they are included here.

The content is important in understanding Delilah's actions. Since her ethnicity is not identified, and she is paid to hand Samson to the Philistines, the suggestion for many is that she is working for monetary gains.[29] Yet such an approach ignores the order of what they say and what happens to Samson's bride. Samson's bride does what the Philistines demand of her, she learns the answer to Samson's riddle and tells them (Judg 14:17). Afterward Samson burns the Philistines fields so the Philistines then burn Samson's former bride and her father (Judg 15:6). It is likely Delilah knows this. When the Philistine lords come up to Delilah and speak to her they use the imperative. They tell her to "open him" to "see" what makes him strong. They do not ask, they command. They also suggest they are only interested in learning what makes him so strong and how to overpower him and make him helpless. Only at the end of the verse do they note that they will each give her money.

Note Delilah is also the object of the verb "give" (נתן) in terms of them giving her money (Judg 16:5). She does not answer them, but the next verse has her asking Samson for the secret to his strength (Judg 16:6). While she does do what they have told her to do, there might be more behind Delilah's actions than greed or Philistine patriotism.[30] By this point in the story, Samson's bride and her entire family have been destroyed by the Philistines because of the whole riddle affair (Judg 15:6). This is not a focus on that situation, but the reality is that Samson's bride delivered the riddle, her people still suffered, and her family is still destroyed because

29. Matthews, *Judges and Ruth*, 159.
30. Matthews, *Judges and Ruth*, 159.

of, one might argue, Samson's temper. This story is connected to Samson's visit to the prostitute in Gaza by the connecting phrase "after this" (Judg 16:4), suggesting there is some relationship. In that case, regardless of what the prostitute knew about the ambush laid by the Philistines, the city of Gaza loses its city gate because of Samson (Judg 16:3). Regardless of who or what Delilah is, a legitimate emotion she might have is fear because all other situations between Samson and the Philistines concerning women end in disaster, usually for the woman and/or the Philistines.

Further proof of this goes back to the command to "open" Samson. The Philistine companions at Samson's wedding also ask his bride to "open" him, using the same verb (Judg 14:15). There appears to be a pattern of enemies of Samson commanding Samson's women. This could suggest further that Delilah is at serious risk. In fact, connecting both of Samson's women with Jael here makes sense as the possibility is high that Jael is a potential victim, in her case, possibly of rape.[31] So Philistine men treat Samson's bride and Delilah the same way. They act differently.

Following this encounter, all of the uses of "said" are in conversation with Samson. Samson "says" to her a series of things that will weaken him, all using this same verb in Judg 16:7, 11, and 17 with the last including the true reason. In Judg 16:15 Delilah's personal speech includes references to him "saying" to her incorrect statements.

The verb for discourse using the root נגד also is used frequently in Samson's and Delilah's discourse. Delilah asks Samson, using the imperative form, which makes him the subject and her the object, when she asks for the secret of his strength in Judg 16:6 and 10. These are the first two times she asks. While the form she uses is the imperative, it is not really an imperative because her speech is tempered by the particle נא suggesting an entreaty or request.[32] In other words, she asks nicely by saying please. In fact, one might argue the difference between a demand and a request is the use of this particle. Where and when translators decide to include "please" or other suggestions of an entreaty is not consistent.[33] In this case, only the NJPS translation does not include the reference to please. The third time Delilah suggests he should tell her, she does not use the term "please," and thus it is a command (Judg 16:13).

---

31. Schneider, Judges, 96.

32. BDB, s.v. "נא."

33. Schneider, Judges, 26–27.

Delilah refers to Samson not telling her in 16:15. This too is in the middle of Delilah's direct speech. It is only in 16:17 that Samson tells her the truth, using this verb. Delilah recognizes that he has finally told her the truth in the following verse (Judg 16:18), again using this verb. This is another example where despite Delilah being the object "her," it is often in her voice and, with this particular verb, used to show how she finally has prevailed.

Another example of Delilah being powerful while the object is when the lords of the Philistines bring up to her the seven tendons Samson suggests will weaken him (Judg 16:8). In this case, Samson tells her they would weaken him and, without having to ask or leave, the Philistine lords bring her what she needs.

The final verbs where Delilah is the object also have her in the power seat. In Judg 16:10, 13, and 15 Delilah tells Samson that he has deceived her (she says, "you have deceived me"). While scholars have suggested that Delilah betrayed Samson, in truth, he is the one who deceives her; her speech is both accurate and accusatory, and while she is grammatically the object of the verb, she is not shying away from him or from her purpose. The trend with other women continues because Delilah's tactic differs fairly considerably from Samson's bride, who cries. The final verb of which Delilah is the object confirms this; she says, "you spoke falsehood" (Judg 16:10). While one may argue against what she is trying to do, her words in this context are accurate.

With one exception, in all of the cases where Delilah is the object of a verb, she is in control, either repeating something that has happened previously or telling/asking Samson to do something to/for her. The one exception is striking and could lay behind her efforts to learn the secret of Samson's strength. The Philistine lords offer her money but only after telling her what to do to weaken Samson. They most certainly do not say please.

Delilah's Relationships

A striking characteristic of Delilah is that she has no family, no men caring for her, and no children needing care. She has no relationship with the Israelite deity and her identity is nebulous at best. As such, one cannot argue for or against any loyalty one might want to impose upon her. It also means that she has very few relationships described in the text.

The most obvious relationship she has, and the reason for the story, is with Samson. He loves her. Since Samson is the focus of the story, this is

clearly an important factor. There is a wide range of discussion from scholars about the impact of Samson loving someone finally, rather than just
taking what he wants.[34] The reality is that the text provides no information
about Delilah's feelings toward Samson. One can argue he has frequent
access to her bedchamber or her home, noted by the frequency with which
he is there and sleeping (though officially there are only two instances
where he is categorically asleep: Judg 16:14 and 19).

Her actions could also be interpreted in a number of ways. When one
likens Delilah to Jael, some have argued that she appears almost like a
savior of the Philistines, at least, until Samson's hair returns.[35] Another
more frequent explanation is that she is doing it for the money.[36] Yet
another option is that she is trying to save herself.[37]

The Philistine lords might be the very people from whom she needs
protection. While this is the first time that lords of the Philistines appear
in the story, the Philistines in general are problematic for the Israelites
prior to Samson's birth (Judg 13:1) and throughout the entire saga (16:30).
They threaten Samson's bride over the riddle (14:15), suffer when Samson
loses (14:19), and take revenge on the bride's family after Samson sets fire
to the fields (15:6). How one might want to define Delilah depends on how
one views her relationship with the Philistines. Is she one? Is she partial
to their side? Is she just interested in the money? Is she happy to play both
sides to succeed? The text provides just enough information to raise these
questions but not enough to solve them categorically.

Finally, there are the other women affiliated with Samson in the saga.
They are all defined as women, a noun that is not necessary for the reader
to understand who they are, thus it links them beyond just being in a relationship with Samson. Despite that, there is little that links them to each
other and especially to Delilah. Samson's mother is his mother, speaks to
a messenger of the deity (Judg 13:3, 9), and wants him to marry a nice
Danite girl (Judg 14:3). Samson's bride is a Philistine (Judg 14:1), is married off to both Samson and then someone else suggesting she has little
power in her life (Judg 14:8; 15:2), and she uses tears to learn the riddle

---

34. Niditch, *Judges*, 168. Cf. Bruce Herzberg, "Samson's Moment of Truth," *BibInt*
18 (2010): 226–50.

35. Mercedes L. Garcia Bachmann, *Judges*, Wisdom Commentary 7 (Collegeville,
MN: Liturgical Press, 2018), 184–85.

36. Bachmann, *Judges*, 184–85.

37. Bachmann, *Judges*, 184–85.

from Samson (Judg 14:17). Despite knowing little about the prostitute in Gaza, the text provides more personal information about her than Delilah: she is a prostitute (Judg 16:1), though that is about all the reader learns. Thus, Delilah stands unique in the book.

Conclusions

The focus of this analysis has been on Delilah and how unique she is in the Samson cycle, in Judges in general and, if there were more space, in the Hebrew Bible writ large. The reality, though, is that, while the events of Judg 16 focus heavily on Delilah, all the characters are flitting around Samson because what he does is the center of those three chapters. Furthermore, as the last judge in the book, everything changes after him. Beginning already in 18:1 the text notes that in those days there was no king in Israel. Note this phrase is at the end of a book where there was no king in Israel at all so to raise such a concept at the end is clearly suggesting something is amiss.

Something is clearly amiss with Israel's last judge. This begins with the deity's limited goals for Samson: to begin to deliver Israel from the Philistines (Judg 13:3). Samson is on a personal downward spiral. His life begins with his mother meeting a messenger of the deity (Judg 13:3). He then goes against his parents (Judg 14:3), marrying a foreign bride, abandoning her, leading to the destruction of her family (Judg 15:6). His visit to the prostitute in Gaza ends in the middle of the night with a missing gate (Judg 16:3).

Elsewhere I argue, along with others, that the book of Judges is a cycle downward and women are the lynchpins that highlight that societal descent.[38] The final stories in Judges depict a woman gang-raped by the man who is supposed to protect her, leading to a civil war where a tribe of Israel is almost wiped out, and the means to continuing that tribe is to force a number of women into marriage (Judg 19–21). Thus, what is striking here is that Delilah is alone. She has no one to protect her and no one to protect. She has no family. She is not of Israel nor is she clearly outside Israel. She is loved by someone whose presence puts her at risk. The leaders of the region tell her to do something. The last time the Philistines gave this task to a woman, she and her family were destroyed. Using nothing

---

38. Schneider, *Judges*, 287.

but her words, Delilah overpowers a man of boundless strength. As soon as she overcomes him, she disappears from the story.

The focus of this volume is intertextuality, and Delilah is a great example because she is clearly connected to the other women in the Samson saga through the character of Samson. Samson is the last judge, and a problematic one at that. Regardless of the original intent of the authors, clearly the Samson and Delilah story, through its connections with some stories and not with the rest, provides an opportunity for those of us living in the twenty-first century to contemplate what and who is right and wrong.

13

"Jonathan's (Great) Grandmother Is a Daughter of a Foreign Priest!" Other Women, Other Priests, and Other Gods in Judges 17–18

Soo Kim Sweeney

And the people of Dan set up the carved image for themselves, and Jonathan the son of Gershom, son of Moses, and his sons were priests to the tribe of the Danites until the day of the captivity of the land.

— Judges 18:30 (ESV)

And the children of Dan set up for themselves the graven image; and Jonathan, the son of Gershom, the son of Manasseh, he and his sons were priests to the tribe of the Danites until the day of the captivity of the land.

— Judges 18:30 (JPS)

It is well known that Judg 17–18 is a polemic against the Danites' cultic practice, but "how so" and "so what" questions are not thoroughly discussed yet.[1] Starting from the observation of the tiny peculiar hanging *nun*

An earlier version of this paper was presented under the title, "In Search of Young Levite Jonathan's Grandfather in Judg 18:30: A Study of the Heuristic Application on the Dialogic Aspect of the Concept Analysis" at the 2013 International Meeting of the Society of Biblical Literature, Saint Andrews University, Scotland. I thank the editors for presenting it to a broader readership.

1. For polemics, Martin Noth is a classic example; Noth, "Background of Judges 17–18," in *Israel's Prophetic Heritage: Essays in Honor of James Muilenburg*, ed. Bernhard W. Anderson and Walter Harrelson (New York: Harper, 1962), 75–76. David Beldman's survey on Judges scholarship regarding compositional issues would be a good place to review the how so and so what questions; Beldman, *The Completion of Judges: Strategies of Ending in Judges 17–21*, Siphrut 21 (Winona Lake, IN: Eisenbrauns, 2017), 10–51.

on Moses's name (מְנַשֶּׁה) in 18:30, I propose two kinds of reading strategies: one is to follow the compositional strategy for the how-so question;
the other is to rethink that agenda for the so-what question.

In "Reading Strategy One," I propose that the text aimed the tempo-
spatial polemic on the entire northern Israel territory beyond the character critics. The hanging *nun* phenomenon is the signal that the author
group abandoned the chronological coherence rule for this stronger
rhetoric.[2] At the same time, however, the text limits our searching
boundary (scope) in four proper names, as Judg 18:30 provides Jonathan, Gershom, and Moses/Manasseh in Jonathan's genealogy. Thus, the
reader's first task is to examine any character who bears one of these
four names in the Hebrew Bible in order to discover the possibility of
building up a common thematic thread from them. Based on the dominant cultic content in Judg 17–18 and Moses's peculiar association with
foreign women, I will first focus on characters related to the foreign
priesthood in Jonathan's maternal genealogy.[3] To help readers connect
this character analysis with the tempo-spatial interpretation, I will also
introduce the text's theological thoughts and rhetorical devices that I
have found from my reading.

"Reading Strategy Two" then evaluates the text's presentation, which
attempted to make the northern tribes the totally Other to the implied
readers. My special attention goes to the author's subtle but undeni-
able mistreatment of women characters. The two women in Jonathan's
genealogy, Zipporah and Aseneth, do not appear in the text, but play
an essential role in binding the male referential characters, Gershom,
Moses, and Manasseh, in Jonathan's genealogy.[4] With the underlying
concept of the foreign and feminine to be forsaken, the text uses those

---

2. A diachronic term, *author group* refers to the entire people involved in produc-
ing the present form of the text. Thus, they include the original writers, scribes, and
compilers; see Soo J. Kim, "Ashamed before the Presence of God," in *Methodological
Studies*, vol. 1 of *Theology of the Hebrew Bible*, ed. Marvin A. Sweeney, RBS 92 (Atlanta:
SBL Press, 2019), 216–21.

3. Except for Moses, all three names refer to multiple characters in the Hebrew
Bible, which means we can choose the best candidates for Manasseh and Gershom,
once we build up the criteria with the thematic threads. However, this is not applicable
to Moses since the name *Moses* is fixed in one character, Moses, son of Amram and
Jochebed. Thus, Moses should be a reference point for the criteria setting.

4. I will explain the referential and linked-in characters below in "1. Characters
Who Have Other Priests and Other Women."

women in order to damage the whole house of Jonathan, the tribe he served, and the land where he stood. Finally, I propose to restore those characters' embracement of others as a suggestive virtue for our so-what question. My effort is restoration rather than creation because the text hides that virtue in it.

The Hanging *Nun* Phenomenon:
Moses? Manasseh? Or Moses and Manasseh?

With the unique device of the hanging *nun* on מֹשֶׁה, the Masoretic Text of Judg 18:30 calls readers to return their reading.[5] It opens two options for who Jonathan's grandfather could be, either Moses or Manasseh. An interpretive choice becomes an issue not only for scribes in the transmission process but also for translators who must work the name into non-Semitic languages.[6] If readers respect the hanging *nun* and accept it as a quasi-regular letter, Manasseh, whoever he might be, becomes Jonathan's grandfather. Nonetheless, if readers treat the suspended *nun* as a later insertion and disregard it, Moses is a grandfather of the Danites' first priest.[7] The ancient author group did not leave us enough information to answer many curious questions like why, when, and how this peculiarity occurred. Accordingly, readers of Judg 17–18 have been eager to make various conjectures according to their preferences, which ironically resemble the narrator's evaluation in Judg 17–18: "Everyone did as they saw fit" (Judg 17:1, 6, NIV).

The most straightforward and popular answer for a long time was that the hanging *nun* was a pious insertion to protect Moses's reputation from the idolatrous Danites' cultic tradition.[8] It looks reasonable at first glance,

---

5. This suspected or raised letter phenomenon occurs two more times in the Hebrew Bible, both with the letter ע in Ps 80:14; Job 38:13, 15. However, these cases do not have a serious issue like the Moses/Manasseh case.

6. The Aleppo Codex and the Leningrad Codex chose the hanging *nun* as a suspended letter, as we see in BHS.

7. The LXX Family B (Codex Vaticanus), JPS, NASB, LUO, LXX (Ralphs) all read מְנַשֶּׁה as Manasseh. Meanwhile, ESV, LXX Family A (Codex Alexandrinus), KRV, Vulg., and REV choose to read it as Moses. Neither Codex Sinaiticus nor the Dead Sea Scrolls contain Judg 18.

8. Generally, scholars attribute this phenomenon to the scribal traditions. For the rabbinic accounts, see b. B. Bat. 109b. For later scholarly discussion, see Karl Budde, *Das Buch der Richter*, KHC 7 (Freiburg im Breisgau: Mohr, 1897), 124–25; Emmanuel

but many ensuing questions quickly arise. For example, did the earlier author make this connection with the evil intention to tarnish the Mushite priesthood reputation?[9] Or did the later groups repaint the initially positive or neutral narratives of the Danites' cultic tradition?[10] This account usually does not answer those questions, probably because interpreters in this position believe in the authenticity of Moses's name in Jonathan's genealogy. However, the Hebrew Bible does not show any corresponding record of the Moses-line up to Jonathan.[11]

The next popular question goes to which Manasseh the author had in mind in the hanging *nun*.[12] Unfortunately, this question also adds another frustration, since the text cannot stand upon the ground of chronological order. Like the lack of a matching name in Moses's genealogy, no Manasseh could be Gershom's father. Therefore, we need to ensure that examining candidates for Manasseh means acknowledging the present text is the result of an image-making product. The author group even gave up the narrative's chronological coherence for their agenda. I suggest employing an image-connection reading, that is, the reader's version of the author's image-making strategy. This will enable us to appreciate the potential ideas that we can generate through combining images of characters.

Tov, *Textual Criticism of the Hebrew Bible* (Minneapolis: Fortress, 1992), 258–85; Susan Niditch, *Judges: A Commentary*, OTL (Louisville: Westminster John Knox, 2008), 184.

9. Gale A. Yee, "Ideological Criticism: Judges 17–21 and the Dismembered Body," in *Judges and Methods: New Approaches in Biblical Studies*, ed. Gale A. Yee, 2nd ed. (Minneapolis: Fortress, 2007), 160.

10. Mark W. Bartusch, *Understanding Dan: An Exegetical Study of a Biblical City, Tribe and Ancestor*, JSOTSup 379 (Sheffield: Sheffield Academic, 2003), 202; Karel van der Toorn, *Family Religion in Babylonia, Syria and Israel*, SHANE 7 (Leiden: Brill, 1996), 305; Jason S. Bray, *Sacred Dan: Religious Tradition and Cultic Practice in Judges 17–18*, LHBOTS 449 (New York: T&T Clark, 2006), 68; also see Trent Butler's discussion on this; Butler, *Judges*, WBC 8 (Nashville: Nelson, 2009), 400.

11. Moreover, 1 Chr 23:16; 26:24 do not mention Gershom's name in the genealogy. It is possible that the family might not want to remember Jonathan as their family member due to his infamous reputation. However, it is also entirely possible that Jonathan's genealogy in Judg 18:30 might be a product of the image-combination agenda.

12. E.g., Steven Weitzman argues that Manasseh in Judg 18:30 reflects the Jewish and Samaritan hostile collective memories from the Second Temple period; Weitzman, "Reopening the Case of the Suspiciously Suspended Nun in Judges 18:30," *CBQ* 61 (1999): 449.

Reading Strategy One: Exploring the Author's Strategy

The author's compositional strategy from my reading includes holding and image-making strategies. To begin with the holding strategy, despite standing on the omniscient viewpoint, the third-person narrator did not inform us of the young Levite's name and genealogy until the end of the story. This holding strategy produces several effects. The indeterminacy keeps readers watching the unnamed Levite at a distance, since both his name and family origin remain unknown even after his joining Micah or the Danites. At the same time, readers hold their growing doubts regarding the legitimacy of Jonathan's priesthood until they burst their held breath with frustration at the end of the story.[13] Ironically, the very frustration also leads readers to take a heuristic attitude and reinvestigate their previous readings, as we do now. Robert O'Connell names this peculiarity in the book of Judges as the author's entrapping strategy, making readers reassess the uncertainty or contradiction in their first reading.[14] Rhetorically speaking, the revelation of Jonathan's familial identity at the end works as a climax in attacking Jonathan and the Danites together.

The second one, the image-making strategy, starts from the author's decision to be free from the narrative's chronological coherence. This is a rare case in the Hebrew Bible. The authorial desire to produce the maximum tempo-spatial polemic against northern Israel prevails over the concerns about the reader's potential confusion. Thus, any reading that sticks to the synchronic reading alone will encounter a problem.[15] As Marvin Sweeney points out, reading the book of Judges as a historical reflection

---

13. Samuel Coleridge named it "suspension of disbelief"; Coleridge, *Biographia Literaria*, ed. James Engell and W. Jackson Bate (Princeton: Princeton University Press, 1983), 6–7.

14. O'Connell, *The Rhetoric of the Book of Judges*, VTSup 63 (Leiden: Brill, 1996), 6–7.

15. E.g., taking the genealogy of Jonathan as Moses's grandson (18:30) literally, Robin Baker argues that the Danites' immigration must have occurred before Samson's birth; therefore, Samson's father Manoah is a representative of the faithful remnant who kept their allocated land; see Baker, *Hollow Man, Strange Women: Riddles, Codes and Otherness in the Book of Judges*, BibInt 143 (Leiden: Brill, 2016), 95–96. However, as Weitzman poses in a rhetorical question to show the dilemma of Manasseh in 18:30 as the son of Joseph, the literal reading on this verse makes a difficult text more difficult; Weitzman, "Suspended Nun in Judges 18:30," 449.

of premonarchic Israel is not recommended.[16] A text such as Judg 17–18 demands that the interpreter actively modify the interpretation scope, even departing from the text's chronological or historical ground. This is the hanging *nun*'s effect.

Then, how far shall we extend our reading scope in picking up candidates of Manasseh from the author's pool? From the time of Aramean king Ben-Hadad's conquest of Dan to the Assyrian conquest or the postexilic edition, proposals on the editorial layers in Judg 17–18 are intrinsically hypothetical and indecisive.[17] Nonetheless, one can easily find the common denominator from each diachronic conjecture: the authorial intention of severe condemnation on the northern tribes.[18] My thesis goes further. I claim that Judg 17–18 aims to make the spatial polemic on the entire northern Israel territory at the horizontal level and the genealogical disparagement on their cultic leadership at the vertical level.

1. Characters Who Have Other Priest and Other Woman

In this section, I will analyze the characters of Judg 17–18. Who are they? My character analysis includes Zipporah and Aseneth as well as Gershom,

---

16. Sweeney, "Davidic Polemics in the Book of Judges," *VT* 47 (1997): 517.

17. For Ben-Hadad's conquest of Dan, see David Ilan and Jonathan Greer, "Dan (Place)," *EBR* 6:62. Based on the reading of 18:30–31 as at least two different layers, Bray argues 18:30 reflects the Assyrian invasion and the exile of northern Israel; Bray, *Sacred Dan*, 21–23. J. Alberto Soggin also argues the demise of the Northern Kingdom by Assyrians must have provided the motive to composite the cultic corruption in the Northern Kingdom; Soggin, *Judges: A Commentary*, trans. John Bowden, 2nd ed., OTL (London: SCM, 1987), 269. Phillippe Guillaume attributes the major edition of Judges 17–18 to King Josiah, based on the anti-Assyrian context and his ambitious project for the annexation of northern Israel. He reads only the last two verses as reflections of the Second Temple period when the competition between Bethel and Jerusalem finally settled; Guillaume, *Waiting for Josiah: The Judges*, JSOTSup 385 (London: T&T Clark, 2004), 135–42. For a postexilic edition, see Yee, "Ideological Criticism," 146. Yairah Amit, "Hidden Polemic in the Conquest of Dan: Judges 17–18," *VT* 40 (1990): 4–20; Uwe F. W. Bauer, "Judges 18 as an Anti-Spy Story in the Context of an Anti-Conquest Story," *JSOT* 25 (2000): 37–47; Nadav Na'aman, "The Danite Campaign Northward (Judges 17–18) and the Migration of the Phocaeans to Massallia (Strabo IV 1, 4)," *VT* 55 (2005): 47–60; Serge Frolov, *Judges*, FOTL 6B (Grand Rapids: Eerdmans, 2013), 287–300.

18. Sweeney, "Davidic Polemics in the Book of Judges," 517; Marc Brettler, *The Book of Judges*, OTR (London: Routledge, 2002), 111.

Moses, and Manasseh. I define *character* as any living entity who can influence the author's story or the reader's understanding of it. Accordingly, they are not necessarily limited to the author's creatures.[19]

Based on this definition, I would like to introduce three kinds of characters for the Judg 17–18 reading. First, characters involved in the plot development at the story's surface-level are *story line characters*. Micah, Micah's mother, Micah's son, Jonathan, the Danites spies, and even the six hundred Danites belong here. Second, characters who are just mentioned by the narrator or characters belong to *referential characters* because their influential power only works at the reference level. The author usually employs this kind of character to control the reader's direction. YHWH/ God (mentioned by story line characters, Micah's mother, Micah, and Jonathan), Gershom, Moses, and Manasseh (mentioned by the narrator) are the referential characters in Judg 17–18. Finally, characters can also be brought or created by the reader. I call them *linked-in characters* because their influence on the readers depends on the individual reader's or interpretive community's intertextual links at the various reading circumstances. Since nobody mentions their names in the text, readers cannot assert that those characters were in the author's mind and should admit that those characters are from the reader's intertextual reading. However, the linked-in characters are not pure creatures from the reader's imagination because they are governed by the shared link(s) that the author group set up through their characters—story line and referential characters.[20]

---

19. My definition is not traditional, but one can find a similar concept to include reader's construction of the character from H. Porter Abbott's narratology; see Abbott, *The Cambridge Introduction to Narrative*, 2nd ed. (Cambridge: Cambridge University Press, 2008), 134–35.

20. The most important condition for the linked-in characters is that they should be in the scope of the author's compositional time line. In other words, the characters whom the reader would bring to the interpretation should be in the shared information pool, the Hebrew Bible in this case. Moreover, the candidates should be corresponding to or serving the theme of the text. The third condition is the strong bond with the story line characters or the reference characters. I will introduce many other characters in this article, including King Jeroboam, Jacob, and Rachel. However, they are not linked-in characters, but examples of my intertextual reading because they are not directly connected with the referential or story line characters. While the referential characters reflect the author's ambition to direct the reader's task, linked-in characters' births are related to the reader's desire to assert that those linked-in characters are indeed standing by in the reading space between the text and the reader.

In search of Jonathan's grandfather in 18:30, we have realized that the text encourages us to conceptualize common thematic images from the given story line and referential characters, Jonathan, Gershom, Moses, and Manasseh. As this article's title shows, "a daughter of a foreign priest" in their genealogy is a thematic thread for both the Moses–Gershom–Jonathan option and the Manasseh–Gershom–Jonathan option. My linked-in characters, Zipporah (the wife of Moses) and Aseneth (the mother of Manasseh), provide a reasonable basis to make sense of the hanging *nun*'s effect in Jonathan's genealogy. This section will unpack how this foreign priest and foreign woman become Others in the author's agenda. The first task is to examine popularly accepted negative characterizations of Micah, Gershom, Moses, and Manasseh, with special attention to their familial and priestly backgrounds in the Hebrew Bible.[21] Strictly speaking, Micah does not belong to this category because his genealogy is not known, and his mother is not a foreign woman. However, Micah, a founder of the house of God in the hill country of Ephraim, provides the primary setting for both Jonathan and the Danites. On the other hand, even though Jonathan belongs to this category, he will be examined in an independent section since he is the ultimate target character.

Micah and the House of Micah

Judges 17:1 introduces Micah as the resident of the hill country of Ephraim (הר אפרים).[22] Interestingly, this famous region always appears with the name Micah in Judg 17–18: one time (17:1) in the introduction of Micah and three times (17:8; 18:2; 18:13) with the phrase "the house of Micah." In other words, the text encourages us to pay attention to the significance of the spatial setting: Micah's (il)legitimate ephod, teraphim, and priest are *in* the house of God (בית אלהים), *in* the house of Micah, *in* the hill country of Ephraim, *on*

---

21. The image connections can be unlimitedly various depending on the reader's accessibility of the information and willingness and may end up with an unwanted subjective reading. Therefore, I set up the reading scope within the biblical characters, hoping to continue to dialogue with the author-oriented intertextual readers.

22. The text presents two forms of his name: Micayehu (17:1, 4) and Micah (17:5, 9, 10, 12, 13; 18:2, 3, 4, 13, 15, 18, 22, 23, 26, 27, 31). The Hebrew Bible informs that many significant cities, mountains, and plains belong to this region: Baal Hazor, Mizpah, Bethel, Samaria, Shiloh, Shechem, Tirzah, Dothan, Jezreel, Ebal, and Gerizim.

the southern border of northern Israel.[23] If I express this setting with Edward Soja's tripartite spatiality, the author group adds the political and religious Secondspace notion to the physical Firstspace, the hill country of Ephraim, to transform the ordinary image into the epicenter image of defilement.[24]

Now, let us look into his family relationship. Most commentators, not in favor of Micah, point out the series of family betrayals surrounding him. Micah stole the money, and by doing so, he betrayed his mother. He fired his son to appoint the Levite a priest. Furthermore, Micah twisted the deal when he changed his promise of making Jonathan a father-like priest to a son-like priest.[25] Finally, his hospitality is betrayed by that priest.

The same rubric has been applied to Micah's mother as a material blessing-driven character. However, as Lillian Klein evaluates her as a "self-sufficient woman," we need to respect our common sense in reading her case.[26] When people lose considerable money, for example, they may curse any imaginable thief. However, when a mother comes to know that the criminal was none but her son, even though the mixed emotions would dominate for a while, she would eventually withdraw the curse, even before the son returns the stolen money. How many more blessings would come from the mother's mouth when the son confesses and returns the silver to her! Her wish is natural in this context.[27] Moreover, her dedication of two hundred pieces of silver to make an image is not necessarily read as a renege from the pledged amount.[28] The text does not use "all"

23. For ephod usage in Judges and the emphasis on the piling up of the illegal objects, see Baker, *Hollow Men, Strange Women*, 101–2. Various translations on בית אלהים reflect translators' perspectives on this narrative: A house of gods (ASV); a shrine (ESV, KRV, NAS, NIV); a house of God (JPS). I chose the capital letter, God; in this because there is no decisive evidence to see this as a house for the other gods. For the detailed discussion, see Barry G. Webb, *The Book of Judges*, NICOT (Grand Rapids: Eerdmans, 2012), 426.

24. Edward Soja, *Thirdspace: Journeys to Los Angeles and Other Real-and-Imagined Places* (Oxford: Blackwell, 1996).

25. Yee, "Ideological Criticism," 159.

26. Klein, "A Spectrum of Female Characters," in *Feminist Companion to Judges*, ed. Athalya Brenner, FCB 4 (Sheffield: JSOT Press, 1993), 30–31.

27. Robert G. Boling, *Judges: A New Translation with Introduction and Commentary*, AB 6A (Garden City, NY: Doubleday, 1975), 255–56.

28. Contra Lillian R. Klein, *The Triumph of Irony in the Book of Judges*, JSOT-Sup 68, BLS 14 (Sheffield: Almond Press, 1988), 147; Baker, *Hollow Man, Strange Women*, 62.

(כל) in 17:3–4; the text never supports that she pledged to use all eleven hundred pieces of silver, but soon changed her mind. Klein's argument to blame the mother for Micah's immoral behavior as her failure to educate her son also seems too harsh.[29] Instead, I encourage my readers to pay attention to the author's ignoring of Micah's mother, even though she is the cofounder of the house of God in the hill country of Ephraim. She is wholly excluded in any deal with the priest appointment or resistance against the Danites' violation, because the author group simply made her disappear after the first four verses. As Luce Irigaray points out, the text limits her in the private zone of the patriarchal culture.[30]

The repetitive inversions regarding the stealing-stolen motif in Judg 17–18 also lead me to read Micah with the Jacob-Rachel couple image in Genesis. Jacob stole (or conned at best) the firstborn birthright from his brother Esau, while Rachel, Jacob's stolen bride, stole the household god from her father, Laban. We know that Micah's foremost characteristic is thievery. Moreover, both Jacob and Rachel had a strong desire for God's blessing, as Micah and his mother had. Yet the Jacob-Rachel couple both suffered from their choices: Jacob endured a long exile in Aram; Rachel lost her own life in her delivery. It is not hard to see that Micah and his mother's various activities regarding the shrine came from their yearning for YHWH's blessing. However, his deity did not even appear at all, and Micah was left with an empty nest in the hill country of Ephraim. Finally, Jacob experienced his favorite son Joseph being stolen by his own sons, just as Micah lost his favorite priest, ephod, and teraphim by force. Unfortunately, the priest whom he hired played a crucial role in this betrayal. Despite the characters' firm conviction that the divine blessing would be granted to them, the subsequent narratives often reveal the opposite result.

Interestingly, this image-connection reading opens two directions. On the one hand, this connection enables me to mitigate Micah's negative image with more neutral characters, Jacob and Rachel, and make him a rather unfortunate or unwise character. On the other hand, this connection may strengthen the author's northern Israel polemic because the Jacob-Rachel family, negatively illustrated in these events, is well known for the association with the northern Israel tradition.

---

29. Lillian R. Klein, "The Book of Judges: Paradigm and Deviation in Images of Women," in Brenner, *Feminist Companion to Judges*, 69.

30. Irigaray, *Sexes et Parentés*, Critique (Paris: Minuit, 1987), 126–27.

How about Micah's characterization in his priestly activity? My overall image-connection reading on Micah concludes that he is one who wanted to be like Moses but ended up like King Jeroboam.[31] As Moses ordered to make an ephod for the priest, Micah did the same thing. As Moses built the tabernacle for the temporary meeting place with the deity in the wilderness, Micah built the house of God in his home when the temple was not yet built. However, whereas Moses appointed Aaron and his sons for the priesthood, not his own sons, Micah first appointed his non-Levitical son a priest and replaced him with the Levite. In all these activities, Judg 17–18 never approves Micah's action as the compliance with the divine commands. In contrast, the pentateuchal narratives do not forget to attach the phrase "as God commanded" to Moses's activities.

These differences call King Jeroboam, another counterpart of Moses, to our discussion table. The parallel starts from a similar pattern in their genealogy. Judges 17:1 introduces Micah with the tribal and regional background instead of the typical formula X, son of Y.[32] This is the first hint that the reader may connect the Ephraimite Micah with the Ephraimite King Jeroboam, the founder of northern Israel and the Bethel shrine. Even though the latter's father is mentioned in the introduction as Nebat (1 Kgs 11:26), the narrator immediately adds his mother's name and widow status. In Micah's case, the implied nuance of Micah's father's absence and his dependence on the mother casts a traditional feminine image on him. Indeed, this conventional feminine image reaches the climax in his confrontation with the Danites' aggressive male image (Judg 18:22–26). Micah cannot go beyond the hill country of Ephraim, even though his precious ephod, teraphim, and priest are all taken before his eyes. Being stuck in one place, he is depicted as the human signpost for the passersby. This static and passive image of Micah is later combined with the similar

---

31. Rainer Albertz, *A History of Israelite Religion in the Old Testament Period*, trans. John Bowden, 2 vols. (Louisville: Westminster John Knox, 1994), 2:141–43.

32. The book of Judges employs several types in the introduction of the main characters. The most popular type is the "X son of Y" style, which occurs for more than eight characters in Judges. However, Micah, the man from the hill country of Ephraim (17:1) belongs to the person with the clan/town origins. Other examples include Jair the Gileadite (10:3); Jephthah the Gileadite (11:1); Ibzan of Bethlehem (12:8); Elon the Zebulunite (12:11). For more detail in this formula, see Mark Leuchter, "'Now There Was a [Certain] Man': Compositional Chronology in Judges–1 Samuel," *CBQ* 69 (2007): 436–38.

image of the conquered land, Laish/Dan. It plays a role in imposing more aggressive images on Jonathan and the Danites as active characters. In this case, the passive feminine image is used to show that the text's real target is Jonathan and the Danites rather than Micah.

Interestingly, the Jeroboam narrative author seems to emphasize Jeroboam's sedentary or even immobile image once he built the golden calves in the two shrines. The narrator just briefly reports his outside activities in the beginning (building activity in 1 Kgs 12:25) and the end (fighting with King Rehoboam in 1Kgs 14:19; 14:30). Like Micah, King Jeroboam wanted the man of God from Judah to stay at his house but could not hold him. Like Micah, who built his shrine for YHWH's blessing but was left in the haunted house, Jeroboam was stuck at the Bethel shrine, which he made for YHWH's blessing to him and his people. Even when his son Abijah was sick, Jeroboam sent his wife to Shiloh instead of leaving to visit the prophet. Micah's priest appointment can even be read as a parody of Jeroboam's non-Levitical priest appointment and his wish to hold the man from Judah to mock both Micah and Jeroboam. Finally, both Micah and Jeroboam made an overlaid image and erected it at their shrine.[33] The clear message from these image-making strategies is that northern Israel, from the previous tenant Micah, is already forsaken as a kingdom created by stolen money and deviant people. Every wish for the blessing, therefore, will be reversed to a curse.

Moses and His Foreign Women

Reading Moses's story with the awareness of gender, genealogy, and geography sharpens a foreign image in Moses. Born in a foreign land, Egypt, he was rescued by pharaoh's daughter, who eventually adopted and raised him in the Egyptian royal family. Moses's lack of confidence with his own people in Exod 2–6 seems a natural consequence; accordingly, the genealogy in Exod 6 seems to emphasize his legitimate status as a full Israelite man, especially as a Levite. Moses seemed to pass this identity trial when YHWH grants him the right to appoint priests and set up various regulations for the newly born nation, Israel. However, the sibling debate regarding Moses's intermarriage with a Cushite woman (Num 12) suggests that

---

33. Butler (*Judges*, 378–82) argues the authorial intention seems explicit to combine Micah's activity with the golden calf idolatry by using the common term מסכה.

the tension from his foreignness might remain even within the core family members. Moreover, his first wife, Zipporah, is not just a foreign woman but a daughter of the Midianite priest, Jethro. As we see in Exod 18 and Num 10, his wife's family was never assimilated into the Israelite community. The anti-Midianite sentiments are strong throughout the book of Judges, as we see in the Ehud and Gideon stories, respectively. In this context, the text surprises us by positioning this Moses in the troublesome Jonathan's genealogy.

Gershom and Zipporah

Besides Gershom, son of Moses and Zipporah, the Hebrew Bible has two more priestly related characters with this name: Gershom, son of Levi, and a descendent of Phinehas.[34] However, based on our commitment to concentrate on the priestly connection and foreignness (or sojourning), our attention goes to the firstborn son of Moses and Zipporah, Gershom. To begin with his name, "Sojourner," Thomas Römer explains two implications of the wordplay on the name Gershom: גר ("sojourner") and שם ("there") and "expulsion" from the verb גרש.[35] While the sojourner concept in Gershom's name in Exod 2:22 reflects his father's status as a sojourner in the foreign land, Gershom, the father of the wandering Levite in Judg 18:30, produces the liminal image throughout his family history. As Exod 2 illustrates, Gershom is a son of a Midianite woman, Zipporah, and a grandson of a Midianite priest, Jethro. Contrary to Exod 4:20, in which all family members of Moses were together on the journey to Egypt, Exod 18:5 informs us that Gershom must have been raised under the Midianite cultic influence, at least for a while, in Moses's absence. As Ken Stone remarks, the Dueteronomistic Historians consistently blame foreign women as a dangerous cause of religious infidelity.[36] We see the

---

34. According to 1 Chr 6:1–2, Gershom is the first son of Levi and the father of Libni and Shimel. Meanwhile, Gershom, a descendent of Phinehas, in Ezra 8:2 is introduced as a returnee from the Babylonian exile.

35. Römer, "Gershom," *EBR* 10:129–30. Frolov also points out that Gershom's name is already hinted as גר (sojourner) and שם (there) in 17:6 (*Judges*, 293).

36. Stone, "'Deuteronomistic History' in Imagery, Gendered," in *Oxford Encyclopedia of the Bible and Gender Studies,* ed. Julia M. O'Brien (Oxford: Oxford University Press, 2014), 1:353–54.

same agenda in Judg 17–18 through the implicit allusion via names on the
male characters.

In sum, Gershom is classified as a not-so-fully qualified priest candidate in Israel due to his foreign mother and even evaluated as somewhat dangerous due to his foreign grandfather, Jethro. His father, Moses,
according to this logic, became the one who caused this problem.

Manasseh and Aseneth

The name Manasseh, including the tribal name, is given to four different
characters in the Hebrew Bible: (1) son of Joseph, (2) king of Judah, (3) a
descendent of Pahath-Moab (Ezra 10:30), and (4) a descendent of Hashum
(Ezra 10:33). Although all these characters are related either to the cultic
or the foreign genealogy issues, Manasseh (1), son of Joseph and Aseneth,
satisfies the criteria the most. Let us review Manassehs (2) to (4) first.

First, King Manasseh (2), despite his full Israelite genealogy, is not
free from our attention due to his illegitimate cultic activity. Deborah
Rooke raises the possibility of the monarch as a functional priest by
emphasizing the sacred image of kings.[37] Christoph Levin also points
out that 2 Kings highlights King Manasseh's child sacrifice as the apex
of cultic abomination.[38] Meanwhile, Francesca Stavrakopoulou conjectures the hanging *nun* might be the reflection of King Manasseh's idolatry.[39] Indeed, King Manasseh's cultic policy and his relationship with the
Assyrian Empire are relevant to the topic in Judg 17–18. Second, the two
Manessehs in Ezra (3 and 4) are contemporary lay returnees who married foreign women. We do not need to assume Manasseh in Ezra 10:30
and 10:33 are the same person by making their ancestor Pahathmoab and
Hashum, the same person.

Meanwhile, the half-tribe of Manasseh in Transjordan is relevant to
this text according to the image-connection reading. According to 1 Chr
7:14, unlike Josh 17 describes, one of Manasseh's two sons, Machir, the

37. Deborah Rooke, "Kingship as Priesthood: The Relationship between the High
Priesthood and the Monarchy," in *King and Messiah in Israel and the Ancient Near
East: Proceedings of the Oxford Old Testament Seminar*, ed. John Day, JSOTSup 270
(Sheffield: Sheffield Academic, 1998), 190–207.

38. Levin, "Manasseh (King of Judah)," *EBR* 17:716–17.

39. Stavrakopoulou, *King Manasseh and Child Sacrifice: Biblical Distortions of
Historical Realities*, BZAW 338 (Berlin: de Gruyter, 2004), 130.

father of Gilead, had the Aramean mother, Maachah. As Erasmus Gaß points out, this Transjordan Manasseh was captured by the Aramean King Hazael of Damascus and later by the Assyrian King Tiglath–pileser III, while the west tribe of Manasseh was scattered by the Assyrian King Sargon II.[40] Finally, in the postbiblical tradition, Manasseh was named the high priest of the Samaritan temple.[41]

As shown above, Manasseh (1), Joseph and Aseneth's son, is the most relevant candidate who satisfies our criteria (a foreign priest's daughter in his maternal line) in the image-connecting reading strategy. Interestingly, like Gershom's name, Manasseh's name also reflects his father's exilic situation. According to Gen 41:51, Joseph confessed that God made him forget all his [my] hardship (כל עמלי) when he had a firstborn son from his Egyptian wife. Joseph's confession seems a positive reflection when we focus on the first direct object, the hardship. Nevertheless, he mentioned another direct object of "forgetting," as "all my father's house" (כל בית אבי), which suggests his awareness of full detachment from the homeland. Overall, the name, Manasseh, produces a more alienated nuance from the denotation "forgetting" since the etymological context in Genesis is not always attached in the collective memory on Manasseh.

How about his genealogy? Unlike Moses, who was involved in the Egyptian court, Manasseh's parents were deeply engaged with the Egyptian religious culture. His Egyptian mother, Aseneth, has an affiliation with the goddess Neith in her name.[42] Three times (Gen 41:45, 50; 46:20), Genesis informs us of her attachment to the Egyptian religion by introducing her as a daughter of Potiphera, priest of On. Genesis does not seem to be bothered by Aseneth's religious and ethnic identity. However, it is also possible to think that the potential polemic on the house of Joseph has already been embedded in this explicit mention of the Egyptian background in her name, her father's name, and occupation.

Aseneth is more well-known in the postbiblical traditions, as we see through the pseudepigraphon, Joseph and Aseneth (ca. first century BCE to the second century CE). As Carsten Burfeind points out, Aseneth in Judaism may reflect "the purity and defilement issue in the religious boundaries." Various solutions for her "foreignness" also suggest that

---

40. Gaß, "Manasseh, Manassites," *EBR* 17:701–2.

41. Weitzman, "Suspended Nun in Judges 18:30," 448–60.

42. Gale A. Yee, "Asenath," *ABD* 1:476; Rivka Ulmer, *Egyptian Cultural Icons in Midrash*, SJ 52 (Berlin: de Gruyter, 2009), 265.

there must be rising concern about the genealogical purity of the tribes of Manasseh and Ephraim. Dinah's adoption of Aseneth is one solution; the story of Aseneth's genuine conversion and faithful life before her marriage to Joseph is another.[43] Jacob's adoption of his grandchildren in Genesis might be an explicit effort to lighten the tension. Unfortunately, however, Manasseh's foreignness must have remained vulnerable to criticism, as his name is used in our text.

2. Stepping Stones for the Tempo-spatial Condemnation

From the beginning, I have argued that Judg 17–18 aims a tempo-spatial condemnation on the northern Israel territory beyond individual character criticism. Now, it is time to puzzle over the logic behind this agenda. How can one argue that the (evil) individuals of a specific time and place permanently defiled the whole country? The quick answer goes to foreign women in the promised land. Through exogamy, these other women produce other sons (who are not Israelites). These other sons soon internalize how to serve other gods or, more importantly, practice different ways of serving the God of Israel and eventually defile their residential place.[44] One may question that Judg 17–18 has only one female character, Micah's mother, and she is not a foreign woman. The observation seems right until we encounter Jonathan's complicated genealogy in 18:30. Here comes the critical role of the linked-in characters. The present text sent enough signals to catch the author group's use of the foreignness in the maternal lineage for the negative image-making against Jonathan. Now, the task falls upon us to discern their indications.

---

43. For Aseneth's adoption, see Ernest Walter Brooks, *Joseph and Asenath: The Confession and Prayer of Asenath, Daughter of Pentephres the Priest* (UK: Society for Promoting Christian Knowledge, 1918). The adoption between the female characters needs our attention, too. As Yitzhak Peleg argues with the Naomi's adoption case of Ruth's son, the identity regarding the son of Israelite father and the foreign mother in the biblical Israel community might be a very serious issue; see Peleg, "Why Didn't Ruth the Moabitess Raise Her Child? 'A Son Is Born to Naomi' (Ruth 4:17)," in *In the Arms of Biblical Women*, ed. John T. Green and Mishael M. Caspi, Biblical Intersections 13 (Piscataway, NJ: Gorgias, 2013), 281–300. For conversion, see Burfeind, "Asenath in Judaism," *EBR* 2:963; Victor Aptowitzer, "Asenath, the Wife of Joseph: A Haggadic Literary-historical Study," *HUCA* 1 (1924): 239–306.

44. Contrary to the explicitly expressed xenophobic misogyny in the priestly writings in the Pentateuch, it works as an underlying concept and subtle rhetoric in Judg 17–18.

From Person X to the House of X

Right after revealing Jonathan's name with the genealogy (18:30), the author provides a unique expression of "captivity of the land" (גלות הארץ), not of the people, and encourages us to delve into the fate of the land.[45] What would be the conceptual ideology on defilement in the Hebrew Bible, which the author group might share with their implied readers? According to Christine Hayes, the promised land can be defiled by the residents through their illegitimate rituals, immoral behaviors, and impure genealogies.[46] Judges 17–18 seems to employ all three sources (ritual, moral, and genealogical) to condemn both the nonpriestly house of Micah and the priestly house of Jonathan. From the plot development, I read that the house of Micah was used to nurture the Danites' first priest, Jonathan, until the Danites could set up the new shrine with all the illegitimate objects from Micah's house. In the transitional moment that the Danites are about to take Jonathan (18:15–18), the narrator already identified Micah's house as the house of the young Levite.[47]

Challenging Saul Olyan's notion of intrinsic impurity, Hayes argues that the Hebrew Bible emphasizes contingent characteristics to lead the audience to keep the covenantal relationship with God. As she points out, the emphasis on the intrinsic aspect, with the notion of "holy seed" and the genealogically defiled Israelites, appears in postexilic texts such as Ezra–Nehemiah.[48] According to her, a strict endogamy requirement to prevent the profanation of the holy seed in the high priest families in the Pentateuch (Lev 21:7) seems to be extending its regulation to ordinary people.[49] This account gives us a more comprehensive safety net to apply the above principle to all characters.

First, Judg 17–18 implicitly presents that the characters surrounding Jonathan—Micah, Gershom, Moses, and Manasseh—are related to two

---

45. O'Connell's emendation to "the captivity of the ark" is understandable but not very persuasive (*Rhetoric of the Book of Judges*, 350).

46. Hayes, *Gentile Impurities and Jewish Identities: Intermarriage and Conversion from the Bible to the Talmud* (Oxford: Oxford University Press, 2002), 19–44.

47. Bartusch translates differently by separating the two words, הנער הלוי, "to the house of the young man, the Levite of the house of Micah"; Bartusch, *Understanding Dan*, 175.

48. Hayes, *Intermarriage and Conversion*, 23–26.

49. Hayes, *Intermarriage and Conversion*, 27.

incompatible things, exogamy and the priestly lineage. More specifically speaking, they are either the appointer of the priest (Micah and Moses) or the grandson of foreign priests (Gershom with Jethro and Manasseh with Potiphera). Second, the text has the underlying ideology that all these cultic-related people, with the higher standard for purity in genealogy, indeed have a familial relationship with the women of others in a ritual or genealogical category. If Micah's mother is checked by a ritual standard, Zipporah and Aseneth are respectively tainted by the genealogical blame, especially as a foreign priest's daughter. I agree with Steffan Mathias, who argues that genealogy is a useful political tool to legitimatize the power structure, especially regarding the land. It uses stories of past names to provoke the reader's memory to figure out stories behind the name.[50] The genealogy in Judg 18:30 is used to delegitimize Jonathan and his company.

Feminine, Foreign, Forsaken: From the House of X to the Land of the House of X

With the recognition of the temporal dimension, we now ask what ideology would connect the inherently defiled people to the defilement of the land. The first bridging concept is a metaphoric connection between the female body and the land.[51] From the goddess of the earth in various creation myths to the body politics of Queen Elizabeth I of England, the female body-land metaphor seems universal throughout history.[52] To

---

50. Mathias, *Paternity, Progeny, and Perpetuation: Creating Lives after Death in the Hebrew Bible*, LHBOTS 696 (London: Bloomsbury, 2020), 78.

51. I prefer the term *female* or *feminine* to *woman* here because this section deals with the ancient author's concepts reflected in Judg 17–18. The ancient author group seemed to take both the biological and social aspects in connecting the metaphor of the woman's body and the land. For more discussion on the female body and land relationship within the Hebrew Bible, see Eve Levavi Feinstein, "Sexual Pollution in the Hebrew Bible: A New Perspective," in *Bodies, Embodiment, and Theology of the Hebrew Bible*, ed. S. Tamar Kamionkowski and Wonil Kim, LHBOTS 465 (London: Bloomsbury, 2010), 114; Alice A. Keefe, "The Female Body, the Body Politic and the Land: A Sociopolitical Reading of Hosea 1–2," in *A Feminist Companion to the Latter Prophets*, ed. Athalya Brenner, FCB 8 (Sheffield: Sheffield Academic, 2004), 99; Lori Hope Lefkovitz, *In Scripture: The First Stories of Jewish Sexual Identities* (Lanham: Rowman & Littlefield, 2010), 143–44.

52. For the creation myth, see Rachel Pollack, *The Body of the Goddess: Sacred Wisdom in Myth, Landscape, and Culture* (Shaftesbury: Element, 1997). For Queen

Irigaray, the womb-earth-factory metaphor for this body politics is a willful example of treating a woman as the receptacle to produce the given seed in it.[53] However, when the author wants to use the passively defiled female body for the extended metaphoric application to the defilement of the land, those passively defiled female characters ironically become the determined culprits. Could ancient Israelite society embrace the foreign women and their multiethnic houses in her community? The answer from the ancient author group of the book of Judges seems no. Indeed, we see that many biblical authors must have used this foreign-feminine-forsaken ideology as a useful weapon to eliminate opponents.

The second concept is more specific, as the covenantal theology is understood through the marital metaphor in many biblical texts. Since the land's purity can be kept through legitimate cultic and ethical practices, the opposite will happen when the residents, especially the cultic-related people, are genealogically defiled.[54] The dichotomous understanding of women with the whore-Madonna complex is applied to the people's fidelity to the deity (Madonna) or idolatry (whore).[55] As we see in Gen 27; Prov 7; Ezek 16 and 23, and other passages, a strange/foreign woman (אשה זרה), a whore (זונה), and an adulterer (האשה המנאפת) are often used interchangeably in the Hebrew Bible. According to Irigaray, a prostitute (neither a virgin nor a mother) shows the community's paradoxical aspect, that is, she is unofficially acceptable but officially condemnable.[56] Irigaray's understanding of prostitute in the patriarchal society is not so different as Other women in the Hebrew Bible, as we just confirmed their semantic proximity. These foreign women's existence suggests that they were once

---

Elizabeth's rhetoric, which emphasizes the weak female body embodying the male monarch's image to make the invincible symbol for the nation, see Rosemary Kegi, *The Rhetoric of Concealment: Figuring Gender and Class in Renaissance Literature* (Ithaca, NY: Cornell University Press, 1994), 28.

53. Luce Irigaray, *Speculum of the Other Woman*, trans. Gillian G. Gill (Ithaca, NY: Cornell University Press, 1985), 18.

54. Feinstein, "Sexual Pollution in the Hebrew Bible," 143.

55. Mieke Heijerman, "Who Would Blame Her? The 'Strange' Woman of Proverbs 7," in *Feminist Companion to Wisdom Literature*, ed. Athalya Brenner-Idan, FCB 9 (Sheffield: Sheffield Academic, 1995), 106. J. Cheryl Exum, "The (M)other's Place," in *Fragmented Women: Feminist (Sub)versions of Biblical Narratives*, JSOTSup 163 (Sheffield: Sheffield Academic, 1993), 92–100.

56. Luce Irigaray, *This Sex Which Is Not One*, trans. Catherine Porter with Carolyn Burke (Ithaca, NY: Cornell University Press, 1985), 185–87.

accepted in various contexts in the ancient Israel community. However, when xenophobia works with exogamy condemnation, this marriage-covenantal metaphor becomes a dangerous missile for the tempo-spatial polemic against one's foreign genealogy.[57] As Cheryl Anderson argues, the other women concept with the cultic violation and the lineage defilement is methodically used in Judg 17–18 for the permanent and destructive polemic.[58] Eva Feinstein's connection of the sexual pollution of the female body to the defilement of the land, city, and nation also supports the tempo-spatial polemic through genealogical defilement.[59]

If Judg 19–21 explicitly uses female body politics by showing the nation's distorted and disconnected reality, Judg 17–18 only provides a nuance through the male referential characters' names.[60] Due to this subtlety, the author's feminine, foreign, and forsaken strategy is hard to catch at first. However, as we have seen, the author group used the rubric of foreignness and feminineness to make rival siblings totally other. With this recognition, let me move to our last character, Jonathan, son of Gershom, grandson of Moses/Manasseh, the first priest of the Danites.

3. Jonathan as the Target

Jonathan is a popular name in the Hebrew Bible; it is given to twenty different characters.[61] We will focus on the Jonathan of our text since he is a

---

57. See Gustav Boström, *Proverbiastudien: Die Weisheit und das fremde Weib* (Lund: Gleerup, 1935); Paul Humbert, "La femme étrangère du livre des Proverbes," *Revue des Etudes Sémitiques* 6 (1937): 49–64; L. A. Snijders, *The Meaning of zar in the Old Testament*, OTS 10 (Leiden: Brill, 1954), 103–4.

58. Anderson, "Reflections in an Interethnic/Racial Ear on Interethnic/Racial Marriage in Ezra," in *They Were All Together in One Place? Toward Minority Biblical Criticism*, ed. Randall C. Bailey, Tat-siong Benny Liew, and Fernando F. Segovia, SemeiaSt 57 (Atlanta: Society of Biblical Literature, 2009), 47–64. See also Randall C. Bailey, "They're Nothing but Incestuous Bastards: The Polemical Use of Sex and Sexuality in Hebrew Canon Narratives," in *Social Location and Biblical Interpretation in the United States*, vol. 1 of *Reading from This Place*, ed. Fernando F. Segovia and Mary Ann Tolbert (Minneapolis: Fortress, 1995), 121–38.

59. Feinstein, "Sexual Pollution in the Hebrew Bible," 125.

60. Lefkovitz, *In Scripture*, 138–39.

61. The most famous Jonathan in the Hebrew Bible must be Prince Jonathan, son of King Saul in 1 Samuel. However, this Jonathan is not qualified in our criteria of foreign priests in the maternal line. His maternal grandfather Ahimaaz has a lack of biblical record, although some scholars conjecture the connection of his genealogy

story line character through whom the author provides enough information to understand characterization. Indeed, it is evident that the author
group's target at the individual level reaches the climax with Jonathan,
since the tempo-spatial condemnation for northern Israel can be derived
from Jonathan's characterization. Just as hunters encircle their prey in all
directions, the author seems to have used a gradual approach to narrow
the distance toward him. In other words, the author's holding strategy can
also be read here as a long-lash policy to allow the live target to practice
limited freedom until the hunters get the decisive evidence to attack. As a
result, the text appears to keep him in the neutral through slightly negative
zone most of the time. Moral and ritual dimensions are not so explicitly
illustrated in the case of Jonathan. For example, the text does not allow
readers to criticize Jonathan's departure from Bethlehem by not revealing
his motive. Likewise, we do not know Jonathan's initial request for living
at Micah's house or the negotiation process for employment. Even though
the text mentions the wages that Micah suggested during the deal (17:10),
it eventually summarizes the reason for Jonathan's satisfaction (ויאל) lies
in his familial relationship with Micah (17:11). The narrator's two-time
comments on Jonathan's emotion appear very selective for making him
the source of potential danger and illegitimacy. According to the narrator,
Jonathan was glad in his two times of promotion: one for the priest of the
house of Micah (17:11) and one for the Danites' priest (18:20). Indeed,
the account of Jonathan's willingness to go with the Danites has affected
my initial impression of his first deal with Micah and made me reconsider

---

with the Jerusalemite Zadokides (cf. Klaus-Peter Adam, "Ahimaaz," *EBR* 1:651). Nevertheless, it is noteworthy to point out that his father King Saul is mostly condemned
by Samuel/YHWH due to the violation of the ritual instructions, once when he caused
people to eat the blood (1 Sam 14:32–35) and then when he himself sacrificed instead
of Samuel (1 Sam 13:8–14). Meanwhile, both Jonathan, son of Abiathar, and Jonathan, son of Asahel, are also partially relevant to our criteria in terms of priest-relation
and intermarriage. Alphonso Groenewald conjectures that King Solomon's expulsion
of Jonathan's father Abiathar in 1 Kgs 2:26–27 implies Jonathan's forced departure
from Jerusalem, too. This opens to conjecture that our Jonathan's unknown departure
from Bethlehem might come from the similar political cause of his time. Meanwhile,
Jonathan, son of Asahel, in Ezra 10:15, draws our attention, too, since he is one who
disagreed with expelling the foreign wives and children. Overall, the three characters
do not have strong backgrounds to replace the image of the story line character, Jonathan, in our text. For the full list, see Groenewald, "Jonathan (Son of Gershom; Son of
Abiathar)," *EBR* 14:605–6.

other unstated motives of him, too. It eventually pushes me to think of the author group's subtle but well-planned strategy against this character. This heuristic reading resembles the hanging *nun* effect to make us reexamine the whole story.

Compared to the criticism of Jonathan's emotional involvement, the tempo-spatial polemic against him is more indirect and comprehensive. It is indirect because it associates with the auras of the temporal and spatial settings surrounding him. It is comprehensive because the target becomes the entire northern Israel beyond the individual or the tribe Jonathan served. A polemic at the spatial dimension pursues Jonathan's movement as he moved from Bethlehem in Judah, through the house of Micah in the hill country of Ephraim, and finally to the Danites' territory. Robin Baker makes an interesting spatial observation in the book of Judges that the character's direction toward north and west corresponds with the intensive otherness, flawed reality, or divine retribution.[62] From the author's perspective, Jonathan's suspicious sojourning is first settled at the house of Micah, another suspicious center of the illegitimate worship for YHWH. When the Danites passed Micah's house, Jonathan proclaimed them a priestly blessing. Ironically, this blessing for the Danites' spies, not for Micah who employed him for the blessing, is the only reported priestly activity of Jonathan in Judg 17–18. Through the detailed depiction of Jonathan's second movement from Micah's house, the text implies that Micah's stealing behavior, self-centered attitude, and (not approved) sacred objects are all together shifted to the new territory, Dan.

Furthermore, the author's image-making strategy works at the temporal dimension too. By assigning the dangerous foreign women and the foreign priests in the genealogy of the first priest at Dan, the text adds the eternal condemnation effect to the existing deleterious spatialization. The author engraves the irrevocable mark through the genealogical defilement and gets the never-expired ticket for the condemnation. This is why the final author group chose the hanging *nun* card to make the maximum synergic effect from both Moses and Manasseh.

Before moving to the conclusion of reading strategy one, I would like to point out the Danites' image by reminding my readers that the Micah-Danites story in Judg 17–18 is positioned after the Samson story in Judg 13–16. It is easy to find that the narrator blames Samson's temporary loss

62. Baker, *Hollow Men, Strange Women*, 117.

of his Nazirite status on his association with the Philistines, especially his intimate relationship with the local women. In other words, the narrator depicts two episodes in detail (14:8–9; 16:9) of how Samson's dedicated body to the holy God of Israel became defiled when being seduced by the foreign women. While Judg 17–18 insinuates blaming Zipporah and Aseneth, two linked-in foreign women characters, the Samson narrative explicitly presents how the foreign women ruined Israel's dedicated body, Samson. The Danites, who took Micah's priest and sacred items and attacked the innocent people for their settlement, are none but the descendants of Samson, who lost his holy status due to the foreign women.

Overall, this scenario serves well for the declaration of illegitimacy at the tempo-spatial dimensions. The author group gradually built up the illegitimacy of the young Levite Jonathan to show that ritually and morally profaned Jonathan defiled all the territory he stepped into, from the hill country of Ephraim to Dan. When the Danites (descendants of Samson who defiled his body twice with the foreign women) and Jonathan (who has two foreign women in his hanging *nun* genealogy) are taken together, the northern Israelite territory, where their footsteps have trod, becomes irrevocably defiled. When the story finally reveals Jonathan's father and grandfather's names, it reaches the climax, and Jonathan is permanently disqualified because he is genealogically profaned through his maternal line, Zipporah or Aseneth. Here, three layers of malicious exclusion wrap around Jonathan: (1) exclusion at the proximate dimension from the contemporary Israel community due to his moral and ritualistic corruption; (2) exclusion at the spatial dimension due to the geographical corruption of his footsteps from the hill country of Ephraim to Dan; (3) exclusion at the temporal dimension due to the genealogical corruption from before his birth to his descendants forever.

Reading Strategy Two:
Learning from the Forsaken Female Foreign Characters

The author group's project to make their siblings totally other seems successful. However, the overly ambitious insertion of a hanging *nun* ironically makes the readers wake to reexamine what they have read. It reveals the author group's bare face; they sacrificed the narrative's chronological coherence for the agenda. In interpreting Isa 63:1–6, Dominic Irudayaraj identifies Edom as the "proximate other" of Israel and explains the reason for Edom's constant and conspicuous appearance in the Bible as an archenemy.[63] A similar principle can be applied to the relationship between southern Judah and northern Israel. The rival sibling, northern Israel, was the archenemy who lived within the promised land, for they are proximate Other to southern Judah.

Now, how shall we read a polemical text like Judg 17–18? Many readers have struggled with this topic and proposed various solutions. Deborah Sawyer suggests "reading against the grain" to reveal the existent reversal factors underneath the sociopolitically structured text.[64] Marianne Kartzow's proposal with the intersectional approach also works the same way to destabilize the fixed hierarchy.[65] In her virtual discussion with Irigaray, Judith Butler suggests recognizing the reality of gender plurality to overcome the masculine and feminine binaries in the given discourses.[66] Butler's efforts for degendering the gendered discourse are valuable for deconstructing the underlying female body politics in Judg 17–18, which connects the foreign female body to the defilement of the land. On the contrary, Irigaray's emphasis on the biological uniqueness of male and female genders gives us guidance on how to adopt the constructive virtue from our women characters.[67] Her focus on gender difference should be understood as a way of learning about each other by respecting the other's horizons. She urges recognition of the other in terms of interrelational subjectivity to avoid imposing one's desire to possess the other.[68] As she argues, we need to educate ourselves to overcome the first impression of the other by moving on from the first sensation to the self-critical perception.[69] I hope my reading strategy can also be the appropriate resistance for this critical reading of the ancient sacred text.

Here is my proposal as an answer to the so-what question. While the Judges' author group searched for Jonathan's grandfather to bury all

63. Irudayaraj, *Violence, Otherness and Identity in Isaiah 63:1–6: The Trampling One Coming from Edom*, LHBOTS 633 (London: Bloomsbury, 2017), 60–61.

64. Sawyer, "Gender," in O'Brien, *Oxford Encyclopedia of the Bible and Gender Studies*, 1:267.

65. Kartzow, "'Asking the Other Question': An Intersectional Approach to Galatians 3:28 and the Colossian Household Codes," *BibInt* 18 (2010): 369–74.

66. Butler, *Bodies That Matter: On the Discursive Limits of "Sex"* (London: Taylor & Francis, 2014), 27–56, esp. 35–49.

67. Luce Irigaray, *J'aime à toi: Esquisse d'une félicité dans l'histoire* (Paris: Grasset & Fasquelles, 1992), 42, 68–70, 84.

68. Luce Irigaray, *Sharing the World* (London: Bloomsbury, 2008), 51, 80.

69. Irigaray, *Sharing the World*, 97.

Jonathan-related people, we are searching for all men and women in the story to see their faces, call their names, and save them from prejudgmental criticism. It will eventually save us from conscious and unconscious biases. As Irigaray suggests making space between *Je* and *Toi* to avoid seeing others as a projection of our own desire, the heuristic intertextual reading would provide space to read the text from multiple perspectives—the author's, characters', and our contexts.[70]

For a more specific discussion, let us call back those who are excluded, criticized, and forsaken based on their gender, geography, or genealogy. Indeed, they are the ones who embraced others. Micah's mother wishes God's blessing for her traitorous son. Pharaoh's daughter saved Moses because of compassion and protected him against the national order to kill all Hebrew baby boys. Zipporah provided all resources to a foreign murderer, Moses, to help him settle in her community and gave birth to two sons for him. Moreover, she saved his life from YHWH's incomprehensible anger in their journey to Egypt. How about her father, Jethro? He accepted a wanted fugitive, Moses, as a family member. When Moses requested to go back to Egypt, Jethro also allowed him to do so, even though he must be aware that his daughter and grandchildren would be left behind by Moses. When Moses and the Israelites stayed at nearby Mt. Sinai, Jethro visited Moses and gave him advice. What could he do more for his son-in-law? How about Aseneth, daughter of a well-known priest in Egypt?[71] She helped the Hebrew immigrant Joseph settle in Egypt and led him to move on from his tortured memory, as reflected in their first-born son's name, Manasseh.

All characters above were indeed in more powerful positions than their beneficiaries but did not abuse their power to oppress vulnerable others. They embraced their other for their survival and settlement. These foreign characters indeed looked after their other from altruistic motives. Moreover, our two linked-in characters, Zipporah and Aseneth, crossed their religious and ethnic boundaries to follow their husbands. In their stories in the Hebrew Bible and beyond, Zipporah and Aseneth are not depicted like Queen Jezebel from Tyre or Solomon's foreign wives, whose activities are explicitly described as idolatrous. Nonetheless, regardless of their piety and obedience to the social norms, the Jonathan polemic in

---

70. Luce Irigaray, "Listening, Thinking, Teaching," in Teaching, ed. Luce Irigaray and Mary Green (London: Bloomsbury, 2008), 231–40.

71. According to Gen 41:45, it was Pharaoh who gave Aseneth to Joseph as a wife.

Judg 17–18 suggests that the Hebrew Bible authors did not welcome these
foreign women. Speaking differently, these foreign women are treated as a
vast pit where the ancient Israelite society might throw all their blame for
religious impiety.

Taking Irigaray's suggestion to make a listening space for the grammar
of discourse and silence in the text, I propose a liminal reading space to
pause our assertion to listen to other voices.[72] The following are my mini-
mum requests for the agreement to make positive silence:

1. Micah's mother provided her unethical son, Micah, (not illegal)
    financial resources to furnish the house of God. She changed her
    curse to the blessing when she realized that her son is the object of
    the curse.
2. There is no support from the biblical text that northern Dan is
    located beyond the promised land. The Danites' departure from
    the initially allotted land has both positive and negative evalua-
    tions in the Hebrew Bible. A problematic theology of total destruc-
    tion in the conquest is a different issue.
3. We do not have enough information to evaluate Jonathan's per-
    sonality, since the text does not tell the reason for Jonathan's
    departure from Bethlehem. Likewise, we should leave his blessing
    for the Danites' spies in the neutral zone, that is, not applicable to
    judge him as a false priest, since the text only shows the perfor-
    mance scene.
4. A polemic based on gender, geography, or genealogy, especially
    against one's siblings, is the systematically evil strategy.

Even if we would start on the same page for the alternative reading, the
unexpected resistance may direct us toward different outcomes. For
example, the longtime traditions have warned us that serving other gods
is not a minor issue. This exclusivism for YHWH is one of the themes that
the Dueteronomistic Historians have planted in the book of Judges. As
Baker rightly explains, the book of Judges applies the concept of otherness
to YHWH of the targeted group and prevents us from imagining other

---

72. Irigaray, *This Sex Which Is Not One*, 75.

images on YHWH.[73] I am aware that the fear of that critique has oppressed our other readings.

Here comes my last comment to remember: We have no God in Judg 17–18! The author group completely controls God's presence not to appear, neither through the narrator's mouth nor through God himself as a character. No miracle or supernatural phenomenon from which readers can conjecture the presence of the deity. Because the text does not provide what YHWH, the God of Israel, thought, talked, and judged, the concept of serving other gods does not have decisive judgmental criteria, at least in our text. This journey to search for Jonathan's family to embrace them will not and should not end in vain. During this journey, I hope to find the other image of the God of Israel, one who comforts the forsaken people based on their gender, geography, and genealogy. Examining scrutinizingly, to be free from any prejudice, and writing the outcome—as I do here—would be one way to start making new rhetoric. Like the catch-phrase in Judg 17–21, "Everyone did as they saw fit," the ethical judgment fell upon the human's hands in the divine absence. Then, we politely ask the postmodern question: why should I think that only yours is right and not mine?

---

73. Baker, *Hollow Men, Strange Women*, 112–14.

14
Lost in the Text(s): The פילגש in Judges 19

Susanne Gillmayr-Bucher

The events told in Judg 19 are situated at the brink of a collapse of the Israelite society as it is depicted in the book of Judges. It all begins when a woman, a פילגש, leaves her Levite husband and returns to her father's house. Read from the end of the book of Judges this action is the final straw, unleashing a series of events leading to civil war. The randomness of this action and the following unusual severity of pointless aggression indicate that Israel is falling apart. Instead of stabilizing its existence, its disintegration is impending.

The textual world as it is presented in Judg 19 is full of gaps and blanks, ambiguities and surprises the readers have to deal with.[1] This applies in particular to the figures of this story, who are not developed as unique literary characters; they even lack names. Thus, the main characters are a nameless Levite from the hill country of Ephraim, who takes a nameless פילגש, the daughter of a nameless father in Bethlehem, and another nameless inhabitant of Gibeah. The vagueness of the figures is further highlighted by rather sparse insights into their perspective: they talk less than in other stories in the book of Judges, and furthermore, their thoughts, plans, and knowledge, or the rules and values they live by, are only partially revealed.[2] This kind of presentation already gives rise to the assumption that the פילגש—like the other figures—is shaped as a

---

1. For an in-depth study on textual incoherence and literary gaps see Kirsten H. Gardner, "Hidden in Plain Sight: Intertextuality and Judges 19," in *Second Wave Intertextuality and the Hebrew Bible*, ed. Marianne Grohmann and Hyun Chul Paul Kim, RBS 93 (Atlanta: SBL Press, 2019), 70.

2. In Judg 19, 33 percent of all utterances are direct speech; the average in the whole book is 39 percent.

typical character.[3] The formulaic introduction "And it happened in these days, and there was no king in Israel" further adds to the impression of an exemplary story.[4]

However, the figures of this story do not act as anticipated by the readers, nor are their transgressions explained. Due to the lack of information on the figures' thoughts and motivations, some of their actions seem to happen without reason, and thus their behavior appears strange or inexplicable.[5] Through their example, peculiar social conditions are portrayed, but it remains the task of the readers to evaluate the narrated world of this story.

However, the lack of orientation characterizing the world of this text also affects the guidance a narration usually offers to the readers. In Judg 19 they are mostly on their own when they try to assess the figures or to determine the function and significance of the story. The virtual absence of rules in the world of the text, and the missing divine perspective, challenges the readers and encourages them to look elsewhere to find some clues how to understand this story.[6] This characteristic of the text could be considered an "intertextual disposition"—as Susanne Holthuis calls it—motivating the readers to search for other biblical texts dealing with similar themes or motives.[7]

---

3. David Moster, "The Levite of Judges 17–18," *JBL* 133 (2014): 729–37; Reinhartz points out that, "her anonymity does more than efface her identity. It highlights her typified role"; Adele Reinhartz, *"Why Ask My Name?" Anonymity and Identity in Biblical Narrative* (New York: Oxford University Press, 1998), 125.

4. Unless otherwise noted, all translations are mine.

5. Susanne Gillmayr-Bucher, *Erzählte Welten im Richterbuch: Narratologische Aspekte eines polyfonen Diskurses*, BibInt 116 (Leiden: Brill, 2013), 216–17.

6. The readers will recognize allusions to other texts, which use similar phrases, motifs, or themes. In doing so, the readers will not only recognize these texts, they will also note the different contexts and connotations of the shared phrases and motifs. In this way, the single elements of the story in Judg 19 can be read and understood on the background of different texts. Especially when Judg 19 does not provide enough information, they have to draw on these other texts to fill in the missing parts. This additional information, in turn, will influence the readers' evaluation and expectations as the story of Judg 19 unfolds.

7. Holthuis, "Intertextuality and Meaning Constitution: An Approach to the Comprehension of Intertextual Poetry," in *Approaches to Poetry: Some Aspects of Textualily, Intertextuality and Intermediality*, ed. János Petöfi and Terry Olivi, Research in Text Theory 20 (Berlin: de Gruyter, 1994), 77–93.

This perspective is the starting point for my essay. Hence, I will search for references and allusions to other texts in order to construct the literary figure of the פילגש on the background of, and in comparison with, other texts. Looking for elements that might trigger an intertextual reading, I will focus on references in the text experienced readers might recognize and consider for their understanding of the story.[8] With such an approach I follow the ideas of Mikhail Bakhtin and Julia Kristeva. Bakhtin assumes all utterances to be dialogic, as they always are connected to an addresser and an addressee. Their meaning depends upon what has previously been said and on how it will be received by others. In his view, every "word is a bridge thrown between myself and another. If one end of the bridge depends on me, then the other depends upon my addressee. A word is territory shared by both addresser and addressee, by the speaker and his interlocutor."[9] Later, Kristeva applied Bakhtin's dialogic concept to a discourse between all texts, which she calls intertext.[10] Kristeva uses another metaphor, describing every text as a mosaic of other texts, and hence a through road and a semantic crossing of many texts. The text becomes a "performative site of engagement with other texts."[11]

Following this line of thought, this contribution aims to look at the portrait of the nameless woman in Judg 19 as such a mosaic or through road of texts. Searching for references to other texts, I will consider the terms used to refer to the women as well as her actions and the action of other figures directly affecting the woman.[12]

---

8. It is, however, not the aim of this paper to look for literary dependencies or to prove that an author intentionally provided a reference.

9. Mikhail Bakhtin, *The Dialogic Imaginations: Four Essays by M. M. Bakhtin*, ed. Michael Holquist, trans. Caryl Emerson and Michael Holquist (Austin: University of Texas Press, 1981), 291; Valentin Volosinov, *Marxism and the Philosophy of Language*, trans. Ladislav Matejka and I. R. Titunik (Cambridge: Harvard University Press, 1986), 86.

10. Julia Kristeva, *Desire in Language: A Semiotic Approach to Language and Art*, ed. Leon S. Roudiez, trans. Thomas Gora, Alice Jardine, and Leon S. Roudiez (New York: Columbia University Press, 1980), 64–91.

11. Susan Friedman, "Weavings: Intertextuality and the (Re)Birth of the Author," in *Influence and Intertextuality in Literary History*, ed. Jay Clayton and Eric Rothstein (Madison: University of Wisconsin Press, 1991), 149.

12. It follows that I will only mention those intertextual references that are relevant to this question. For a more comprehensive discussion of intertextual references in Judg 19 see, e.g., Gardner, "Hidden in Plain Sight"; Sara J. Milstein, "Saul the Levite

The Nameless Woman in the Story

In absence of a name, the woman in Judg 19 is called a secondary wife (פילגש), a young woman (נערה), a slave (אמה), and a woman (אשה). Each of these terms describes the woman within a specific relation: her husband, her father, or the host in Gibeah; only the term אשה depicts her without any relation.

Distribution of Terms

Verse	Terms	Voice	Focalization
1	אשה פילגש	narrator	Levite
2	פילגשו	narrator	Levite
3	אבי הנערה	narrator	father
4	אבי הנערה	narrator	father
5	אבי הנערה	narrator	father
6	אבי הנערה	narrator	father
7	אבי הנערה	narrator	father
9	פילגשו	narrator	Levite
	אבי הנערה	narrator	father
10	פילגשו	narrator	Levite
19	אמתך	Levite addressing the host in Gibeah	host in Gibeah
24	פילגשהו	host in Gibeah addressing the men outside	host in Gibeah/Levite
25	פילגשו	narrator	Levite/host in Gibeah
26	אשה	narrator	narrator
27	האשה פילגשו	narrator	Levite
29	פילגשו	narrator	Levite

---

and His Concubine: The 'Allusive' Quality of Judges 19," *VT* 66 (2016): 95–116; Daniel I. Block, "Echo Narrative Technique in Hebrew Literature: A Study in Judges 19," *WTJ* 52 (1990): 325–41.

פילגש A

The way by which the Levite and the nameless woman are introduced in Judg 19:1 already points to a first deviation from an expected norm: The Levite takes a פילגש, a secondary wife, although his first wife is not mentioned. The readers either have to assume that they are given incomplete information, or that the Levite could not yet find a wife and meanwhile takes a פילגש-wife. Within Judg 19, the nameless woman is called פילגש whenever she is mentioned in connection with the Levite or from his point of view (Judg 19:1, 2, 9, 10, 24, 25, 27, 29; see also 20:4, 5, 6).

The exact legal status of a פילגש-wife cannot be ascertained.[13] These women usually do not receive much attention and, furthermore, the few biblical narrations featuring פילגש-wives offer quite different images of their status and fate. They are, for example, mentioned when they give birth (so Reumah [Gen 22:24], Keturah [1 Chr 1:32], and Timna [Gen 36:12]). Especially as a mother, a פילגש is not insignificant, as the example of Abimelech shows. He is introduced as the son of Gideon's פילגש (8:31), who, as we are later informed, comes from an (influential) family in Shechem and thus Abimelech is able to use his mother's relations to gain power (Judg 9:1–3) and to kill all the other sons of Gideon (Judg 9:5). The story of Rizpah, Saul's פילגש, presents an active and very courageous woman and mother, who, after Saul died and David had her sons executed, guards their corpses until David gave them a proper burial (2 Sam 21:11–14).[14] Second-rank wives are not only presented in their role as mothers, the mentioning of their numbers is also used to highlight the glory and wealth of a king.[15] Despite the lower status, a פילגש-wife also belongs to her husband and any harm inflicted on her concerns the husband.[16]

Pointing out that this woman is a פילגש, the narration in Judg 19 does not deny her the possibility to act or to exert influence, but her husband

---

13. See Isabelle Hamley, "'Dis(re)membered and Unaccounted For': פילגש in the Hebrew Bible," *JSOT* 42 (2018): 416–20.

14. The fact that Rizpah is special is also emphasized by her being called daughter of Aja (2 Sam 3:7; 21:8, 10, 11) and not just Saul's פילגש. In this way her father and family of origin is highlighted.

15. See, e.g., 2 Sam 5:13; 15:16; 16:21–22; 19:6; 20:3 (David); 1 Kgs 11:3 (Solomon); 2 Chr 11:21 (Rehoboam); or Esth 2:14 (Ahasuerus).

16. See, e.g., Ahithophel, who advises Absalom to humiliate David by lying with his wives (2 Sam 16:21–22); see also Gen 35:22.

denies her a privileged position. At least from the Levite's point of view, she remains a woman on the margins.

Furthermore, the woman's classification as פילגש distinguishes the Levite and his second-rank wife in Judg 19 from another story in Exod 2 that starts in a similar way introducing "a man, a Levite … who took a wife." However, in Exod 2 the wife is not a פילגש. Nonetheless, this allusion could point the readers to expect a hero's birth. However, such expectations will not be fulfilled. In contrast to other texts mentioning פילגש-wives, the woman in Judg 19 is not connected to motherhood, she is neither presented as a mother, nor as a childless woman.[17] Hence, from the start of this story, this woman evades a clear classification, as she does not fit into a traditional female role.

זנה To Do

The first action the story ascribes to the woman is that she did זנה, but no further information is provided. Hence, the meaning of the verb זנה in 19:3 is highly discussed. Was the woman unfaithful, literally or metaphorically, or was she just angry, as already the LXX and later Vetus Latina (*irata est*) suggested?[18]

References to other texts featuring זנה are numerous, however the construction of the verb with the preposition (על) is only used here and in Ezek 16:15–16. There, the preposition על introduces both, a literal place, the high places (במות), which are the scene of her wrongdoing, and a metaphorical

---

17. See Mercedes L. García Bachmann, *Judges*, Wisdom Commentary 7 (Collegeville, MN: Liturgical Press, 2018), 217–18.

18. Following this reading, there are several attempts to argue for a homonym verb זנה II, with the meaning "to be angry, to hate"; see Mieke Bal, *Death and Dissymmetry: The Politics of Coherence in the Book of Judges*, CSHJ (Chicago: University of Chicago Press, 1988), 87; Hermann-Josef Stipp, "Richter 19: Ein frühes Beispiel schriftgestützter politischer Propaganda in Israel," in *Ein Herz so weit wie der Sand am Ufer des Meeres: Festschrift für Georg Hentschel*, ed. Susanne Gillmayr-Bucher, Annett Gierke, and Christina Nießen, ETS 90 (Würzburg: Echter, 2007), 137–38; Eynikel points out that the original Hebrew reading behind the LXX reading could have been זנח, "to reject." This reading fits the reaction of the Levite, who "spoke to her heart"; Erik Eynikel, "Judges 19–21, an 'Appendix': Rape, Murder, War and Abduction," *CV* 47 (2005): 104. For a detailed discussion, see also Isabelle Hamley, "What's Wrong with 'Playing the Harlot'? The Meaning of זנה in Judges 19:2," *TynBul* 66 (2015): 41–62.

place, namely her name or reputation, that is: "by means of" her beauty and her status she seduced other men.[19]

In Judg 19, however, it is difficult to translate she committed fornication "on/by means of" the Levite. Nonetheless, the verb זנה might be used in this context to devalue the woman's behavior, but not to call her a prostitute. When she leaves her husband and returns to her father's house, she claims autonomy and the right to decide where to live. This behavior does not correspond with the expectations on a פילגש, and thus is evaluated as זנה, a prostitute.[20] The statement on the woman's behavior is not necessarily an explanation; it can also be an evaluation of the following description of her action: "She did זנה by going away." Nonetheless, such behavior, which violates social role expectations, bears a certain risk. By leaving her husband the woman chooses to dissocialize herself.[21] On the other hand, זנה in the meaning of "committing fornication" might also fit into the context.[22] In this understanding, the פילגש's character matches the other morally dubious figures of the story.

Whatever meaning the readers ascribe to the woman's first action, it attracts attention and thus provokes thought. Although the woman might not be accused of adultery in the eyes of the readers, the allusion to Ezek 16 initiated by the phrase ותזנה עליו hints at terrible events to come. Furthermore, this reference indicates that the figure of the woman is transparent to Israel. In this way, a double-voiced dialogue starts between the story of a woman and the allusion to Israel's fate.

---

19. In Ezekiel, this behavior is considered improper, as her actions do not correspond with the standards of her reputation. Furthermore, the new space she created on the high places became the scene of her wrongdoing.

20. Cf. J. Cheryl Exum, *Fragmented Women: Feminist (Sub)versions of Biblical Narratives* (Valley Forge, PA: Trinity Press International, 1993), 179; Ilse Müllner, "Tödliche Differenzen: Sexuelle Gewalt als Gewalt gegen Andere in Ri 19," in *Von der Wurzel getragen: Christlich-feministische Exegese in Auseinandersetzung mit Antijudaismus*, ed. Luise Schottroff and Marie-Theres Wacker, BibInt 17 (Leiden: Brill, 1996), 93; Ken Stone, "Gender and Homosexuality in Judges 19: Subject-Honor, Object-Shame?," *JSOT* 20 (1995): 90–91.

21. Johan H. Coetzee, "The 'Outcry' of the Dissected Woman in Judges 19–21: Embodiment of a Society," *OTE* 15 (2002): 54.

22. See Hamley, "What's Wrong with 'Playing the Harlot'?," 43–45.

The Woman Goes

The woman's second action, immediately following the first, is "to go" (הלך). The combination of the verbs ותזנה and ותלך is only used in contexts where Israel, a metaphorical woman, is accused of being unfaithful, that is, worshiping other deities, and going in wrong ways, or to go up on every hill to prostitute herself.[23] In this way, the combination of these two verbs further adds to the allusions that the פילגש does something wrong and that she represents Israel.

However, the further development of the story does not encourage such allusions. The way the woman goes does not lead her to any forbidden place nor any misdoing, but straight to the house of her father. She returns to her family. Setting out for such a journey gives rise to allusions to initiative and to courageous women, who decide for themselves what they are going to do. This action thus encourages readers to expect the portrait of a self-determined woman.

Other women that decide on their own to set out and go are, for example, Deborah who not only instructs Barak to fight the enemy, but also goes with Barak and accompanies him on the way to the battle (Judg 4). Another woman, whose decision to go forms an essential part of the story, is Rebekah. Not until she agrees to go with the servant, to follow him to an unknown country and to become Isaac's wife, does the story reach its hoped-for ending (Gen 24). When Ruth decides to go with Naomi (Ruth 1:16), it is an action she pursues against Naomi's explicit advice. Throughout the story, Ruth is depicted as the more active woman, who takes the initiative and goes out (Ruth 2:2–3). This series of women is continued by Abigail. To prevent immanent bloodshed, she sets out to meet David, to offer him what he asked for, and to instruct him on his way to become king (1 Sam 25:42). Women also travel some distances on their own. Jeroboam's wife travels to Shiloh to meet the prophet Ahijah (1 Kgs 14); and the woman of Shunem goes to Carmel to fetch Elisha (2 Kgs 4). Yet another story, that might come into view, is the story of Tamar. She is sent away by her father-in-law and returns/goes to the house of her own father (Gen 38:11); later she dresses up as a harlot and conceives a child by Judah.

---

23. For going wrong ways, see Judg 2:18; 2 Chr 21:13. Without (זנה): who does not follow God's ways, but goes on the wrong ways: Jer 15:6, Ezek 16:47; 23:31, or goes after her lovers Hos 2:15. For going up every hill, cf. Jer 3:6, 8; Hos 2:7.

She acts against Judah's unjust behavior, claiming her rights, and is justified in the end.

Based on these stories, women taking the initiative to go seem to be
outstanding. They decide freely and independently, initiate changes, or
fight for their rights. Hence, the allusions initiated by 19:2 already hint
that the story of this woman will be extraordinary. However, they do not
help to clarify the estimation of the woman.

Speaking to Her Heart

When the Levite follows his פילגש-wife a few months later, the narrating voice calls him "her man" (אישה), and in this way defines him by his
relationship with the woman, thus seemingly confirming the expectations
raised before. The Levite's intention is to speak to the woman's heart (Judg
19:3). This phrase is usually used when somebody needs encouragement,
consolation, or forgiveness. Ruth, for example, calls Boaz's friendly and
encouraging words "speaking to her heart" (Ruth 2:13). In Gen 34:3, this
phrase is used to express consolation, maybe even a plea for forgiveness, as
Shechem speaks to Dinah's heart after he had raped her. In Hos 2:16 and
Isa 40:2, God promises forgiveness and a new start after the punishment
with these words.

References to these texts thus may raise the readers' expectations that
the Levite intends to restore the relation to his פילגש. Nonetheless, the
hoped-for outcome remains ambivalent. Does the Levite want to speak to
her in order "to make it (the heart) turn back" (*ketiv*) or "to make her (the
woman) turn back" (*qere*)?[24] The readers thus may come to the conclusion
that the woman is forgiven and the Levite wants her to come back, or that
her heart turns back to the Levite.

And She Brought Him into the House of Her Father

While the story does not tell if the woman's heart turned toward the Levite,
she obviously does not go back with him immediately. She rather takes the
initiative and brings the Levite into her father's house (19:3). Although
this scene is only mentioned and not unfolded in detail, a vague allusion

---

24. Usually, the combination of the verb שוב (*hiphil*) with the object לב is formu-
lated with the preposition אל or על to clarify the relation (cf. Mal 3:24; 1 Kgs 12:27).

to wooing scenes come to mind. A man arrives at a place, he is met by
the daughter of a resident and introduced to the family. However, unlike
Rebekah (Gen 24:28) and Rachel (Gen 29:12), or the daughters of Reuel
(Exod 2:18–20), who do not know the traveler, the Levite is no stranger.
Thus, the woman seems to be free to bring him into her father's house
herself, and her initiative is immediately approved by the joyful reaction
of her father. The delight of the father seeing the Levite and the allusion to
a wooing scene let the reader expect a happy family reunion.

The Implicit Daughter

The woman's father is only known by his role as father and father-in-law.[25]
Six times this man is called the "father of the young woman" (אבי הנערה),
although his daughter is a married woman. This term is otherwise only
used in Deut 22:15–29 for the father of a raped daughter negotiating the
consequences of such a violent act.[26] This allusion replaces the act of זנה
by another inappropriate behavior. Promiscuity and rape are both sexual
transgressions, but regarding the question of guilt they represent quite
the opposite. Nonetheless, the references point to a highly problematic
although ambiguous situation, where the husband of an allegedly promiscuous woman meets the father of a supposedly raped daughter, whereby
the woman and the daughter are identical. Like the reference to the woman's wrongdoing, this hint remains vague and is not unfolded on the level
of the narration. Both accusations only provide a background, whereas the
main story unfolds quite pleasantly, depicting the encounter of a very hos-
pitable father and an unobtrusive Levite guest.[27] It also fits this picture that
neither the father nor the Levite put pressure on the woman or demand an
explanation from her. The two men seem oblivious to any transgression,
be it adultery or rape.

---

25. The relationship between the father and the husband of the anonymous
woman is referred to as father-in-law and son-in-law, thus pointing to a legal relationship between the Levite and his פילגש-wife; see Hameley, "Dis(re)membered," 423.

26. Cf. Mercedes L. García Bachman, *Women at Work in the Deuteronomistic History*, IVBS 4 (Atlanta: Society of Biblical Literature, 2013), 153 n. 102.

27. Gardner points out that the description of the father's exaggerated hospitality,
that led to five days of eating and drinking, might point to a *marzēaḥ* feast (Gardner,
"Hidden in Plain Sight," 57–58).

However, as soon as the woman brings the Levite into the house of her father, she disappears as an independent figure.[28] Her father never speaks to her, nor is she explicitly called his daughter. For the rest of her stay, she is only mentioned together with the Levite.[29]

Your Slave

The next time the woman is explicitly mentioned is when the Levite talks to the man in Gibeah. The term אמה that the Levite uses for his פילגש addressing the man in Gibeah (19:19) is an act of courtesy; likewise, he refers to the male members of the group as עבד.[30] However, the man does not return this courtesy, rather he will soon act on it in the most literal sense (19:24–25).

Being Pushed Out

The woman's independent action of leaving her husband and returning to her father's house is now contrasted by her being kicked out.[31] The formulation in 19:25 leaves it open whether the Levite or the host seized the פילגש and forced her out.[32]

---

28. Edenburg points out that, although the scene in the house of the father bears some resemblance to the hospitality offered to Abraham's servant in Gen 24, the nameless woman in Judg 19 is portrayed in contrast to Rebekah, who is asked whether or not she is willing to depart; Cynthia Edenburg, *Dismembering the Whole: Composition and Purpose of Judges 19–21*, AIL 24 (Atlanta: SBL Press, 2016), 279.

29. The fatal decision to depart and to set out in the late afternoon is also made by the Levite alone. Left on her own, the woman was able to negotiate an unknown space and to travel safely to her father's house. On the return journey, however, when the Levite takes responsibility, this changes dramatically.

30. Women and men use this kind of courtesy when talking to someone superior, or when they want to honor the other. E.g., Abigail speaking to David (1 Sam 25), Bathsheba talking to David (1 Kgs 1), Ruth speaking with Boaz (Ruth 3), David addressing Saul (1 Sam 17). Also, Abraham and Lot call themselves עבד when speaking to the angelic travelers (Gen 18:3; 19:19).

31. Like Gen 19, this story describes a society where only men are protected by the rules of hospitality; see Block, "Echo Narrative Technique in Hebrew Literature," 334.

32. The verb חזק is used three times in this story. The father holds the Levite with his hospitality (19:4); the host in Gibeah or the Levite takes hold of the פילגש and forces her out (19:25); the Levite takes a knife, takes hold of the woman's body, and dismembers her (19:29).

Nonetheless, references to other texts using the phrase ויחזק ... ויצא
suggest that she might be spared the worst. Genesis 19 describes a similar
threatening scene, but no harm is done, because the angelic travelers inter-
vene. They seize (חזק) Lot, his wife, and two daughters and bring them out
(יצא), thus rescuing Lot's family (Gen 19:16). This phrase is also used in Jer
31:32 to remember God bringing the Israelites out of Egypt.

However, once it becomes obvious that the woman is not rescued, any
expectations of a reunion are betrayed. The Levite persuaded her to come
back with him, but he does not hesitate to put her in harm's way in order
to protect himself.

As before, references to prophetic texts (e.g., Hos 2; Ezek 16) might
come to mind. Could the rape be a belated punishment reversing the
sequence of marriage-punishment-forgiveness (Hos 2)?[33] Compared to
these prophetic texts, the merciless rigor of Judg 19 stands out. While
Hos 2 offers an existence, even reconciliation after the punishment,
and Ezek 16:60–63 adds that God remembers his covenant, Judg 19
does not offer any future for the woman. The allusions rather seem to
unmask the friendly words of the Levite as a means to lure the woman
away from her refuge, her father's house, into a space where she will
have no protection.

Raped and Disbanded

The woman's behavior described as זנה and the implied sexual connotation is now acted upon. However, it is not the פילגש who, like
the woman in Ezek 16 or Hos 2, acts as a prostitute, rather the roles
are reversed: The woman is not offering her body; the men take it by
force. The woman is victimized and finally depersonalized. The פילגש is
turned into a woman who belongs to no one and thus her body belongs
to every man. When the men of Gibeah take possession of her, they

---

33. Exum suggests that the text finds the פילגש deserving of this terrorizing fate.
Perhaps the patriarchal narrator has given this פילגש a necessary punishment. Exum
adds that this is not the purposeful misogynist intention from the narrator; rather, the
"gender-motivated subtext" naturally functions as a product of the writer's Umwelt:
"independent women should understand this story as a warning" (Exum, *Fragmented
Women*, 181) In Hos 1–2, the divine request: "take a wife of whoredom [אשת זנונים]"
(Hos 1:2) is later continued with a threat of punishment and finally completed with
the promise of a reconciliation "I will allure her, … I will speak to her heart" (2:16).

are not invited and they are not a prostitute's clients. They are not even seeking pleasure, but they viciously take possession of her and brutalize her in order to prove their power, their domination, and to humiliate and destroy the woman and her husband.[34] It is noteworthy that even in her role as a victim of sexual violence, gender aspects are secondary. She is not abused because she is a woman, but because she is offered and used as a substitute for the Levite.

After she has been gang raped, the woman is not dead. As dawn began to break, the violators sent her away (19:25). She came back to the house, yet she lacks the strength to cross the doorsill, her hands only touch the border. This is the last action ascribed to the woman. At this point in the story, when the woman is totally on her own, she is just called אשה. When she breaks down at the doorstep, she has no relations left and there is no way back. Her disintegration, however, has not yet ended.

Dismembering the Woman's Body

When the Levite comes out of the house in the morning (Judg 19:27) his upright position presents a strong contrast to the collapsed woman. The moment, the Levite is confronted by the events outside is marked with הנה. In the following, the narrating voice describes his perception: First, he first sees the woman (אשה), and only on a second glance his relation to this woman is added, calling her his פילגש-wife. Nonetheless, the Levite shows no signs of compassion for the woman but only asks her to get up and move on.[35] His reaction recognizes the woman's body only as an obstacle in his way. Her body that had kept him safe has served its purpose. When the woman does not respond to his request, he does not try to nurse her to health, nor does he bury her appropriately.[36] Rather, he picks her body up and brings her back to his house. Once there, he takes a knife, dismembers the פילגש's body, and in this way continues the work

---

34. Cf. Alice Bach, "Rereading the Body Politic: Women and Violence in Judges 21," *BibInt* 6 (1998): 1–19; Susanne Scholz, *Sacred Witness: Rape in the Hebrew Bible* (Minneapolis: Fortress, 2010), 139, points out that rape is a destructive force.

35. A similar phrase is used by Amnon (2 Sam 13:15) when he orders Tamar to "get up and go" after the rape.

36. Julie Faith Parker, "Re-membering the Dismembered: Piecing Together Meaning from Stories of Women and Body Parts in Ancient Near Eastern Literature," *BibInt* 23 (2015): 176.

of destruction. The Levite cuts her body into twelve pieces, treating it like a sacrificial animal.[37]

Again, several allusions link this episode to other texts. The phrasing "and he took the knife" (ויקח את המאכלת) refers to Abraham in Gen 22 and thus insinuates that the Levite is offering the woman as a sacrifice. This aspect is supported by the verb נתח (*piel*), to cut into pieces, which is almost exclusively used in the context of a sacrifice.[38] But the Levite is not preparing an offering—God is still strikingly absent from the plans and the imagination of the protagonists of this story—he rather sends the body parts throughout all the territory of Israel. The Levite exploits the פילגש's body as "body-matter." The purpose of this action, however, is not explained. The only other story where someone sends out body parts is Saul, sending out parts of his oxen (1 Sam 11). Unlike Saul (11:7)—who seeks to gather the troops in self-defense against the Ammonites—the Levite does not attach a message or a demand, thus, an adequate reaction is left to the addressees. There is yet another text the woman's fate alludes to, namely Jezebel, who is also dismembered and her body left as fragmented refuse (2 Kgs 9:30–37). In contrast to the Levite's פילגש, however, Jezebel is characterized as a warrior, she is a powerful queen, and thus dismembering her is part of the victory.[39]

The allusions to other texts depicting a dismemberment leave the readers with more questions than insights: Is the dismembering of the woman another horrible and misguided sacrifice like Jephthah's nameless daughter (Judg 11:31, 39)? Or is sending the body parts a provocation, a brutal reminder of what has become possible in Israel? Does the Levite request Israel to take the place of a divine judge (cf. Gen 18:20–21)? And why is the Levite fighting his פילגש-wife? Why does he make sure nothing remains of her?

Raising these questions, the references to other texts highlight the strange reaction of the Levite in this final scene. Correspondingly, the Israelites' response further emphasizes the uniqueness of the events: "(Such a

---

37. See Talia Sutskover, "The Frame of Sacrificing in Judges," *VT* 64 (2014): 266–78. She shows the importance of the semantic frame for sacrificing in the book of Judges.

38. Exod 29:17: consecration of Aaron and his sons, bull as burnt offering; Lev 1:4–6: sacrifice to make atonement; 8:20: burnt offering; 1 Kgs 18:23, 33: Elijah.

39. See Parker, "Re-membering the Dismembered." She points out that Anat dismembers her enemies in battle.

thing) has not happened nor been seen from the day the Israelites went up out of the land of Egypt until this day" (19:30).

Summary

The story of the Levite's nameless פילגש offers yet another disturbing aspect within the book of Judges' dire portrait of the people. The striking absence of guidelines, obligations, and common values turns this story into a critical commentary on the state of the society in the eyes of the readers. Because the story withholds an explicit valuation, the readers have to assume this responsibility. The full extent of what is going wrong in this story becomes obvious when the readers follow the references to other biblical texts. Once the readers engage in an intertextual reading, the different texts linked to the story of the Levite's פילגש emphasize the deviation from a normal behavior. Although some allusions might tempt the readers to hope for a positive turn, in the end, they only increase their dismay. Like the metaphorical women in the prophetic texts, the פילגש is brutalized. However, she is not punished in this story, nor is the violence inflicted by a deity, rather she suffers and dies by the hand of her own people: the host, and men of Gibeah, and her husband. She is the victim of unwarranted violence and lack of compassion.

When the relationships between husband and wife, father and daughter, guest and host do not offer stability but dissolve into chaos and violence, these social roles and their underlying gender constructions are fundamentally called into question. The story of the פילגש challenges the readers' images of the social structure by forcing them to recognize the woman's limited room for maneuver and her endangered living space. Although the woman is given a prominent role in the story, she remains a character on the margins; she is not given an appropriate status, either as a wife or as a daughter. Even though the woman is portrayed as active, and at least occasionally acting on her own, yet she remains vulnerable, as there is no one to guide, warn, protect, or save her—quite the contrary, she is sacrificed for the safety and the honor of the Levite.

As the story unfolds, the egocentric and unregulated behavior of the protagonists leads to an escalating violence, hence any illusion of a functioning society is eliminated. Thereby the woman's fragmented body becomes a metaphor for the menacing destiny of Israel. While following the woman on her journey, idealized images of hospitality, solidarity, and compassion, of being one people, but also of being courageous and fighting for one's rights, are deconstructed before the eyes of the readers, revealing Israel's fragile constructions of its identity.[40] In this line of thought, Judg 19 is more than just a tragic story in dangerous times; it rather is a parable on Israel's way to self-destruction, insinuating a possible extinction.

---

40. See Gillmayr-Bucher, *Erzählte Welten*, 259–60.

15

The Poverty of Parallels:
Reading Judges 19 with Ezekiel 16 via the Song of Songs

Serge Frolov

Introduction

It is common knowledge that the term *intertextuality* was coined by the French-Bulgarian philosopher and literary critic Julia Kristeva in a 1969 publication where she famously proclaimed, "Any text is constructed as a mosaic of quotations; any text is the absorption and transformation of another. The notion of *intertextuality* replaces that of intersubjectivity, and poetic language is read as at least *double*."[1] It is less well known, however, that barely five years later Kristeva tried to distance herself from the term, to the point of (rather disingenuously) disowning it:

> As we know, Freud specifies two fundamental "processes" in the work of the unconscious: *displacement* and *condensation*.... To these we must add a third "process"—*the passage from one sign system to another*.... In this connection we examined the formation of a specific signifying system—the novel—as the result of a redistribution of several different sign systems: carnival, courtly poetry, scholastic discourse. The term *inter-textuality* denotes the transposition of one (or several) sign system(s) into another; but since this term has often been understood in the banal sense of "study of sources," we prefer the term *transposition* because it specifies that the passage from one signifying system to

---

1. Julia Kristeva, "Word, Dialogue, and Novel," in *Desire in Language: A Semiotic Approach to Literature and Art*, ed. Leon S. Roudiez, trans. Thomas Gora, Alice Jardine, and Leon S. Roudiez (New York: Columbia University Press, 1980), 66, emphasis original (originally published in French in 1969).

another demands a new articulation of the thetic—of enunciative and denotative positionality. If one grants that every signifying practice is a field of transpositions of various signifying systems (an inter-textuality), one then understands that its "place" of enunciation and its denoted "object" are never single, complete, and identical to themselves, but always plural, shattered, capable of being tabulated. In this way polysemy can also be seen as the result of a semiotic polyvalence—an adherence to different sign systems.[2]

This about-face is more than just a curious case of a postmodern theoretician chagrined by finding out that a crucial assumption underlying her thinking is actually true: the creator of the text has little to no control over its interpretation. It goes, rather, to the very heart of what the present article, indeed, this entire volume, is about—because the understanding of intertextuality that disgusted Kristeva into trying (belatedly) to jettison the term remains prevalent in biblical studies.

In this broad (to Kristeva, illegitimately so) understanding, intertextuality loomed large in modern Hebrew Bible scholarship long before Kristeva was even born. Starting already in the eighteenth century, and on a massive scale in the nineteenth and twentieth, biblical critics have used similarities of diction, style, and thought in arguing that certain passages belong to the same source, tradition, or redactional layer and therefore should be read together despite not being contiguous in the Bible as we know it. Somewhat later, when cuneiform and hieroglyphic writings became available and legible, a similar set of tools was used to trace the Hebrew Bible's origins in ancient Near Eastern literatures—the quest epitomized by Friedrich Delitzsch's unexpectedly, and undeservedly, controversial *Babel und Bibel* and James Pritchard's celebrated (and still highly utile) *Ancient Near Eastern Texts Pertaining to the Old Testament*.[3] With time, the pursuit of provenance through parallels became so ubiquitous

2. Julia Kristeva, *Revolution in Poetic Language*, trans. Margaret Waller (New York: Columbia University Press, 1984), 59–60, emphasis original (originally published in French in 1974). Cf. Leon S. Roudiez, "Introduction," in Kristeva, *Desire in Language*, 15: "The concept [of intertextuality] ... has been generally misunderstood. It has nothing to do with matters of influence by one writer upon another, or with the sources of a literary work."

3. Friedrich Delitzsch, *Babel und Bibel: Ein Vortrag* (Leipzig: Hinrichs, 1902) (ET: Friedrich Delitzsch, *Babel and Bible: Two Lectures*, Ancient Near East: Classic Studies [Eugene, OR: Wipf & Stock, 2007]); *ANET* (first published 1950).

that in 1962 Samuel Sandmel found it necessary to decry its worst excesses as "parallelomania" from the bully pulpit of a Society of Biblical Literature presidential address.[4]

In the late twentieth century, interpretive focus began to shift—under heavy influence of late modern and especially postmodern literary criticism—from establishing authorship and background of biblical texts to plumbing their meaning. Yet, two crucial and interrelated assumptions remained firmly in place. First, in order to read two or more texts together, a plausible generative pathway should be traced between them, in terms of either origin (common authorship, borrowing, etc.) or authorial intent (quotation, allusion, mimesis, parody, etc.). Second, shared formal and/or conceptual elements constitute both indispensable and sufficient evidence that such a pathway does exist. In other words, there is no intertextuality without parallels.

Granted, Kristeva left the door open for such assumptions by using poorly considered language in her initial description of intertextuality:

> To investigate the status of the word is to study its articulations (as semic complex) with other words in the sentence, and then to look for the same functions or relationships at the articulatory level of larger sequences. Confronted with this spatial conception of language's poetic operation, we must first define the three dimensions of textual space where various semic sets and poetic sequences function. These three dimensions or coordinates of dialogue are writing subject, addressee, and exterior texts. The word's status is thus defined *horizontally* (the word in the text belongs to both writing subject and addressee) as well as *vertically* (the word in the text is oriented toward an anterior or synchronic literary corpus).[5]

With this in the background, the (already-quoted) statement in Kristeva's next paragraph that "any text is constructed of a mosaic of quotations; any text is the absorption and transformation of another" reads as presupposing a process that takes place when the text is produced, not when it is consumed, and leaves traces in it; connections between texts are to be discovered rather than drawn.[6] This made it possible for biblical scholars to

4. Samuel Sandmel, "Parallelomania," *JBL* 81 (1962): 1–13.
5. Kristeva, "Word, Dialogue, and Novel," 65–66, emphasis original.
6. Similarly with Roland Barthes: "Any text is a *new tissue* of *past citations*" ("Theory of the Text," in *Untying the Text: A Post-Structuralist Reader*, ed. Robert

happily continue doing what they have been doing all along, only under a fancier heading. However, already here Kristeva indicates that what really matters for her is the *reader's* ability to see the text as carrying more than one meaning. In the above quotation from *Revolution in Poetic Language*, she leaves no doubt that the importance of "transposition" lies in semiotic destabilization that leads to polyvalence and thence to polysemy.

The purpose of the present article is to test-drive Kristeva's (better understood) theoretical model by transposing a biblical text rich in gender issues—Judg 19—to the gender-based metaphorical space of another biblical text—Ezek 16—with which it shares several major planks of theological agenda but displays no parallels. As a result, new meaning will emerge, exposing weaknesses of this agenda and therefore clearly unintended by the authors of both pieces but potentially stimulating for the Bible's post-Holocaust readership.

Discussion

One notable peculiarity of Judg 19 is that not a single one of its characters has a name. It is, of course, perfectly normal that minor characters, the Levite's servant, his father-in-law, and the only resident of Gibeah to extend hospitality to the party, remain anonymous: the Hebrew Bible is generally quite selective in awarding personal names. That the Levite's concubine is anonymous as well is also less than surprising; so is Micah's mother just two chapters earlier, and so is Samson's mother, referred to in Judg 13 only as "Manoah's wife." But it *is* surprising that the Levite is not named as well—in contrast to his colleague featured in chapters 17–18, who is revealed at the very end as Jonathan the son of Gershom the son of Moses (Judg 18:30). Anonymous characters are plentiful in the Hebrew Bible. Fully anonymous casts, not so much. In fact, the Song of Songs is the only other biblical text to feature a fully anonymous couple.[7]

In both Jewish and Christian traditions, the anonymous lovers of the Song of Songs are identified as the male deity (YHWH or Jesus) and the female community of faith (the Jewish people or the church). That, in turn, brings to mind the representation of God and Lady Israel as husband and

---

Young [Boston: Routledge; Kegan Paul, 1981], 39, emphasis added); "A text is *made* of multiple writings" (Barthes, *Image, Music, Text: Essays*, trans. Stephen Heath [New York: Hill & Wang, 1977], 148, emphasis added).

7. This is a parallel, of course, but not between Judg 19 and Ezek 16.

wife that is commonly found in prophetic literature, including Isa 49–50; 52; 54; 62; 66; Jer 2–3; Hos 1–3; and especially Ezekiel where the metaphor mushrooms in chapters 16 and 23 into over a hundred verses rich in detail that would make Larry Flint blush. What if in Judg 19 we deal with the same couple?

At first blush, this may seem random, if not preposterous. In recent studies, Judg 19 presents itself as a virtual treasure trove of parallels with a vast array of various biblical texts. In particular, it resembles Gen 19 so strongly as to become known as the "second story of Sodom." In both texts, a mob of townsfolk surrounds the house of a resident alien where a small bunch of strangers, whom initially no one wanted to put up for the night, had finally found shelter. In both cases, the attackers clamor to rape a male visitor or visitors. In both cases, the host offers two women instead. Ultimately, both cities are destroyed, and all their inhabitants die (in Judges, it happens in chapters 20–21).[8] In addition, various commentators have claimed that Judg 19 displays connections to a large number of other biblical texts, including Gen 16:8; 18:2; 21:12; 22:6, 10; 24:4, 25, 32, 54; 50:21; Deut 13:14; 22:13–29; Judg 1–2; 9:19, 27; 14:14; 17–18; 20:47; 1 Sam 1:16; 11:7; 2 Sam 3:16; 13:12–15; 15:16; 16:1; 20:3; Isa 40:2; Hos 2:16; Prov 31:20.[9] But Ezek 16 is not among them. At most, there is a second-

---

8. See esp. Cynthia Edenburg, *Dismembering the Whole: Composition and Purpose of Judges 19–21*, AIL 24 (Atlanta: SBL Press, 2016), 174–95.

9. Edenburg, *Dismembering the Whole*, 221–55, 274–80, 286–312; Kirsten H. Gardner, "Hidden in Plain Sight: Intertextuality and Judges 19," in *Second Wave Intertextuality and the Hebrew Bible*, ed. Marianne Grohmann and Hyun Chul Paul Kim, RBS 93 (Atlanta: SBL Press, 2019), 56–63. I say "claimed" rather than "demonstrated" because herein lies yet another problem inherent in the understanding of intertextuality that remains prevalent in current biblical scholarship: What qualifies as a parallel between two texts? In the case of Judg 19, these range from the numerous and massive similarities to Gen 19 discussed by Edenburg (above note) and many others to Gardner's contention that the presence of the root שׁמח in Judg 19:3 connects the chapter to Judg 9:19 where the same root is used (why not to its other 267 occurrences in the Hebrew Bible?). Texts written in one language are bound to share lexemes, grammatical forms, syntactic structure, idioms, stock expressions, and so on; if all such sharing becomes indication of intertextuality, the concept would lose all its heuristic value. (In this respect, I am reminded of a joke about David Mamet, an American playwright whose dialogue contains a lot of profanity. A panhandler approaches a distinguished looking gentleman and asks for money. The man replies pompously, "To quote William Shakespeare, 'Neither a borrower nor a lender be.'" The beggar looks at him and says, "To quote David Mamet, 'F-ck you'"). Jeffrey Leonard, "Identifying Inner-Bibli-

degree connection, in that Hos 2:16 shares Ezekiel's metaphor of God and
Israel as husband and wife and has the former "speak to the heart" of the
latter in the same way that the anonymous Levite intends לדבר על־לב of
his concubine in Judg 19:3.[10] Yet, the expression is not uniquely tied to
the metaphor: in Gen 34:3, Prince Shechem "speaks to the heart" of Dinah
(who is referred to, just like the Levite's concubine, as הנערה); in Ruth 2:13,
Ruth thanks Boaz for "speaking to her heart"; and in 1 Sam 1:13, Hannah
even speaks to her own heart.

In the sense of the term that Kristeva decries in *Revolution in Poetic
Language*, all this means that there is no intertextuality between Judg 19
and Ezek 16. By the same token, there is none between the Song of Songs
and any biblical text that implicitly employs the conjugal metaphor. The
former displays parallels with Proverbs, religious love poetry of ancient
Mesopotamia, secular love poetry of ancient Egypt, Theocritus's idylls,
Syrian wedding songs, and even South Asian literature, including the
Gita-Govinda and Tamil love poetry—in short, almost anything but the
biblical prophetic corpus.[11] In part for this reason, since early modern

cal Allusions: Psalm 78 as a Test Case," *JBL* 127 (2008): 241–65, has tried to formulate
principles of establishing connections between biblical texts; and Dennis MacDonald,
The Homeric Epics and the Gospel of Mark (New Haven: Yale University Press, 2000),
8–9 (see also MacDonald, *Does the New Testament Imitate Homer? Four Cases from the
Acts of the Apostles* [New Haven: Yale University Press, 2003], 2–7), has offered criteria
for identifying mimesis, but their heroic efforts have yet to find broad recognition.

10. Isa 40:2, where the addressees are urged to "speak to the heart" of feminine Jerusalem, may have the same metaphor in mind, but the city is not explicitly
described as the deity's consort.

11. On a strong verbal parallel between Cant 8:7b and Prov 6:31, see Wilhelm
Wittekindt, *Das Hohelied und seine Beziehungen zum Ištarkult* (Hannover: Lafaire,
1926), 58. For the Song's parallels with Mesopotamian love poetry, much of it dedicated to Inanna, see COS 1:445–46, 540–43; with (predominantly secular) Egyptian
love poetry, Miriam Lichtheim, *The New Kingdom*, vol. 2 of *Ancient Egyptian Literature* (Berkeley: University of California Press, 1976), 181–93; Michael V. Fox, *The Song
of Songs and the Egyptian Love Songs* (Madison: University of Wisconsin Press, 1985);
with Theocritus's idylls, Marco Treves, *The Song of Solomon* (Florence: Fortunée,
2004), 29–32 and references there; with Syrian wedding songs, Karl Budde, "Was ist
das Hohelied?" in *Preußische Jahrbücher* 78 (1894), 92–117; Budde, "Das Hohelied
erklärt," in *Die fünf Megillot (Das Hohelied, Das Buch Ruth, Die Klagelieder, Der Prediger, Das Buch Esther)*, ed. Karl Budde, Alfred Bertolet, and D. G. Wildeboer, KHC 17
(Freiburg im Breisgau: Mohr, 1898), x–xii; with the Gita-Govinda, Marvin H. Pope,
Song of Songs: A New Translation with Introduction and Commentary, AB 7C (New

times biblical scholarship has tended to pooh-pooh the traditional reading; among others, the otherwise magisterial and highly informative treatise by Egyptologist Donald Redford famously blasts "purblind and unfeeling exegetes" who "spiritualized" the Song of Songs without asking for his permission.[12]

Yet, the alternatives that scholars have come up with are just as unsatisfactory, only for a different reason—on account of their being exegetically barren. The male lover of the Song of Songs has been identified as King Solomon and his paramour as the pharaoh's daughter whom he married according to 1 Kgs 9:16, a shepherdess, or an Arabian princess.[13] More recently, the tendency has been to eschew any specific identifications, treating the Song as a celebration of love in general.[14] If the book existed on its own—as it may have been the case originally, although I have my doubts—this could suffice. But what is *the Bible* trying to tell us through it? Okay, Solomon had a tryst with a cowgirl or unsuccessfully tried to woo her. Okay, sex is fun, especially if you do not have to get married or worry about possible pregnancy. So what? It is only under the traditional identification of the Song's lovers that its cup begins to brim with meaning. If they are God and Lady Israel, the book becomes capable of adding a major new aspect to their relationship as described elsewhere in the Bible, and especially a healthy counterbalance to the essentially misogynistic presentation of this relationship by the prophets.[15] As I have argued elsewhere,

---

York: Doubleday, 1977), 85–89; with Tamil love poetry, Chaim Rabin, "The Song of Songs and Tamil Poetry," *SR* 3 (1973): 205–19.

12. Donald B. Redford, *Egypt, Canaan, and Israel in Ancient Times* (Princeton: Princeton University Press, 1992), 389. For Pope's similarly minded but much more nuanced and better-argued treatment of the issue, see *Song of Songs*, 89–90.

13. Pharaoh's daughter: e.g., Jacques Bénigne Bossuet, "Praefatio in Canticum Canticorum," in *Œuvres complètes de Bossuet*, 31 vols. (Paris: Librairie de Louis Vivès, 1862; first published 1693), 571–74; shepherdess: e.g., Christian D. Ginsburg, *The Song of Songs: Translated from the Original Hebrew* (London: Longman, 1857); Arabian princess: Michael Goulder, *The Song of Fourteen Songs*, JSOTSup 36 (Sheffield: JSOT Press, 1986).

14. E.g., Othmar Keel, *Das Hohelied*, ZBK 19 (Zurich: TVZ, 1986); André LaCocque, *Romance She Wrote: A Hermeneutical Essay on Song of Songs* (Harrisburg, PA: Trinity Press International, 1998); J. Cheryl Exum, *Song of Songs: A Commentary*, OTL (Louisville: Westminster John Knox, 2005).

15. Admittedly, while boldly easing the Song of Songs onto the semiotic field of the prophetic conjugal metaphor, the traditional commentators decline—for obvious

this aspect is especially consequential given that the Song of Songs mostly relates a woman's experience—which makes it a unique exposition of the relationship between the people and their deity from Israel's standpoint.[16]

It is similar with Judg 19. The intent that underlies its most conspicuous parallels with other texts is not in much doubt. It is reasonably clear why the author of Judg 19 would want to refer the readers back to Gen 19—to indicate that the Israelites' moral condition has hit the rock bottom. After several rounds of apostasy that dominate the book of Judges, they are no better than the people of Sodom and Gomorrah—the only cities in the entire Hebrew Bible that God destroys personally rather than using a human agent.[17] That, in turn, indicates that the time is ripe for regime change—as transparently hinted by the reference to the absence of a king in Israel that opens the chapter and also closes its sequel in Judg 20–21. Connections to the account of Saul's rise to power—which, in addition to the dismemberment of the murdered woman in Judg 19:29 (cf. 1 Sam 11:7) and the setting of the crime in Gibeah (cf. 1 Sam 11:4), include the persistent but otherwise redundant references to the Levite's donkeys and his servant (Judg 19:3, 9–13, 19; cf. 1 Sam 9:3–8)—also make much sense as foreshadowing the ultimate failure of Israel's first king. All these, however, are what Kristeva would define as "singular" meanings because they neatly fit in with the theological agenda pursued not just by Judges, but also by the entire Enneateuch, and strongly supported—and metaphorized in conjugal terms—by the prophets.

Arguably the most naked—in both senses of the word—and most concentrated expression of this agenda can be found in Ezek 16. Here, God is quoted as complaining about Lady Israel's mind-boggling ingrati-

---

reasons—to reveal this metaphor's underside. However, they do pave the way to reading the prophets' poetic language as at least double.

16. Serge Frolov, "The Comeback of Comebacks: David, Bathsheba, and the Prophets in the Song of Songs," in *On Prophets, Warriors, and Kings: Former Prophets through the Eyes of Their Interpreters*, ed. George J. Brooke and Ariel Feldman, BZAW 470 (Berlin: de Gruyter, 2016), 51–61.

17. Virtually all commentaries and studies of the last quarter century agree that in addition to the obvious cycles of apostasy, oppression, repentance, and deliverance, there is a more implicit linear trend of deterioration running through almost the entire book of Judges. Among the first to highlight this trend were J. Cheryl Exum, "The Centre Cannot Hold: Thematic and Textual Instabilities in Judges," *CBQ* 52 (1990): 410–31; and Marvin A. Sweeney, "Davidic Polemics in the Book of Judges," *VT* 47 (1997): 517–29.

tude. He rescued her when she was an abandoned child wallowing in her own blood (16:4–7), married her despite her questionable ancestry (16:8; cf. v. 3), and lavished expensive gifts upon her (16:9–14). Yet she cheated on him with every pool guy and cable repairman (16:15–34). Following on this sordid account is a twofold promise—to punish the unfaithful wife severely but also to reconcile with her after she is sufficiently chastened (16:35–63). This very pattern is especially prominent in Judges where apostasy—explicitly described as "playing the harlot" (2:17; 8:27, 33)—takes place not once, not twice, but six times, and where God forgives Israel every single time, even without her asking for help (as is the case in Judg 13 where the people never "cry to YHWH," but the deity fields a deliverer regardless).

One major stress point of this agenda that gives way when the Levite and his concubine are identified as God and Lady Israel is that when the latter suffers, she suffers for her transgressions—moreover, that she is penalized by getting too much of what she sinfully used to enjoy. In Ezek 16, after accusing Lady Israel of lavishing her favors on every passerby, God vows to gather all her lovers against her, "open her nakedness before them so that they see all her nakedness," and to "give her into their hand" (16:37 and 39). With Lev 18, 20 establishing beyond reasonable doubt that "opening the nakedness" is a circumlocution for sexual intercourse, it is clear that here the supposedly promiscuous woman is being punished by gang rape—which is, among other things, a common plot, almost a subgenre, of porn videos. Several feminist exegetes have claimed that something similar happens to the woman in Judg 19: The patriarchal writer has her gang-raped because she "played the harlot" on her husband and left the safety of her house—in other words, displayed sexual and social independence.[18] Yet there is no indication in the story that this was her male partner's intent. Unless we imagine a highly elaborate and highly cynical conspiracy behind the scenes, it looks as though the Levite was genuinely trying to reconcile with his concubine and avoid trouble while traveling with her—as indicated by his determination to spend the night in an Israelite town rather than in Jebusite Jerusalem (Judg 19:11–15). What happens in Gibeah is a nasty surprise not just for her but for him as well.

---

18. E.g., Mieke Bal, *Death and Dissymmetry: The Politics of Coherence in the Hebrew Bible*, CSHJ (Chicago: University of Chicago Press, 1988), 169–96; J. Cheryl Exum, *Fragmented Women: Feminist (Sub)versions of Biblical Narratives* (Valley Forge, PA: Trinity Press International, 1993), 177–98.

He does not want his partner to be gang-raped. He is just powerless to prevent this from happening—or, perhaps, not caring enough to try. With the Holocaust in mind, this is both good and bad news. The good news is that God did not want six million Jews and countless others to die. The bad news is that the deity, for one reason or another, was insufficiently involved to save them.

At this point, I am reminded of the fact that in addition to multiple parallels between Judg 19 and Gen 19, there is a major difference between the two texts: while in Gen 19 sexual violence is prevented altogether by miraculous means, in Judg 19 a woman is gang-raped and dies as a result. This raises a simple but all-important question: Where is God this time? The intertextual reading pursued here provides a disturbing—but also edifying—answer: cowering behind the locked door, or perhaps even blithely going back to the rudely interrupted banquet.

Related to that is the marked contrast between God's attitude toward Israel as touted by the prophets, and less explicitly by the Enneateuch, including Judges, and the Levite's attitude toward his partner. God in Ezek 16 is a model divine being: He saves the newborn Israel from almost certain death and enthusiastically showers riches upon her when they become a couple. If he is willing to orchestrate sexual violence against her, that is only because she has left him no choice, and he repeatedly promises that reconciliation would follow. The Levite of Judg 19 also comes out of the gate as a model husband, prepared to overlook the woman playing the harlot, in other words, to swallow his male pride for the sake of reconciliation. Yet, when the concubine needs him most, the Levite waxes cruel and aloof. Even though the mob refuses to listen to the host's proposal to give them two women instead of the man for whom they clamor, the Levite "seizes" (ויחזק) his concubine and drags her outside (19:25). With Deut 22:25 in mind (which also uses the root חזק), this makes him a participant of the gang rape. In the morning, instead of frantically looking for her, he prepares to leave; it looks as though for him it is business as usual. Upon finding her prostrate on the threshold, all that he has to say is, "Up, let's go." When there is no answer, instead of trying to revive her or call for help, he loads the concubine on the donkey and upon returning home dismembers her—perhaps while she is still alive.[19] Seemingly unconscionable in a person who is less than a full-fledged psychopath (but in fact

19. Exum, "Centre Cannot Hold," 428.

well-attested in a variety of patriarchal cultures where the stigma of rape is always on the woman), this pattern is unavoidably imputed to a monotheistic deity by the sum total of humanity's empirical experience. The God-administered world, not only physical but also social, merrily continued on its track when the mutilated body of Ashkenazic Jewry was discovered on Europe's doorstep. (It is an open question whether having pieces of this body on display in dozens of Holocaust memorials and museums the world over makes things better.)

The Levite's behavior becomes especially striking when we realize that he sacrificed the woman in order to save his own hide. The mob did not clamor for the concubine or, for that matter, for any woman; as already mentioned, they refused to listen when offered two. They wanted the Levite, and in all probability not for the sake of sexual gratification but rather to assert power over him by turning him, to use a modern term, into a prison bitch.[20] (Incidentally, the Sodomites were likely after the same thing when they tried to rape God through his proxies—which amply explains fire and brimstone.) This calls into question another basic premise of the Enneateuch and the prophets, especially of Ezek 16—that Lady Israel only suffers when she abandons her numinous spouse. In Judg 19, when the concubine plays the whore upon the Levite and leaves him, she apparently travels alone from Mount Ephraim to Bethlehem, perhaps even through Gibeah, without a single incident. It is only when they are reunited that she is exposed to gang rape and ultimately death, and, in more ways than one, it happens because of her husband. Likewise, empirically speaking, over the course of two millennia Jews suffered precisely because they stuck to their God, with their faith being the mob's primary target. Until the birth of racial anti-Semitism (which itself was an outgrowth of religious anti-Judaism) they had ample opportunities to escape the suffering by abandoning God—in terms of Judg 19, avoiding the bad company by becoming a whore (and isn't that a paradox!).

Arguably, these layers of meaning are richer and more relevant today than those yielded by the parallels between Judg 19 and other biblical texts. Instead of political theology that today is of largely antiquarian interest, we face the evergreen problem of theodicy; and we do so by emphasizing the woman's perspective suppressed or neglected by both the Enneateuch and

---

20. Cf. Katharina von Kellenbach, "Am I a Murderer? Judges 19–21 as a Parable of Meaningless Suffering," in *Strange Fire: Reading the Bible after the Holocaust*, ed. Tod Linafelt, BibSem 71 (Sheffield: Sheffield Academic, 2000), 176–91.

the prophets.[21] What is more, these concerns are very much in sync with those that stem, as noted above, from the traditional interpretation of the Song of Songs.

All this is not to say that gratifying exegetical yield is sufficient to render intertextuality valid: Any interpretation worthy of the name needs to be grounded in the interpreted text or texts. In the case of Judg 19, this grounding comes in the form of multiple signals that support identification of the Levite and his concubine with God and Lady Israel.

First, it may not be by accident that the story begins with the Levite's concubine doing something described by the verb זנה, usually translated into English along the lines of "playing the harlot." It stands to reason that the main function of this verb in Hebrew vernacular of the biblical times was to describe certain, most likely poorly defined, kinds of human, more specifically female, sexual behavior. However, in the Hebrew Bible proper זנה and its derivatives are used of human women in less than 10 percent of the cases, and with the single exception of Amos 7:17 all of these women are daughters or daughters-in-law, not wives. Overwhelmingly, the root is used of Israel worshiping foreign gods—which, again not accidentally, happens time and again in Judges and which the prophets describe as marital infidelity.

Second, the term אדון "master, lord," twice used of the Levite in Judg 19 (vv. 26, 27), is almost never employed elsewhere in the Hebrew Bible to denote a husband in relation to the wife—unless she is a slave (as is the case in Exod 21:4, 8). The only exception overall is Gen 18:12, where Sarah calls Abraham אדוני "my master," and there are no clear exceptions specifically in narratorial discourse.[22] By contrast, the lexeme is repeatedly applied to YHWH, both in its own right (Exod 23:17; 34:23; Deut 10:17; Josh 3:11, 13; Isa 1:24; 3:1; 10:16, 33; 19:4; Zech 4:14; 6:5; Mal 1:6; 3:1; Ps 8:2, 10; 97:5; 114:7; 135:5; 136:3; 147:5; Neh 8:10; 10:30) and especially in the specialized form אדני (425 occurrences overall).

Third, neither the falling-out between the Levite and his concubine nor their apparent reconciliation play any discernible role in the larger plot of Judg 19 and chapters 19–21 as a whole. The concubine זנה-ing on

---

21. On the blatant silencing of Lady Israel, as represented by the prophet's wife Gomer, in Hosea, see Marvin A. Sweeney, *Reading the Hebrew Bible after the Shoah: Engaging Holocaust Theology* (Minneapolis: Fortress, 2008), 154–55.

22. In Amos 4:1, the reference may be to the husbands of the "Bashan cows" or to their Lord, i.e., YHWH.

the Levite and leaving him and the Levite going to Bethlehem to retrieve her is superfluous in launching the gruesome plot of the chapter—and of Judg 19–21 as a whole—and specifically in demonstrating that Israel is now worse than Sodom and Gomorrah. The couple could get into trouble while traveling through Gibeah for any number of reasons or for no explicit reason at all. Conversely, Israel playing the harlot and God being eager to reconcile with her are central to the prophetic metaphorization of the relationship between the two as reported by the Enneateuch.

Fourth, the Levite and his concubine are the counterparts of the two visitors who come to Sodom in Gen 19.[23] Although those visitors apparently look like regular humans and the text mostly refers to them as "men," they are anything but. The narrator not only explicitly describes them as angels from the outset (19:1) but also blurs the distinction between them and God: for example, in Gen 19:13, they say, "we are destroying this place because … YHWH sent us" but in 19:24–25 it is God who does the job. Likewise, although the couple that comes to Gibeah in Judg 19 looks like regular humans, they might be more than that.

Fifth, within the framework of Judg 19–21 as a whole there is notable stage dynamic between the Levite and YHWH. The Levite is massively present in chapter 19 and the beginning of chapter 20 but completely disappears from the picture after 20:7. The deity is completely absent from chapter 19 and the beginning of chapter 20, making its first appearance in 20:18. It is as though the two cannot occupy the same space-time continuum (notably, although in 20:1 the people come "to YHWH in Mizpah," the deity does not show up here), suggesting that, after the manner of classic vaudeville, the former is the latter in disguise.

Finally, as insightfully noted by Gale A. Yee, the concubine's dismembered body serves as a symbol of Israel's disjointed body politic.[24] In other words, she is the embodiment of Israel—just like the woman in the Song of Songs as per the book's traditional interpretation.

With these signals in place, the interpretation of Judg 19 offered here cannot be dismissed as arbitrary. Yet, they only come to light when the chapter is transposed onto the semiotic field of the prophetic conjugal metaphor despite the nearly total lack of parallels with the texts that

---

23. Again, this is a parallel, but not between Judg 19 and Ezek 16.

24. Yee, "Ideological Criticism: Judges 17–21 and the Dismembered Body," in *Judges and Method: New Approaches to Biblical Studies*, ed. Gale A. Yee, 2nd ed. (Minneapolis: Fortress, 2007), 146–70.

deploy this metaphor. That is why I took the unconventional step of discussing these signals last rather than first. Intertextuality is constructed, not excavated; it originates in the reader's desire for a rewarding meaning, not in the author's agenda. But like any edifice it would not stand without support.[25]

Conclusion

The results of the exercise undertaken in the present essay suggest that the identification of intertextuality with parallels, still implicit in much of biblical scholarship, is in need of substantial correction. Their absence is not a reason to eschew what Kristeva called transposition, and their presence is not a reason to undertake it (which is, in particular, the case with most of the putative parallels between Judg 19 and other biblical texts).[26]

The discussion above also demonstrates that biblical exegesis is uniquely positioned to practice intertextuality as Kristeva envisioned it. If *text* is understood expansively (something that Kristeva seems to do when she lists carnival as such), the semiotic spaces that intersect and interact in my reading of Judg 19 do not include just Ezek 16 and the Song of Songs (which already is a handful). Massively involved alongside these are the interpretive traditions of the Bible-based communities of faith, the historical experiences of these communities as particularly exemplified by the Holocaust (which in its turn falls into three interrelated but distinctive texts—Holocaust history, Holocaust literature, and post-Holocaust theology), and the contemporary discourse on gender. What makes this

---

25. It is somewhat different with the Song of Songs. Its only aspect that supports the traditional interpretation is the anonymity of the featured couple. At the same time, nothing in it precludes this interpretation; in a way, it is all about filling a yawning, book-scale gap. Also, while it is well-nigh impossible that the creator of Judg 19 had the prophetic conjugal metaphor in mind, this may well be—although not necessarily is—the case with the Song of Songs. That would be in line with the overall trend in the Writings section of the Masoretic canon, much, if not all, of which is easily construable as a human response or riposte to the Enneateuch's impersonal narration and the divine discourse in the prophetic books (see Frolov, "Comeback," 51). In this sense, while the present chapter reads "double" the poetics of Judg 19, the traditional interpretation of the Song of Songs does the same to the poetics of the Hebrew Bible as a whole.

26. As demonstrated by Gardner's efforts to make sense of as many of them as possible ("Hidden in Plain Sight," 68–72).

exuberance possible is the fact that while being a product of a culture that ceased to exist millennia ago, the Bible retains massive presence in today's world. Since civilization can also be described as a text, this means that biblical scholarship could be intertextual throughout if it abandoned its ultimately futile and irrelevant quest for sources and authorial intent.

16

Synchrony versus Diachrony—Reader- versus Author-Centered: Shall the Twain Ever Meet?

Gregory T. K. Wong

For about three decades now, among scholars who research relationships between biblical texts, which approach makes better sense and has legitimacy remains an issue of contention. Historical-critical scholars who for over a century have collectively honed their skills using the historical comparative method have continued using that method in their study of textual relationships. In their view, the main task of such studies is to determine the direction of influence between related texts so that one may discern the meaning an author wishes to convey by referencing another text. The essence of such an approach is thus diachronic and author-centered.

But pointing to an inherent interconnectedness that binds all texts, literary critics argue that every time a reader approaches a text, that text will inevitably interact with other texts in that reader's textual universe, such that meaning is more a product of such multifaceted interactions than a linear one-to-one relationship that depends on a reader's ability to recover the original intent of the text's author. Meaning is thus created by readers rather than authors, and the focus of intertextual studies should be on how two texts dialogue with each other in the mind of a reader to produce new meaning and significance. To the extent that diachronic issues such as relative chronology of texts do not matter in this kind of dialogue, a reader-centered approach is invariably synchronic, even though a synchronic reading does not have to be reader-centered.[1]

---

1. A synchronic reading simply refers to a reading strategy that focuses on the final form of a text without regard for the redaction processes that produced that final form.

Gregory T. K. Wong

From this brief summary of the two approaches, it is evident that they represent diametrically opposing reading strategies, so much so that in the minds of many, reconciliation between the two appears a lost cause.[2] But are the two really so incompatible as to render dialogue utterly impossible? To answer this question, I have decided to conduct an experiment using two related texts, to see if points of contact can be found that would open up a dialogue between these two seemingly opposing approaches.

In keeping with the focus on gender and Judges in this volume, I have chosen to examine two narratives from Judges about pledges that ended up victimizing women: the narrative about Jephthah's daughter in Judg 11 and the one about finding wives for Benjaminites in Judg 21. While I have briefly written about the relationship between these two narratives before, in what follows I will be examining that relationship in far greater detail, focusing especially on the possible interplay of reading strategies that are equally applicable in the analysis of the relationship between these two texts.[3] In terms of approach, I will begin by first embracing a reading strategy associated with the diachronic, author-centered approach, but will, in the end, also be looking at the two texts from a synchronic, reader-centered perspective.

A Diachronic, Author-Centered Analysis:
Establishing Allusive Links, Determining a Likely Direction of Dependence, and Exploring Redactional Implications

To begin, consider the literary context of the two narratives. The narrative about Jephthah's daughter is found in a section containing hero stories that, under the Deuteronomistic History hypothesis, is generally regarded as belonging to the Deuteronomistic core of Judges. The narrative about finding wives for Benjaminites, on the other hand, is found within the last five chapters of Judges, in a section generally considered an appendix artificially tagged on to the book's core at a later stage of Judges' redaction history.[4] Thus, one can perhaps begin with the assumption that the two

---

2. Geoffrey D. Miller ("Intertextuality in Old Testament Research," *CBR* 9 [2011]: 304) declares hope of reconciliation between the two approaches bleak.

3. For my earlier analysis of these two texts, see Gregory T. K. Wong, *Compositional Strategy of the Book of Judges: An Inductive, Rhetorical Study*, VTSup 111 (Leiden: Brill, 2006), 132–35.

4. The classic 1943 view of Martin Noth (*The Deuteronomistic History*, 2nd ed., JSOTSup 15 [Sheffield: JSOT Press, 1991], 69–85) regarding the overall process of

narratives in question came from different hands, even though in their current state, they have now become parts of the same book.

Despite their distinct redaction histories, plot-wise, the two narratives share certain similarities. First, both narratives involve a pledge made in advance of war.[5] Second, after the battles were fought and won, both parties began regretting their pledges when it became clear that honoring these pledges would bring catastrophic consequences. Finally, those who ended up being victimized by both pledges turned out to be women: while Jephthah's daughter was presumably offered up as a burnt offering in fulfillment of her father's prewar vow, six hundred women from Jabesh-Gilead and Shiloh were allowed to be forcibly taken as wives as the Israelites tried to circumvent their prewar oath not to give their daughters to Benjaminites.

But not only do the two narratives share similarities plot-wise, in terms of characterization, the female victims of the pledges are also described in remarkably similar terms. The unintended victim of Jephthah's vow is characterized in two ways. First, she is identified as a "daughter" (בת) both by Jephthah in 11:35 and by the narrator in 11:34, 40. Then she is also presented as a virgin, her virginity (בתולים) being referred to both by herself in 11:37 and by the narrator in 11:38. In fact, to emphasize that her virginity lasted until the very end, in 11:39 the narrator further describes her as "not having known a man" (לא־ידעה איש) when her father did to her as he had pledged.

---

redaction for Judges within DtrH is still generally affirmed by scholars today. For Noth's view of the last five chapters of Judges, see his one-sentence comment in Noth, *Deuteronomistic History*, 77 n. 2.

5. Although Jephthah's pledge is characterized in 11:30 as a vow (נדר נדר), while Israel's pledge is characterized in 21:1, 7, 18 as an oath (שבע), the two roots are considered largely synonymous. In fact, not only are the two used in a parallel synonymous pair in Ps 132:2, both referring to the same pledge David made to build a house for YHWH, in a passage particularly relevant to the narratives in question, the roots are also used synonymously in Num 30:3, where YHWH commanded that regardless of whether a man has vowed a vow (נדר נדר) or sworn an oath (שבע שבעה) to YHWH, his word must not be broken, but he must do according to all that comes out of his mouth. It is precisely the irrevocable nature of such pledges as stipulated in this command that brought grief to both Jephthah and the Israelites as they faced the unforeseen consequences of their pledges. Incidentally, in 11:36, when Jephthah's daughter urged her father to "do to me according to that which came out of your mouth" (עשה לי כאשר יצא מפיך), she may have been directly referencing this command in Num 30:3 to "do according to all that comes out of his mouth" (ככל־היצא מפיו יעשה).

In the narrative about finding wives for Benjaminites, similar descriptions are also used to characterize the two groups of women who fell victim to Israel's collective oath. First, the young women from Shiloh are twice referred to in 21:21 as "daughters of Shiloh" (בנות־שילו), a description that connects them with Jephthah's daughter. Second, that they are presented as coming out (יצאו) to celebrate a festival of YHWH "with dancing" (במחלות) mirrors Jephthah's daughter, who in 11:34 was also coming out (יצאת) to celebrate her father's victory "with dancing" (במחלות), both parties innocently oblivious of the fate that would await them.

But if the daughters of Shiloh mirror Jephthah's daughter in being innocent dancing daughters, the young women of Jabesh-Gilead likewise mirror Jephthah's daughter. For not only are they referred to in 21:12 as virgins (בתולה), a description that reminds one of the virginity (בתולים) of Jephthah's daughter (11:38), they are further tagged with the exact same "have not known a man" (לא־ידעה איש) that describes Jephthah's daughter (11:39).

These similarities, both plot-wise and pertaining to specific word choice in characterization, suggest that the two narratives are perhaps more intricately related than what was initially assumed. But do these similarities result from each drawing from the same shared tradition, or do they reflect conscious literary dependence?

To answer this question, it should be noted that, since there seems to be no other narrative of a prewar pledge that ended up dooming virgin daughters within the tradition of the Hebrew Bible, it is likely that the similarities noted here are specifically designed to elicit association between these very two narratives.[6] Furthermore, that some of the associative links involve highly marked linguistic features further increases the likelihood that they result from conscious literary dependence where one narrative is alluding to the other.

For example, 11:34 and 21:21 represent the only two times the noun מחלה ("dance") appears in Judges. As for לא־ידעה איש ("she has not known a man"), 11:39 and 21:12 are the only two times this exact formulation appears within the Hebrew Bible.[7] As Cynthia Edenburg points out in her

---

6. Although one can conceivably postulate the existence of a common source no longer extant, Cynthia Edenburg ("How [Not] to Murder a King," *SJOT* 12 [1998]: 71) correctly argues that methodologically, the conjectural nature of hypothetical sources makes it imperative that only known sources be regarded as evidence.

7. A similar clause appears in Gen 19:18, but with the subject and corresponding verb form in the plural instead of the singular. The clause does appear in the singular in Num 31:17, albeit without the negation particle.

empirical study differentiating between intertextual echoes based on oral tradition and text-based literary compositions, texts that elicit intertextual associations stemming from parallel accounts, allusion, and so on, were generally designed by highly literate scribes for *reading* audiences who could reread texts in order to recognize the associative device, and then, to identify the alluded text.[8]

But if the similarities between the two accounts indeed result from conscious *textual* dependence, then what is the direction of dependence? In cases such as this where absolute dating of texts seems impossible, Edenburg's notion of ungrammaticality proves helpful. Pointing out that the placement of associative markers in alluding texts to signal the presence of an allusion often involves elements borrowed from the alluded text, Edenburg argues that these borrowed markers will inevitably introduce a degree of foreignness into the alluding text, breaking that text's own narrative grammar.[9] The presence of such ungrammaticality thus enables one to distinguish the alluding text from the alluded text.[10]

Unfortunately, Edenburg has not provided further clarification regarding the scope and nature of such ungrammaticalities, although the examples she cites in the article that introduces this concept appear to be focused primarily on textual incongruities having to do with plot logic.[11]

---

8. Cynthia Edenburg, "Intertextuality, Literary Competence and Question of Readership: Some Preliminary Observations," *JSOT* 35 (2010): 147.

9. Edenburg, "How (Not) to Murder a King," 68–69. While the overall direction of Edenburg's assertion is surely correct, one wonders, however, if such associative markers must *inevitably* display an obvious foreignness or ungrammaticality. After all, if the source text is deemed sufficiently familiar to an intended audience and hence readily recognizable, a skillful author may not need to resort to overt ungrammaticality to signal the presence of an allusion, but can afford to weave their associative markers more seamlessly into their text without awkwardness. After all, the presence of ungrammaticalities, while helpful in most cases for signaling the presence of an allusion, also has the potential of becoming a distraction, thus reducing the overall rhetorical effectiveness of the author's own text.

10. Edenburg, "How (Not) to Murder a King," 73.

11. In the two examples she cites from 1 Sam 24 and 26 in her 1998 article, Edenburg argues for the dependence of 1 Sam 24 on 1 Sam 26 based on plot incongruities in the 1 Sam 24 account ("How [Not] to Murder a King," 76–77). In her most recent work on Judges, in discussing criteria for evaluating literary relationships between texts, Edenburg (*Dismembering the Whole: Composition and Purpose of Judges 19–21*, AIL 24 [Atlanta: SBL Press, 2016], 172) casually speaks of ungrammaticalities as arising from disrupting language norms and dysfunctional or blind motifs but has still not

But one suspects that this notion of ungrammaticality can also be applied to literary issues. Here, I am thinking specifically about the laconic style and principle of economy that especially characterize biblical narrative, such that in general, only information relevant to further plot development is disclosed.[12] Thus, if an allusive marker in a narrative text introduces information that, although not logically at odds within that text, is nonetheless superfluous to or holds no further relevance toward subsequent plot development, then in a way it should also constitute an ungrammaticality.

If so, then where our two narratives are concerned, evidence seems to suggest that the narrative about Jephthah's daughter is the source text while the narrative about finding wives for Benjaminites is the alluding text.

As was pointed out earlier, the allusive markers linking Jephthah's daughter to the virgins of Jabesh-Gilead include the women's shared status as virgins (בתולה/בתולים) who had not known a man (לא־ידעה איש). A careful consideration of these two markers seem to show a degree of ungrammaticality in the narrative about finding wives for Benjaminites.

First, in 21:11, the married women of Jabesh-Gilead who were to be killed are set in contrast with the virgins who were to be spared. Since the former are described as "every woman having known a man's bed" (כל־אשה ידעת משכב־זכר), one would expect the description of the latter to involve a negation of that fact using a similar formula. Indeed, the full description of the virgins in 21:12 is "four hundred young women, virgins who had not known a man with respect to a man's bed" (ארבע מאות נערה בתולה אשר לא־ידעה איש למשכב זכר). But note that although the basic formulation of the two descriptions is similar, in the latter, the insertion of a superfluous איש makes the description unnecessarily wordy, yet adds nothing not already communicated through משכב־זכר. Thus, one may infer that this איש may have been inserted solely for the purpose of establishing an allusive link to Jephthah's daughter, so that לא־ידעה איש למשכב זכר in 21:12 would form a stronger parallel with the description of Jephthah's daughter in 11:39 as והיא לא־ידעה איש.

---

provided further clarification regarding what exactly constitutes a disruptive norm or a dysfunctional motif. One wonders if the plot incongruities cited in her 1998 article would fall under the category of a dysfunctional motif or if that constitutes yet another category of ungrammaticality.

12. Shimon Bar-Efrat, *Narrative Art in the Bible*, trans. Dorothea Shefer-Vanson, JSOTSup 70 (Sheffield: Sheffield Academic, 1989), 114.

In addition, it is possible that even the description of the virgins of Jabesh-Gilead as בתולה in 21:12 constitutes an ungrammaticality. For although the two main allusive markers that link the virgins of Jabesh-Gilead to Jephthah's daughter, namely, בתולים/בתולה and לא־ידעה איש, essentially communicate the same basic fact, these two markers are used differently in the two texts. In the narrative about Jephthah's daughter, these two characterizations are used synonymously to express the same idea, albeit in different contexts. In 11:37, Jephthah's daughter had asked for two months to mourn her בתולים and 11:38 reports her doing so after permission was granted by her father. Then in 11:39, the narrator reports Jephthah carrying out his vow regarding her, and, in a parenthetical comment, highlights her virgin status remaining until the very end through the disjunctive clause והיא לא־ידעה איש.

But in the narrative about the virgins of Jabesh-Gilead, לא־ידעה איש occurs in a relative clause, the main function of which is apparently to qualify the immediately preceding בתולה. But such a qualification is entirely unnecessary because the fact that a בתולה is someone who has never sexually known a man is self-evident.[13] In fact, in the great majority of the sixty-plus occasions where בתולה or בתולים appears in the Hebrew Bible, no such qualification is needed.[14] When it is necessary to specify whether a woman has sexually known a man, the antecedents are invariably nouns like בנות (Gen 19:8) or נשים/אשה (Num

---

13. Joel 1:8 appears to be the only occurrence where בתולה may have been used to refer to a married woman, as she is depicted as being in sackcloth over the husband of her youth. However, it is not entirely clear that בעל נעוריה indeed refers to a husband, as some commentators understand the term merely as a reference to a fiancé to whom the בתולה has long been engaged.

14. The only two times when the mention of a בתולה is further clarified with respect to her relationship with men are Gen 24:16 and Lev 21:3. In Gen 24:16, the qualification comes immediately after the disclosure of Rebecca's virgin status in the form of a parenthetical comment through a disjunctive clause, the focus being on no man having known Rebecca sexually rather than on her not having known a man. The function of this clause is likely deliberately reiterative for emphatic purposes. In Lev 21:3, the qualification relates to a virgin sister of a priest who does not have a husband. The focus here, however, is not so much on her sexual status as it is on her marital status. Because she was unmarried, her brother, the priest, would then be counted as among her closest male family members and hence, be allowed to defile himself for her funeral. Therefore, in neither case does "not having had sexual relationship with a man" serve as a direct explanation of בתולה through a relative clause as in Judg 21:12.

31:17, 18, 35; Judg 21:11), in which the woman's sexual status is not inherently implicit.

Furthermore, the antecedent בתולה in 21:12 that renders the following relative clause superfluous is itself in apposition with an immediately preceding נערה ("young woman"). Since נערה, like בת or אשה, does not inherently communicate a woman's sexual status, on occasions where it is necessary to specify that a particular נערה is a virgin, בתולה usually follows immediately in apposition, and no further qualification is needed (cf. 1 Kgs 1:2; Esth 2:2–3; and the *qere* reading of Deut 22:23, 28).[15] Thus, the only time an appositional בתולה is followed by further qualification specifying she has not sexually known a man is in Judg 21:12. Therefore, one suspects that the description אשר לא־ידעה איש למשכב זכר perhaps originally exists to qualify נערה, with the superfluous appositional בתולה being an allusive marker inserted primarily to link these virgins with Jephthah's daughter.

Likewise, one of the allusive markers that link Jephthah's daughter to the daughters of Shiloh also seems to display a similar superfluous quality. In instructing the Benjaminites to go and each snatch a daughter of Shiloh for himself as wife in 21:21, that these daughters would be dancing is already made clear through the verb חול ("to dance"), such that the immediately following qualification במחלות ("with dancing") is entirely unnecessary. In fact, in 21:23, when the narrator reports the Benjaminites doing exactly as told, only the *polel* participle of חול is used to describe these dancing daughters. This suggests that במחלות in 21:21 may have been introduced primarily to serve as an allusive link to Jephthah's daughter, so that in both narratives, the female victims are portrayed as coming out dancing using almost identical terms.

What the above observations suggest is that of the two narratives, the one about finding wives for Benjaminites is the alluding text while the one about Jephthah's daughter is its source. For while all the allusive markers are contextually functional in the narrative about Jephthah's daughter, most of them seem superfluous and awkwardly placed in the narrative about finding wives for Benjaminites.

---

15. That נערה can refer to a married woman is apparent in Judg 19, where six times in 19:2–9, the Levite's concubine is referred to as הנערה. In Ruth 2:6; 4:12, Ruth is also referred to as נערה even though those referring to her as such were clearly aware of her status as Naomi's widowed daughter-in-law.

But having arrived at this conclusion, what significance does it hold? First, for those interested in historical issues, the ability to identify this innerbiblical allusion and determine a plausible direction of dependence provides invaluable insight regarding how Judges in its current form was put together. In fact, it may have given us reason to rethink some widely held assumptions about the relationship between the Deuteronomistic core of the book and its last five chapters. For as has been pointed out, while the section of Judges featuring stories about the various judges is often considered the book's Deuteronomistic core, the last five chapters are often considered an independent work artificially appended to the Deuteronomistic core primarily because events narrated in these chapters occurred in the same historical period.

But if it is true that a narrative in the epilogue of Judges contains conscious allusions to a narrative found in the Deuteronomistic core of the book, and if similar instances can be found in which other narratives in Judges' epilogue also make conscious allusions to the narratives about the various judges in the book's Deuteronomistic core, then the implication is that, whatever form the book may have taken in its prior life as part of DtrH, the form it currently takes may not have come about by sheer historical happenstance.[16] Instead, one may even argue that Judges' epilogue was composed/redacted with the narratives of the various judges in mind specifically to serve as conclusion to the book. If so, a new and different approach to the study of the last five chapters of Judges is called for, such

---

16. Incidentally, other such instances of allusion to the judges can be found within Judges' epilogue. One example would be the description in 20:16 of some among the Benjaminite army as אטר יד־ימינו ("restricted in his right hand"). This identical phrase, also used to describe Ehud in 3:15, is highly marked, as it involves the rare root אטר, which is found only three times within the Hebrew Bible. That in both instances in Judges the expression describes someone from the tribe of Benjamin and constitutes a pun on the tribe's name suggests that these two occurrences likely represent an attempt to establish an allusive link. But while this description is integral to the plot of the Ehud narrative since his left-handedness plays a critical role in his successful assassination of Eglon, the mention of the left-handed stone-slinging Benjaminites who took part in the civil war has no apparent plot relevance within that narrative, as these Benjaminites were not mentioned again in the remainder of that narrative. This suggests that the author/redactor of the narrative of the Benjaminite war was consciously alluding to the Ehud narrative. For other examples of narratives in the epilogue alluding to the narratives of the judges, see Wong, *Compositional Strategy*, 79–135.

that insights on the historical perspective or theology of these chapters ought not to be sought solely from within these five chapters, but must also include considerations of how these chapters relate to and flow from the narratives of the various judges that immediately precede.

A Second Look: The Validation of a Synchronic, Reader-Centered Reading Strategy

But in addition to historical implications regarding the redactional process of the book, surprisingly, there is also insight to be gained regarding matters of interest to those who embrace a synchronic, reader-centered approach to textual relationships. For in the process of recovering the point the author/redactor of Judges' epilogue was trying to make through the setting up of this allusion, one actually discovers evidence that affirms a synchronic, reader-centered approach as a valid reading strategy.

As mentioned earlier, in a reader-centered approach to textual relationship, the primary interest is not so much on discovering any historical relationship that may have existed between two texts or how an author conceives that relationship, but on how a reader takes the texts in question and allows them to dialogue with each other synchronically to create new meaning and significance. But in speaking of readers, Ellen van Wolde reminds us that even authors/redactors are themselves readers and digesters of texts and not just producers.[17] This is especially true for authors/redactors who reference other texts to bring out their own perspective.

If so, then a case can be made that, in setting up the allusion between the narrative about Jephthah's daughter and the narrative about finding wives for Benjaminites, the author/redactor of Judges' epilogue may in fact have engaged in a synchronic, reader-centered reading of the two texts.

Allow me to explain. Concerning the narrative about finding wives for Benjaminites, commentators have suggested that the two episodes concerning the virgins of Jabesh-Gilead and the daughters of Shiloh were originally independent traditions brought together under the common theme of "bringing women in to reconstitute the tribe of Benjamin."[18] Whether

---

17. Ellen van Wolde, "Trendy Intertextuality," in *Intertextuality in Biblical Writings: Essays in Honour of Bas van Iersel*, ed. Sipke Draisma (Kampen: Kok, 1989), 46.

18. J. Alberto Soggin, *Judges*, trans. John Bowden, 2nd ed., OTL (London, SCM, 1987), 300; Robert G. Boling, *Judges: A New Translation with Introduction and Commentary*, AB 6A (Garden City, NY: Doubleday, 1975), 294.

it was the author/redactor of Judges' epilogue who brought these episodes together or whether the episodes came already combined is almost impossible to ascertain. But from our earlier observation that some of the allusive markers planted into this narrative seem superfluous and awkwardly placed, such that their deletion would have no effect on the overall flow of the narrative except to make for a smoother reading, one surmises that the author/redactor of Judges' epilogue was very likely working with preexisting material, the integrity of which the author/redactor was trying to preserve with minimal modification.[19] For had this narrative originated from the author/redactor of Judges' epilogue, those allusive markers could easily have been woven seamlessly into the text without the present awkwardness. But if the author/redactor of Judges' epilogue was indeed working out of a preexisting text, and through the insertion of allusive markers, was trying to set up a dialogue between that text and the narrative about Jephthah's daughter, then the author/redactor of Judges' epilogue may have been engaging in a reader-centered reading of the relevant texts.

When the two narratives in question are examined on their own, it appears that apart from some very superficial similarities, such as both involving prewar pledges that ended up victimizing women, there is no clear point of contact between the two, as neither seems to represent an attempt to comment on the other. But through the insertion of allusive marks that artificially drew the two narratives into a literary dialogue, the author/redactor of Judges' epilogue had in fact transformed both narratives and imbued them with new significance they did not have on their own.

Consider the narrative about finding wives for Benjaminites. Read on its own, one of its foci appears to be on how women ended up falling victim to war and to the pledges of men who instigated war as they foolishly courted divine approval in hope of securing a favorable outcome. In the context of its appearance in the epilogue of Judges, it probably highlights the kind of chaos that had befallen Israelite society as her leaders thought nothing of sacrificing women on the altar of war. But through the setting up of allusive markers that drew it into a dialogue with the narrative about Jephthah's daughter, the author/redactor of Judges' epilogue was in fact encouraging their readers to view the female victims in this

---

19. By preexisting material, I am here referring to already-existing fixed textual traditions of the two episodes that make up the current narrative about finding wives for Benjaminites.

narrative as a version of Jephthah's daughter, who, incidentally, also fell victim to her father's pledge uttered in advance of war in hope of securing a favorable outcome. In that light, what happened to the female victims in the aftermath of the Benjaminite war had become more than isolated incidents, but a recurring injustice. Furthermore, to the extent that those who sanctioned this injustice in this narrative were nameless Israelites, whereas the victimizer in the case of Jephthah's daughter was her father, a named judge presumably raised up by YHWH to deliver and lead the nation, what the author/redactor of Judges' epilogue seems to be implying is that the root of this victimization can be traced all the way to the highest level of leadership within the nation. Thus, if Israelite society had succumbed to the kind of chaos that included victimization of women on the altar of war, it is because one of the nation's top leaders had set a very bad precedent that somehow got filtered down and replicated itself in society at large. Thus, the dialogue between the two texts has subtly transformed what may have originally been construed as isolated incidents in the narrative about finding wives for Benjaminites not only into part of a pattern, but also into a likely indirect consequence of an earlier injustice.

But this dialogue between the two texts has also subtly transformed the narrative about Jephthah's daughter and imbued it with a new level of significance. For taken solely in the context of the Jephthah cycle, the focus of this narrative appears to be on the personal tragedy that had befallen Jephthah and his daughter because of a rash and inappropriate vow that never should have made, had Jephthah not been plagued by a deep thirst for recognition, combined with an abject sense of insecurity. But through this intertextual dialogue, this personal tragedy has now been transformed into something with far greater significance, as the mistake Jephthah made has now become not just a personal failure, but a failure that had national repercussions as it turned into a bad precedent that opened the way to further victimizations of women on the altar of war.[20]

---

20. As this piece constitutes part of a collection of essays, one focus of which is gender, it is perhaps only appropriate for me to make the following observations. First, if what I have argued here about the reading strategy of the author/redactor of Judges' epilogue and the message conveyed through the new text being constructed are valid, then contrary to oft-repeated accusations by some feminist scholars that the Hebrew Bible is patriarchal, misogynist, and androcentric, what we have here is a biblical author/redactor who has taken pains to craft an indictment against the vic-

From the above observations, it seems the author/redactor of Judges' epilogue had been engaging in a synchronic, reader-centered reading of the two relevant texts. For in setting up this dialogue between two apparently independent, originally unrelated texts, the author/redactor of Judges' epilogue seems to have shown interest neither in the relative chronology of the texts in question, nor any linear historical relationship that may have existed between the two texts. In fact, apparently unconcerned about whether the original authors of these texts ever knew of the existence of the other or intended for them to be read together, the author/redactor of Judges' epilogue seems simply to have noticed parallels between the two texts that warranted them being brought together, and so, planted allusive markers into the one being adapted to create a dialogue so that a new level of significance could emerge. In this respect, the reading strategy adopted was decidedly synchronic and reader-centered.

But having engaged in such a reading, this author/redactor of Judges' epilogue had apparently also taken pains to make sure readers of those texts would be able to arrive at the same perspective. For why else would this author/redactor take the trouble to plant allusive markers into the narrative before them, if not to make sure that through these markers, readers would also be led to participate in this dialogue? But by enshrining this reader-centered reading through the introduction of allusive markers into the text being adapted, this author/redactor had effectively created a new text with its own set of meaning and significance.

---

timization of women on the altar of war. To the extent that the source of this victimization is pointed right at the men who occupy authoritative leadership positions in Israelite society, even to a named judge at the highest level of leadership who was likely deemed a national hero in his day, this biblical author/redactor, at least, was far from leaving the exploitation of the Israelite male hierarchy unchallenged, even as the narratives appear to be simply recounting historical facts. Second, to the extent that this biblical author/redactor's subversive agenda is discoverable largely through a historical-critical analysis of the texts that does not proceed from a predetermined political/ideological starting point, it perhaps furnishes some evidence that, contrary to what some feminist and postcolonial scholars such as Musa W. Dube (*Postcolonial Feminist Interpretation of the Bible* [Saint Louis, MO: Chalice, 2000]) and Susanne Scholz ("'Tandoori Reindeer' and the Limitations of Historical Criticism," in *Her Master's Tools? Feminist and Postcolonial Engagements of Historical-Critical Discourse*, ed. Caroline Vander Stichele and Todd C. Penner, GPBS 9 [Atlanta: Society of Biblical Literature, 2005], 47–69) claim, when it comes to having something relevant to say about contemporary social issues, historical criticism may not be quite obsolete yet.

Conclusion

So what do all these tell us? They tell us that a synchronic, reader-centered approach is a valid reading strategy that even ancient authors/ redactors of biblical texts engaged in. But they also tell us that the very same author/redactor who engaged in such a reading was also concerned enough about preserving this insight for future readers that pains would be taken to leave clues to help those readers retrace the necessary steps. In other words, what we seem to have here is diachrony in the service of synchrony, in which an ancient reader-centered reading is preserved and recoverable largely through a diachronic, authored-centered analysis of the relevant texts.

So, synchrony and diachrony, reader- and author-centered approaches. Perhaps the twain do meet after all.

Bibliography

Abbott, H. Porter. *The Cambridge Introduction to Narrative*. 2nd ed. Cambridge: Cambridge University Press, 2008.

Ackerman, Susan. *Warrior, Dancer, Seductress, Queen: Women in Judges and Biblical Israel*. ABRL. New York: Doubleday, 1998.

———. "What If Judges Had Been Written by a Philistine?" *BibInt* 8 (2000): 33–41.

Adam, Klaus-Peter. "Ahimaaz." *EBR* 1:651.

Aguilar, Grace. *The Women of Israel*. 2 vols. New York: Appleton, 1872.

Albertz, Rainer. *A History of Israelite Religion in the Old Testament Period*. Translated by John Bowden. 2 vols. Louisville: Westminster John Knox, 1994.

Alkier, Stefan. "Intertextualität—Annäherung an ein texttheoretisches Paradigma." Pages 1–26 in *Heiligkeit und Herrschaft: Intertextuelle Studien zu Heiligkeitsvorstellungen und zu Psalm 110*. Edited by Dieter Sänger. Biblisch-theologische Studien 55. Neukirchen-Vluyn: Neukirchener Verlag, 2003.

———. "Intertextuality and the Semiotics of Biblical Texts." Pages 3–21 in *Reading the Bible Intertextually*. Edited by Richard B. Hays, Stefan Alkier, and Leroy A. Huizenga. Waco, TX: Baylor University Press, 2009.

Alter, Robert. *The Art of Biblical Poetry*. New York: Basic Books, 1985.

Amit, Yairah. *The Book of Judges: The Art of Editing* [Hebrew]. Biblical Encyclopaedia Library 6. Jerusalem: Bialik, 1992.

———. "Hidden Polemic in the Conquest of Dan: Judges 17–18." *VT* 40 (1990): 4–20.

———. *Judges: A Commentary* [Hebrew]. Mikra LeYisra'el. Tel Aviv: Am Oved; Jerusalem: Magnes, 1999.

———. "'Manoah Promptly Followed His Wife' (Judges 13:11): On the Place of the Woman in Birth Narratives." Pages 146–56 in *A Femi-*

nist Companion to Judges. Edited by Athalya Brenner. FCB 4. Sheffield: JSOT Press, 1993.

———. *Reading Biblical Narratives: Literary Criticism and the Hebrew Bible.* Translated by Yael Lotan. Minneapolis: Fortress, 2001.

Anderson, Cheryl B. "Reflections in an Interethnic/Racial Era on Interethnic/Racial Marriage in Ezra." Pages 47–64 in *They Were All Together in One Place? Toward Minority Biblical Criticism.* Edited by Randall C. Bailey, Tat-siong Benny Liew, and Fernando F. Segovia. SemeiaSt 57. Atlanta: Society of Biblical Literature, 2009.

Aptowitzer, Victor. "Asenath, the Wife of Joseph: A Haggadic Literary-Historical Study." *HUCA* 1 (1924): 239–306.

Aschkenasy, Nehama. *Eve's Journey: Feminine Images in Hebraic Literary Tradition.* Philadelphia: University of Pennsylvania Press, 1986.

Ashmon, Scott. "Birth Annunciations in the Hebrew Bible and Ancient Near East: A Synchronic and Diachronic Comparison of Their Forms and Functions." PhD diss., Hebrew Union College-Jewish Institute of Religion, 2010.

Auld, A. Graeme. "Gideon: Hacking at the Heart of the Old Testament." *VT* 39 (1989): 257–67.

———. *Joshua, Judges, and Ruth.* Daily Study Bible. Philadelphia: Westminster, 1984.

Bach, Alice. "Rereading the Body Politic: Women and Violence in Judges 21." *BibInt* 6 (1998): 1–19.

Bachmann, Mercedes L. García. *Judges.* Wisdom Commentary 7. Collegeville, MN: Liturgical Press, 2018.

———. *Women at Work in the Deuteronomistic History.* IVBS 4. Atlanta: Society of Biblical Literature, 2013.

Bailey, Randall C. "They're Nothing but Incestuous Bastards: The Polemical Use of Sex and Sexuality in Hebrew Canon Narratives." Pages 121–38 in *Social Location and Biblical Interpretation in the United States.* Vol. 1 of *Reading from This Place.* Edited by Fernando F. Segovia and Mary Ann Tolbert. Minneapolis: Fortress, 1995.

Baker, Robin. "Double Trouble: Counting the Cost of Jephthah." *JBL* 137 (2018): 29–50.

———. *Hollow Men, Strange Women: Riddles, Codes and Otherness in the Book of Judges.* BibInt 143. Leiden: Brill, 2016.

Bakhtin, Mikhail. *The Dialogic Imagination: Four Essays by M. M. Bakhtin.* Edited by Michael Holquist. Translated by Caryl Emerson and Michael Holquist. Austin: University of Texas Press, 1981.

Bal, Mieke. "A Body of Writing: Judges 19." Pages 208–30 in *A Feminist Companion to Judges*. Edited by Athalya Brenner. FCB 4. Sheffield: JSOT Press, 1993.

———. *Death and Dissymmetry: The Politics of Coherence in the Book of Judges*. CSHJ. Chicago: University of Chicago Press, 1988.

———. *Murder and Difference: Gender, Genre, and Scholarship on Sisera's Death*. Translated by Matthew Gumpert. ISBL. Bloomington: Indiana University Press, 1988.

Bank, Michaela. *Women of Two Countries: German-American Women, Women's Rights, and Nativism, 1848–1890*. Transatlantic Perspectives 2. New York: Berghahn, 2012.

Bar-Efrat, Shimon. *Narrative Art in the Bible*. Translated by Dorothea Shefer-Vanson. JSOTSup 70. Sheffield: Sheffield Academic, 1989.

Barthes, Roland. *Image, Music, Text: Essays*. Translated by Stephen Heath. New York: Hill & Wang, 1977.

———. "Theory of the Text." Pages 31–47 in *Untying the Text: A Post-Structuralist Reader*. Edited by Robert Young. Boston: Routledge; Kegan Paul, 1981.

Bartusch, Mark W. *Understanding Dan: An Exegetical Study of a Biblical City, Tribe and Ancestor*. JSOTSup 379. Sheffield: Sheffield Academic, 2003.

Basch, Norma. *In the Eyes of the Law: Women, Marriage and Property in Nineteenth-Century New York*. Ithaca, NY: Cornell University Press, 1982.

Bauer, Uwe F. W. "Judges 18 as an Anti-Spy Story in the Context of an Anti-Conquest Story: The Creative Usage of Literary Genres." *JSOT* 25 (2000): 37–47.

Bekker, Marrie H. J., and Ad J. J. M. Vingerhoets. "Adam's Tears: The Relationships between Crying, Biological Sex and Gender from Various Perspectives." *Psychology, Evolution and Gender* 1 (1999): 11–31.

Beldman, David J. H. *The Completion of Judges: Strategies of Ending in Judges 17–21*. Siphrut 21. Winona Lake, IN: Eisenbrauns, 2017.

Ben-Smit, Peter. *Masculinity and the Bible: Survey, Models, and Perspectives*. Leiden: Brill, 2017.

Beuken, W. "שָׁכַב." *TDOT* 14:659–71.

Bhabha, Homi K. *The Location of Culture*. New York: Routledge, 1994.

Biddle, Mark E. *Reading Judges: A Literary and Theological Commentary*. Reading the Old Testament. Macon, GA: Smyth & Helwys, 2012.

Bird, Phyllis A. "Prostitution in the Social World and Religious Rhetoric of Ancient Israel." Pages 40–58 in *Prostitutes and Courtesans in the Ancient World*. Edited by Christopher A. Faraone and Laura K. McClure. Wisconsin Studies in Classics. Madison: University of Wisconsin Press, 2006.

Bledstein, Adrien J. "Is Judges a Woman's Satire of Men Who Play God?" Pages 34–54 in *A Feminist Companion to Judges*. Edited by Athalya Brenner. FCB 4. Sheffield: JSOT Press, 1993.

Block, Daniel I. "Echo Narrative Technique in Hebrew Literature: A Study in Judges 19." *WTJ* 52 (1990): 325–41.

———. *Judges, Ruth*. NAC 6. Nashville: Broadman & Holman, 1999.

Bohmbach, Karla G. "Conventions/Contraventions: The Meanings of Public and Private for the Judges 19 Concubine." *JSOT* 24 (1999): 83–98.

Boling, Robert G. *Judges: A New Translation with Introduction and Commentary*. AB 6A. Garden City, NY: Doubleday, 1975.

Bossuet, Jacques Bénigne. "Praefatio in Canticum Canticorum." Pages 571–74 in *Œuvres complètes de Bossuet*. 31 vols. Paris: Librairie de Louis Vivès, 1862.

Boström, Gustav. *Proverbiastudien: Die Weisheit und das fremde Weib in Spr. 1–9*. Lund: Gleerup, 1935.

Bray, Jason. S. *Sacred Dan: Religious Tradition and Cultic Practice in Judges 17–18*. LHBOTS 449. New York: T&T Clark, 2006.

Brayford, Susan A. *Genesis*. Septuagint Commentary Series. Leiden: Brill, 2007.

Breed, Brennan W. *The Nomadic Text: A Theory of Biblical Reception History*. ISBL. Bloomington: Indiana University Press, 2014.

Brenner, Athalya, ed. *A Feminist Companion to Judges*. FCB 4. Sheffield: JSOT Press, 1993.

———. "Introduction." Pages 13–17 in *Judges: Feminist Companion to the Bible*. Edited by Athalya Brenner. FCB 2/4. Sheffield: Sheffield Academic, 1999.

———, ed. *Judges: Feminist Companion to the Bible*. FCB 2/4. Sheffield: Sheffield Academic, 1999.

———. "A Triangle and a Rhombus in Narrative Structure: A Proposed Integrative Reading of Judges 4 and 5." Pages 98–109 in *A Feminist Companion to Judges*. FCB 4. Edited by Athalya Brenner. Sheffield: JSOT Press, 1993.

———. "Women Frame the Book of Judges—How and Why?" Pages 125–38 in *Joshua and Judges*. Edited by Athalya Brenner and Gale Yee. Texts and Contexts. Minneapolis: Fortress, 2013.

Brett, Mark G. *Genesis: Procreation and the Politics of Identity*. OTR. London: Routledge, 2000.

Brettler, Marc Zvi. *The Book of Judges*. OTR. London: Routledge, 2002.

———. "The Book of Judges: Literature as Politics." *JBL* 108 (1989): 395–418.

Bronner, Leila Leah. "Valorized or Vilified? The Women of Judges in Midrashic Sources." Pages 72–95 in *A Feminist Companion to Judges*. Edited by Athalya Brenner. FCB 4. Sheffield: JSOT Press, 1993.

Brooks, Ernest Walter. *Joseph and Asenath: The Confession and Prayer of Asenath, Daughter of Pentephres the Priest*. London: SPCK, 1918.

Budde, Karl. *Das Buch der Richter*. KHC 7. Freiburg im Breisgau: Mohr, 1897.

———. "Das Hohelied erklärt." Pages x–xii in *Die fünf Megillot (Das Hohelied, Das Buch Ruth, Die Klagelieder, Der Prediger, Das Buch Esther)*. Edited by Karl Budde, Alfred Bertholet, and D. G. Wildeboer. KHC 17. Freiburg im Breisgau: Mohr, 1898.

———. "Was ist das Hohelied?" *Preußische Jahrbücher* 78 (1894): 92–117.

Bull, Robert J., and Edward F. Campbell Jr. "The Sixth Campaign Balaṭah (Shechem)." *BASOR* 190 (1968): 2–41.

Burfeind, Carsten. "Asenath in Judaism." *EBR* 2:963.

Butler, Judith. *Bodies That Matter: On the Discursive Limits of "Sex."* London: Taylor & Francis, 2014.

———. *Gender Trouble: Feminism and the Subversion of Identity*. New York: Routledge, 1990.

Butler, Trent C. *Judges*. WBC 8. Nashville: Nelson, 2009.

Camp, Claudia V. "The Wise Women of 2 Samuel: A Role Model for Women in Early Israel?" *CBQ* 43 (1981): 14–29.

Cassel, Paulus. *The Book of Judges*. Translated by Peter H. Steenstra. Vol. 4. of *A Commentary on the Holy Scriptures: Critical Doctrinal and Homiletical*. Edited by John Peter Lange. New York: Scribner, 1872.

Castelbajac, Isabelle de. "Histoire de la rédaction de Juges IX: Une solution." *VT* 51 (2001): 166–85.

Chaudhuri, Supriya. "Dangerous Liaisons: Desire and Limit in the Home and the World." Pages 87–100 in *Thinking on Thresholds: The Poetics of Transitive Spaces*. Edited by Subha Mukherji. London: Anthem, 2013.

Chisholm, Robert B., Jr. *A Commentary on Judges and Ruth*. Kregel Exegetical Library. Grand Rapids: Kregel Academic, 2013.

———. "The Role of Women in the Rhetorical Strategy in the Book of Judges." Pages 34–49 in *Integrity of Heart, Skillfulness of Hands: Biblical and Leadership Studies in Honor of Donald K. Campbell*. Edited by Charles H. Dyer and Roy B. Zuck. Grand Rapids: Baker, 1994.

———. "What Went on in Jael's Tent? The Collocation תכסהו בשמיכהו in Judges 4,18." *SJOT* 24 (2010): 143–44.

———. "What Went on in Jael's Tent? [Part Two]" *SJOT* 27 (2013): 216–18.

Chodorow, Nancy. "Family Structure and Feminine Personality." Pages 43–66 in *Woman, Culture, and Society*. Edited by Michelle Z. Rosaldo and Louise Lamphere. Stanford: Stanford University Press, 1974.

Christianson, Eric. "The Big Sleep: Strategic Ambiguity in Judges 4–5 and in Classic Film Noir." *BibInt* 15 (2007): 519–48.

Clines, David J. A. "David the Man: The Construction of Masculinity in the Hebrew Bible." Pages 212–41 in *Interested Parties: The Ideology of Writers and Readers of the Hebrew Bible*. Edited by David J. A. Clines. JSOTSup 205. Sheffield: Sheffield Academic, 1995.

———. *I, He, We, and They: A Literary Approach to Isaiah 53*. JSOTSup 1. Sheffield: JSOT Press, 1976.

Coetzee, Johan H. "The 'Outcry' of the Dissected Woman in Judges 19–21: Embodiment of a Society." *OTE* 15 (2002): 52–63.

Coleridge, Samuel Taylor. *Biographia Literaria*. Edited by James Engell and W. Jackson Bate. Princeton: Princeton University Press, 1983.

Collins, Patricia Hill, and Valerie Chepp. "Intersectionality." Pages 57–87 in *The Oxford Handbook of Gender and Politics*. Edited by Georgina Waylen, Karen Celis, Johanna Kantola, and S. Laurel Weldon. Oxford: Oxford University Press, 2013.

Conway, Colleen M. *Sex and Slaughter in the Tent of Jael: A Cultural History of a Biblical Story*. Oxford: Oxford University Press, 2017.

Craig, Kenneth M., Jr. "Judges in Recent Research." *CurBR* 1 (2003): 159–85.

Creangă, Ovidiu, and Peter Ben-Smit, eds. *Biblical Masculinities Foregrounded*. HBM 62. Sheffield: Sheffield Phoenix, 2014.

Crenshaw, James L. *Samson: A Secret Betrayed, a Vow Ignored*. Atlanta: John Knox, 1978.

Cundall, Arthur E., and Leon Morris. *Judges and Ruth: An Introduction and Commentary*. TOTC 7. Downers Grove, IL: InterVarsity Press, 1968.

Dahmen, V. "שִׁיר." *TDOT* 14:609–46.

Daly, Brenda O., and Maureen T. Reddy, eds. *Narrating Mothers: Theorizing Maternal Subjectivities.* Knoxville: University of Tennessee Press, 1991.

Day, Peggy L., ed. *Gender and Difference in Ancient Israel.* Minneapolis: Fortress, 1989.

De Pury, Albert. "Le raid de Gédéon (Juges 6, 25–32) et l'histoire de l'exclusivisme yahwiste." Pages 173–205 in *Lectio difficilior probabilior? L'exégèse comme expérience de décloisonnement: Mélanges offerts à Françoise Smyth-Florentin.* Edited by Thomas Römer. Heidelberg: Wissenschaftliches theologisches Seminar, 1991.

Delitzsch, Friedrich. *Babel and Bible: Two Lectures.* Ancient Near East: Classic Studies. Eugene, OR: Wipf & Stock, 2007.

———. *Babel und Bibel: Ein Vortrag.* Leipzig: Hinrichs, 1902.

DeMaris, Richard E., and Carolyn S. Leeb. "Judges—(Dis)Honor and Ritual Enactment: The Jephthah Story; Judges 10:16–12:1." Pages 177–90 in *Ancient Israel: The Old Testament in Its Social Context.* Edited by Philip F. Esler. Minneapolis: Fortress, 2006.

Denis the Carthusian. "Enarratio in Librum Josue." Pages 1–105 in *Enarrationes in libros Josue, Judicum, Ruth, Regum, Paralipomenon.* Vol. 3 of *Doctoris Ecstatici D. Dionysii Cartusiani Opera Omnia.* 41 vols. De Monstreuil: Typis Cartusiae Sanctae Mariae de Pratis, 1897.

Dijk-Hemmes, Fokkelien van. "Mothers and a Mediator in the Song of Deborah." Pages 110–14 in *A Feminist Companion to Judges.* Edited by Athalya Brenner. FCB 4. Sheffield: JSOT Press, 1993.

Dolansky, Shawna, and Sarah Shetman. "Introduction: What Is Gendered Historiography and How Do You Do It?" *JHebS* 19 (2019): 3–18.

Douglas, Mary. *Purity and Danger: An Analysis of Concepts of Pollution and Taboo.* New York: Praeger, 1966.

Driver, G. R. "Problems of Interpretation in the Heptateuch." Pages 66–76 in *Mélanges bibliques: Rédigés en l'honneur de André Robert.* Travaux de l'Institut Catholique de Paris 4. Paris: Bloud & Gay, 1957.

Dube, Musa W. *Postcolonial Feminist Interpretation of the Bible.* St. Louis, MO: Chalice, 2000.

Edenburg, Cynthia. *Dismembering the Whole: Composition and Purpose of Judges 19–21.* AIL 24. Atlanta: SBL Press, 2016.

———. "How (Not) to Murder a King." *SJOT* 12 (1998): 64–85.

———. "Intertextuality, Literary Competence and Question of Readership: Some Preliminary Observations." *JSOT* 35 (2010): 131–48.

Emerton, John A. "Gideon and Jerubbaal." *JTS* 27 (1976): 289–312.

Engar, Ann W. "Old Testament Women as Tricksters." Pages 143–57 in *Mappings of the Biblical Terrain: The Bible as Text*. Edited by Vincent L. Tollers and John Maier. Bucknell Review 33.2. Lewisburg, PA: Bucknell University Press, 1990.

Evans, Mary J. *Judges and Ruth: An Introduction and Commentary*. TOTC 7. Downers Grove, IL: InterVarsity Press, 2017.

Exum, J. Cheryl. "The Centre Cannot Hold: Thematic and Textual Instabilities in Judges." *CBQ* 52 (1990): 410–31.

———. "Encoded Messages to Women." Pages 112–27 in *Feminist Biblical Interpretation: A Compendium of Critical Commentary on the Books of the Bible and Related Literature*. Edited by Luise Schottroff, Marie-Theres Wacker, and Martin Rumscheidt. Grand Rapids: Eerdmans, 2012.

———. "Feminist Criticism: Whose Interests Are Being Served?" Pages 65–90 in *Judges and Method: New Approaches in Biblical Studies*. Edited by Gale A. Yee. 2nd ed. Minneapolis: Fortress, 2007.

———. *Fragmented Women: Feminist (Sub)versions of Biblical Narratives*. Valley Forge, PA: Trinity Press International, 1993.

———. "'Mother in Israel': A Familiar Figure Reconsidered." Pages 73–85 in *Feminist Interpretation of the Bible*. Edited by Letty M. Russell. Philadelphia: Westminster, 1985.

———. "The (M)other's Place." Pages 94–147 in *Fragmented Women: Feminist (Sub)versions of Biblical Narratives*. JSOTSup 163. Sheffield: Sheffield Academic, 1993.

———. "Promise and Fulfillment: Narrative Art in Judges 13." *JBL* 99 (1980): 43–59.

———. *Song of Songs: A Commentary*. OTL. Louisville: Westminster John Knox, 2005.

———. *Was sagt das Richterbuch den Frauen?* SBS 169. Stuttgart: Katholisches Bibelwerk, 1997.

Eynikel, Erik. "Judges 19–21, an 'Appendix': Rape, Murder, War and Abduction." *CV* 47 (2005): 101–15.

Fabry, Heinz-Josef. "כָּרַע." *TDOT* 7:336–39.

Farber, Zev I. "Jerubaal, Jacob, and the Battle for Shechem: A Tradition History." *JHebS* 13 (2013): 1–26.

———. "Snippets from a Lost Joshua Cycle: The Prehistory of an Israelite Legendary Hero." Pages 43–60 in vol. 1 of *"Now It Happened in Those Days": Studies in Biblical, Assyrian, and Other Ancient Near Eastern*

Historiography Presented to Mordechai Cogan on His Seventy-Fifth Birthday. Edited by Amitai Baruchi-Unna, Tova Forti, Shmuel Aḥituv, Israel Eph'al, and Jeffrey H. Tigay. 2 vols. Winona Lake, IN: Eisenbrauns, 2017.

Feinstein, Eva Levavi. "Sexual Pollution in the Hebrew Bible: A New Perspective." Pages 114–45 in *Bodies, Embodiment, and Theology of the Hebrew Bible.* Edited by S. Tamar Kamionkowski and Wonil Kim. LHBOTS 465. London: Bloomsbury, 2010.

Fewell, Danna Nolan. "Deconstructive Criticism: Achsah and the (E)razed City of Writing." Pages 115–37 in *Judges and Method: New Approaches in Biblical Studies.* Edited by Gale A. Yee. 2nd ed. Minneapolis: Fortress, 2007.

———. "Judges." Pages 67–77 in *The Women's Bible Commentary.* Edited by Carol A. Newsom and Sharon H. Ringe. Louisville: Westminster John Knox, 1992.

Fewell, Danna Nolan, and David M. Gunn. "Controlling Perspectives: Women, Men, and the Authority of Violence in Judges 4 and 5." *JAAR* 58 (1990): 389–411.

———. *Gender, Power, and Promise: The Subject of the Bible's First Story.* Nashville: Abingdon, 1993.

Finlay, Timothy D. *The Birth Report Genre in the Hebrew Bible.* FAT 2/12. Tübingen: Mohr Siebeck, 2005.

Fischer, Agneta H., and Antony S. R. Manstead. "The Relation between Gender and Emotion in Different Cultures." Pages 71–94 in *Gender and Emotion: Social Psychological Perspectives.* Edited by Agneta H. Fischer. Studies in Emotion and Social Interaction. Cambridge: Cambridge University Press, 2000.

Fishbane, Michael. *Biblical Interpretation in Ancient Israel.* Oxford: Clarendon, 1985.

Fleenor, Rob. "Manoah's Wife: Gender Inversion in a Patriarchal Birth Narrative." Pages 24–34 in *Women in the Biblical World, 2: A Survey of Old and New Testament Perspectives.* Edited by Elizabeth A. McCabe. Lanham, MD: University Press of America, 2011.

Fleishman, Joseph. "A Daughter's Demand and a Father's Compliance: The Legal Background to Achsah's Claim and Caleb's Agreement (Joshua 15,16–19; Judges 1,12–15)." *ZAW* 118 (2006): 354–73.

Fox, Michael V. *The Song of Songs and the Egyptian Love Songs.* Madison: University of Wisconsin Press, 1985.

Franke, John R. ed. *Joshua, Judges, Ruth, 1–2 Samuel.* ACCS 4. Downers Grove, IL: InterVarsity Press, 2005.

Friedman, Susan. "Weavings: Intertextuality and the (Re)Birth of the Author." Pages 146–80 in *Influence and Intertextuality in Literary History.* Edited by Jay Clayton and Eric Rothstein. Madison: University of Wisconsin Press, 1991.

Frolov, Serge. "The Comeback of Comebacks: David, Bathsheba, and the Prophets in the Song of Songs." Pages 41–64 in *On Prophets, Warriors, and Kings: Former Prophets through the Eyes of Their Interpreters.* Edited by George J. Brooke and Ariel Feldman. BZAW 470. Berlin: de Gruyter, 2016.

———. *Judges.* FOTL 6B. Grand Rapids: Eerdmans, 2013.

———. "Sleeping with the Enemy: Recent Scholarship on Sexuality in the Book of Judges." *CurBR* 11 (2013): 308–27.

Fuchs, Esther. "The Literary Characterization of Mothers and Sexual Politics in the Hebrew Bible." Pages 117–36 in *Feminist Perspectives on Biblical Scholarship.* Edited by Adele Yarbro Collins. BSNA 10. Chico, CA: Scholars Press, 1985.

———. "The Literary Characterization of Mothers and Sexual Politics in the HB." *Semeia* 46 (1989): 151–66.

Gafney, Wilda C. *Daughters of Miriam: Women Prophets in Ancient Israel.* Minneapolis: Fortress, 2008.

Gardner, Kirsten H. "Hidden in Plain Sight: Intertextuality and Judges 19." Pages 53–72 in *Second Wave Intertextuality and the Hebrew Bible.* Edited by Marianne Grohmann and Hyun Chul Paul Kim. RBS 93. Atlanta: SBL Press, 2019.

Gaspey, Thomas. *Tallis's Illustrated Scripture History for the Improvement of Youth.* 2 vols. London: Tallis, 1851.

Gaß, Erasmus. *Die Ortsnamen des Richterbuchs in historischer und redaktioneller Perspektive.* ADPV 35. Wiesbaden: Harrassowitz, 2005.

———. "Manasseh, Manassites." *EBR* 17:701–4.

Gennep, Arnold van. *The Rites of Passage.* Chicago: University of Chicago Press, 1960.

Gibson, Arthur. "ṣnḥ in Judges i 14: NEB and AV Translations." *VT* 26 (1976): 275–83.

Gillmayr-Bucher, Susanne. *Erzählte Welten im Richterbuch: Narratologische Aspekte eines polyfonen Diskurses.* BibInt 116. Leiden: Brill, 2013.

Ginsburg, Christian D. *The Song of Songs: Translated from the Original Hebrew.* London: Longman, 1857.

Globe, Alexander. "'Enemies Round About': Disintegrative Structure in the Book of Judges." Pages 233–51 in *Mappings of the Biblical Terrain: The Bible as Text*. Edited by Vincent L. Tollers and John Maier. Bucknell Review 33.2. Lewisburg, PA: Bucknell University Press, 1990.

Gooding, D. W. "The Composition of the Book of Judges." *ErIsr* 16 (1982): 70*–79*.

Gottlieb, Freema. "Three Mothers." *Judaism* 30 (1981): 194–203.

Gottstein, M. H. "A Note on צנח." *VT* 6 (1956): 99–100.

Goulder, Michael. *The Song of Fourteen Songs*. JSOTSup 36. Sheffield: JSOT Press, 1986.

Graybill, Rhiannon. *Are We Not Men? Unstable Masculinity in the Hebrew Prophets*. New York: Oxford University Press, 2016.

Green, Barbara. *Mikhail Bakhtin and Biblical Scholarship: An Introduction*. SemeiaSt 38. Atlanta: Society of Biblical Literature, 2000.

Groenewald, Alphonso. "Jonathan (Son of Gershom; Son of Abiathar)." *EBR* 14:605–6.

Groß, Walter. *Richter: Übersetzt und ausgelegt*. HThKAT. Freiburg im Breisgau: Herder, 2009.

Guest, Deryn. *Beyond Feminist Biblical Studies*. Bible in the Modern World 47. Sheffield: Sheffield Phoenix, 2012.

———. "From Gender Reversal to Genderfuck: Reading Jael through a Lesbian Lens." Pages 9–43 in *Bible Trouble: Queer Readings at the Boundaries of Biblical Scholarship*. Edited by Teresa J. Hornsby and Ken Stone. SemeiaSt 67. Atlanta: Society of Biblical Literature, 2011.

Guillaume, Philippe. "An Anti-Judean Manifesto in Judges 1?" *BN* 95 (1998): 12–17.

———. *Waiting for Josiah: The Judges*. JSOTSup 385. London: T&T Clark, 2004.

Gunn, David M. "Joshua and Judges." Pages 102–21 in *The Literary Guide to the Bible*. Edited by Robert Alter and Frank Kermode. Cambridge: Belknap, 1987.

———. *Judges*. Blackwell Bible Commentaries. Malden, MA: Blackwell, 2004.

Haag, Herbert. "Gideon—Jerubbaal—Abimelek." *ZAW* 79 (1967): 305–14.

Hackett, Jo Ann. "In the Days of Jael: Reclaiming the History of Women in Ancient Israel." Pages 15–38 in *Immaculate and Powerful: The Female in Sacred Image and Social Reality*. Edited by Clarissa W. Atkinson, Constance H. Buchanan, and Margaret R. Miles. Boston: Beacon, 1985.

———. "Violence and Women's Lives in the Book of Judges." *Int* 58 (2004): 356–64.

———. "Women's Studies and the Hebrew Bible." Pages 141–64 in *The Future of Biblical Studies: The Hebrew Scriptures*. Edited by Richard Elliott Friedman and H. G. M. Williamson. SemeiaSt 16. Atlanta: Scholars Press, 1987.

Hallo, William W. "New Light on the Story of Achsah." Pages 330–35 in *Inspired Speech: Prophecy in the Ancient Near East; Essays in Honor of Herbert B. Huffmon*. Edited by John Kaltner and Louis Stulman. JSOTSup 378. New York: T&T Clark, 2004.

Halpern, Baruch. "The Rise of Abimelek Ben-Jerubbaal." *HAR* 2 (1978): 79–100.

Hamley, Isabelle. "'Dis(re)membered and Unaccounted For': פילגש in the Hebrew Bible." *JSOT* 42 (2018): 415–34.

———. "What's Wrong with 'Playing the Harlot'? The Meaning of זנה in Judges 19:2." *TynBul* 66 (2015): 41–62.

Hayes, Christine E. *Gentile Impurities and Jewish Identities: Intermarriage and Conversion from the Bible to the Talmud*. Oxford: Oxford University Press, 2002.

Heijerman, Mieke. "Who Would Blame Her? The 'Strange' Woman of Proverbs 7." Pages 100–109 in *Feminist Companion to Wisdom Literature*. Edited by Athalya Brenner-Idan. FCB 9. Sheffield: Sheffield Academic, 1995.

Henriks, Michelle C. P., Marcel A. Croon, and Ad J. J. M. Vingerhoets. "Social Reactions to Adult Crying: The Help-Soliciting Function of Tears." *Journal of Social Psychology* 148 (2008): 22–42.

Henry, Matthew. *An Exposition of the Old and New Testament*. Vol. 2. London: Robinson, 1839.

Herdt, Gilbert H. *Guardians of the Flutes: Idioms of Masculinity*. New York: McGraw-Hill, 1981.

Hermert, Dianne A. van, Fons J. R. van de Vijver, and Ad J. J. M. Vingerhoets. "Culture and Crying: Prevalences and Gender Differences." *Cross-Cultural Research* 45 (2011): 399–431.

Herzberg, Bruce. "Samson's Moment of Truth." *BibInt* 18 (2010): 226–50.

Hoenig, Sidney, and A. J. Rosenberg, eds. *The Book of Joshua: A New English Translation of the Text and Rashi*. Translated by P. Oratz, A. J. Rosenberg, and Sidney Shulman. New York: Judaica, 1969.

Hogan, Susan. "Breasts and the Beestings: Rethinking Breast-Feeding Practices, Maternity Rituals, and Maternal Attachment in Britain & Ireland." *Journal of International Women's Studies* 10 (2008): 141–60.

Holthuis, Susanne. "Intertextuality and Meaning Constitution: An Approach to the Comprehension of Intertextual Poetry." Pages 77–93 in *Approaches to Poetry: Some Aspects of Textuality, Intertextuality and Intermediality*. Edited by János Petöfi and Terry Olivi. Research in Text Theory 20. Berlin: de Gruyter, 1994.

hooks, bell. *Feminist Theory: From Margin to Center*. 3rd ed. New York: Routledge, 2015.

Hornsby, Teresa J., and Deryn Guest. *Transgender, Intersex, and Biblical Interpretation*. SemeiaSt 83. Atlanta: SBL Press, 2016.

Hornsby, Teresa J., and Ken Stone, eds. *Bible Trouble: Queer Reading at the Boundaries of Biblical Scholarship*. SemeiaSt 62. Atlanta: Society of Biblical Literature, 2011.

Hugh of St. Cher. *Postilla super Librum Josue*. Pages 177r–195r in vol. 1 of *Opera Omnia in Universum Vetus & Novum Testamentum*. Venice: Pezzana, 1754.

Humbert, Paul. "La femme étrangère du livre des Proverbes." *Revue des Études Sémitiques* 6 (1937): 49–64.

Hurvitz, Avi. "The Chronological Significance of 'Aramaisms' in Biblical Hebrew." *IEJ* 18 (1968): 234–40.

Ilan, David, and Jonathan Greer. "Dan (Place)." *EBR* 6:61–63.

Imparati, Fiorella. "Private Life among the Hittites." *CANE* 1:571–86.

Irigaray, Luce. *J'aime à toi: Esquisse d'une félicité dans l'histoire*. Paris: Grasset & Fasquelles, 1992.

———. "Listening, Thinking, Teaching." Pages 231–40 in *Teaching*. Edited by Luce Irigaray and Mary Green. London: Bloomsbury, 2008.

———. *Sexes et Parentés*. Critique. Paris: Minuit, 1987.

———. *Sharing the World*. London: Bloomsbury, 2008.

———. *Speculum of the Other Woman*. Translated by Gillian G. Gill. Ithaca, NY: Cornell University Press, 1985.

———. *This Sex Which Is Not One*. Translated by Catherine Porter with Carolyn Burke. Ithaca, NY: Cornell University Press, 1985.

Irudayaraj, Dominic S. *Violence, Otherness and Identity in Isaiah 63:1–6: The Trampling One Coming from Edom*. LHBOTS 633. London: Bloomsbury, 2017.

Irwin, William. "Against Intertextuality." *Philosophy and Literature* 28 (2004): 227–42.

Jans, Edgar. *Abimelech und sein Königtum: Diachrone und synchrone Untersuchungen zu Ri 9.* ATSAT 66. St. Ottilien: EOS, 2001.

Janzen, J. Gerald. "A Certain Woman in the Rhetoric of Judges 9." *JSOT* 12 (1987): 33–37.

Johnson, Benjamin. "What Type of Son Is Samson? Reading Judges 13 as a Biblical Type-Scene." *JETS* 53 (2010): 269–86.

Jobling, David. "Structuralist Criticism: The Text's World of Meaning." Pages 90–114 in *Judges and Method: New Approaches in Biblical Studies.* Edited by Gale A. Yee. 2nd ed. Minneapolis: Fortress, 2007.

Jost, Renate. "Achsas Quellen: Feministisch-sozialgeschichtliche Überlegungen in Jos 15, 15–20/Ri 1, 12–15." Pages 110–25 in *"Ihr Völker alle, Klatscht in die Hände!": Festschrift für Erhard S. Gerstenberger zum 65. Geburtstag.* Edited by Rainer Kessler. Exegese in unserer Zeit 3. Münster: LIT, 1997.

———. *Gender, Sexualität und Macht in der Anthropologie des Richterbuches.* BWANT 9.4. Stuttgart: Kohlhammer, 2006.

Kaiser, Otto. "נָדַר." *TDOT* 9:242–55.

Kalmanofsky, Amy. *Gender-Play in the Hebrew Bible: The Ways the Bible Challenges Its Gender Norms.* Routledge Interdisciplinary Perspectives on Biblical Criticism 2. New York: Routledge, 2017.

Kaltner, John. "Abraham's Sons: How the Bible and the Qur'an See the Same Story Differently." *BRev* 18 (2002): 16–23, 45–46.

Kartzow, Marianne Bjelland. "'Asking the Other Question': An Intersectional Approach to Galatians 3:28 and the Colossian Household Codes." *BibInt* 18 (2010): 364–89.

Keefe, Alice A. "The Female Body, the Body Politic and the Land: A Sociopolitical Reading of Hosea 1–2." Pages 70–100 in *A Feminist Companion to the Latter Prophets.* Edited by Athalya Brenner. FCB 8. Sheffield: Sheffield Academic, 2004.

———. "Rapes of Women/Wars of Men." *Semeia* 61 (1993): 79–97.

Keel, Othmar. *Das Hohelied.* ZBK 19. Zurich: TVZ, 1986.

Kegi, Rosemary. *The Rhetoric of Concealment: Figuring Gender and Class in Renaissance Literature.* Ithaca, NY: Cornell University Press, 1994.

Kellenbach, Katharina von. "Am I a Murderer? Judges 19–21 as a Parable of Meaningless Suffering." Pages 176–91 in *Strange Fire: Reading the Bible after the Holocaust.* Edited by Tod Linafelt. BibSem 71. Sheffield: Sheffield Academic, 2000.

Kim, Soo J. "Ashamed before the Presence of God." Pages 213–44 in *Theology of the Hebrew Bible, Volume 1: Methodological Studies*. Edited by Marvin A. Sweeney. RBS 92. Atlanta: SBL Press, 2019.

King, Philip J., and Lawrence E. Stager, *Life in Biblical Israel*. LAI. Louisville: Westminster John Knox, 2001.

Klein, Lillian R. "The Book of Judges: Paradigm and Deviation in Images of Women." Pages 55–71 in *A Feminist Companion to Judges*. Edited by Athalya Brenner. FCB 4. Sheffield: JSOT Press, 1993.

———. *From Deborah to Esther: Sexual Politics in the Hebrew Bible*. Minneapolis: Fortress, 2003.

———. "A Spectrum of Female Characters." Pages 24–33 in *A Feminist Companion to Judges*. Edited by Athalya Brenner. FCB 4. Sheffield: JSOT Press, 1993.

———. *The Triumph of Irony in the Book of Judges*. JSOTSup 68. BLS 14. Sheffield: Almond Press, 1988.

Knauf, Ernst A. *Richter*. ZBK 7. Zurich: TVZ, 2016.

Kooij, Arie van der. "On Male and Female Views in Judges 4 and 5." Pages 135–52 in *On Reading Prophetic Texts: Gender-Specific and Related Studies in Memory of Fokkelien van Dijk-Hemmes*. Edited by Bob Becking and Meindert Dijkstra. BibInt 18. Leiden: Brill, 1996.

Kottsieper, Ingo. "שָׁבַע." *TDOT* 14:311–36.

Kristeva, Julia. "Bakhtine, le mot, le dialogue et le roman." *Critique* 23.239 (1967): 438–65.

———. *Desire in Language: A Semiotic Approach to Language and Art*. Edited by Leon S. Roudiez. Translated by Thomas Gora, Alice Jardine, and Leon S. Roudiez. New York: Columbia University Press, 1980.

———. *Revolution in Poetic Language*. Translated by Margaret Waller. New York: Columbia University Press, 1984.

———. "Word, Dialogue, and Novel." Pages 64–91 in *Desire in Language: A Semiotic Approach to Language and Art*. Edited by Leon S. Roudiez. Translated by Thomas Gora, Alice Jardine, and Leon S. Roudiez. New York: Columbia University Press, 1980.

LaCocque, André. *Romance She Wrote: A Hermeneutical Essay on Song of Songs*. Harrisburg, PA: Trinity Press International, 1998.

Lambdin, Thomas O. *Introduction to Biblical Hebrew*. New York: Scribner, 1971.

Lanoir, Corinne. *Femmes fatales, filles rebelles: Figures féminines dans le livre des Juges*. Actes et recherches. Geneva: Labor et Fides, 2005.

Lasine, Stuart. "Guest and Host in Judges 19: Lot's Hospitality in an Inverted World." *JSOT* 9 (1984): 37–59.

Lefkovitz, Lori Hope. *In Scripture: The First Stories of Jewish Sexual Identities*. Lanham, MD: Rowman & Littlefield, 2010.

Leonard, Jeffrey M. "Identifying Inner-Biblical Allusions: Psalm 78 as a Test Case." *JBL* 127 (2008): 241–65.

Leuchter, Mark. "'Now There Was a [Certain] Man': Compositional Chronology in Judges–1 Samuel." *CBQ* 69 (2007): 429–39.

Levin, Christoph. "Manasseh (King of Judah)." *EBR* 17:716–17.

Lindars, Barnabas. "Gideon and Kingship." *JTS* 16 (1965): 315–26.

———. *Judges 1–5: A New Translation and Commentary*. Edinburgh: T&T Clark, 1995.

Lichtheim, Miriam. *The New Kingdom*. Vol. 2 of *Ancient Egyptian Literature*. Berkeley: University of California Press, 1976.

Lockyer, Herbert. *The Women of the Bible*. Grand Rapids: Zondervan, 1967.

Logan, Alice. "Rehabilitating Jephthah." *JBL* 128 (2009): 665–85.

Lydia [pseudonym]. "Female Biography of the Scriptures: Achsah." *The Christian Lady's Magazine* 10 (1838): 156–63.

MacDonald, Dennis. *Does the New Testament Imitate Homer? Four Cases from the Acts of the Apostles*. New Haven: Yale University Press, 2003.

———. *The Homeric Epics and the Gospel of Mark*. New Haven: Yale University Press, 2000.

Mackay, W. Mackintosh. *Bible Types of Modern Women*. Garden City, NY: Doubleday, 1929.

Magness, Jodi. "New Mosaics from the Huqoq Synagogue." *BAR* 39.5 (2013): 66–68.

Malamat, Abraham. *History of Biblical Israel: Major Problems and Minor Issues*. CHANE 7. Leiden: Brill, 2001.

Mathias, Steffan. *Paternity, Progeny, and Perpetuation: Creating Lives after Death in the Hebrew Bible*. LHBOTS 696. London: Bloomsbury, 2020.

Matthews, Victor H. "Hospitality and Hostility in Judges 4." *BTB* 21 (1991): 13–21.

———. *Judges and Ruth*. NCBC. Cambridge: Cambridge University Press, 2004.

McCann, J. Clinton. *Judges*. IBC. Louisville: Westminster John Knox, 2011.

McKinlay, Judith. "Meeting Achsah on Achsah's Land." *Bible and Critical Theory* 5 (2009): 1–11.

Meyers, Carol. *Discovering Eve: Ancient Israelite Women in Context*. New York: Oxford University Press, 1988.

Miller, Geoffrey D. "Intertextuality in Old Testament Research." *CurBR* 9 (2011): 283–309.

Miller, Robert D. *Chieftains of the Highland Clans: A History of Israel in the Twelfth and Eleventh Centuries B.C.* Bible in Its World. Grand Rapids: Eerdmans, 2005.

Milstein, Sara J. "Delusions of Grandeur: Revision through Introduction in Judges 6–9." Pages 147–73 in *Tracking the Master Scribe: Revision through Introduction in Biblical and Mesopotamian Literature*. New York: Oxford University Press, 2016.

———. "Saul the Levite and His Concubine: The 'Allusive' Quality of Judges 19." *VT* 66 (2016): 95–116.

Mosca, Paul G. "Who Seduced Whom? A Note on Joshua 15,18 // Judges 1,14." *CBQ* 46 (1984): 18–22.

Moster, David Z. "The Levite of Judges 17–18." *JBL* 133 (2014): 729–37.

Müller, Reinhard. "Gefahren im Umgang mit Macht: Midraschim und Paradigmata in Jdc 8 und 9." Pages 93–118 in *Königtum und Gottesherrschaft: Untersuchungen zur alttestamentlichen Monarchiekritik*. FAT 2/3. Tübingen: Mohr Siebeck, 2004.

Mukherji, Subha. "Introduction." Pages xvii–xxviii in *Thinking on Thresholds: The Poetics of Transitive Spaces*. Edited by Subha Mukherji. London: Anthem Press, 2013.

Müllner, Ilse. "Tödliche Differenzen: Sexuelle Gewalt als Gewalt gegen Andere in Ri 19." Pages 81–100 in *Von der Wurzel getragen: Christlich-feministische Exegese in Auseinandersetzung mit Antijudaismus*. Edited by Luise Schottroff and Marie-Theres Wacker. BibInt 17. Leiden: Brill, 1996.

Murphy, Kelly J. "Judges in Recent Research." *CurBR* 15 (2017): 179–213.

Murphy, Fredrick J. *Pseudo-Philo: Rewriting the Bible*. Oxford: Oxford University Press, 1993.

Na'aman, Nadav. "The Danite Campaign Northward (Judges 17–18) and the Migration of the Phocaeans to Massalia (Strabo IV 1, 4)." *VT* 55 (2005): 47–60.

———. "A Hidden Anti-Samaritan Polemic in the Story of Abimelech and Shechem (Judges 9)." *BZ* 55 (2011): 1–20.

———. "Rediscovering a Lost North Israelite Conquest Story." Pages 287–302 in *Rethinking Israel: Studies in the History and Archaeology of Ancient Israel in Honor of Israel Finkelstein*. Edited by Oded Lipschits,

Yuval Gadot, and Matthew J. Adams. Winona Lake, IN: Eisenbrauns, 2017.

———. "The Tower of Shechem and the House of El-Berith" [Hebrew]. *Zion* 51 (1986): 259–80.

Neef, Hans-Dieter. "Jephta und seine Tochter (Jdc. xi 29–40)." *VT* 49 (1999): 206–17.

Niehr, H. "שָׁפַט." *TDOT* 15:411–31.

Nelson, Richard D. *Judges: A Critical and Rhetorical Commentary*. New York: Bloomsbury T&T Clark, 2017.

———. "What Is Achsah Doing in Judges?" Pages 12–22 in *The Impartial God: Essays in Biblical Studies in Honor of Jouette M. Bassler*. Edited by Calvin J. Roetzel and Robert L. Foster. New Testament Monographs 22. Sheffield: Sheffield Phoenix, 2007.

Nicholas of Lyra. *Postilla in Librum Iosue*. In *Biblia sacra cum glossa ordinaria … et postilla Nicholai Lyrani*. Venice, 1603.

Nicholson, E. W. "The Problem of צנח." *ZAW* 89 (1977): 259–66.

Nicholson, L. J. "Feminist Theory: The Private and the Public." Pages 221–30 in *Beyond Domination: New Perspectives on Women and Philosophy*. Edited by Carol C. Gould. Totowa, NJ: Rowman & Allanheld, 1984.

Niditch, Susan. "Eroticism and Death in the Tale of Jael." Pages 305–17 in *Women in the Hebrew Bible: A Reader*. Edited by Alice Bach. New York: Routledge, 1999.

———. *Judges: A Commentary*. OTL. Louisville: Westminster John Knox, 2008.

Noort, Ed. "Genesis 22: Human Sacrifice and Theology in the Hebrew Bible." Pages 1–20 in *The Sacrifice of Isaac: The Aqedah (Genesis 22) and Its Interpretations*. Edited by Ed Noort and Eibert Tigchelaar. TBN 4. Leiden: Brill, 2002.

Noth, Martin. "Background of Judges 17–18." Pages 68–85 in *Israel's Prophetic Heritage: Essays in Honor of James Muilenburg*. Edited by Bernhard W. Anderson and Walter Harrelson. New York: Harper, 1962.

———. *The Deuteronomistic History*. 2nd ed. JSOTSup 15. Sheffield: Sheffield Academic, 1991.

O'Connell, Robert H. *Rhetoric of the Book of Judges*. VTSup 63. Leiden: Brill, 1996.

O'Connor, Kathleen M. *Genesis 1–25A*. SHBC 1A. Macon, GA: Smyth & Helwys, 2018.

O'Connor, Michael. "The Women in the Book of Judges." *HAR* 10 (1986): 276–93.

Olson, Dennis T. "The Book of Judges." *NIB* 2:721–888.

Olyan, Saul M. *Biblical Mourning: Ritual and Social Dimensions.* Oxford: Oxford University Press, 2004.

Ottosson, Magnus Y. "הָרָה." *TDOT* 3:458–61.

Parker, Julie F. "Re-Membering the Dismembered: Piecing Together Meaning from Stories of Women and Body Parts in Ancient Near Eastern Literature." *BibInt* 23 (2015): 174–90.

Patrick, Symon. *A Commentary upon the Historical Books of the Old Testament.* 5th ed. 2 vols. London: Midwinter, 1738.

Peleg, Yitzhak. "Why Didn't Ruth the Moabitess Raise Her Child? 'A Son Is Born to Naomi' (Ruth 4:17)." Pages 281–300 in *In the Arms of Biblical Women.* Edited by John T. Green and Mishael M. Caspi. Biblical Intersections 13. Piscataway, NJ: Gorgias, 2013.

Peter, Mathell, Ad J. J. M. Vingerhoets, and Guus L. Van Heck. "Personality, Gender, and Crying." *European Journal of Personality* 15 (2001): 19–28.

Pinch, Geraldine. "Private Life in Ancient Egypt." *CANE* 1:363–82.

Pollack, Rachel. *The Body of the Goddess: Sacred Wisdom in Myth, Landscape, and Culture.* Shaftesbury: Element, 1997.

Polzin, Robert. *Late Biblical Hebrew: Toward an Historical Typology of Biblical Hebrew Prose.* HSM 12. Missoula, MT: Scholars Press, 1976.

———. *Moses and the Deuteronomist: A Literary Study of the Deuteronomistic History, Part 1; Deuteronomy, Joshua and Judges.* New York: Seabury Press, 1980.

Pope, Marvin H. *Song of Songs: A New Translation with Introduction and Commentary.* AB 7C. New York: Doubleday, 1977.

Pope-Levison, Priscilla. "Elizabeth Cady Stanton." Pages 469–73 in *Handbook of Women Biblical Interpreters: A Historical and Biographical Guide.* Edited by Marion Ann Taylor and Agnes Choi. Grand Rapids: Baker Academic, 2012.

Portier-Young, Anathea. "I Sing the Body Politic: Stillborn Desire and the Birth of Israel in Judges 5." Pages 375–95 in *Celebrate Her for the Fruit of Her Hands: Studies in Honor of Carol L. Meyers.* Edited by Susan Ackerman, Charles E. Carter, and Beth Alpert Nakhai. Winona Lake, IN: Eisenbrauns, 2015.

Pressler, Carolyn. *Joshua, Judges, and Ruth.* Westminster Bible Companion. Louisville: Westminster John Knox, 2002.

Preuss, Horst D. "עָצַי." *TDOT* 6:225–50.

Rabin, Chaim. "The Song of Songs and Tamil Poetry." *SR* 3 (1973): 205–19.

Rake, Mareike. "'Schreiende Widersprüche' in Ri 1:1–21." Pages 74–90 in *"Juda wird aufsteigen!" Untersuchungen zum ersten Kapitel des Richterbuches*. BZAW 367. Berlin: de Gruyter, 2006.

Ratner, Tsila. "Playing Fathers' Games: The Story of Achsah, Daughter of Caleb, and the Princess's Blank Sheet." *JMJS* 3 (2004): 147–61.

Reeder, Caryn A. "Deuteronomy 21.10–14 and/as Wartime Rape." *JSOT* 41 (2017): 313–36.

Redford, Donald B. *Egypt, Canaan, and Israel in Ancient Times*. Princeton: Princeton University Press, 1992.

Reinhartz, Adele. "Anonymity and Character in the Books of Samuel." Pages 117–42 in *Characterization in Biblical Literature*. Edited by Elizabeth Struthers Malbon and Adele Berlin. SemeiaSt 63. Atlanta: Society of Biblical Literature, 1993.

———. "Samson's Mother: An Unnamed Protagonist." Pages 157–70 in *A Feminist Companion to Judges*. Edited by Athalya Brenner. FCB 4. Sheffield: JSOT Press, 1993.

———. *"Why Ask My Name?" Anonymity and Identity in Biblical Narrative*. New York: Oxford University Press, 1998.

Reis, Pamela Tamarkin. "Uncovering Jael and Sisera: A New Reading." *SJOT* 19 (2005): 24–47.

Rich, Adrienne. *Of Woman Born: Motherhood as Experience and Institution*. New York: Norton, 1976.

Richter, Wolfgang. *Traditionsgeschichtliche Untersuchungen zum Richterbuch*. BBB 18. Bonn: Hanstein, 1963.

Roi, Micha. "Conditional Vows—Where They Are Made and Paid." *BN* 167 (2015): 3–24.

Römer, Thomas. "Gershom." *EBR* 10:129–30.

Rooke, Deborah W. "Kingship as Priesthood: The Relationship between the High Priesthood and the Monarchy." Pages 187–208 in *King and Messiah in Israel and the Ancient Near East: Proceedings of the Oxford Old Testament Seminar*. Edited by John Day. JSOTSup 270. Sheffield: Sheffield Academic, 1998.

———. "Sex and Death, or, the Death of Sex: Three Versions of Jephthah's Daughter (Judges 11:29–40)." Pages 249–71 in *Biblical Traditions in Transmission: Essays in Honour of Michael A. Knibb*. Edited by Charlotte Hempel and Judith M. Lieu. JSJSup 111. Leiden: Brill, 2006.

Rooker, Mark F. *Biblical Hebrew in Transition: The Language of the Book of Ezekiel.* JSOTSup 90. Sheffield: JSOT Press, 1990.

Rothstein, Jay, and Eric Clayton. *Influence and Intertextuality in Literary History.* Madison: University of Wisconsin Press, 1991.

Roudiez, Leon S. "Introduction." Pages 1–22 in *Desire in Language: A Semiotic Approach to Literature and Art.* By Julia Kristeva. Edited by Leon S. Roudiez. Translated by Thomas Gora, Alice Jardine, and Leon S. Roudiez. New York: Columbia University Press, 1980.

Ryan, Roger. *Judges.* Readings, a New Biblical Commentary. Sheffield: Sheffield Phoenix, 2007.

Salmon, Marilyn. *Women and the Law of Property in Early America.* Studies in Legal History. Chapel Hill: University of North Carolina Press, 1986.

Sandmel, Samuel. "Parallelomania." *JBL* 81 (1962): 1–13.

Sarna, Nahum M. *Genesis: The Traditional Hebrew Text with the New JPS Translation.* JPS Torah Commentary. Philadelphia: Jewish Publication Society of America, 1989.

Sasson, Jack M. *Judges 1–12: A New Translation with Introduction and Commentary.* AB 6D. New Haven: Yale University Press, 2014.

Sawyer, Deborah F. "Gender." Pages 264–73 in vol. 1 of *Oxford Encyclopedia of the Bible and Gender Studies.* Edited by Julia M. O'Brien. 2 vols. Oxford: Oxford University Press, 2014.

Schneider, Tammi J. "Achsah, the Raped *Pîlegeš*, and the Book of Judges." Pages 43–57 in *Women in the Biblical World: A Survey of Old and New Testament Perspectives.* Edited by Elizabeth A. McCabe. Lanham, MD: University Press of America, 2009.

———. *Judges: Studies in Hebrew Narrative and Poetry.* Berit Olam. Collegeville, MN: Liturgical Press, 2000.

———. *Mother of Promise: Women in the Book of Genesis.* Grand Rapids: Baker Academic, 2008.

Scholz, Susanne. *The Bible as Political Artifact: On the Feminist Study of the Hebrew Bible.* Dispatches. Minneapolis: Fortress, 2017.

———. *Sacred Witness: Rape in the Hebrew Bible.* Minneapolis: Fortress, 2010.

———. "'Tandoori Reindeer' and the Limitations of Historical Criticism." Pages 47–69 in *Her Master's Tools? Feminist and Postcolonial Engagements of Historical-Critical Discourse.* Edited by Caroline Vander Stichele and Todd C. Penner. GPBS 9. Atlanta: Society of Biblical Literature, 2005.

Schöpflin, Karin. "Jotham's Speech and Fable as Prophetic Comment on Abimelech's Story: The Genesis of Judges 9." *SJOT* 18 (2004): 3–22.

Schreiner, J. "עור." *TDOT* 10:568–74.

Schroeder, Joy A. "Elizabeth Wilson, the Bible, and Legal Rights of Women in the Nineteenth Century." *Postscripts* 5 (2009): 219–32.

Seeman, Don. "The Watcher at the Window: Cultural Poetics of a Biblical Motif." *Prooftexts* 24 (2004): 1–50.

Sellin, Ernst. *Wie wurde Sichem eine israelitische Stadt?* Leipzig: Deichert, 1922.

Shalom-Guy, Hava. "Three-Way Intertextuality: Some Reflections of Abimelech's Death at Thebez in Biblical Narrative." *JSOT* 34 (2010): 419–32.

———. "Why Recall Abimelech's Death in the David and Bathsheba Narrative?" [Hebrew]. *Beit Mikra* 54 (2009): 5–13.

Sharistanian, Janet. "Conclusion: The Public/Domestic Model and the Study of Contemporary Women's Lives." Pages 179–84 in *Beyond the Public/Domestic Dichotomy: Contemporary Perspectives on Women's Public Lives*. Edited by Janet Sharistanian. Contributions in Women's Studies 78. New York: Greenwood, 1987.

———. "Introduction: Women's Lives in the Public and Domestic Spheres." Pages 1–10, in *Beyond the Public/Domestic Dichotomy: Contemporary Perspectives on Women's Public Lives*. Edited by Janet Sharistanian. Contributions in Women's Studies 78. New York: Greenwood, 1987.

Sherwood, Yvonne. "Binding–Unbinding: Divided Responses of Judaism, Christianity, and Islam to the 'Sacrifice' of Abraham's Beloved Son." *JAAR* 72 (2004): 821–61.

Shields, Stephanie A. "Thinking about Gender, Thinking about Theory: Gender and Emotional Experience." Pages 3–23 in *Gender and Emotion: Social Psychological Perspectives*. Edited by Agneta H. Fischer. Studies in Emotion and Social Interaction. Cambridge: Cambridge University Press, 2000.

Sima, Alexander. "Nochmals zur Deutung des hebräischen Namens ʿOṯniʾēl." *BN* 106 (2001): 47–51.

Simon, Maurice, trans. "Megillah 14a." Pages 81–83 in *The Babylonian Talmud: Seder Moʾed*. Edited by Rabbi Dr. I. Epstein. London: Soncino, 1938.

Smith, D. Charles. *The Role of Mothers in the Genealogical Lists of Jacob's Sons*. CBET 90. Leuven: Peeters, 2018.

Smith, Mark S. *Poetic Heroes: Literary Commemorations of Warriors and Warrior Culture in the Early Biblical World*. Grand Rapids: Eerdmans, 2014.

Smith, Michael J. "The Failure of the Family in Judges, Part 2: Samson." *BSac* 162 (2005): 424–36.

Snijders, L. A. *The Meaning of zar in the Old Testament*. OTS 10. Leiden: Brill, 1954.

Soggin, J. Alberto. *Judges: A Commentary*. Translated by John Bowden. 2nd ed. OTL. London, SCM, 1987.

Soja, Edward. *Thirdspace: Journeys to Los Angeles and Other Real-and-Imagined Places*. Oxford: Blackwell, 1996.

Speiser, Ephraim A. *Genesis: A New Translation with Introduction and Commentary*. AB 1. Garden City, NY: Doubleday, 1964.

Speth, Linda E. "The Married Women's Property Acts, 1839–1865: Reform, Reaction, or Revolution?" Pages 69–91 in *Property, Family, and the Legal Profession*. Volume 2 of *Women and the Law: A Social Historical Perspective*. Edited by D. Kelly Weisberg. Cambridge, MA: Schenkman, 1982.

Spronk, Klaas. *Judges*. HCOT 7. Leuven: Peeters, 2019.

———. "Judging Jephthah: The Contribution of Syntactic Analysis to the Interpretation of Judges 11:29–40." Pages 299–316 in *Tradition and Innovation in Biblical Interpretation: Studies Presented to Professor Eep Talstra on the Occasion of His Sixty-Fifth Birthday*. Edited by Wido Th. van Peursen and Janet Dyk. SSN 57. Leiden: Brill, 2011.

Spurgeon, Charles Haddon. *Spurgeon's Sermons on Great Prayers of the Bible*. Grand Rapids: Kregel, 1995.

Stanton, Elizabeth Cady. *The Woman's Bible*. 2 vols. New York: European Publishing Company, 1895–1898.

Stavrakopoulou, Francesca. *King Manasseh and Child Sacrifice: Biblical Distortions of Historical Realities*. BZAW 338. Berlin: de Gruyter, 2004.

Steibart, Johanna. "Human Conception in Antiquity: The Hebrew Bible in Context." *Theology and Sexuality* 16 (2010): 209–27.

Steinberg, Naomi. "Kinship and Gender in Genesis." *BR* 39 (1994): 46–56.

Stendebach, F. J. "רֶגֶל." *TDOT* 13:309–24.

Stipp, Hermann-Josef. "Richter 19: Ein frühes Beispiel schriftgestützter politischer Propaganda in Israel." Pages 127–64 in *Ein Herz so weit wie der Sand am Ufer des Meeres: Festschrift für Georg Hentschel*. Edited by Susanne Gillmayr-Bucher, Annette Gierke, and Christina Nießen. ETS 90. Würzburg: Echter, 2007.

Stone, Ken. "'Dueteronomistic History' in Imagery, Gendered." Pages 349–55 in vol. 1 of *Oxford Encyclopedia of the Bible and Gender Studies*. Edited by Julia M. O'Brien. 2 vols. Oxford: Oxford University Press, 2014.

———. "Gender and Homosexuality in Judges 19: Subject-Honor, Object-Shame?" *JSOT* 20 (1995): 87–107.

———. "Gender Criticism: The Un-Manning of Abimelech." Pages 183–201 in *Judges and Method: New Approaches in Biblical Studies*. Edited by Gale A. Yee. 2nd ed. Minneapolis: Fortress, 2007.

———. "What Happens When Achsah Gets Off Her Ass? Queer Reading and Judges 1:11–15." Pages 409–20 in *Sacred Tropes: Tanakh, New Testament, and Qur'an as Literature and Culture*. Edited by Roberta Sterman Sabbath. BibInt 98. Leiden: Brill. 2009.

Streck, Michael, and Stefan Weninger. "Zur Deutung des hebräischen Namens ʿOṭnīʾēl." *BN* 96 (1999): 21–29.

Sutskover, Talia. "The Frame of Sacrificing in Judges." *VT* 64 (2014): 266–78.

Sweeney, Marvin A. "Davidic Polemics in the Book of Judges." *VT* 47 (1997): 517–29.

———. *Reading the Hebrew Bible after the Shoah: Engaging Holocaust Theology*. Minneapolis: Fortress, 2008.

Syrén, Roger. *The Forsaken First-Born: A Study of a Recurrent Motif in the Patriarchal Narratives*. JSOTSup 133. Sheffield: JSOT Press, 1993.

Szpek, Heidi M. "Achsah's Story: A Metaphor for Societal Transition." *AUSS* 40 (2002): 245–56.

Tapp, Anne Michele. "An Ideology of Expendability: Virgin Daughter Sacrifice in Genesis 19:1–11, Judges 11:30–39 and 19:22–26." Pages 157–74 in *Anti-Covenant: Counter-Reading Women's Lives in the Hebrew Bible*. Edited by Mieke Bal. JSOTSup 81. BLS 22. Sheffield: Almond Press, 1989.

Talshir, Zipporah. "Narrative Ties in Early Biblical Historiography" [Hebrew]. *Shnaton* 5–6 (1982): 69–78.

Tamber-Rosenau, Caryn. *Women in Drag: Gender and Performance in the Hebrew Bible and Early Jewish Literature*. Piscataway, NJ: Gorgias, 2018.

Taylor, Marion Ann, and Christiana de Groot, eds. *Women of War, Women of Woe: Joshua and Judges through the Eyes of Nineteenth-Century Female Biblical Interpreters*. Grand Rapids: Eerdmans, 2016.

Thelle, Rannfrid Irene. "Matrices of Motherhood in Judges 5." *JSOT* 43 (2019) 436–52.

Toorn, Karel van der. *Family Religion in Babylonia, Syria and Israel.* SHANE 7. Leiden: Brill, 1996.

Tov, Emmanuel. *Textual Criticism of the Hebrew Bible.* Minneapolis: Fortress, 1992.

Towner, W. Sibley. *Genesis.* Westminster Bible Companion. Louisville: Westminster John Knox, 2001.

Trapp, John. *Genesis to Second Chronicles.* Vol. 1 of *A Commentary on the Old and New Testaments.* Edited by W. Webster and Hugh Martin. London: Dickinson, 1866.

Treves, Marco. *The Song of Solomon.* Florence: Fortunée, 2004.

Trible, Phyllis. *Texts of Terror: A Literary-Feminist Reading of Biblical Narratives.* OBT 13. Philadelphia: Fortress, 1984.

Tull, Patricia K. "Mikhail M. Bakhtin and Dialogical Approaches to Biblical Interpretation." Pages 175–89 in *Second Wave Intertextuality and the Hebrew Bible.* Edited by Marianne Grohmann and Hyun Chul Paul Kim. RBS 93. Atlanta: SBL Press, 2019.

Turner, Victor W. *The Ritual Process: Structure and Anti-Structure.* Chicago: Aldine, 1969.

Ulmer, Rivka. *Egyptian Cultural Icons in Midrash.* SJ 52. Berlin: de Gruyter, 2009.

Vermigli, Peter Martyr. *In Librum Iudicum.* Zurich: Froschauer, 1571.

Victor, Royce M. "Delilah—A Forgotten Hero (Judges 16:4–21): A Cross-Cultural Narrative Reading." Pages 235–56 in *Joshua and Judges.* Edited by Athalya Brenner and Gale Yee. Texts @ Contexts. Minneapolis: Fortress, 2013.

Vingerhoets, Ad, and Jan Scheirs. "Sex Differences in Crying: Empirical Findings and Possible Explanations." Pages 143–65 in *Gender and Emotion: Social Psychological Perspectives.* Edited by Agneta H. Fischer. Studies in Emotion and Social Interaction. Cambridge: Cambridge University Press, 2000.

Volosinov, Valentin. *Marxism and the Philosophy of Language.* Translated by Ladislav Matejka and I. R. Titunik. Cambridge: Harvard University Press, 1986.

Vos, J. Cornelis de. *Das Los Judas: Über Entstehung und Ziele der Landbeschreibung in Josua 15.* VTSup 95. Leiden: Brill, 2003.

———. "Violence in the Book of Joshua." Pages 161–76 in *Violence in the Hebrew Bible: Between Text and Reception*. Edited by Jacques van Ruiten and Koert van Bekkum. OTS 79. Brill: Leiden, 2020.

Webb, Barry G. *The Book of Judges*. NICOT. Grand Rapids: Eerdmans, 2012.

———. *The Book of Judges: An Integrated Reading*. JSOTSup 46. Sheffield: JSOT Press, 1987.

Weitzman, Steven. "Reopening the Case of the Suspiciously Suspended Nun in Judges 18:30." *CBQ* 61 (1999): 448–60.

Weyde, Karl William. "Inner-Biblical Interpretation: Methodological Reflections on the Relationship between Texts in the Hebrew Bible." *SEÅ 70* (2005): 287–300.

Williams, D. G. "Weeping by Adults: Personality Correlates and Sex Differences." *Journal of Psychology* 110 (1982): 217–26.

Wilson, Stephen. *Making Men: The Male Coming-of-Age Theme in the Hebrew Bible*. New York: Oxford University Press, 2015.

Wittekindt, Wilhem. *Das Hohe Lied und seine Beziehungen zum Ištarkult*. Hanover: Lafaire, 1926.

Wolde, Ellen van. "Trendy Intertextuality." Pages 43–49 in *Intertextuality in Biblical Writings: Essays in Honour of Bas van Iersel*. Edited by Sipke Draisma. Kampen: Kok, 1989.

———. "Ya'el in Judges 4." *ZAW* 107 (1995): 240–46.

Wong, Gregory T. K. *Compositional Strategy of the Book of Judges: An Inductive, Rhetorical Study*. VTSup 111. Leiden: Brill, 2006.

———. "Is There a Direct Pro-Judah Polemic in Judges." *SJOT* 19 (2005): 84–110.

Wright, Jacob L. "Yael and the Subversion of Male Leaders in Judges." *TheTorah.com*. 2017. https://tinyurl.com/SBL03109a.

Würthwein, Ernst. "Abimelech und der Untergang Sichems: Studien zu Jdc 9." Pages 12–28 in *Studien zum Deuteronomistischen Geschichtswerk*. BZAW 227. Berlin: de Gruyter, 1994.

Yeatman, A. "Gender and the Differentiation of Social Life into Public and Domestic Domains." *Social Analysis* 15 (1984): 32–49.

Yee, Gale A. "Asenath." *ABD* 1:476.

———. "By the Hand of a Woman: The Metaphor of the Woman Warrior in Judges 4." Pages 99–132 in *Women, War, and Metaphor: Language and Society in the Study of the Hebrew Bible*. Edited by Claudia V. Camp and Carole R. Fontaine. SemeiaSt 61. Atlanta: Scholars Press, 1993.

———. "Gender, Race, Class, and the Etceteras of Our Discipline." *JBL* 139 (2020): 7–26.

———. "Ideological Criticism: Judges 17–21 and the Dismembered Body." Pages 138–60 in *Judges and Method: New Approaches in Biblical Studies*. Edited by Gale A. Yee. 2nd ed. Minneapolis: Fortress, 2007.

Yoo, Philip Y. "Hagar the Egyptian: Wife, Handmaid, and Concubine." *CBQ* 78 (2016): 215–35.

Younger, K. Lawson, Jr. *Judges/Ruth*. NIV Application Commentary. Grand Rapids: Zondervan, 2002.

Zakovitch, Yair. "Inner-Biblical Interpretation." Pages 92–118 in *Reading Genesis: Ten Methods*. Edited by Ronald Hendel. Cambridge: Cambridge University Press, 2010.

———. *Through the Looking Glass: Reflection Stories in the Bible* [Hebrew]. Tel Aviv: Hakibbutz Hameuchad, 1995.

Zammuner, Vanda L. "Men's and Women's Lay Theories of Emotion." Pages 48–70 in *Gender and Emotion: Social Psychological Perspectives*. Edited by Agneta H. Fischer. Studies in Emotion and Social Interaction. Cambridge: Cambridge University Press, 2000.

Zertal, Adam. *A Nation Is Born: The Altar on Mount Ebal and the Origins of Israel* [Hebrew]. Tel Aviv: Yedioth Aharonot, 2000.

———. *The Eastern Valleys and the Fringes of the Desert*. Vol. 2 of *The Manasseh Hill Country Survey*. CHANE 21.2. Leiden: Brill, 2001.

Contributors

Elizabeth H. P. Backfish is assistant professor of Hebrew Bible at William Jessup University in Rocklin, California, USA.

Shelley L. Birdsong is associate professor of religious studies at North Central College in Naperville, Illinois, USA.

Zev Farber is senior editor for TheTorah.com and a research fellow at the Shalom Hartman Institute's Kogod Center, Jerusalem, Israel.

Serge Frolov is professor of religious studies and Nate and Ann Levine Endowed Chair in Jewish Studies at Southern Methodist University, Dallas, Texas, USA.

Susanne Gillmayr-Bucher is professor of biblical studies/Old Testament at Catholic Private University, Linz, Austria.

Susan E. Haddox is professor of philosophy and religious studies at University of Mount Union in Alliance, Ohio, USA.

Hyun Chul Paul Kim is Harold B. Williams Professor of Hebrew Bible at Methodist Theological School in Ohio (MTSO), Delaware, Ohio, USA.

Richard D. Nelson is professor emeritus of Biblical Hebrew and Old Testament interpretation at Southern Methodist University, Dallas, Texas, USA.

Pamela J. W. Nourse is a PhD student at Claremont School of Theology, Claremont, California, USA.

Tammi J. Schneider is professor of religion at Claremont Graduate University, Claremont, California, USA.

Joy A. Schroeder is professor of church history at Trinity Lutheran Seminary at Capital University, Columbus, Ohio, USA.

Soo Kim Sweeney is adjunct faculty of Hebrew Bible at Claremont School of Theology at Willamette University in Salem, Oregon, USA and supplemental faculty at Central Seminary in Shawnee, Kansas, USA.

Rannfrid I. Lasine Thelle is associate professor of religion at Wichita State University, Wichita, Kansas, USA.

J. Cornelis de Vos is professor of New Testament and Ancient Judaism at the Institutum Judaicum Delitzschianum, University of Münster, Münster, Germany.

Jennifer J. Williams is an assistant professor of religious studies at Linfield University, McMinnville, Oregon, USA.

Gregory T. K. Wong is associate professor of biblical studies at Evangel Seminary, Hong Kong.

Ancient Sources Index

Modern Authors Index

CPSIA information can be obtained
at www.ICGtesting.com
Printed in the USA
JSHW021948290323
39658JS00003B/67